"So how does one teach hope and agency during our climate crisis? Gifted educator Maggie Favretti provides some powerful answers in this remarkable book. Read it, then teach it for the sake of our future on earth."

Tony Wagner, *Senior Research Fellow, Learning Policy Institute and best-selling author*

"Young people know that we're in the fight for our lives—for our collective future. The climate crisis has contributed to the mental health crisis among teens because we've responded so inadequately. In this book Maggie Favretti outlines what school could be if focused on our collective and regenerative resilience: Personhood, People, Place, Purpose, Process, and Positivity. This is a must read for school communities searching for what's next and what Favretti calls 'cultures of coherence, belonging and agency.'"

Tom Vander Ark, *CEO, Getting Smart, author of* Difference Making at the Heart of Learning

"*Learning in the Age of Climate Disasters* offers a fresh and empowering ecological view of design, infused with systems thinking, and most importantly, community wisdom. This book invites us to reimagine design-based solutions to societal and environmental problems with a decolonial mindset. It is a gift of change-making with an equity and justice lens."

Yerko Sepúlveda, PhD, *Educator, Diversity, Equity, Inclusion, & Justice leader, Project Zero's Introduction to Maker-Centered Learning coach*

"'Process is not a linear or single pathway, but a tapestry of potential for transformation that emerges from relationships and collective knowledges...' Yes, yes, yes! It's what I found myself saying as I read *Learning in the Age of Climate Disasters*. Maggie Favretti offers profound intelligence and goodness in her book and I am so grateful she is pointing the way to engage learning and design mindsets to revitalize the Earth."

Wise, *Author of* Design for Belonging, *Founder of d.school K12 Lab*

"In the face of the complex and overwhelming challenges we face, youth and the adults that support and stand with them need a vision for how to cultivate hope and empower action. Favretti's powerful and eloquent book provides just that. Favretti explores the power of place, purpose, and processes to offer a transformative vision for education in the age of the climate crises. With love, creativity, and a deep sense of justice and equity her narrative shines a light on an actionable pathway of hope and possibility."

Robin Cox, PhD, *Royal Roads University Professor &*
Program Head, Climate Action Leadership;
Director, Resilience By Design (RbD) Lab

"*Learning in the Age of Climate Disasters* tackles the specter of climate change with moral clarity and abundant hope. By centering the voices of children and educators, this inspiring book illuminates the great power that exists within each of us to save this precious planet we call home. This is a must read for anyone searching for actionable guidance on how to respond to crisis with courage."

Lori Peek, *Professor of Sociology and Director of the*
Natural Hazards Center, University of
Colorado Boulder, U.S.A., co-author of
Children of Katrina

Learning in the Age of Climate Disasters

Learn how to infuse learning with deeper purpose, connectedness, and engagement, so students feel more empowered and less anxious about their futures. In *Learning in the Age of Climate Disasters*, author and award-winning teacher Maggie Favretti outlines the contexts and causes of "futurephobia" and then offers Regenerative Learning strategies rooted in nature's principles for repair and redesign. She explains how tending the soil and cultivating the roots of (re)generative power (Love, Personhood, People, Place, Purpose, Process, Positivity) help us disrupt degenerative hierarchical fragmentation. She also explores methods for co-empowering youth creativity, agency, and hope. Chapters include interviews with and contributions by children and young people, as well as key takeaways (Seeds for Planting), and tools to help you implement the ideas. With this book's thought-provoking concepts, you'll be able to help students overcome eco-anxiety and find healing connection and meaning for more sustained, regenerative change.

Maggie Favretti conspires with younger learners and colleagues from around the world to democratize and deepen learning and to build agency for transformative systemic change-making. Her next steps include Earth and indigenous rights advocacy, and helping to further emancipatory and regenerative learning and civic action networks in the interest of peaceful and interrelated life. She plans to keep asking, what kind of ancestor will I be?

Learning in the Age of Climate Disasters

Teacher and Student Empowerment Beyond Futurephobia

Maggie Favretti

Routledge
Taylor & Francis Group

NEW YORK AND LONDON

Designed cover image: © Maggie Favretti

First published 2023
by Routledge
605 Third Avenue, New York, NY 10158

and by Routledge
4 Park Square, Milton Park, Abingdon, Oxon, OX14 4RN

Routledge is an imprint of the Taylor & Francis Group, an informa business

© 2023 Maggie Favretti

Library of Congress Cataloging-in-Publication Data
Names: Favretti, Maggie, author.
Title: Learning in the age of climate disasters : teacher and student empowerment beyond futurephobia / Maggie Favretti.
Description: New York, NY : Routledge, 2023. | Includes bibliographical references. |
Identifiers: LCCN 2022025167 | ISBN 9781032105352 (hardback) | ISBN 9781032048086 (paperback) | ISBN 9781003215806 (ebook)
Subjects: LCSH: Emotions and cognition. | Anxiety in children. | Future, The--Psychological aspects. | Environmental disasters--Psychological aspects.
Classification: LCC LB1073 .F38 2023 | DDC 370.15/34--dc23/eng/20220713
LC record available at https://lccn.loc.gov/2022025167

ISBN: 978-1-032-10535-2 (hbk)
ISBN: 978-1-032-04808-6 (pbk)
ISBN: 978-1-003-21580-6 (ebk)

DOI: 10.4324/9781003215806

Typeset in Palatino
by MPS Limited, Dehradun

Access the Support Material: www.routledge.com/9781032048086

Note to readers: The weblinks in the eBook are not active. Please type or cut and paste the entire URL into your browser in order to access the source

Contents

Support Material

Bonus: There are several additional resources on our website to accompany the book.

- ◆ **Don't Anticipate, Participate: Youth Perspective on the Climate Crisis (Resource 1)**
- ◆ **Creating Listening Circles (Resource 2)**
- ◆ **Activities for Educators and Students to Help Invite and Sustain Coherence (Resource 3)**
- ◆ **Design Process Benefits and Pitfalls (Resource 4)**
- ◆ **Reflections on Individual Growth (Resource 5)**

To access these resources, visit the book's product page at www.routledge.com/9781032048086 and click on the link that says "Support Material."

Author and Youth Contributor Bios

Author

Maggie Favretti has been conspiring with younger learners to build their agency for change-making, and democratizing and deepening learning for a long time now. (At the time of printing, 37 years.) Maggie believes that she has learned more from her students than they probably did from her. With her husband Paul Duddy, Maggie gratefully works and plays and humbly seeks lessons from our Mother Earth and her relations on the traditional lands and coastal areas of the Mashuntucket and Eastern Pequot Tribal Nations in what is now called Mystic, CT. Her next steps include advocacy for return of public lands and shared land management wherever possible, as well as helping to further emancipatory and regenerative learning, and experiential, agency-building learning and civic action networks in the interest of peaceful and interrelated life on Earth.

Maggie's educational background is mostly at Yale University (BA in History of Art) and Middlebury (MA English). She has been honored as a cultural historian and educator of "history by doing" in three professional organizations, participated in the establishment of the World History Association as a place where high school and university educators could collaborate, received community-based experiential education and teaching awards, recognition from the Obama Administration for Environmental Education (community gardens and civic agency), and an invitation from NASEM to make education part of the conversation on empowered community resilience. It is one of Maggie's deepest honors to be a trusted member of a beautiful community of regenerative and emancipatory educators and youth in Puerto Rico.

Wisdom Contributors

Joe Rice (Choctaw) assumed the Executive Director position at Center School in July 2001. Previously, he taught high school in South Dakota for 17 years, first at Little Wound High School on the Pine Ridge reservation for nine years, followed by eight years at Central High School in Rapid City. He serves on the Board of Directors of the Minneapolis Urban Indian Directors and the Metropolitan Federation of Alternative Schools. He also lectures on Native American education and related issues. He helped to launch and acts as coordinator of Phillips Indian Educators (PIE) which convenes teachers to discuss best practices in Indian education and was a key player in developing a website to post information and curriculum on Best Practices in Indian Education. www.pieducators.com Joe has taken numerous graduate-level courses in Native American issues and has been learning to speak his language as well as Dakota. He graduated from Macalester College with a B.A. in History. In addition to PIE, Joe successfully manages a number of internal and collaborative projects including the Healthy Choices Program, and the Children of the Seventh Fire Initiative. He is currently overseeing a $1.25 million five-year SAMSHAA federal grant supporting experiential education.

Dra. Sandra L. Soto-Santiago has a BA in English Literature and a MA in English Education from the University of Puerto Rico at Mayagüez. She completed her PhD in Language, Reading and Culture at the University of Arizona in Tucson. Dr. Soto-Santiago teaches ESL courses as well as graduate and undergraduate courses in Applied Linguistics, Language Acquisition, Education and Research Methods. Her research interests include Social and Educational Justice, Anthropology and Education, Critical Literacies, Transnationalism, Translanguaging and Language Acquisition, Agroecology and Decoloniality.

Eduardo A. Lugo Hernández, PhD, Dr. Lugo is an Associate Professor at the Department of Psychology of the University of Puerto Rico, Mayagüez Campus. He possesses a PhD in Clinical-Community Psychology from DePaul University in Chicago. His work centers around child and youth civic engagement through the use of Community Based Participatory Research (CBPR). Currently, Dr. Lugo is the Director of the Impacto Juventud Project, which has the goal of promoting youth civic and political engagement through the use of social media and the arts. Dr. Lugo collaborates in public policy initiatives and has worked as an international consultant in educational and violence prevention projects. He is co-founder of Aula en la Montaña and host of a radio show raising awareness about social justice issues.

Youth Contributors

I am Anirudh, 10th grade, Army Public School in Hisar, India. I strive to achieve excellence in every field. My ambition is to become a scientist and create cost effective inventions which are accessible to all.

Parker Carrus (he/him/his) 10th grade, at Hawken Upper School in Cleveland, Ohio. Parker is of Colombian descent and is very passionate about the environment as well as developmental disabilities in youth. He is especially interested in data science, which he hopes to use to make positive impacts on the world. Parker is an avid Cross Country and Track athlete.

Annabelle Clark, 5, CT
Elliott Clark, 8, expert tree climber, CT

Sam Cohen (he/him/his), 10th grade, Hawken Upper School, in Cleveland, Ohio. Sam is enthusiastic about advocating for climate change and supporting the betterment of the community he is in. He hopes to pursue a career in science in which he can better the world. Sam is also an athlete as he participates in Cross Country and Track.

Isabel A. Colón-Borges, 12th grade, Edison School in Caguas, PR. My interests are painting, gardening, and volunteering. I will be majoring in psychology. I hope that in the future I can achieve all the goals I set for myself.

Karina I. Gonzalez-Alvarez, 7th grade, Edison School in Caguas, PR.
My hope is that we find green energy sources and stop deforestation.

I am Gunav, 3rd grade, Army Public School, in Hisar, India and I want to create a world where technology is in sync with nature.

Beatrice (Bea) Hardacre (she/her/hers) is currently a student at Hawken Upper School in Cleveland, Ohio. Bea's passions include, but are not limited to: DEIJ work, the outdoors & traveling, language, and environmentalism. She is a co-architect of Hawken's first ever Gender Non-Conforming Locker Room. Bea hopes to use her talents in DEIJ work, mathematics, and science to create positive change in the world.

Amelia Kearney, 12th grade, homeschooled, CT, is passionate about environmental protection and exploring the outdoors, is currently a member of the Sunrise CT leadership team, loves writing, and hopes to continue to help make the world a better place through activism.

Javier Moscoso-Cabrera (UPR-Mayagüez) is a student committed to Puerto Rico's sustainable future by studying and implementing solar energy systems, educating about energy consumption and renewable sources while recently combining interests with agriculture to create alternatives to address energy and food security as well as the needs and well-being of the people he engages with.

Ajahni Nedrick, 11th grade, Eagle Academy For Young Men II, Green Team. I like to play basketball and play video games with my friends. I enjoy spending time with my family. I also like to watch scary movies and documentaries about things that are interesting to me. I also like going out and making new friends. I enjoy learning about animals.

José Obregón (UC-Berkeley) (See Interview)

Génesis Ramos (UPR-Mayagüez 2021) (See Interview)

I am Rehan Raza, 9th grade, Army Public School, in Hisar, India. I hope to become one of the future world leaders and contribute my ideas towards creating a better world for the upcoming generations.

I am Serena, 5th grade, Army Public School, in Hisar, India and I believe that we can make a difference by living a more mindful and organised lifestyle. It is the small changes that can create the biggest impact.

I am Pawandeep Singh, 7th grade, Army Public School, in Hisar, India. I enjoy expressing my ideas through art and wish to be recognised all over the world for my art someday.

My name is Dubar Smalls, Jr. from the Eagle Academy For Young Men II, Green Team. My interests include entrepreneurship, playing video games, and watching various TV shows. I think the best trait about me is my work ethic and getting things done. Overall, I love to learn new skills and I am continually gaining knowledge on how to grow in my academic career.

David Warren, Ogiek Nation, Kenya. Youth from Ogiek community, living alongside Mau forest in Kenya. Environmentalist & climate change Activist. Journalist and nurseryman for indigenous plants and trees.

Sena Wazer is an 18 year old climate justice activist from CT and is passionate about engaging young people in climate action, specifically around policy change. She is currently a Truman Scholar at the University of Connecticut.

Raymond Woolery, 11th grade, I enjoy playing sports, primarily basketball and football. I also enjoy spending time with my friends and family and socializing. I also enjoy going outside and experiencing new things that benefit my mental and physical health. I also love to learn new things by researching.

Roberta Kubik's students are in grade 6 at Myrtle Philip Community School, SD 48 Sea to Sky, Whistler, BC. The students took it upon themselves to study species at risk in their community.

Student artists at Nawayee Center School, Minneapolis, MN

Special thanks to their teachers/school administrators, who not only collected these students' contributions, but are creating the conditions in their learning environments so that these students can learn holistically and achieve their dreams.

Dr. Kavitha Jakher, Principal, Army Public School, Hisar, India

Mr. Sean McFadden, Eagle Academy for Young Men II, Brooklyn, New York

Dra. María Elena Velásquez- Dean of Students, Thomas Alva Edison School, Caguas, Puerto Rico

Dr. Yerko Sepúlveda, Hawken Upper School, Cleveland, Ohio

Ms. Roberta Kubik, Principal, Myrtle Phillips Community School, SD #48 Sea to Sky, Whistler, British Columbia, Canada

Mr. Joseph C. Rice, Executive Director, Nawayee Center School, Minneapolis, MN and Coordinator Phillips Indigneous Educator network (www.pieducators.com)

For students and teachers shining through injustice and disaster everywhere
Who are weaving the future, out of love and joy, life and fortitude every minute of every day

For my parents
Who taught me to recognize my ancestors
Who led me to love Earth and let her love me back
Who showed me how to nourish neighborly relationships with all living beings

Preface

"Is it too soon to worry?
Or do we have some time left-
For choosing amongst abundance or
Leaving our earth bereft?

...Is it too soon to worry?
Or can we have time to ourselves-
To defer the serious discussions and
Ignore flooded crops and parched wells?..."
From "Too Soon?" by Rehan Raza,
9th grade, Hisar, India

With accelerating frequency, the scientists on the International Panel on Climate Change (IPCC) issue reports based on evidence and consensus that the window of opportunity to prevent runaway global warming is closing. Achievable carbon-reduction goals have already been overshot and without sweeping actions by those wielding the power to make decisions, especially regarding continuing extraction from and destruction of the planet, as well as individual and community actions, we are looking at continuing intensification of widespread suffering and displacement within existing human lifetimes. The prognosis: the number of years we have left to make significant systemic changes to avert the "worst picture" has dropped to single digits.

At the end of 2021, UNESCO (United Nations Educational, Cultural, and Scientific Organization) released a report calling on all educational institutions to stop business as usual and focus on the four existential challenges confronting life on earth: climate change, inequality, fragmentation, and struggling democracies. Education is the only local and global institution that touches almost everyone, and as a result education is the most effective and interconnected lever for transformative change. There has never been a more important time for societies and communities to embrace and empower educators and learners of all kinds to take a leading role in addressing these complex, interwoven imperatives for life. The big question is: how can we confront the realities of climate change in schools and universities and not sink into hopelessness?

The complexity of the situation is daunting, but there are five essential simplicities to hold on to within the tangle. When confronted with overwhelming powerlessness, teach agency. When confronted with extinction, teach closer to the roots of life. Educators hold the keys to cultural transformation. Our Mother Earth takes care of us and so we must take care of her. The best news of all: Nature has given us everything we need.

The culture of separation and destruction is strong and its systems of harm (colonialism, racism, sexism, extractivist capitalism) are resilient. It has governments and money and powerful narratives (materialism, patriarchy, fatalism) on its side. It has spent centuries colonizing lands and species and peoples, and fracturing bonds with living natural systems, within ourselves, and with each other. It extracts, pollutes, enslaves, traffics, incarcerates, and kills. It breeds suspicion and hatred, fear, corruption, and lies. There have always been strong people fighting against the cultures of destruction and holding fast to the wisdoms of love and life. They show us pathways to justice and care, abundance and hope. Pathways to return home to the powers we already have.

On these paths, we can revitalize our learning and revive Earth by accepting what life has given us. Infinite interrelatedness. Coherence. Regeneration. Unities of diversities. Collective success. Continuous change. These regenerative principles are like a living vision on the puzzle box that reminds us how, when we focus more on how the pieces fit together, we can bring into being something much more beautiful than its parts. In the hands of educators and their young (and old) allies, life's principles are already helping us to move and act beyond *futurephobia*, that sticky toxic mix of fear, fatalism, guilt, anger, blame, and above all powerlessness that has many of us stuck and carrying on with a futureless 'business as usual.' One caveat: regenerative learning is a journey, not a destination. You don't get a grade in it and move on to something else. Nature teaches us that life is change. No one can claim they are done learning, that they are now an expert at regenerative learning and can teach it to you in a workshop and then you will be an expert, too. We are always learning and changing together, going deeper, understanding more of how we can be better at being human and playing our part in the pluriverse of infinitely changing relationships.

So join us in the next chapters, where we will explore ways in which teachers are already aligning with life and tapping into all ways of knowing and being and shifting the paradigm for learning to make it more liberatory and just. We will explore new frameworks for thinking about life and love (the teacher's superpower), emotional well-being, and safety in school and build those into everything we do. Our young thought partners will show us what matters to them. We will identify the sources of (re)generative power (Power To, Power With) within and among us–the efficacy resources we already have to drive change and strengthen collective resilience: our Personhood, People, Place, Purpose, Process, and Positivity. We will imagine and see some living examples of what school could look like if it was designed to do what it should–to cultivate cultures of coherence, belonging and agency and the love of change and learning and the sense of possibility that goes with them. When all of our resources for power are built into our learning environments, a positive sense of well-being, interconnectedness and efficacy becomes the basis for thriving. Together, we can co-create regenerative, living worlds.

There are big trees in this welcoming forest, trees whose roots share sustenance below ground and whose arching branches show us the way. These tall oaks are the foundation of the liberatory regenerative learning ecosystem–scholars and thinkers and givers like Paolo Freire, bell hooks, and Robin Wall Kimmerer. And they are accompanied by all of the strong new wonder-ers and do-ers in this space, and all of the fractal ways we interconnect are held together and strengthened by our ancestors and their ancient wisdoms, with love and life. Without them, the saplings like me could not thrive. Enter this green and sheltering space. Give yourself the permission to slow down, breathe and listen deeply. Maybe you will hear something that will make you feel stronger about what you already are doing, maybe you will see something totally different from what you know. Together we will find ways to co-create our contributions. The culture of destruction and separation is very loud, and so it is hard to hear the love in the voices of our ancestors sometimes. But they have not abandoned us.

This book was almost finished before I fully gave myself permission to write it. I am the seventh generation from my nearest Kanien'kehaka (Mohawk) ancestor who used his Indigenous name, Itsychosaquachka. He also used a Dutch name, and after the intervening years of colonization and assimilation, I was raised in the shelter of Whiteness. When I started this book I felt I had grown up far from the challenges he and his mother Ots-toch met, and was troubled about how to humbly honor their traditions without also appropriating something that was not mine. But the privilege of knowing the names of my ancestors helps me to understand that they are not locked away in the past. In my heart I hear them asking, what are the seeds you will plant that will nourish the next seven generations? How can you braid together the teachings of *all* of your ancestors to decide how best to support life? What I do now, and the quality of my gratitude and respect will determine what kind of ancestor I will become. Educators and learners of all kinds, administrators and policy makers and parents, please accept this book as my humble offering, one voice among many, to energize and focus our efforts. We are alive and connected and becoming. The seeds I plant today came from generations of love. What kind of ancestor do you want to become?

1   Futurephobia and Renewal

What is the relationship between climate change, powerlessness, and futurephobia, and why does it make us stuck?

How does life itself generate the agency and healing to get unstuck?

> "After [Hurricane] María, I couldn't speak. All I could do was draw, and I drew and drew. Design Lab has given me my voice back. Now I know I have ideas that can help."
>
> —Ayana, age 15

In a crisis, the most dangerous position to be in is one without the power to improve your situation. Sometimes powerlessness comes from being too young or too old. Sometimes powerlessness emerges from the oppressions we suffer, and sometimes it emerges from the stories we tell ourselves. Sometimes a feeling of powerlessness overwhelms and becomes trauma and hopelessness. Children are the most powerless of all, and climate change is making them even more worried than you might think. They are experiencing the same disasters and injustices as you are. They are absorbing the same media, no matter how young and untouched we may wish them to be. Towers of flames. Texas frozen to a standstill. Swarms of tornados. People picking through the rubble of

DOI: 10.4324/9781003215806-1

their homes. Fossil fuels funding war crimes and choking life. Inundated neighborhoods. Millions of people leaving their homes with only hope to keep them going. Meteorologists saying, "we've never seen anything like this," and the United Nations Secretary General and the IPCC scientists declaring "Code Red" for Earth and giving us a handful of years to get our act together—or, as they might say in New York City, "fuggedaboutit."

Overall, 2021 saw google searches for "climate anxiety" skyrocket 565% from the years 2004 to 2020. In the weeks following the 2021 IPCC report, searches for "mapping sea level rise" and "what can I do about climate change" increased by 1,000% and 2600%, respectively.[1] According to the Yale Center for Climate Change Communication's report, nearly three-quarters of Americans are concerned or very concerned about humanity's impact on our planet.[2] For "GenZ," concerns about the planet lead all others. And the story of doom and dystopia we tell, the fear that it might be too late, the layers of confusing complexity in the challenge itself, and the many ways in which we are failing to rectify human-designed injustices and narratives that are destroying our lives and the interrelated life of the biocollective around us, can be debilitating.

When Faced With Extinction, Root Teaching in Life

But we humans are more powerful than we sometimes think. The growing level of acceptance that humans play the leading role in climate change acceleration is good news. We know a lot about fear, grief, guilt, and anger. We know how systems change. Most importantly, humans are imaginative and reflective and can choose from and weave together many paths, intentionally tapping into more than one understanding of power and many kinds of love. We can embrace and unpack complexity and learn, unlearn, and relearn in many ways. There is only one purpose for education now: life itself. We need to get from here (Figure 1.1):

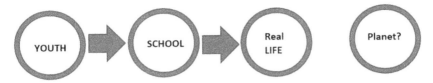

FIGURE 1.1 We need to get from here: Youth> School> Real Life...Planet?

To here: (Figure 1.2)

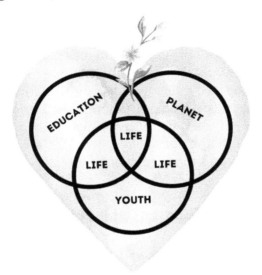

FIGURE 1.2 To here: When the purpose of school is life

What we cultivate today will shape how we grow into tomorrow. We can get unstuck from patterns of overconsumption and overproductivity and consider slowing down and moving toward the fulfillment of relatedness and interconnection in new (and very old) social and economic patterns. We can grow out of the industrial idea that school is about creating an obedient workforce and a stratified society. We can grow together to get from "this will never work" to "we know we can because we already are." From "someone should" to "we will." When faced with powerlessness, teach agency. When faced with extinction, teach closer to the roots of life. And school, university, and community learning ecosystems are the best ways to get us there.

Learning ecosystems touch every aspect of society. Imagine if we replaced fragmentation with coherence, and unyielding hierarchies and exclusions with unity and interrelationship. Regenerative (i.e., based on principles of life) learning empowers us by helping us to embrace opportunities to heal, to deepen our understanding, and to expand our agency by sharing and honing and sharing again the tools and skills and dispositions needed to make a difference now, in the present moment. "If we want to make a better future," one of my students once said, "we have to make a better now." In Chapters 2 and 3, we will explore the gifts Nature has given us and how the essential and inseparable principles of life (interrelatedness, coherence, diversity, regenerativity, and iterative change) not only guide us toward our full potential as human beings but empower us in (at least) ten different ways. Chapters 4–10 help us understand the roots of our regenerative power and how to reconnect learning to those sources of life and agency.

A Crisis of Agency: Educators and Futurephobia

Futurephobia is a term that does not (yet) exist in the lexicon of climate psychology, but it definitely exists. It describes what happens when there is a convergence of powerful emotions relating to the predicted future—in this case reflecting experiences of disaster and injustice now, projecting them into the future, and layering worsening and unequal climate impacts into the mix. Those emotions are not simple or transitory: fear, grief, guilt, love, betrayal, anger, mistrust, moral shock, and more. Any one of them by themselves could require professional assistance, and taken together can be overwhelmingly complex. The stress of carrying these emotions is exhausting and is not only making people sick but causing them to fear thinking about the future. To make matters more complicated still, this convergence of emotions relating to climate change and the future is felt *collectively*. But collective doesn't mean it affects everyone the same way. Children are exposed to the harm and to the emotions around it before their cognitive development can catch up and help them process and resolve what they can. Whole groups of people are feeling *something* about climate change. Intersectional cultural, social, and personal identities, inherited traumas, and systemic oppressions create a complex context into which these intense emotions flow. Underlying all of it is a pervasive feeling of powerlessness—that we can't do anything about it, or that others who have the power will not do anything about it—and this sets us on a path of trauma, disengagement, and fatalism.

Futurephobia is fundamentally a crisis of agency. Those students who are already experiencing "natural" disasters, individual and collective oppressions and traumas because of historical and systemic racism, sexism, colonialism, and educational injustice are even more likely to be feeling powerless and futurephobic. In any given disaster, kids usually make up more than half of those who are affected but they typically have no voice or choice or opportunities to contribute to the care and recovery of their families and communities. In school it's the same. Why would they think they have any control over what happens next in their lives?

As educators (and here I mean informal ones, too, such as parents), we generally assume our primary concern is helping young people to engage in the world in such a way as to thrive, but we ourselves are in the same predicament. Educators are also futurephobic. We are scared for ourselves and our offspring, and we are scared for the future reflected in the faces of the children and young adults in our care. We are burning out trying to do what's right in an outmoded educational system that invests in compliance and oppressions of self, others, and the planet. Most of us thought, when we "signed up for this job," that we would engage with "our kids" in resisting or changing whatever was harming them. We felt passionately about protecting our young from the racism, sexism, colonialism, poverty, ableism, materialism, etc. that is undermining their well-being and sapping their hope. We wanted to make a difference and contribute to the well-being of society and democracy. For many decades, educators have hacked pathways through the static and cleared out some of the barriers to healthy lives for youth, but have remained unable (rendered powerless?) to change the mechanistic structures of daily schooling and the seeming ignorance of the education system's policy makers "upstream" whose decisions seem to serve other purposes.

And now this. Climate change, with all of the emotions and all of the converging "disciplines" and cultural impacts that go with it, simply does not fit our usual educational structures or pedagogies. Here is what one teacher colleague shared with me:

> "I have been feeling guilty for a long time. I feel like they need something better than we are giving them. If I do what I'm *supposed* to do, teach them (air quotes) the curriculum, there's no way they'll be ready. And I'm not just talking about ready for college, or whatever. I'm talking about LIFE. Now. The future, too. Being flexible, critical thinkers. Being kind. Finding a reason to engage. Finding and solving problems together, and on the fly. But when I look at them, my own kids, too, that's what I see: A giant train wreck about to happen, and I'm not able to stop it. I wonder if they see it, too, and blame me for not being able to stop it. I don't dare ask. They're right when they say school is wasting their time and stressing them out. The truth is, we don't *have* a vision for the long game. And it's so sad, because there's all these good people, creative and smart people, are in this system that is harming our kids. I'm so tired of trying to push against it and not getting anywhere. I just need to walk away. I can't keep doing this."

Many educators, parents and youth are feeling both the incoherence and the crisis of agency that causes futurephobia. We all need to Do Something Different. But WHAT? There are lots of ideas and loud voices and initiatives overloading our circuits. Too many sites and webinars and not enough hours in the day. Where will we get some clarity and consensus? We can't "buy it and apply it" or add it on, that's for sure. Inequities are magnified and inefficacies are deepened when we don't grow and iterate integrated solutions ourselves. But wait—this is a crisis!

We need to fix it fast! We don't have time (or the knowledge!) to re-invent the wheel! But the truth is—we don't need to. Nature has given us great gifts, and we already know what to do. If we can create empowered and resilient cultures of change and care in our learning ecosystems, we won't need to scramble when the next crisis happens, either.

As Joanna Macy said in Christopher Landry's intense film *The Great Turning*, "There has never been a guarantee of human life. All the wise ones tell us that. But it's that knife edge of uncertainty where we come alive to our truest power."[3] If climate disaster and oppression bring forward the futility and powerlessness of futurephobia, then we can help each other to function fully beyond it by drawing out six of the creative, generative powers that we already have: our Personhood, our People, our Place, our Purpose, our Processes, and our Positivity. Our "deep-rooted powers" are these, and along with other gifts such as imagination, reflection, collaboration, and historical wisdom, they make up the generative powers to co-create change. When these powers that come from our humanness are also focused on life's principles (interrelatedness, coherence, diversity, regenerativity, and continuous change) and become the basis of school, a culture shift toward power-full belonging, purpose, and abundance occurs. Schools of all kinds, which affect nearly all children and youth and therefore the community as a whole, can become community change centers that establish the well-being that comes with our power-full sense of agency—our ability to effect change in the world around us.

Learning From Those Who Know Means We Are Never Alone

I believe in doing what we can with what we have and learning from those who know. I've already said we'll be learning from life and letting it guide and be the rich soil into which we grow.

Nature Is Our Best Teacher

Nature is our life, our extended family, the original designer, and our best teacher. These basic principles of life—interrelationship, coherence, diversity, regeneration, and evolution—enable us to understand our strength and they give us hope. It is difficult to put something like these on a chart, because they are interconnected and inseparable, as we see when we look closely at the marvel of living systems. But let me try to explain them so you, too, will be able to identify their presence in the vitality of your work, and then we will try to chart the implications for life-based education. The Earth is a living system (a biosphere, or biocollective of beings). In order for "living systems" to be alive, all of the following basic principles (and more, such as all of it is powered by the sun) have to be present, and taken together, they are the basis of infinite liveliness, joy, awe, beauty, and well-being. In later chapters, we will investigate these more, as well as estimate how we might base ecosystems of learning and co-empowerment on them. (Figure 1.3)

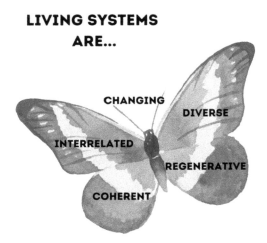

LIVING SYSTEMS ARE...

CHANGING
DIVERSE
INTERRELATED
REGENERATIVE
COHERENT

FIGURE 1.3 Inseparable principles of life in living systems

Living Systems Are ...

Interrelated—everything/everyone is connected to/related to everything/everyone else, co-existing "in relation" in an infinite web of interconnected nesting systems of interrelationship. Remove or damage, heal or restore one part, and the rest is affected. No individual can survive on its own. In human terms, "I relate, therefore I am."

Coherent—everything/everyone fits together in a mutual and reciprocal relationship in living systems without any waste or uselessness. Everything/everyone in the living system has a purpose in the present and over time.

(Bio)Diverse—every one of the millions of species that make up life on Earth has a good reason for being there. A single eco-system's species each has its own niche, or role to play. The ecosystem becomes weaker and more vulnerable if any are re-moved. Monoculture (where everyone/everything is the same) cannot survive.

Regenerative—it is said that "life creates the conditions for more life." Interrelationship and coherence and diversity make it possible for self-sustaining and autonomous living systems to continue infinitely. When the term "regenerative" is used in front of agriculture, architecture, or education, it means that the farming, building, or learning experience is intentionally using life's principles to create the conditions for more life.

Changing—living systems are constantly changing. In infinitely interconnected living systems, conditions are changing and learning and adaptation is happening in dynamic relation all the time. If to be alive means to be changing and learning, then learning is life. And that's why life's foundational principles should intentionally undergird everything we do as educators. See what I mean in Figure 1.4.

Living Systems Are...	So Regenerative Learning Is...
Interrelated – nothing lives by itself alone; all relationships are present all of the time	Multi-disciplinary and collaborative Focused on relationships as much as separate parts Collective and shared success Based on relational awareness and critical systems thinking/feeling with time built in for full listening, caring and compassion
Coherent – wholeness means all fits together and nothing is wasted	Holistic (head, heart, hands/body, spirit) Healing and restorative Life—'real world' experience, driven by curiosity and wonder, deep reflection and authentic accountability to others
Biodiverse — thriving only possible through difference. Unity, not uniformity.	Safe for all beings Welcoming and encouraging of individual difference as contributing to whole community Cultural brilliance held by individual beings adds to cultural 'wealth' of the whole ecosystem
Regenerative — life creates the conditions for more life to occur	Learning that draws learners deeper into learning Lifelong and intergenerational/interage/ancestral
Changing — continuous adaptation and change	Iterative and flexible, embracing of mistakes and failing as learning opportunities Growth-based rather than fixed or deficit-based Seeking of opportunities and challenges to support change Guided by regenerative values—see above and below
Power-diffuse — ecosystems are self-governing	Democratic--Lead learners (educators) and learners co-create learning experiences Focused on building agency and civic responsibility by enabling space and opportunity for collective self-direction Authentic accountability determines success

FIGURE 1.4 Regenerative learning at the roots of life: living systems in education

And there are human guides, too, who can help us get to the integration of learning and life:

1. People whose sustenance is Indigenous wisdom passed on through the land and sea and whose ancestral love is the reason we all are here today. Our Indigenous neighbors lived in good familial relation with Nature for hundreds of millennia and are actively and generously engaged in restoration, teaching, and advocacy today. Their ways of understanding the universe and our presence in it underpin the philosophy of this book.

2. People who are living in an existential exigency, in the teeth of climate injustice and under additional layers of moral, political, economic, and social violence against them. In Puerto Rico, a colony of the United States (US) and one of the most disaster-affected places in the world, they are living what many fear the most from the future, and they are charting new and finding old pathways to thriving. Many of the lights shining brightly along the path will come to us from there.

3. Science and technology and academic research can help us too, to see more and prove more of what we have suspected to be true all along, especially when it is balanced by the coherence of life.

4. Children and Youth, who embody the best of human nature: imagination, curiosity, compassion, joy, love, and whose alignment with Nature, ingenuity and critical questioning is too often ignored or actively stifled. From age 4 to 25, you will hear from them directly in these pages about what really matters.

5. Elders, whose learned and inherited wisdom is frequently wasted. Some of them make their voices heard; many think no one cares to hear them. This book seeks to ensure that we integrate the healing wisdom of our elders so we don't re-enact the traumas of their childhoods, and so we can learn the best of what they learned from their ancestors, too.

6. Educators, who turned on a dime when COVID-19 hit and moved forward together to reimagine the purpose of schooling and align learning more closely with life. Educators carry expertise and practical experience of all sorts, heal fragmentation when they can, and build bridges connecting silos and other kinds of divides to confront integrated and complex challenges.

This book focuses on the United States because it is what I know best and because it is leading the world in extraction, consumption, and waste. Its attitudes towards schooling have also spread around the world. The United States is capable of leading with humanitarian concern, contributes significantly to climate scholarship and research, and could step forward as a global partner in making the systemic changes called for by the realities we are living and the imperatives those realities bring to the fore. The examples in this book from around the world show us we are not alone and give us opportunities to connect.

My own subjectivity as the inheritor of settler colonial privileges and as a White woman educated in an elite college in the 1980s, where becoming a teacher was belittled as a "waste of a good education," might be influencing my thinking in ways I am still learning how to suss out. It may have produced blind spots or blocked traumas or pain that I am still trying to understand but that might creep into my biases. So it is with humility and gratitude that I quote people who resist being shoved to "the margins," and present the voices and images of young people and regenerative educators directly and indirectly—with the promise of my lifelong commitment to center the knowledge, the wisdom, and *La Brega*, the everyday struggle to thrive that defines your truths. I am dedicated to the vision of a world, as pluralist Arturo Escobar put it, in which all worlds fit.

Living in Disaster-Land

A word about "natural" disasters: the ones that come on suddenly, like the storms and fires and earthquakes, are usually the intensified effects of the slow ones—global warming, sea level rise, and drought, for example. The impacts of both are created and magnified by earlier-occurring human activity and systemic injustices such as poverty, environmental degradation, and racism, for example. Following-on human activity can further compound the disasters, through such systemic injustices as disaster capitalism, colonialism, and corruption. Almost all disasters have cascading and associated co-disasters that occur predictably like the falling of dominos, as we are seeing with the COVID-19 pandemic precipitating an economic crisis, a housing and employment crisis, inflation and a widespread though uneven physical and mental health downturn.

All "natural" disasters are compound and complex, and while all people are affected, some are affected much more seriously than others. There are still people in deciding positions (including in education) who believe that if we do just a little bit, add on one more initiative, tweak the methodology just a little, we will be okay, even as the earth's biodiversity collapses and ecosystems come apart. That is a stance only a privileged person (or one who doesn't think about systemic relationships) could take. Indeed, most books about well-being and climate discuss climate anxiety from a position of privilege, as if this is the first time anyone has confronted an "existential threat." But the majority of people who share this earth have never been FREE of existential threats, and they should be the focus of our learning and our efforts to establish different narratives and systems based on life.

Puerto Rico Teaches the World

Most US educators, like most Americans, don't spend much time thinking about Puerto Rico. They have their own issues to deal with, and besides, Puerto Rico is "over there" somewhere in their consciousness. A lot of studies, research data, media, and story gathering skip right over it. Aside from the fact that there are more Puerto Ricans living in the United States now than in PR (and more children and youth than adults), shouldn't we *want* to know what they know about surviving and thriving, situated as they are in the teeth of climate change? What are their sources of power to resist harm? How are they doing now? What works and what doesn't? Joining with the people and other beings who inhabit the most disaster-affected places strips down the layers of denial, willful ignorance, and reluctance to risk change, and shows us our shared pathways forward.

(Heart-) Breaking News: Everyday Climate Impacts in Puerto Rico are worsened because of its colonial status and the fact that polluters and developers continue to get away with environmental (and therefore humanitarian) crimes. Puerto Rican's everyday health is declining. Human activity, both local and global, make the impacts of repeated climatological disasters even worse. For example, human safety is compromised by both flooding and erosion. Removal of protective dunes and mangrove wetlands, and construction of hardscape too close to the shore causes the destruction of coral reefs and other food-producing ecosystems. Food and water security are also compromised by drought in half of the island, interrupted periodically by severe rainstorms which cause landslides destroying homes and transportation routes. Since the 1960s, the number of days over 90F degrees has increased from a handful to nearly a hundred in urban areas (where most people live). Increasing heat and humidity, worsened by urban paving and heat-absorbing construction, contributes to the most climate-related deaths on a day-to-day basis. Climate anxiety and depression and a sense of futurelessness are the traumatic results of repeated disasters with catastrophic effects due to government ineffectiveness and betrayal, combined with not enough available and accessible systemic mental health care.

Puerto Rico is one of the most disaster-affected places on the planet.[4] In September of 2017, over 3 million people were struck by two devastating hurricanes (Irma and María) in the span of two weeks, resulting in over 3,000 deaths (officially, closer to 5,000 by local count), the most significant loss of life of any US "natural" disaster in more than 100 years. No part of the island went unscathed. Two category 4 and 5 hurricanes in two weeks could be enough to stagger the most resilient and well-funded community, but in the case of Puerto Rico, they came after over 500 years of colonialism, skyrocketing poverty rates, and years of anunrelenting colonial austerity program put in place to pay banks back over 100B in predatory loans.

Puerto Rico is also the oldest colony in the world, and it has been a territory of the United States since the US took it from Spain in 1898. Puerto Ricans have a "special" (second class) citizenship status. They can be drafted into military service (and have been since 1917), and by law [the Jones Act (1920)] must only accept goods shipped by the US merchant marine on ships built in the United States, and flying a US flag, which makes all goods very expensive. They may travel to and work in the United States freely, though they are frequently hassled by TSA (Transportation Security Administration) agents and police who don't understand this. Puerto Rican students are often considered "international," and disqualified from scholarships and opportunities for recognition, funding, and mentoring. Puerto Rico has its own legislature and executive branch, both of which can and do manage domestic affairs but are ultimately answerable to the United States, and cannot receive aid from or negotiate with any state or agency (such as the UN) outside of the United States. The colonial austerity "debt restructuring" plan (enacted by the Fiscal Board, made up of the very people who connived to create the debt crisis at gains of hundreds of millions to themselves) has slashed school and university budgets, as well as pay and public pensions and the social safety net, creating a spiraling humanitarian crisis of skyrocketing poverty and a demographic crisis that begins with outmigration and forestalls future thriving. The wealth gap there is larger than in any US state. If we want to see what climate impacts look like in the context of unfettered and degenerate "Power Over," we need not search any further.

Colonialism and the austerity plan will suffocate Puerto Rico's capacity to recover from, prepare for, and mitigate climate impacts directly for many decades yet. Over a third of the island's schools were closed at the beginning of the school year in 2018 because of the predatory debt's austerity budgeting, dislocating and scattering children away from the security of their communities. In early 2020, a swarm of severe earthquakes began in the southwest of the main island, toppling and destabilizing churches, schools, and homes. And then COVID-19 began taking its toll, sending them into a longer and more complete lockdown (in 2020) than any US state. With a child poverty rate close to 60% (58% compared to a still embarrassing national average of 13%), and with over 35% living in severe poverty and relying on a shaky energy grid at best, lockdown meant tens of thousands of children had little access to food or school and some also lost access to relief from unsafe homes.[5]

Puerto Ricans have been through a lot, and they are tired. But they are also proving the old adage true—that the people closest to the problems are also the ones closest to the solutions.[6] They are more masked and vaccinated than any US state. In spite of (and in resistance to) colonial misgovernance and disaster capitalism, communities both rural and urban have come together to build proactive climate resilience and well-being based on local knowledge and relationships. On average, a similar percentage of the adult population is college educated in comparison to the United States, and their university scholars are global leaders in environmental and social sciences, among other fields. Puerto Rican architects and engineers are leaders in structural and infrastructural resilience, and they frequently work with community leaders to bring together ways of knowing and being and to bridge the gap between academe and real life. They understand climate migration and the impact on families and social systems firsthand. They are expert multi-disciplinary problem-solvers and genius innovators, and daily young people and their adult allies question the status quo and advocate for justice. Young people and their communities have generated solutions ranging from social and climate justice initiatives and regenerative farming on land and sea, to nano-grid solar-powered water filtration, touchless hand-washing, and refrigerated lockers for medicine. They've teamed up with teachers to redesign schooling. They've researched landslides and earthquakes and created new geo-stability assessment guides and curriculum plans for resilient community centers. Children figured out how to get food across raging rivers and water to their grandparents trapped on the 16th floor. Joanna Macy is right. The truest Boricua strengths are showing. After the double hurricanes, a group of college students including Génesis Ramos (see Interview pp. 45–50) created a social justice action and advocacy group called Impacto Juventud. Today, it is a leader in community empowerment and child well-being, and a strong voice in advocacy for children's and gender rights, as well as fighting against "poverty by policy." As one educator put it, "kids here have been solving complex problems and fighting for what should be their right for as long as they've been alive. They could teach us all."

 **Mending News!**

ResilientSEE-PR Assists Long-Term Recovery in Puerto Rico

When Yanel DeAngel returned to Puerto Rico from her work at Perkins & Will in Boston after the double hurricanes of 2017, she identified some significant problems that would hamper recovery and long-term resilience. For one thing, most government agencies and engineers work with fairly narrow definitions of the term resilience—either building back to what it was, or future-proofing structures. From a community perspective, however, resiliency means the integrated abilities to pull together what and who you need to change your situation for the better. A related problem was that communities would get stuck without access to engineers and architects who could do some basic needs assessment and data gathering, preventing access to recovery funds. ResilientSEE was born. Now a global organization, ResilientSEE spearheads a group of professionals, including architects, engineers, planners, and educators, who donate their expertise to communities in Puerto Rico who are reimagining and re-empowering their resilience. https://www.resilientsee-pr.com/

Living Without a Future

Puerto Rican students were the first to teach me about futurephobia, my name for the whole bucket of distress rooted in the collective trauma of climate and social injustice, and they were also the first to show me a path forward.[7] I knew kids were getting anxious, that rates of serious depression and even suicide were climbing and that things had gotten much worse after the storms, but I had no idea how bad it was until May of 2019. Maybe, like many of my teaching colleagues, I had held back from asking. Perhaps I was afraid to know. During a high school project in urban Bayamón, students revealed the depth of their concern. I had challenged my design lab students to tell a story about change, any story they wanted to tell, in a four-minute video. They declared, "We want to tell the story of how design thinking[8] is helping us to believe we have a future."

> I asked, "When you say you do not believe you have a future, what do you mean?"

> "That's simple," they said with some force. "The world is going to end, because the adults are playing games with our lives."

> "Would you say a lot of you feel this way?"

Thus began an unscientific but nonetheless powerful and revealing informal survey of their peers. Every single student they interviewed was readily able to identify the threats in their lives that darkened or shut out their thinking about the future (they had a much harder time identifying their strengths and dreams). Most of them named global warming or its impacts. Further, 8 out of 10 said they were interrupted at least once a day and sometimes couldn't sleep because of their concerns. Many had stopped attending school except occasionally for social reasons because it "wasn't helping much." But together they were using their own version of empathy and place-based problem-solving process (design thinking—more on this later) to build hope by transforming their school. That was the story they told in their film (https://www.designed4resilience.org/puerto-rico).[9] Take four minutes to watch it now. Look for and reflect on the examples of how they add to their agency to effect change and their overall well-being, with their powers of Purpose and Process.

Why Do Young People Think Their Future Is Disappearing?

The glib answer is because it is. As we've seen, human life is based on an infinity of nesting and interlocking living systems, which also determine climate and the ability of the planet to sustain life. If one of those systems is damaged or comes apart, it will affect all the nested and interrelated systems around it, such as when a respiratory system problem (e.g., lack of clean air and oxygen) causes circulatory, neurological, and structural impacts. On a larger scale, deforestation results in the loss of trees as carbon sequestration agents, contributing to the greenhouse gas load in the atmosphere. It also damages the earth's freshwater filtration capacity, encourages drought and soil loss, and, oh, by the way, trees breathe out oxygen and other chemicals necessary to human health. Living systems can also heal and regenerate, as long as the conditions are created and sustained for the damaged system to recover and replenish itself. Everything exists in relation.

We are doing the right things to slow warming, just not fast enough. And even if we succeed at keeping global temperature rise since the industrial age to 1.5 degrees C (by some measures we've already zoomed past it) it will take decades to stop the accumulated effects of warming. Fear about our future is a reasonable and totally healthy response. Even if we have not experienced disasters directly, most feel a sense of eerie unease when it is too warm in January, or we don't see the birds we are used to seeing. How old will our kindergartners be by the end of the century? Or your children or grandchildren? What emotions are you feeling? Name them. Pause. This is normal. We can't avoid thinking about it. Take a few deep breaths and look at or listen to something that brings you joy before you go on. Climate psychologist Lisa Davenport frames the key question in her indispensable book, *Emotional Resiliency in the Era of Climate Change* (2017), "How can we open our eyes and hearts and minds to the losses associated with climate change without sinking into despair?"

The future orientation of youth requires them to confront the reality that what we (adults) are deciding to do now is and will DEFINITELY affect their lives, and we are getting a vote of no confidence. Globally, many children believe that the world will end in their lifetime, either from climate change or conflict. The World Economic Forum's 2019 study of 30,000 youths under 30 (in 186 countries) showed the greatest concerns were climate and the destruction of Nature.[10] In 2018, 82% of 10- to 12-year-olds felt fear, sadness, and anger when they considered the environment.[11] And these were kids who had no direct experience of disaster. Their anguish simply came from what they had heard or seen in media and popular culture, and the dread of what many feel is an inevitable future, given how the adults in the world have acted in the past and are acting now.

Many youth just do not think adults are taking this seriously enough to do what needs to be done. Some well-meaning adults rave about youth "these days" and how they will tap into their "fight" response to save the world. But this evades accountability, and let's face it, puts our own moral and ethical responsibility onto the ones who are and will be the most affected.

In fact, the recent study of 10,000 youths ages 16–25 in 10 countries in the "global south (4) and north (6)" revealed that not only do 3:4 fear for our future but they also have little faith in the adults in charge. More than half (58%) felt that the adults in charge were lying to them regularly, and overall their sense of betrayal was much stronger than their sense of reassurance.[12] What I'm calling *futurephobia* is not an abnormal or pathological response. It's the normal, predictable, and healthy response, and it is growing.

No More Blah, Blah, Blah: Youth Activists Meet Unyielding Hierarchies of Power

For most people in the world, the lived realities of inequality and injustice make up the body of the story they've been trying to get across to powerful decision-makers all along. To address climate change adequately is to address social injustices of all kinds, but young people, who are the most affected and also the most justice oriented, are also the least directly engaged in decision making. Outside the COP26 (nations at least nominally committed to taking action on climate change have met 26 times) conference in late 2021, Greta Thunberg expressed her frustration on Twitter. "This is a Global North greenwash festival. A two-week celebration of business as usual and blah blah blah."[13] The decision-making adults seem to be "playing games" instead of focusing on solving the challenges of our times. Youth are on the margins and not in the deciding circles, but they will bear the long-term consequences of decisions made today.

Disasters put the painful results of environmental and social racism, colonialism, and immoral decision-making on full display. There is no hiding it or ducking the moral responsibility. Climate impact disasters are man-made, and the decision-makers whose policies and actions have *caused* much of the destruction are also the ones who are now in a position to "help." While young people are driving the largest social movement in human history for change and justice, they still stand outside the rooms where the actual decisions are made, and feel like they are the hens being asked to trust the foxes to do the right thing. Young people need to be at the center of the decision-making conversation.

"They Don't Seem Stressed *Enough*": Futurephobia Causes Disengagement

"But the students in my class do not *seem* stressed," said a university engineer and dear friend of mine, "if anything, they don't seem stressed enough. I tried to shock them into action. I told them that hey, I'll be dead, so it won't matter to me, but if they don't get off their butts and do something, they will just be running from disaster to disaster." "Did that help?" I asked. "They just looked at me. They are SO apathetic. I don't want to sugar-coat the truth. I think we are doomed." By "just looking at him," my friend's students were sending him a loud and clear message. When climate change thought leader and author of *Hope Matters*, Elin Kelsey appears at conferences and in front of large audiences, she always asks them to describe how they are feeling about climate change, in a word.[14] While they do not *appear* to be *any* of these things, the most commonly heard words are, "Scared, numb, hopeless, overwhelmed, paralyzed, depressed, angry, guilty," and I could add from my own experience of doing this with colleagues and students, "alone, anxious, powerless, mistrustful." If you ask trauma psychologists to identify the most often used words to describe the feelings associated with trauma, they would be identical.

My friend's students were not outwardly reacting to his shedding his own fears and cynicism onto them—they were trying to tune him out and think about something else. Disengagement (and dissociation) can look like indifference or apathy and is a legitimate protective response to upsetting realities we can't control. It embodies both the typical "freeze" and "flight" responses to the threat. It is a key paralytic factor in futurephobia. Many people suffering from futurephobia either can't think about the future at all or it interrupts them multiple times a day. Trauma is our brain's response to extreme powerlessness—the inability to protect oneself or others from harm.[15] Our deeper intelligence, our emotional/body brain (we will explore our interconnected nervous system in Chapter 4), protects us from trauma with emotional numbing and blocking, tuning out, dissociation, and disengagement, from both present and future.

The dominant narrative in school is "preparation for your future." When I asked the students in Bayamón whether they felt a disconnect between the future-orientation of school and their own concerns about their future, they said, "we just try not to think about it. A lot of times we just don't come to school." As researchers from the University of Puerto Rico-Rio Piedras confirm, absenteeism of both students and teachers has climbed steeply since the double hurricanes (Irma and Maria) and then the school closures and then the earthquakes and then COVID-19.[16] As Elin Kelsey points out in *Hope Matters*, "when we believe nothing will change for the better, then any positive action can feel pointless." Instead of "getting ready for opportunities," the students' school narrative shifts to, "what's the point?" Many teachers and students alike are feeling useless and drained. Futurephobia and all that goes with it *could* prevent us from doing anything at all.

The Impact on Science Teachers

One of the many good things about my engineer friend is that he loves his students, and they love him. He's open to learning and listening. Progress is being made. At the very least, he has committed to the not-so-simple first step of keeping his futurephobic fatalism to himself. One thing my friend finds a little bit helpful is that he knows he is not alone in his frustration. Many scientists are on the frontline of the climate crisis. They have been seeing both the science and the injustice, but not seeing enough substantial policy or societal responses. They are the main contributors to the IPCC reports that tell us the shrinking number of years we have left before we reach "runaway" global warming, leading to mass suffering and accelerating extinctions.[17] They know what they know, and much of it is terrifying, and it doesn't automatically come with feasible solutions. Since the 1990s, they've been the ones trying to help the rest of us see we'd better get going, using their science to confirm what Indigenous peoples and nations have been telling extraction-minded settler colonials for centuries, and trying to focus on affecting policy changes without being dismissed as "political" and therefore unscientific.[18] By the early 2000s, they found themselves on the frontier of a new mental health field—the early adopters and first raison d'etre of "climate psychology."

 **Mending News!**

Scientists Find Seeds of Hope in Nature Herself

"If hope had a color," begins the *Washington Post* article, "it would be the pale green of a newly sprouted seed." In her work at Dream of Wild Health, Seneca Hope Flanagan assures us that we have a lot to learn from our elders, those animals and plants and insects who have been around a lot longer than we have, and that they have the answers we need. Ayana Elizabeth Johnson, co-founder of Urban Ocean Lab, shares her view. All we have to do is look at how ecosystems form in columns in the sea, and see what conditions enable coral to heal to know how to restore them. And look at how effective regenerative ocean farming is at generating food and restoring ecosystems simultaneously! For more information, see https://urbanoceanlab. org/ and Bren Smith's Green Wave https://www.green wave.org/team. From Washington Post Staff, "Seeds of Hope: How Nature Inspires Scientists To Confront Climate Change." *Washington Post*, 26 April 2022.

The climate science we teach in most schools and universities focuses on "this is what's happening and why" which scientifically speaking, leads to "soon we really WILL be powerless to stop terrible suffering and possible extinction no matter *what* we do." Many feel that the proper role of a professor or a teacher is to provide students with the latest scientific research about the causes and magnitude of the problems, and once the students know all the science, they can get to work on solutions. Emotional care and social well-being are often not in our training or comfort zone. Students, eager to sign up for courses in environmental sciences, leave our classrooms in a slouch, saying, "I love learning about this but it is terrifying and depressing." In her undergraduate course at Humboldt State University, Sarah Jaquette Ray started out by asking her students to visualize a future in which their wishes for the climate had come to pass. Most of them didn't do it. After digging into it with them, she came to the realization that "the generation growing up in this age of global warming is not lazy or feigning powerlessness … they are so frozen that they are unable to desire—or yes, even imagine—the future."[19] My friend wanted to see the "fight" response grow among his students. He wanted to encourage all of his students to be activists. Now he is exploring more effective ways to go about it.

Teen Amelia Kearney is all for that. Like many whose families feel that typical schooling needs to readjust its focus, she is homeschooled. Her life has been defined by her interest in the outdoors and her passion for the world. She writes, "*It is hard to escape this fear of what we are doing as humans to other people, to the earth, and to our future. Solutions for the climate crisis are extremely important, but we also need to work on managing the side effects that this crisis has on our mental health. Even now, after decades of knowing that climate change is real and caused by human activities, we still don't talk about it enough. This needs to change in all aspects of society, but especially in education because it reaches so many young people. Climate anxiety and depression need to be validated right away. ... Educators, communities, society as a whole, need to let young people know that these feelings are legitimate and normal, and need to provide resources and support to help. Climate education is so important, but we need to be sure that support for climate anxiety and depression is built into the curriculum. While working to resolve the climate crisis, we need to take care of ourselves and each other, too."*

 Mending News!

You Are Not Alone: The Climate Psychology Alliance of North America Has Your Back

The Climate Psychology Alliance of North America brings together climate psychology research and clinical experience to provide connection, conversation, articles, and tips on how to stay stable in the Age of Climate Disasters. https://www.climatepsychology.us/

I'd like for you to come with me to a little thought exercise right now. On a scale of 1 to 10, with 10 being the most motivating to **individual and collective** action, rank the power of these emotions to motivate you to action over time. Think deeply about this and make it personal. Add definitions, drawings, and musings if you wish. You don't have to show this to anyone. You may wish to return to it after you read this book, just to reflect on how your personal motivations evolve, or to use it with colleagues, school boards, students, and parents. (Figure 1.5)

Emotion or Mindset	Short Term Motivation 1-10	Long Term Motivation 1-10
Fear		
Guilt		
Belonging		
Confidence		
Compassion		
It Feels Good		
Ambition for Wealth		

FIGURE 1.5 What feelings or mindsets motivate you for the long haul?

If one of your top choices was compassion, then you fall into the category of fear response that usually gets left off the fight, flight, or freeze list. If you look at life in disaster-land, what you see most in communities that have been struck is the "Tend and Befriend" response. First written about by positive psychologist and trauma stress expert Dr. Shelley Taylor, this part of the fear response deepens social contacts around caring for others and also releases the same healthy well-being hormones that love and nurturing does. I like to add, Tend, Befriend, *and Mend*, because in the disaster recovery context as well as the context of accelerating climate change, the shared agency of working together to repair the earth generally and our home communities specifically, is actually good for us physiologically and helps to make us more resilient as well, especially when confronted by daily hardship or frightening news.[20]

The Stories We Tell Ourselves Are Self-Fulfilling Prophecies

We are consuming a lot more news from all kinds of sources with the advent of social media and the 24/7 news cycle. Added to this is the "crowdsourced" emotional immediacy of personal reporting from disaster sites and the *intensity* of social media. The news media, which gets most of its climate change stories either from disasters themselves, or from scientific journals, regularly and frequently repeats the emotionally charged narrative of disaster, urgency, failure, and loss. According to a Pew Research study, close to 70% of Americans feel worn out and stressed by the news.[21] Many have to take "newsbreaks" just to "stay sane." And it's not just lived experience and headlines and viral videos about climate disasters that are contributing to paralyzing futurephobia—it's also popular culture's fascination with dystopian narratives, confirming our fear that the world is already and fatally trapped in a dystopian web of harm. Many young people feel the way the student who created the drawing in Figure 1.6 feels.

FIGURE 1.6 *Futurephobia*. Xion Torres Luccas, Guayanilla, Puerto Rico

In Xion's view, we can't turn back, but we can't get through, either. We humans know we created the mess we're in, the powerful "economic growth at all costs" narrative that influences everything we do, even when we are fighting against it, as Indigenous and marginalized people have been doing for hundreds of years.[22] We can see where we're headed, but can't seem to get unstuck while there's still time. Some tell us that we will have to give up certain foods or cars or long showers or whatever that we love, and that's hard to get people to do. Mostly, we are told (or we tell our governing bodies) that needed changes cost too much and that we can't afford it. Or at least those are the public narratives we are focusing on.

The stories we ingest and those we tell ourselves matter because they can become self-fulfilling. We've all heard about the "power of positive thinking" (or, the "placebo effect") in medical healing. Or in the negative, if we keep telling ourselves we will fail, or have failed already, or because we "always" do, we make it much harder to succeed or even to try. In that scenario, even when we are successful, we can't quite believe it. There are plenty of stories of success that need more and louder telling, of inventive alternatives and Nature's own resilience … but confirmation bias kicks in. This is often referred to as our "gut feeling," because like fear and anxiety, it is deeply situated in our "body brain," hard to reach by our reasoning and critical thinking brain. Essentially, it causes us to accept or reject narratives as "true" or not, based on whether it seems or feels right to us. Even if we are surrounded by examples of positive changes in the world of restorative climate action, we might not be able to notice or absorb them and continue to believe that we are powerless to Do Something that might make a difference.

What Educators Can Do to Change the Doom Narrative

While the majority of adults believe that climate change is real and we need to do something about it, there are significant differences of opinion about how we should proceed and who should foot the bill. Both large corporations and nations who have committed to carbon reductions are hiding the truth of their emissions.[23] The oil and natural gas industry in the US funds field trips, distributes teaching materials through professional teaching organizations, and even sends school ambassadors extolling the virtues of fossil fuels. They also work hard to raise concerns about renewable energy and spread misinformation about the safety and security of pipelines, methane releases, fracking, and oil drilling and transport, even though thousands of spills occur each year. Textbook publishers, such as Random House and Pearson, sell textbooks and supporting teaching materials widely which sow doubt about climate change in the name of neutrality.[24]

Those immoral acts and heated disputes leave many young people despairing that any agreement will come in time. Some world, national, and state policy makers seem bent on economic and political domination at the expense of morality, truth, and life itself. The good news, even big news about new economic systems and innovations in environmental restoration and food or energy systems, can get drowned out. That leaves the door open for those who are benefiting most from the status quo, who have never had the public good in mind, to invest in and benefit from the narrative of doom. The "we can't afford it" and "besides, it's too late" narrative needs to be witnessed and called out and questioned from the perspectives of those who are already and will end up paying the most. Doom is a choice we make when we as educators and school systems "stay neutral." We can choose a different path. We can help young people see the stories of empowered hope and justice, *and to find their way to contribute.*

I am not suggesting that saving the world is all on teachers' shoulders. Instead, I am hoping that this book can empower you to find a connection with others, to feel the emergent power and the collective wisdom of interrelationship, and to feel the energizing force of creative companionship to Do Something based on love and life. Regenerative learning is revitalizing for teachers, too.

For this, we need to see climate as a multidisciplinary endeavor. It is not a science class alone. Focusing on how to get engaged in both creating and furthering solutions opens the doors for students (and teachers!) to bring their disciplines and interests together to generate hope. You'll have noticed that I'm sprinkling Mending News (instead of Breaking News) throughout this book, to give you ideas and feed hope as you are reading. In his essay "To Remake the World," Paul Hawken estimates based on his contact list and research that there are at least a million, maybe two million, non-governmental organizations trying to restore, sustain, and heal the planet and the injustices that have brought us to this point.[25] The Solutions Journalism Network (https://www.solutionsjournalism.org/) aims to help shift the stories from Breaking News to Mending News, especially to help tell a social justice story. Do you receive newsletters that bring you realistic hope as well as reporting on the situation? Consider Civil Eats, or Food and Water Resilience, or joining the UN Sustainable Development Goals education network. Inside Climate, the Climate Museum, the American Society for Engineering Education, the National Adaptation Network, the Urban Sustainability Directors' Network, and the Stanford Social Innovation Network will fill your box with examples and events to share. Follow organizations on social media, like WECAN, the Women's Earth Alliance, Engineering for Change, Social Justice+Engineering Initiative, Design for Change, and other non-profits who are doing good work. In Resource 1 (See Support Materials), you will find a well-researched essay by 10th graders at the Hawken School, filled with suggestions for actions young people can take. It also provides important perspectives on adult alliances. Their work could be as inspiring, kid-to-kid, as anything. You will also find there links to the sources I just mentioned and more—just a few of the sources you can use to get ideas for projects, civic actions, and supporting mental health. Figure 1.7 includes some encouragement from Earth herself. But the essential starting questions are these: Who is doing good work locally, and how can the students be resources for their work? Is there a university or community college nearby that is involved in community climate work? This practice will not only give you an emotional boost and locate potential partners for you and your students, but it will also give your students ideas about how to take action. If your students are not already engaged in the good work that will build their civic confidence, use this book as a starting place!

FIGURE 1.7 Climate change, by Pawandeep Singh, grade 7, Hisar India

Futurephobia's Crisis of Agency Leads to Fatalism

Anthony Leiserowitz of Yale's Project on Climate Change Communication notes that a "perceived threat *without efficacy of response* [my italics] is usually a recipe for disengagement, and fatalism."[26] Taken together, disengagement and fatalism are the twin paralyzing elements of futurephobia. That fatalistic "it's already too late—we humans will not be able to get our act together in time" aspect of futurephobia is dangerous because fear and powerlessness combined is a strong drug that makes it harder for us to succeed when we need it most. If we are mistrustful of ourselves and each other and don't believe we have the power to change our world, we are less likely to take creative risks and less likely to collaborate positively. We can more easily be driven to turn away from each other and toward demagogues (including gang leaders, cults, authoritarians, warlords, and dictators) who compel our fearful emotions about other people, distract us from the true challenges, and create chaos while promising order. Powerlessness to change our situation causes us to block our critical thinking and crave "normal," however insufficient or unjust that may be.

Futurephobia is natural and legitimate for a human being to feel in the face of injustice and climate change. But the chronic stress and anxiety associated with it causes isolation and depression, also lowers our immune responses, and damages our organs and internal systems. Climate disaster-induced trauma and secondary trauma can last for decades and even extend across generations. Climate anxiety aggravates and magnifies other illnesses and mental illnesses, and exacerbates the difficulties caused by racial and ethnic inequality and the global pandemic of COVID-19. By October of 2021 in the United States, a coalition of 77,000 physicians and psychologists had declared youth mental health a national emergency. Dr. Gabrielle Carlson, president of the American Academy of Child and Adolescent Psychiatry said in an interview with National Public Radio's Deepa Shivaram, "We are caring for young people with soaring rates of depression, anxiety, trauma, loneliness, and suicidality that will have lasting impacts on them, their families, their communities, and all of our futures."[27] And the pain is not at all evenly distributed. Indigenous children are 4.5 times more likely than White children to have lost a parent or grandparent caregiver to COVID-19, Black children 2.4%, and Latinx children twice as likely. Girls, by some accounts the most future-oriented element of human society,[28] from across all demographic groups are experiencing significantly higher rates of anxiety, depression, suicidal thoughts, and suicide.

However, it didn't take a global pandemic to sound the alarm bells. In 2020, the CDC (Center for Disease Control) called attention to striking increases over the previous decade in severe emotional distress (including anxiety, Post Traumatic Stress Disorder (PTSD), and depression), with overall youth suicide rates in the United States increasing from 2007 to 2017 by 56%. In some states, the suicide rate doubled during that time.[29] In 2018, the US Congressional Black Caucus convened a Task Force, whose 2019 report showed that suicides among Black children of both sexes were rising faster than any other group, increasing 73% from 1991 to 2017.[30] After the double hurricanes in Puerto Rico in 2017, almost two-thirds of children had experienced the loss or out-migration of a family member, nearly half reported damage to their home, and a third felt that their lives were at risk during the storm as well as experiencing shortages of food and water afterwards. Suicide rates spiked and children suffered PTSD at more than twice the rate of those in the states.[31] Stress levels continued to rise after austerity measures closed nearly a third of the schools in Puerto Rico. Families shared with me that the school closings were "even harder for us than María. We can eventually recover from a hurricane. We'll never recover from this." Then the earthquakes began, followed by COVID-19.

Efficacy and Agency: "Now I Know I Have Ideas That Can Help."

An important caution: we would not want to make the mistake of pathologizing or catastrophizing our students and ourselves into a position of helplessness. Instead, we can be motivated and empowered to act once we recognize that the causes of stress, climate and health vulnerabilities are mostly human-designed. Anything designed by people can be redesigned by people. Nothing is inevitable. After an unimaginable pair of devastating hurricanes flattened Ayana's world, she lost her words. It wasn't until she collaborated with her team in the Design Lab (see Chapter 8) and saw that she had ideas to help others that she found her voice again. She never stopped listening and drawing and growing, and will not sideline her civic courage now.

Dr. Leiserowitz and the kids in Puerto Rico (and many many more people in the teeth of crisis) are showing us how to proceed. A "perceived threat *without efficacy of response* [my italics] is usually a recipe for disengagement, or fatalism." So the best place to intervene and use the leverage of education is clear: "Efficacy of response." Meet futurephobia with agency. We all need to feel our power to effect change. Impacto Juventud brings young people together to make a difference now. As Génesis Ramos attests in her Interview (p. 45), we feel better, and grow stronger together when we are able to do something about it.

> *What this planetary predicament calls for is regenerative (life-principled) education that prioritizes both individual and collective agency.*
> *What if young people ... (and old ones) found meaningful, healing purpose, and connected with nature and other people to create a more equitable and sustainable world?*
> *What if that happened "in school?"*

It seems now is the time (the last chance?) for the old guard to step aside or welcome new ideas for more appropriate schools, more equitable economic and social paradigms, and new participatory decision-making models. This is beginning to happen on the local and geo-political and geo-economic stage. Schooling is lagging behind, but it's still the best lever we have for transformative change at the level of lived community and individual experience. Too often we acculturate youth to adult expectations and ask them to wait and comply—it's time for adults to attune to the expectations youth have of us. Schooling can instead establish and support cultures of healthy, caring difference makers.

What's the New Story?

By redesigning education and how we engage with it, we want to change the dystopian story of our present-day lives to one that brings us together around something that inspires, revitalizes, and empowers us. We want to ensure our survival and co-create the best possible future we can imagine for and with our children and theirs. We want to be good ancestors, and so we want to tell a new story to our children that shows how we, the people that brought us back from the edge,

shifted from deficiencies, threats, and compliance to foundations of belonging, growth and evolutionary vitality.

allowed the challenges and opportunities in our communities to be the organizing principles of learning and change-making curricula.

invested in collaborative knowledge and meaning creation, and in truth and reconciliation.

energized purposeful and meaningful civic participation and planetary understanding.

reoriented from a "top-down" to "co-creative companionship" learning approach.

healed from fragmentation, and the splitting apart from self, others, ideas and the world, by restoring holistic (whole-istic) and regenerative habits of mind and becoming.

redesigned the whole idea of school into a lifelong learning ecosystem, in which schools and universities merged with community hubs for the exchange of relevant learning experiences and the tools, skills, and dispositions to influence change.

redefined success.

We have a lot of work to do, because in most school systems still, many teachers have to fight hard to "lift the elephant" of the Inevitability Narrative—possibly the most destructive one there is. Instead of accepting the narrative of the 'inevitability' of harm ("don't some have to fail in order to make the testing/grading valid?" "Isn't it more efficient to close and consolidate schools?" "We'll never be able to change this"), parents, students, educators at all levels could join those who are already asking, collectively, *why are we doing this and whose interests does it serve?*

Why Education Policymakers Should Read This Book, Too

Education policymakers flirt dangerously with the concept of neutrality, all the while participating in establishing the powerlessness educators and students feel. Neutrality might *sound* nice, but not every idea, no matter how loudly expressed, will foster the growth of kind, healthy, happy, and engaged citizens. Schools must stand for truth and life, and be welcoming, safe places to form the relationships and take the risks needed for learning. Schools must embody the principles of life and generative empowerment that will enable the people in them to have a future. Education is a civic responsibility with which we must lead. We cannot afford to be neutral. As the late Archbishop Desmond Tutu wrote in the *Book of Forgiving*, "If you are neutral in situations of injustice, you have chosen the side of the oppressor. If an elephant has its foot on the tail of a mouse, and you say that you are neutral, the mouse will not appreciate your neutrality."[32] We know what we need to do, we already have the knowledge, tools, and technologies to do it, so there's no moral basis for denying that we have to lead with vision. If you are a policy maker, join with educators, both inside the system and out, both formal and informal, and with students and their families to listen deeply. Do it now, and emerge as co-designers of new systems and better stories.

Schools and universities are the most important levers we have to lift up youth, build collective efficacy, and shift cultural attitudes and harmful systems. For one thing, schools are the only institution that touches nearly every child, nearly every family, and nearly every community. Young people spend more waking hours involved with school than they do engaging with their families. Schools and universities represent the main opportunity for human beings to bring together multiple perspectives and ways of knowing to build stronger and more just communities. Schools are future oriented and ought to share a future-oriented purpose, to foster learning that is foundational to thriving in conditions of change.

Education has the most potential to create sustained and regenerative change—by hosting, facilitating, and iterating social and cultural transformation. Education both shapes and draws out individual and collective genius. It can liberate our minds and our hearts. Paul Hawken's uplifting book *Regeneration: Ending the Climate Crisis in One Generation* shows us how to apply the tools we already have to transform every ecosystem type and every major "industry."[33] Unfortunately, like many thought leaders in the policy arena, he doesn't include education directly as one of the transforming and transformative "industries." Similarly, education policy-making in the United States falls into a strange wormhole unlike any other sector, because in education, decision-making is not in the hands of experts in teaching and learning. Neither expert practitioners nor the "end users" of the system are driving the policymaking or holding it accountable. Essentially, any taxpayer or politician is qualified and the experts are often closed out; hence, policy decisions are commonly driven by short-term financial considerations first, political considerations second, efficiencies third, and the needs and hopes of the children now and in the future somewhere back in the pack. Underpaying and undermining teachers and professors, privatizing public education, the overtesting and sorting of children and youth are all mechanisms to improve education's bottom line, not to help to create the educated, capable, confident, and interconnected citizenry needed to save us.

The UN includes education among the Sustainable Development Goals (SDGs), and in one of my SDG Academy[34] classes, we did a little thought experiment. Which of the 17 goals did we think should be attended to first? After rousing breakout sessions, we came back together and discovered that almost all of the groups noticed that long-term, sustained, and evolving change in all 16 of the *other* SDG areas hinged on education. When Admiral Thad Allen, Co-Chair of the NASEM Measuring Community Resilience project[35] invited me to attend the New York portion of their listening tour, he said, "the problem is that education is everywhere and nowhere in conversations about climate resilience." Education policymakers should want to be held accountable to the children whose futures we shape. It is the most important civic responsibility they have (arguably the most important civic responsibility ANYONE has). This book aims to give policymakers some ideas for change, too, including working collaboratively in creative co-governance with teachers and youth to fulfill opportunities to change the story of human life from one of doom to one of empowered hope.

A Matter of Doing Our Part in the Web of Life

This is a book that offers lots of "What If" questions and takes up many threads of research and experience, weaving them together with different perspectives and ways of being into possible pathways forward. It humbly and respectfully draws on many ancestral traditions and ways of being. This book will also ask as many questions as it answers, and your learning communities will keep the inquiry going. It is not a recipe book or a curriculum plan. Your consideration of the questions will generate and regenerate deep-rooted change. There is a lot to do, in a short period of time, but the good news is that we are not having to "start from scratch." We (remember mine is not the only voice heard in these pages) have given you some starting places and suggestions and examples, some steps you can take tomorrow, and some goals for further off, mostly from my own experience and from the many teachers, school leaders, professors, community leaders, elders, parents, youth, and kids who are already acting on what they know to be true. They have already established a shared momentum, and are proving that *collectively*, we humans (at some level) *already know how* to do what we need to do. We just need to give ourselves the permission to do it and find energy and strength, beauty and solidarity in the powers that we have.

This book re-situates education at the center of industrialized humanity's need to internalize or relocate narratives of agency, coherence, belonging, and care. It prioritizes our ability to realign with Nature and to read and assess power structures and our roles in them. Once we can name our generative powers, we are well on the way to individual and collective change making. Most importantly, this book re-centers creative energy with educators and learners and facilitates tapping into pre-existing courage, knowledge, and skills to nourish well-being, civic action, and climate learning. We educators are not bystanders.

How Do I Know We Can Do This? Because ...

Because educators and youth are already leading school transformation. We are not alone or even "at the starting line." You can feel the momentum and the gathering up of creative companions on platforms like Edutopia, Getting Smart, or Design for Change. You can feel it in transformative books such as *Worldwise Learning*, *Street Data*, *Timeless Learning*, and *Cultivating Genius*.[36] Educators are already building elements of healing and restoration, multi-disciplinary and holistic systems thinking into their work.

Because life is on our side. Everywhere we turn, we can see and learn from the resilience of life. From our ancestors, whose tenacity and ingenuity brought us alive to today. From our earth-family, whose elements ARE us, who feed us and water us and whose species and systems heal and regenerate with alacrity, if given the chance. From ways of knowing and being that kept humanity in the right relationships with nature for all those millennia. From the strength of the interconnected ecosystems within our own bodies and the way they resonate and heal with others.

Because turning toward each other makes us healthy and whole. There are many ways to belong, and belonging makes us powerful enough to shift whole systems. Research shows that consistently helping others not only improves confidence and relevance, responsibility and belonging, it improves cognitive functioning, planning, focus, immune system response, and longevity.[37] Student self-image and well-being will improve.

A 17-year-old in Guayanilla (PR), one of the areas hardest hit by ongoing earthquakes, wrote, "I used to avoid thinking about my future because I didn't think I could do anything about it under the circumstances. Designing Our Lives helped me to see that I am powerful because of what I know about myself. We are powerful because of our community."

Because participation in change also enables us to be part of something and to become comfortable with risk, uncertainty, and iteration. What Buddhists would call "Joyous Participation" in positive change generates creative companionship and belonging, and especially with compassion driving our motivation, empowers us to act.

Because creative minds, compassionate hearts, open spirits, and willing hands can change the world, especially when they work together. We've done it before.

In a 2003 speech called, "Confronting Empire," award-winning Indian author Arundhati Roy famously said, "Another world is not only possible, she's on her way, and, on a quiet day, I can hear her breathing." As I write this 20 years later, I might add, she's already here. Within us, between us, embracing us. We just have to make the contribution that is within our life-given power to make. We are the generations our ancestors hoped for.

Our best allies and closest conspirators in this are our students and the youths with whom we imagine and build a better future. Their voices resound in this book, too. They will inspire you and your team to keep going and give you ideas to guide you through this. Some are thriving in the midst of multiple layers of catastrophe, colonialism, and racism of both socio-economic and environmental kinds. All have the courage of their convictions and the joyful experience of doing something that matters. All can show us different yet clear pathways through the paralysis of futurephobia. I am humbled to know them, grateful for their time and talent, awed by the depth of their love for this world, inspired by their insight and wit and so totally motivated by them that they are the reason this book is here.

You will find that building on the efforts of educators who are already moving this way, climate-solutions-orientation and school-supported civic engagement improves young peoples' attitudes towards school and towards themselves and each other (and the planet). They will be more likely to show up, and to show up with their most inspired selves. You will be re-energized, too. Soon other teachers and the students in your classes will want to go deeper and learn more. Remember, it doesn't have to be perfect. You and your students will change it and make it better as you go. Vaclav Havel wrote, "Hope is not the conviction that something will turn out well, but the certainty that something makes sense, regardless of how it turns out."[38] If it makes sense, we should try it, and then keep learning as we go.

In the learning, thinking, sharing, and writing of this book, it has ceased to be "mine." Really, it is ours—not only young people, but teachers, professors, and parents from Puerto Rico, the United States, and around the world have weighed in. And when you and your team take this up, it will be yours, too. Update and regenerate it. Make it work for your school, university, and community. There is consensus. We have good reason to believe that if we work together, we can do this.

Seeds to Plant (Key Ideas)

Climate change is creating powerful individual and collective emotions such as fear, grief, guilt, anger, mistrust, and underlying them all, powerlessness.

Powerlessness creates disengagement and fatalism. Too many doom stories make this worse.

Nature has given us inseperable (re)generative powers—in the coherent self (Personhood), in interrelationship with other People (and beings), in Place, Purpose, and Process. All lead to the agency to act beyond futurephobia, which in turn enacts a cycle of Positivity.

We have guides for this transformative time. Nature is our best teacher and can show us through living systems how we can thrive. Living systems are Interrelated, Coherent, Biodiverse, Regenerative, and Continuously Changing. Power is distributed, not concentrated. These attributes translate easily into regenerative learning.

We can also depend on other people: those who are living in the teeth of climate injustice, those who hold ancestral and experiential wisdom, children and youth, each other.

We know how to do this, and we know *that* because we already are. There are many ways to change the story.

Notes

1 Yoder 2021.
2 Leiserowitz, et al., 2021.
3 Landry 2022.
4 The Climate Risk Index, created in Germany, established that PR was the region most affected by climate disasters between 1999 and 2018. See: https://germanwatch.org/sites/default/files/Global%20Climate%20Risk%20Index%202021_1.pdf
5 For Puerto Rico Child Services Data Bases 2019 See: https://www2.census.gov/programs-surveys/acs/tech_docs/accuracy/PRCS_Accuracy_of_Data_2019.pdf October 2021
6 Johnson and Wilkinson 2020. If you teach middle or high school, you will want to use these beautiful essays directly. In any case, you will want not to miss this collection of feminist climate voices. What's important about the feminist angle? Aside from the fact that women are an underused resource and are more affected by climate change, they are also more likely to think long-term (like mothers do), act collectively and creatively from compassion, and limit competitiveness so as to stay focused on the challenges (p. xviii-xx). Thousands of copies of this book are already being used in schools and colleges across the world, including boys' schools. Why? Because boys and men are oppressed by certain kinds of hyper-competitive and extractive masculinity as well. *All We Can Save* demonstrates that the climate movement is multi-racial and multi-ethnic, intersectional and multidisciplinary.
7 By September of 2017, when the twin hurricanes Irma and María struck Puerto Rico exactly 14 days apart, I was teaching a public policy class in community resilience called City 2.0. That class had a history of bringing together high school students and community members, government officials and other organizations to engage in enacting our learning about what makes a community resilient and how we might use design thinking to address threats both slow and sudden. The American Superintendents Association asked me to go to PR ten days after María (along with three superintendents), to see how we might help. My aim was to listen to and support educators. More about this story in Chapter 8. You can find out how those initial contacts and relationships developed into collaborative action on my website, https://www.designEd4resilience.org. One of those collaborations brought me into an exciting series of design thinking intersessions at Escuela Francisco Manrique Cabrera in Bayamón. They were part of a student-led public school transformation supported by the Center

for Design Thinking and Innovation in Education (CD-TIE), which was then El Pueblo Unido Program. The teachers there are still cultivating youth-empowered learning, and CD-TIE continues to collaborate with schools around the island. https://sites.google.com/view/elpueblounido

8 **Design thinking** is a way of thinking about simple and complex problems that cultivates resilience-building agency and innovators' mindsets, as well as providing a process that begins with listening and empathizing. Much more about this in later chapters.

9 Command Z 2019.

10 Pierce 2019.

11 Burke, et al., 2018.

12 Nugent 2021. Nugent, Ciara. 2021. "75% of the Young People Around the World are Frightened of the Future Because of Climate Change." *TIME*. 14 September 2021. https://time.com/6097677/young-people-climatechange-anxiety/ The author caught a pre-print look at the article due out soon from *Lancet Planetary Health*.

13 Thunberg 2021.

14 Kelsey 2020.

15 Menakem 2017.

16 Segarra-Alméstica, Eileen V., et al., 2021.

17 Intergovernmental Panel on Climate Change (IPCC) 2021.

18 And women scientists, too, have been trying to tell us what was coming. In **1856**, Eunice Newton Foote's paper about how CO2 in the atmosphere could affect the earth's temperature was, well, ignored. After all, Foote had signed on to the women's rights Declaration of Sentiments (1848, Seneca Falls). Johnson and Wilkinson 2020.

19 Ray 2020.

20 Taylor 2006.

21 Gottfried 2020.

22 Mooney, Chris, et al., 2021.

23 Michaels 2011.

24 Worth 2021.

25 Hawken 2007.

26 Leiserowitz, et al., 2021.

27 Shivaram 2021. The statistics about inequity in the sentences that follow the quote are also from this article.

28 Kristof and WuDunn 2009.

29 Curtin 2020.

30 Coleman 2019.

31 Abrams 2019.

32 Tutu 2014.

33 Hawken 2021. Whenever you are having doubts or are in need of ideas, read this book. You can read one or two pages at a time. It is packed with solutions that are in action now.

34 The 17 UN Sustainable Development Goals are by no means complete but can serve as excellent categories for communities and schools to jumpstart conversations about topics for challenge-based learning and civic action. https://sdgs.un.org/goals There are also MOOC classes available on many of the topics in the SDG Academy, and an Academy community to go along with it. https://sdgacademy.org/

35 National Academies of Science, Engineering, and Medicine, 2017.

36 A starting reading list might include Safir, Shane, and Jamila Dugan. *Street Data: A Next Generation Model for Equity, Pedagogy, and School Transformation.* Corwin, 2021. Socol, Ira; Moran, Pam; and Ratliff, Chad. *Timeless Learning.* Jossey-Bass, 2018. Muhammad, Gholdy. *Cultivating Genius: An Equity Framework for Culturally and Historically Responsive Literacy.* Scholastic, 2020; Pledger, Michelle Sadrena. *LIBERATE! Pocket-Sized Paradigms for Liberatory Learning.* 2022.

37 The benefits of altruism, helping others, pitching in in an emergency, volunteerism, and generosity are well-documented. All result in our brains releasing positivity hormones that make us not only feel better about ourselves but also assist in physiological and psychological healing and healthy functioning.

38 Havel 1991.

Interview: Génesis Ramos Rosado

After the storms in 2017, Dr. Lugo's students wanted to Do Something about the injustices all around them. When he asked what they wanted to do, they concluded that engaging youth ages 15–25 in community-empowering social justice (i.e., anti-poverty, gender-violence, youth rights, climate, and food justice) awareness and action would not only create long-lasting positive change, it would benefit their own healing and well-being. "Because real change is up to us" is not only Impacto Juventud's motto, in Puerto Rico it is a statement of fact.

Génesis Ramos is one of the co-founding leaders of Impacto Juventud. She also works, attends school full time, and is a youth leader in Hijos de Borinquen, a group dedicated to the elimination of child poverty. She gave me a beautiful hour. I want you to hear how she and Impacto Juventud move beyond futurephobia and build coherence and power, so we might apply similar tools in our contexts. Génesis's story is a root story for the lessons in this book. It demonstrates moving toward coherence in the midst of chaos and how to gather the generative power needed to go beyond futurephobia. Since she gave me this interview, Génesis has graduated with the highest honors and earned the Student of the Year Award from the Puerto Rico Psychological Association. She is currently a Fellow with Mentes Puertorriqueñas en Acción and is attending graduate school at Arizona State University. Listen in, look for those moments that resonate with you, and feel free to underline.

Génesis Ramos Tells It Like It Is. 7 October 2020.

Edited for length.

Limits now limit the future?—The hardest part is what the Bayamón kids said about their future. We often don't think there is a way out. At night, there's a constant thing—I worry about whether what I am doing is enough, not just for me and my family, but for society in general. Because every day we see

DOI: 10.4324/9781003215806-2

that the opportunities we thought we had are being limited. Some kids don't have computers or the Internet. I don't have Internet. I only have my phone and a hotspot, but that doesn't work too well when you're connected to zoom meetings every day, four hours a day. My family always says that money should not be an obstacle to achieving your goals, but it is.

My goal right now is to survive this year. First, this year started with the earthquakes and now the pandemic, and there seems to be no happy ending. When you visualize your future, you think, "oh, I'd like to be a professional, and work here, and do this and that," but when you come to reality, it's like, I don't know if I am even going to be alive.

The pandemic has heightened a sense of helplessness in every possible way. Among college kids too. They say, we can't be looking for graduate schools because there is no way we can get out of this. Not just COVID, but all the other hardships here in Puerto Rico. In my case, I have a very supportive family, a family of teachers, and they have always encouraged me to look forward and to try to get the money and help me think of ways to get by, but every time it gets harder and bigger. I have friends who are working, too, and when they finish their Bachelors, they think they will not find a job.

There are no limits—Before I started University I worked in a summer camp as a teacher's assistant. It was about recycling, and we made a dress out of newspaper. It was very fun and also very complex, because it was mainly for children of different learning abilities, like dyslexia, ADHD [Attention Deficit and Hyperactivity Disorder], etc. All the kids in the camp have different exceptionalities, and they were all part of the Special Ed program. I also worked with Camp Ability, with blind kids, and that was the highlight of my life. I have my five senses, and I think, "oh, I can't do this," and then you see them and they go out there and do all this stuff ... they paddleboard, go kayaking, they play tennis ... they did all these activities. I learned that sometimes you are the one who puts the limits to yourself! For them, there were no limits. It was very empowering. That was one of the things that got me involved in these kinds of projects. It made me believe that there are no limits if you put your mind to it.

Reciprocal impact—It's very sad, too, here in PR, because you need to have certain resources in order to accomplish those things, but I think that through Impacto Juventud and Hijos de Borinquen, we want that inequality to end. We want everyone to have the same chance of succeeding in what they want to do in life. Through Impacto Juventud and Hijos de Borinquen, I think I have the power and opportunity to empower others and to be a little bit of guidance through our videos and informational content and give other people the same skills we are gaining here. It's not only to educate others it's about self-education because you have to read, research, and look for all this information to be able to share it, because we don't want to give anything that's not scientifically based, and we learn from these experiences.

Impacto Juventud—It started as a psychology class that Dr. Eduardo Lugo gave after Hurricane Maria, and the main point back then was to give information to people and to make possible access to the rights of children,[1,2] so that people could know more about them. Here in Puerto Rico, not even the parents know about them, and this is a challenge for the dynamics between parents and kids—here there is a dynamic that children should be quiet and on the side. We don't validate their opinion that much, and it's very important that they know from a very young age that they have the power to say what they are feeling, and the power to have a say in how their life is going to go.

I was very happy to join this journey because, basically, Impacto Juventud is for everything that's fair—we also do lots of activities. I see Impacto Juventud as a skill, and as an asset in my life, that it helped me to empower myself and educate myself too. A lot of the stuff that I'm still learning, I did not even imagine existed before. A lot of what I have gotten to do is community outreach and advocacy.

We have visited different schools and communities with lots of problems, but not as a savior or an expert coming in to drop knowledge off and just go, but to do this in a way that they feel that we're equals. We give you this information and we also want to know about you—about the different skills you have, what do you need, or what do you think you can give back to the community, or to the country in general.

You also see that the municipalities and schools also do not give youth the space to explore and develop those skills they have. So I also like open mike nights—it's more creative and outgoing and people express themselves in a very spontaneous way. Here, at school sometimes art is not valued, but you can do so much through art, not only to express your feelings but also to show the different problems we're facing and you can show solutions, too. At Impacto Juventud, we value that very much, and we try to give everyone a space to grow and to show what they're made of and what they have.

A sense of belonging—And I think that's the beauty of it. Everybody feels welcome, and even though we have a lot going on, we try to give everyone a space so that they can do what is their passion, or their way to contribute to the world. Also, we have people who follow us from different countries. We've been trying to expand ourselves. I know that our situation is very particular because of our status as a colony, but there are other countries that are having similar problems, and we can help each other and learn from each other, too.

What restores me and fuels me—One of the things that helps me the most to calm myself is to spend time with my family, my dancing, and other forms of exercise. I try to blow off some steam that way.

My aunt has a house that belonged to my great-grandmother, secluded in the woods. There's nobody around, it's very small, but it's very peaceful. We go once a month and stay a weekend—there's no wifi, it's just in nature. We put up our hammocks and we take naps in there, and we just breathe for a moment. The most beautiful thing about it is that it has been passed down through generations. We all took care of her. We also feel like that place reconnected us all around her, and we won't lose that unity we have as a family.

When the family is split—Something else that fuels me to keep fighting for the changes that we need for this country—most of my dad's family went to the States to find jobs, and they always dream of the idea of coming back to PR, because they don't feel as a part of the United States. They feel lonely and we feel like a part of us is missing. And this makes me want to keep fighting to make this a better place so that they can come back here. Even if they can't raise their kids here, because they are already living there, at least maybe their grandchildren can come here and live and see the beauties of Puerto Rico, because it is very sad that they don't get to enjoy their heritage there because they are afraid they will be discriminated against. It is very clear why they feel that way because every day we see all the things that are happening there. So that fuels me.

Impacto Juventud is family—The family that Impacto Juventud has given me plays a key role in fuelling me too, not only because I relate their story with mine, but also because I see that my fellow friends are going through some things that are even worse, and we don't want that for anybody. It's about trying to find the hope and that ray of light in all of this darkness. Even during the pandemic, we have created a support network among each other. It's not just an assignment or a means to an end. We are a real team that not only supports each other in the activities of Impacto Juventud but in general.

Sometimes we disagree too, but we know how to respect each other, and to elaborate on our ideas in a respectful way. We want to show that people with different perspectives can work together to make new spaces and opportunities.

On improving systems—We know there is a large group of people that want to do better—for themselves and the country, and I know maybe it seems like a tunnel with no end, but if I give up and promote the idea that there's no way out, then how will the change happen? Hence, I keep fighting and sharing that vision with my friends and family so they don't lose hope because that's the last thing we can hold onto.

It's not going to be easy, from one day to another, but if we work for it, it will go forward. Things will change. We have to start somewhere, and we can't be complaining about it because that doesn't bring anything good to the situation. We have to find our own way of how we can give back and help in this process. That's something that Impacto Juventud helped me realize—how I could contribute and also that it's our responsibility as citizens to do something.

Even though we don't see ourselves as an individualistic culture, sometimes we are. It's like, if I and my family are ok, I am going to do nothing because that's not affecting me. But we shouldn't be that way, because everything we do or don't do affects others, like a never-ending circle. I think that's what Impacto Juventud is trying to do, too. To help people see that their lives have meaning. And that what they do can have an impact not just on themselves but on the whole system and the whole community.

Notes

1 Instituto del Desarrollo de la Juventud, Child and Youth Well-Being Index, 2020 http://juventudpr.org/inicio.html. IDJ is the most respected social data-gathering agency on the island and is focused exclusively on the impacts of child poverty and advocating to eliminate it. Spend some time exploring their informative site if you're curious about what's going on with kids in PR.
2 The United Nations Declaration of the Rights of Children (1959) makes it simple. Five. Protection, Education, Health Care, Shelter, and Good Nutrition. Many organizations around the world use these fundamental needs and rights of children as the basis for their work. https://www.un.org/en/sections/issues-depth/children/index.html#:~:text=In%201959%2C%20the%20UN%20General,%2C%20shelter%2C%20and%20good%20nutrition The1989 OHCHR (Office of the High Commissioner on Human Rights) Convention on the Rights of the Child includes the importance of considering youth opinions and involving them in decisions touching on their lives. https://www.ohchr.org/en/professionalinterest/pages/crc.aspx in 2003, UNICEF's State of the World's Children emphasized the same point, and prioritized child and youth participation in decision making. https://www.unicef.org/publications/index_4810.html#:~:text=The%20State%20of%20the%20World's%20Children%202003%20reports%20on%20child,appreciation%20of%20diversity%20and%20peace.

2 The Power of Love: Unity in the Universe

What is the role of love in the universe?
What does learning based on love (unity) and life look like?
How can we co-create regenerative learning ecosystems?

One of the first things you might notice about living ecosystems is that power is distributed. There is no outside agency monitoring development. "Straighten up, tree! Tomato, put out another root!" The second thing we notice is just how resilient this way of doing things is. The ecosystem can absorb and adapt much more effectively precisely *because* power and agency are distributed instead of being in the hands of an outside agent or in one species who owns or runs the ecosystem. What if the powerful agent or species did not have the interests of the whole in mind? What if something happened to the most powerful species? Or if it was just not paying attention? Concentrating power in living systems such as humans have done, in fact makes them more vulnerable. But wait! Without a centralized authority figure, what holds life together? Just as gravity keeps the Earth and all of its systems sticking together instead of flying off into space and entropy, love is the universal unifying principle of life. Few people understand this better than educators.

DOI: 10.4324/9781003215806-3

Love Is a Teacher's Superpower

Teachers might say they "love their kids," or that they feel a calling to teach. Teachers build community inside and outside of their classrooms, and they do their best to defend that community. Teachers like to be trusted, and they do their best to deserve that trust. Most teachers love to learn, are excited about what they've learned and are eager to learn more. They want to share that energy with their students. Most teachers are aware of the ways in which what they do and say affects these young peoples' lives, both individually and collectively. Many would say they went into teaching because they wanted to make a positive difference, and so they look for opportunities, even within restrictive and oppressive systems, to protect and empower their students. Most would agree that what is supporting and energizing them is the power of love. Even before there is real learning , there is trust, safety, and belonging. Our regenerative powers of Personhood, People, Place, Purpose, Process, and Positivity, as well as our foundational human capacities for imagination, reflection (metacognition), research, and long-range planning evolve in the context of a dynamic relationship that reflects the essential principles of life. And because love is that element of our being that craves unity and connectedness, the essential unifying force of the natural world, it is the soil in which all human agency that is based on and conducive to life, grows. It is also a teacher's superpower.

In his book *Power and Love: A Theory and Practice of Social Change*[1], Adam Kahane, a globally sought-after facilitator for solving the stickiest of complex problems, outlines a paradigm of power combined with love that gives words to what I think most teachers feel. Going back to theologian and philosopher Paul Tillich,[2] Kahane borrows the paradigm that power can be either generative or degenerative. Degenerative power is easy to spot, and we will explore it further in Chapter 3. Suffice it to say here that degenerative "Power Over," weakens and harms those around and under it and therefore eventually itself. In the scheme of life, it is the opposite of "regenerative," which by definition creates the conditions for more life. It must be said that "Power Over," is not always degenerative. It can be tempered by love and may be helpful in small doses, out of recognition of expertise or wisdom. But in rigidly hierarchical organizational structures and at the scale of socio-political-economic and military history, degenerative power is aggressive and oppressive. Simply put, it denies or ignores the fully actualized agency that belongs to a person or people or lands or beings it encounters. For one example on the global scale (which we'll revisit in Chapter 6), when European colonizers settled far away from their origins, for example, they viewed both the land and the people they encountered as empty, or "undeveloped." On the scale of a school, when a teacher or a professor or outside consultant enters the learners' space with the attitude that the learners are empty vessels or only partially developed people, there is already a degenerative power balance in the room. Kahane asserts that love can be generative or degenerative, too. When a parent (or a teacher), perhaps hoping to protect, makes all the decisions on behalf of the child, and does not allow the child to carry actual age-appropriate responsibility within the family that brings on real results, there is a degenerative power balance within the loving relationship. The child will have lower self-esteem and might not become a self-confident and secure adult.

Regenerative Power Is Rooted in Love

Regenerative power, of the kind we will investigate in detail in the next chapter, the kind that Paul Tillich's mentee Rev. Dr. Martin Luther King, Jr. said "... is the strength required to bring about social, political and economic change ... ,"[3] and is rooted in love, or that force that, like gravity, pulls toward unity, but not uniformity. A teacher's love creates trust and belonging. A teacher's love guarantees that the student's uniqueness will be lifted up, seen, heard, and valued. Their special brilliance will shine, and they will contribute their gifts to the whole. A teacher's love opens the relational bridge of reciprocity between teacher and learner, learner and teacher, and allows the student's Self to emerge in the "conversation." A teacher's love empowers real growth, draws out strengths, gives space to wonder, to struggle, and thereby to learn. A teacher's expertise might be enacted in the way they balance love and power (more than the content they "deliver"), so that each energizes and strengthens the other. A teacher's love is the soil in which the roots of agency and life can thrive in the process of learning and change. When confronted with futurephobia, the love shared in a learning community helps us to activate our "Tend, Befriend, and Mend" response, or motivates us to advocate strongly, fighting hard for life.

Love without power is degenerative. Teachers with lots of love but without change-making agency cannot transfer agency to their students. Love without the power to effect change in school might attract students to school to see their friends or to please their parents, and might even lead obedient students in, but unless they have efficacy and agency, students eventually disengage with school. Dr. King said, " ... One of the great problems of history is that the concepts of love and power have usually been contrasted as opposites—polar opposites—so that love is identified with the resignation of power, and power with the denial of love. Now we've got to get this thing right."[4] Empowered love is regenerative, and it enables interconnectedness, holistic (coherent) learning, and comfort with continuous change. In the age of climate disasters, it is the audacious antidote to futility, fatalism, and futurephobia.

The triple literacies of life, love, and power then become the basis of learning and essential matters for educators' consideration. How best to explore the unifying principle of love? Clearly, we are not talking about romantic love or even familial love, although you can see power in all its forms in those matters of the heart too, but rather something both more expansive and pragmatic. How does love, as a universal principle governing life itself, nourish and strengthen both life and the regenerative powers available to humans?

In her book, *Biomimicry*, biologist Janine Benyus writes, "Virtually all cultures that have survived without fouling their nests have acknowledged that nature knows best, and have had the humility to ask the bears and wolves and ravens and redwoods for guidance."[5] So let's turn again to the basic principles of life, to see how they reflect the unifying pull of love and how they might enable the human agency to flourish. What might they look like in learning ecosystems? Here's a more detailed exploration of regenerative learning than the chart in the last chapter (Figure 1.3). Look for evidence of the unifying force of love, and reflect on it in the third column. I provided one example. (Figure 2.1)

Living Systems Are…	So Regenerative Learning Is…	And Love Holds It Together
Interrelated – nothing lives by itself alone; all relationships are present all of the time	Multi-disciplinary and collaborative Focused on relationships as much as separate parts Collective and shared success Based on relational awareness and critical systems thinking/feeling with time builtin for full listening, caring and compassion	An example in learning : Mutuality and reciprocity in collaborative relationships built through listening and creative companionship at all stages of development
Coherent – wholeness means all fits together and nothing is wasted	Holistic (head, heart, hands/body, spirit) Healing and restorative Life—'real world' experience, driven by curiosity and wonder, deep reflection and authentic accountability to others	
Biodiverse — thriving only possible through difference. Unity, not uniformity.	Safe for all beings Welcoming and encouraging of individual difference as contributing to whole community Cultural brilliance held by individual beings adds to cultural 'wealth' of the whole ecosystem	
Regenerative — life creates the conditions for more life to occur	Learning that draws learners deeper into learning Lifelong and intergenerational/interage/ancestral	
Changing — continuous adaptation and change	Iterative and flexible, embracing of mistakes and failing as learning opportunities Growth-based rather than fixed or deficit-based Seeking of opportunities and challenges to support change Guided by regenerative values— see above and below	
Power-diffuse — ecosystems are self-governing	Democratic--Lead learners (educators) and learners co-create learning experiences Focused on building agency and civic responsibility by enabling space and opportunity for collective self-direction Authentic accountability determines success	

FIGURE 2.1 Love as the essential principle of life and learning

The word "education" grows from **both** of its Latin roots: *educare*, to shape, and *educere*, to draw out. Plants, too, are adapted to draw out the best, the fittest elements of themselves and those beings around them. When Darwin wrote about the fittest surviving, what he meant was that those organisms who could both shape (adapt) themselves to contribute to their ecosystem and could also draw out the contributions of others would thrive. How can we create a learning community where everyone has something to contribute, and where every being is known and valued? Where unified wins out over uniform? Where the creative energy whizzing back and forth among and between learners and teachers draws out the essence of the self in relation to others? The climate justice crisis (and the mental health and efficacy crisis that go with it) is an invitation to those of us who have not already done so, to accept the greatest gift of all—Nature's ways of knowing and being to inform and empower (from the roots!) our learning and being, too.

Everything/Everyone Is Mutually Interrelated

If we narrow the scale of this enduring unifying (loving) element in Nature, we can see how it works in a very personal way. Take the human body. We are made up of interconnected ecosystems of living organisms, the vast majority of which have non-human DNA. In fact, only a tiny portion of our *own* DNA is specific to humans. Totally, 96% of our mass is due to the four organic elements, hydrogen, oxygen, carbon, nitrogen (mostly in the form of water), shared with all life. This makes us relatives with our whole living biocollective community and all the systems and processes in it. Buddhists and Taoists call this Interbeing. How would our relationship with the natural world be different if we thought of all in our biocollective as relatives? We'll explore this further in Chapter 5. We depend on our connection with other living things to survive, and they in turn on their connections with the ecosystems around them. This is why maintaining habitats for pollinators and biodiversity in our food-producing ecosystems is of critical importance to us.

Not only that, we also depend on human bodies including our own to cultivate, harvest, perhaps transport and market, and prepare the food. If we cut out any part of those interconnected systems, or alter or fragment them in such a way that an imbalance or outright breakdown occurs, we will become ill and possibly die off.

 Mending News!

Student Project Promotes Cross-Sector Relationships

US Coast Guard Academy Junior Christine Groves wondered why a huge offshore wind energy project failed to come to fruition (even though it would have energized 400,000 homes). What she found was that the project planners had not considered the balance of the relationships in the ecosystem (migration routes, transportation and fishing zones, recreation, etc.) and had not included those with knowledge and experience early enough in the process. Without their inclusion, they resisted until the project broke down. Cadet 2nd Class Groves created a pre-project research and risk-assessment model to help planners understand the relationships, how they can inform the likelihood of project success or failure, and how to identify important voices to invite to the decision-making table. If they had had Christine's insights in hand and acted upon them, the planners would have saved over 100 million dollars!

Historically speaking, our school systems grew out of the industrial age (Committee of 10, 1892), when efficiency (one teacher, many students) and the development of specific skills and hierarchies were what mattered, not the integrity of interrelating systems. *Homo praeceptorus industrialis* (the industrialized school teacher) works in an odd kind of isolation (as there are people all around), with closed classroom doors and departments that do not interact with one another. Students are frequently sorted by both age and ability (for efficiency's sake?), stratifying schooling and splitting the community, frequently reflecting the socio-economic and racial stratification outside the building's thick walls. The resulting fracturing of multi-disciplinary systems thinking and holistic well-being in schools creates systemic illness and exacerbates vulnerabilities to disaster. I did my student teaching in a typical industrialized school.

Day 1: I walked into the old, small, hot, smelly classroom with my heart beating fast. The first day of student teaching, 1984. My "master teacher" was nowhere to be seen, and the kids were all over the place. One was yelling and flapping his shirt because he had scorched his belly on the radiator while trying to lean out the window. Two girls were insulting each other's taste in music in escalating tones near the door ("now that shit's going to be stuck in my head..."). A few boys were making a mess at the chalkboard and trying to make the chalk screech by pushing it against the slate. One kid was seeing if he could sit upside down in his chair. Some were singing and clapping. The others were mostly watching to see what I would do. I had no idea. I had my lesson all drawn out (with Plans A, B, and C depending on their likely questions), knew the goals and objectives and what content I was supposed to "teach." There was nothing in there about how I was going to BE with them and how they might BE with me.

So, maybe just to buy time, I turned off the glaring lights. I went to the kid nearest to me and said, my parents named me Margarita Augusta Favretti, but they wrote Margaret on my birth certificate because my immigrant grandmother who had nearly died as a prisoner of war in northern Italy did not want me to sound too Italian. But I am not a Margarita or a Margaret. I've named myself Maggie because it seems to fit. What is your name today?

Thus began our mutual learning journey. I had no idea how to teach differently from how I was taught, and neither did they. It turned out we were all accustomed to a model of schooling that didn't make room for us to be us or for us to be *together*. Without any of us setting out to do so, by naming ourselves, we were unintentionally stepping into mutuality, giving each other space to be ourselves (love) and to challenge the assumptions and the systems around us (regenerative power). I never told them that their teacher introduced them to me as his "unteachables," and I had seen him spend half of every class getting them to sit down, hold their pencils right, and quietly take notes while he taught them about ancient civilizations from the textbook—all before he had learned their names. By the end of the day, they had started to teach me their signature hand-shakes (that was big back then).

Day 2: After learning more signature handshakes and a few students updating their names, I showed them a map of Africa to locate Egypt. They gathered around it. "Egypt is in *Africa*?" one of them yelped in surprise. "These gods and pharaohs were *Black*?" "So you're saying that civilization got started by *Black* people?" "Why don't you people *tell* us these things?!"

Why Don't You People Tell Us These Things?

Suddenly our curriculum in story-telling (who gets to tell it), critical thinking, civic courage (based on ancient civilizations and ours), and historical meaning began to take shape. These kids helped me to think about history in their terms: how people make sense of the world and shape their participation in it; how events affect people and people affect events. I began to think in "triple-meta," how history is really all about change, and change is all about learning, with plenty of critical thinking about how we know what we know (and why) and how we approach challenges and opportunities to take up our places in evolution from multiple perspectives and subjectivities. Together we were beginning to appreciate how we stand at the intersection of past and future, inheriting the love and wisdom (and the pain and fortitude) of our ancestors and how we, too, can decide what kind of ancestors we want to be. These kids were teaching me how to think about teaching, learning, love, and interrelationship, and how my position of privilege and the way I participated in the system of schooling could either lock down or liberate. Who learned more that day? Probably me.

Through this unplanned reciprocity, I became aware of an-other essential lesson about regenerative teaching from life: teachers are learners and learners are teachers. Together, we create change. *None can do it alone.* Teaching-learning, like life, is fundamentally and infinitely relational.

What would happen if teachers relied on their pedagogical expertise to build relationships full of love, mutuality, and reciprocity with learners at all levels and all ages?

Coherence Means That Nothing/No One Is Wasted

In Nature, coherence in living systems means that everything is there for a reason and has a relevant purpose. Everything fits together and nothing is left out. Even what dies brings life to another. No waste. The beauty of this is its wholeness. And the wholeness itself is more than the sum of its parts—it is expansive and abundant with the unified love we call life. Thus, *coherence* is one of the most important regenerative (living and changing) and unifying (loving) transformations needed for restoring our biosphere to health. As we will see in the next chapter, fragmentation is one of the greatest threats to living power-full and dynamic lives. Fragmentation (incoherence) is felt in school in the emphasis on academic achievement over well-being, "efficient" rushed school schedules, the siloing of knowledge, the separation of age groups, and the demands to move through the requirements of the curriculum in spite of emotional upset, to name a few. We will explore fragmentation further in Chapter 3. The broader context of social media extends the problem of fragmentation. Smartphones and their texting apps have replaced most forms of communication, and while it does provide opportunities for creativity, amplification, and at least superficial connectedness across long distances, it cannot replace in-person connectedness felt in the body, mind, heart, and spirit. The projected self is often not the authentic one, and nuance is impossible in a text. To make matters worse, the stratifying and polarizing of people is being accelerated by the algorithms created for artificial intelligence.[6]

What if we reimagined school based on coherence and wholeness? Could deeper learning take place if well-being and interconnectedness were top priorities?

How to Stop Wasting People and Our Planet-Mates

Colonists inserted the morally abhorrent notion of disposable people inhabiting the "empty" spaces as yet untouched by "civilization." Environmentally racist policymakers and neo-liberal policies of "uncare" have continued, creating "sacrifice zones" where dumping and destruction of people and our larger living community goes unregulated. Industrial Development (including industrial agriculture) has eroded the number of species on the planet by close to a million. However, college students in Puerto Rico are filming and documenting the damage, using new sampling technologies, data analytics, and drone observation. School children are learning to measure air and water quality and to create the conditions to restore coral reefs and mangrove swamps. High school students in Arizona are working with college professors to turn things around. Children are suing the government to force them to take action.

 Mending News!

High School Students Design Climate Solutions at ASU

Arizona State University created ASU Prep and ASU Digital Prep to help students and their families to gain access to college experience. They currently have over 3100 enrolled, in both elementary and secondary schools. Many teams were invited to work with ASU professors on a climate issue of their choosing. First, they had to observe human impacts in their chosen setting … one group decided to focus on the relationship between climate change impacts and those living on the streets. After developing their solutions, one student said in a podcast, "we went into the situation with puny plans and narrow mindedness. We needed to think about the long run." She credited the program with giving her the independence and confidence to be a change maker.

From Tom Vander Ark, "ASU Prep: Experiencing College Success in High School." *Getting Smart*, 4 April 2022.

Children in the Verdi EcoSchool in Melbourne, Florida are helping NASA to experiment with plants that can grow in outer space. (see p. 196)

Sena Wazer (see pp. 262–264) was 5 when she became an activist on behalf of whales getting caught in fishing nets.

Sophia Kianni (see p. 279 and 353) was 16 when she started Climate Cardinals, once she discovered that most of the conversation and information about climate change was in English, but most of the people most affected by climate impacts are not English speakers. https://www.climatecardinals.org/

Alexandra Villaseñor started Earth Uprising at 15 to help other kids learn about climate change and find pathways to action. https://earthuprising.org/

Elders in Barrio Rucio, Peñuelas, Puerto Rico are thriving by showing eager elementary school students how they grew food and medicine in the old days, helping to build food sovereignty and security in their town.

Helena Gualinga, a Sarayaku-Finnish 20-year-old, began her climate activism by defending her remote Indigenous community through video storytelling, a project begun as a teen. She is now one of the leading spokespeople for Indigenous land rights and the natural rights of land and water in the Escazú Agreement (See Chapter 9) region.

What if the curricula of "schools" or community change studios were based on multi-generational alliances to address the environmental justice challenges facing the community?

How Not to Waste Children

Somehow, perhaps especially in the West, we got the idea that the first couple of decades of life should be about learning how to be productive, the middle decades should be productive, and the last decades should be spent in unproductive retirement. One of my students, a young person named Chris, once vented his exasperation, "why are we always told to wait? I'm alive NOW." Children are changemakers, too. Children are affected by the world's big challenges and can learn about big ideas and how to make the world better. In India, industrial designer and parent Kiran Bir Sethi shared Chris's and her own child's frustration when she saw the lack of choice and authentic impact afforded to young children. She felt her son's "I Can" mindset disappearing. She created The Riverside School in Ahmedabad (2001) and developed a simple design thinking process, "Feel, Imagine, Do, Share," that has become the basis of Design for Change (2009), now a global design thinking community and neighborhood "I Can" action phenomenon primarily for young children. This is from their website:[7]

> For the longest time, education has believed that children are the future, that 'ONE day' they will grow up and make the world a better place. And in waiting for that 'One day', education has deferred the promise that it made to its children to help them become creative, proactive, empathetic and responsible citizens. This resulted in children graduating saying 'I CAN'T.'

Love Your Kids With Big Ideas

Studies have shown that the ideal time to engage young people's excitement about citizenship and participation in their neighborhoods and beyond is from the beginning. In her *National Civic Review* article, social scientist Diann Cameron Kelly wrote, "The greatest resource our nation has is our engaged, hopeful youth."[8] Her article goes on to say how important enlisting toddler and early elementary schoolchildren in bettering the world around them can be—to them and to their families and communities. In their book *Unpack Your Impact*, elementary educators Naomi O'Brien and Lanesha Tabb show how little kids can take on big ideas with surprising clarity, and if they can be involved in making a difference, are empowered by the challenges.[9] When you hear young people talking about their projects and their ideas, they fill the room with their energy. When they see the impact of their ideas in action, they come to understand their regenerative power—and how they fit into the coherence of life. Their agency and efficacy takes root. The next time there is a challenge, they will step up and say, "we got this." They won't shy away from a future full of volatility, uncertainty, complexity, and ambiguity (VUCA). Gunav, a 3rd grader, is trying to educate the adults in his life about the possibilities of Artificial Intelligence to help us understand the workings of the world and how to work together better. He writes, "Let's step into/the streets where a new kind of intelligence awaits/In the garden of our days/Where man and machine finally converge/As dawn climbs the sky/With computer vision machine learning/Where the 3Rs count ratified strategy/ With smart sorting and bins alarming/AI helps prevent tragedy." In Gunav's vision, we will use ALL of our ways of knowing, think and act flexibly and with confidence, embracing the unknown and seeking challenges such as injustice and climate change as opportunities to contribute.

How Not to Waste Elders

Disaster response and recovery research has identified collaborative problem-solving and participation across generations as one of the leading catalysts for smooth recovery.[10] Research also shows that older people who continue to engage with society, feel a strong sense of purpose, and spend time with younger people have less occurrence of dementia and other cognitive diseases, and live longer, more fulfilling lives. They are more energetic and joyous and able to contribute more to society than they draw from it. Communities that build cross-generational collaboration are significantly more likely to bring about positive change and withstand high-impact disasters.[11] Can you imagine the regenerative power and love and creative companionship embodied in teams of grandparents and grandchildren , tapping into all of their sources of ancestral inspiration, life experience, and youthful ingenuity to bring to life ideas about the world's challenges? Re-imagining learning (lifelong!) in the age of climate disruption calls for re-engaging everyone and not leaving anyone's potential "on the bench."

 **Mending News!**

Where Do Old Leaders With Justice in Mind Go?

Not just "former" leaders, The Elders is a group founded in 2007 by the late Nelson Mandela that includes humanitarian leaders and some present and many retired heads of state. All are committed to leaving the world a better place for future generations. Their membership has included the late Archbishop Desmond Tutu, Kofi Annan, and emeritus Jimmy Carter. It is currently chaired by Mary Robinson, the first female president of the Republic of Ireland, and co-chaired by former UN Sec'y General Ban Ki-Moon and Graca Marchel, Education Minister of Mozambique. Through quiet diplomacy and a focus on gender equality, they help to forge peace and justice and protect the planet. https://theelders.org/

How Not to Waste Teachers, Either

In *Where Do We Go From Here*, Dr. King wrote, "power without love is reckless and abusive, and love without power is sentimental and anemic."[12] Teacher-Love without power also causes cognitive dissonance, stress, and burnout. Teachers' efficacy and agency is at a low point, and this needs to change if we hope to facilitate students and their families in deeply engaging learning. We are not going to have healthy kids if we don't have healthy teachers. And if what we're after is student agency and efficacy, the teachers have to have agency, too, to co-create the coherent holistic environments that will support deeply engaging and efficacy-building learning. In the Hattie Research Studies on the relative impacts of hundreds of educational interventions and strategies used with thousands of students over several years, by far the intervention with the most positive impact on students was the collective efficacy of the teachers.[13]

   In the United States since the 1970s, the typical length of time a new teacher stays in teaching, gathering experience, and adding to their repertoires, has shortened considerably, to 2.5 years. When researchers investigate the leading causes for teachers to leave teaching, pay is certainly significant (pay has gradually declined over this period as well), but the most pressing issue is "working conditions." This means a lot of things—from excessive class sizes to having too many responsibilities unrelated to teaching, but by far the most recurrent is lack of agency.[14] For most teachers, advocacy for school improvement centers on the students and their needs. One sign frequently carried in the 2020 teachers' strikes read, "Our working conditions are your child's learning conditions."[15] But teachers are often not in the deciding circles, and when they are, their inputs are dismissed as "self-serving," emphasizing their powerlessness to effect change in the system.

Most teachers began to suffer signs of severe stress during COVID-19. The "always on" and multiple role-juggling expectations of on-again/off-again hybrid schools and staff shortages, schools and states that did not adjust their standards, threatening attacks by parents, and deepening and traumatic social and environmental injustices made it even harder to stay healthy. The Surgeon General's office in the United States broke from its usual calm and joined the CDC (Centers for Disease Control) in proclaiming a mental health crisis among children and adolescents in 2021, and violence, threats of violence, and disruptive acts occurred in school with disturbing frequency. In the fall of 2021 a new COVID-19 variant (omicron) emerged, and school psychologists, administrators, and teachers' prevailing responses to my "How are you doing?" were "I'm exhausted." "Running on fumes." "I need a break."[16] In November, "nearly half (48%) of the 6,000 teachers surveyed said they had considered changing jobs in the past month, up from 32% in June."[17]

Teachers Are First Responders

For many children, school is a reprieve from violence elsewhere in their lives. Under normal circumstances in the United States, according to SAMSHA (Substance Abuse and Mental Health

Services Administration), more than two-thirds of children report at least one traumatic event before age 16. In a 2008
"Update for Mental Health Professionals," witnessing community violence affected between 39 and 85 percent of children,
and up to 43% have experienced sexual abuse.[18] Who do students turn to FIRST when they feel a conversation with a parent
is not possible? Teachers are often the first to notice when
something is wrong, in recognition of which teachers are required to report suspected abuse or self-harm or the potential to
harm others. During COVID-19 stay-at-home orders, the school
could no longer be the place to seek comfort or to practice being
in social relationships, and so once schools reopened fully in
person, the individual and collective traumatic impacts of the
pandemic began to be understood. During a "natural" disaster,
children frequently make up the majority of those affected (and the
majority of children affected are children from marginalized
groups).

In these COVID- and "natural" disaster-affected days, it is
striking to see the ways in which teachers are intervening with
love and care, pushing to have children and youth tended to,
making sure their basic needs are met, and innovating new
ways to help all of them heal. This has been true for a long time,
and in the age of climate disasters, we need to shift our institutional attention to caring for our teachers and building
administrators first and foremost. We will not have healthy
children or youth without healthy educators (in fact, we won't
have schools at all). As emotional health first-responders, more
than three-quarters of teachers are struggling with toxic stress
themselves.

In 2020, Denny Taylor released an important guide for teachers as first responders during COVID-19, which also applies
to most climate crises. In it, she writes, "Children need schools
to be safe, joyful places *before disasters occur* [my italics] if they
are going to have the opportunity to recover when catastrophes
take place. Trans-system approaches are critical … . Build
strong communities, incorporate health and well-being into
pedagogical initiatives. Every attempt should be made to take
care of the whole child, every child, and make school a joyful

place for children to be. This is the basis for school and community *preparedness* [my italics] for catastrophes."[19]

Let's pay and treat teachers, too, as fully actualized professionals. They *know what they need in order to be at their best* for their students, and as communities let's do our best to provide that and to honor their expertise. Let's support them as frontline first responders (with free access to primary *and secondary* trauma care and training, and heightened access to students). Teachers need to be loved so that THEY can enable their own regenerative powers by tapping into love, trust, and belonging too. And teachers are the experts in constructing and iterating learning experiences for their students, though they might need some companionship and support to go beyond what they've been taught to do.

There are thousands of teachers who are extending themselves beyond the confines of the classroom to engage students in collaborative, creative problem-solving that matters. Their teaching is full of both power and love, and their students see and feel the ways in which their own personhood is valued and the ways in which they belong. The students have real responsibilities and are making a difference in the lives of others. They are building coherence and social and emotional learning into everything they do. And we know that those communities that already act with empowered love prove to be much more resilient when disaster strikes.

Natural Systems Only Thrive When There Is Diversity

In natural living systems, life only exists when there is diversity. A healthy ecosystem will have hundreds of visible species and hundreds more that you can't see. All of them are different, but working together in the unity (love) of diversity called life. One of the hardest things for school leaders to do during the COVID-19 pandemic was to bring people together and build consensus when the stresses of the disaster were pulling them apart. The schools that do best in any crisis are those where there is already a commonly understood vision and inclusive decision-making process in place to be followed from the beginning. Those schools are more resilient because they have ready access to their own unifying resources, and have already done some work to break down the walls that make us vulnerable: between kids and adults, school and community, primarily, but also between different age groups, community sectors, and political, demographic, and social groups. Younger and older children become accustomed to learning and working together and working with adults to chart the course of the school and keep it focused on its vision. Transparency and mutual understanding leads to deepening trust and willingness to work together in spite of potentially distracting disagreement. Listening circles often prevent loud voices that falsely claim to be representing many from dominating public meetings, and disagreement without being disagreeable in turn leads to greater empathy, effort, and creativity. Schools and communities that already think of themselves as learning together stay open to many ways of thinking and being, and to trying out new and different approaches together. They do better in addressing all kinds of challenges.

Assistant Superintendent Jammie Behrendt of the Menlo Park City School District in CA cheered their years of community collaboration to co-create their Whole-Child Learning and Development Framework when COVID-19 descended on them because it had already strengthened trust and relationships. They already had clear priorities and protocols for transparent and inclusive communication. And everyone knew that the Framework prioritized Healthy Relationships and Integrated Well-Being through learner-centered, meaningful work, and competencies. They were NOT going to "let the important get ruined by the urgent,"[20] and stuck to their priorities and vision while remaining committed to putting in place all of the county health and locally trusted doctor-recommended safety protocols to ensure everyone's safety. A face-to-face summer 2020 program with teachers who felt comfortable participating (Behrendt joined in, too) piloted the new measures and demonstrated that face-to-face school could happen. One case and no spread. People from very different perspectives could get behind that.

In a time of pandemic or climate disruption and disaster, it is the job of leadership and educators to provide a safe "container," to borrow a term from Adam Kahane, for students and community groups to safely explore complexity from diverse (and self-critical) perspectives. "Our society is full of diverse, strong, competing voices and ideas and cultures. This *fullness* is the fundamental reason why we need to address the world's toughest challenges with both power and love."[21] And this fullness is the main reason we can be hopeful. In the way that greater biodiversity strengthens ecosystems, the diversity of beings and ways of knowing co-empowers our continued co-existence.

How can we create safe and radically inclusive spaces for addressing complexity and uncertainty, for learning together?

I put this question to my community resilience design lab. We learned about what makes climate change so complex and also how and when people of different backgrounds feel unsafe. We deeply considered how climate change affects different people and other living beings differently, even though we have experienced the same disaster—and how social injustice makes people unsafe in many contexts. We learned about learning and stress, and how our minds and bodies work differently when we are not safe.

And then we came up with the 5-Point Safety Framework for Schools. Students felt that schools should ensure Physical, Emotional, Cultural, Social, and Environmental safety as a prerequisite to learning (see Chapter 4, Figure 4.4). Some of us wanted to call it the 5-Point Safety Harness, because of car seats and rock climbing, but a harness just seemed too binding. In order to live fully and learn well, we propose that schools prioritize safety, for teachers, students, and living communities.

"When people feel safe, they feel like they belong," they said, "they share their differences and hear others kindly. There's no othering. They are more creative and open-minded. They work together better. And they can learn because they are not always on edge." And I would add that people who are safe feel less stressed and exhausted. There is more love in their learning space. I pressed a little on environmental safety in school. "We want to know that our school is participating with us in making sure that our learning environment is healthy (safe) and sustainable. Beyond sustainable if possible. We want the school to advocate for us."[22] Most importantly, we articulated the link between feeling safe and diversity. Diversity doesn't mean much if people can't show up with their full selves.

 Mending News!

Green Schools Advocate for Environmental Safety

Trailblazers for Whole School Sustainability: Case Studies of Educators in Action (Seydel, et al., editors, 2022), presents 16 different ways of protecting students' environmental well-being by making sure that the whole school is "practicing what it preaches." This kind of consistency is important. If learners are taught in one class or at home that they should be recycling or even waste-free, and then the school does not take it seriously, that undermines trust. Vending machines on all night. Computers and screens on all night. Long gas-fuelled school bus runs. Processed food. Some teachers who share youth concerns and others who dismiss them. A curriculum that's climate-blind. What is your school's environmental footprint? Try the Green Schools Network's GreenPrint guide! Greening your school district presents your students with civic action opportunities at a manageable scale.

Unity Is Not Uniformity: Standardization Undermines Diversity

… just as monoculture undermines ecosystems.

Another question came up in the resilience design lab. If diversity is so important to the resilience of life, then why are we teaching a centralized curriculum and using standardizing testing to determine who gets what? Many teachers are courageously teaching their students how to think critically, and about how their unique genius and collective power can stand up to systemic injustice, even while the school system's standardized, one-size-fits-all curriculum and testing demands compliance in the name "hard data," inaccurate though it may be. Will we squash our students' ingenuity and passion when our survival depends on it?

In late 2020, a longitudinal study of 150,000 Chicago 9th graders from various socio-economic backgrounds demonstrated the incompleteness of testing as a measure of school effectiveness. Instead, for all students, holistic and competency-based assessment and schooling that emphasized social and emotional development, such as self-awareness, belonging, relationship-building, and listening resulted in improved graduation rates and college matriculation at significantly greater rates than schools that emphasized test scores. Said lead researcher C. Kirabo Jackson in an *Edutopia* interview, "these impacts are particularly large for vulnerable students who don't tend to do very well in the education system."[23] Does that mean that the tests are not providing reliably constructive data that can actually improve children's unique and diverse learning pathways and experiences? If not, and if the "unifying energy" of standardization has no useful purpose other than artificially sorting students into haves and have-nots, then why are we allowing it to continue to hold us back?

What if "assessment" had more to do with a person's unique growth and contribution to the whole, and accountability had to do with authentic engagement in civic life?

Regenerativity—All of It Works (Generates More Life) When All of It Is Working Together

Most gardeners know that plants work together and collaborate with other organisms underground to reduce vulnerability and enhance well-being, not only for themselves but also for the soil itself. A tree thrives in the right reciprocal relation to its environment. It takes in and generates energy. It takes up and also filters water. It sequesters carbon and emits oxygen. The bacteria and fungi around its roots thrive in symbiosis. Its roots are connected with other trees and plants and it is host to other species who live in it and eat from it and, in the end, fertilize the soil around it and help to spread its seeds. *All of it works when all of it is working together, and it keeps working (and changing) infinitely.* That's basic regenerative integrity. Life creates the conditions for more life. A gardener's job is to facilitate, and most especially, not get in the way.

If we can create our learning systems in accord with the logic of living ecological systems, we will be working with the power of love toward interrelated coherence, regenerative integrity and unity, and schools will help all of us (and Earth) to thrive. Teaching and learning with regenerative power/love facilitates the student's evolving self "in right relation" with others and with life itself.

The loving and regenerative purpose of schools and universities alike could be to curate those experiences that allow people's strengths to emerge, such as emotional well-being, belonging, efficacy, purpose, change making, collaborative knowledge creation, and co-governance. We can seek opportunities to align well-being with learning, to connect research with community know-how, to empower youth, teachers, and elders through authentic participation in decision-making in a five-point safe environment. We can deepen motivation and critical thinking, unleash our collective creativity, and flex our agency to make the world a more just and peaceful place.

Cultivate Vision *Together*

Some communities have a bias toward quick solutions, often purchased from consultants or "off the shelf" (see Adam Robb's story in Chapter 10). They'll even spend millions of dollars, depending on the size of the District, to avoid spending the time to

uncover complex local thoughts, feelings, and potentially controversial ideas. It took Menlo Park City School District years and
at least 50 collaborative thought sessions and Board meetings to
fully uncover their Whole Child Learning Framework. As a result, people have confidence in it and each other. Taking the time
to listen and learn, and crafting your own solutions saves a LOT
of time and money later on. Additionally, listening closely and
carefully is more likely to result in culturally responsive, deeply
rooted transformation.[24] Prepare the soil and do it well. Then you
can get out of the way. My father says, "If you put a $10 plant in
a $1 hole, you end up with a $1 plant. But it is possible to put a
$1 plant in a $10 hole and end up with some beautiful fruit." Why
not spend those funds listening and learning together, both from
what's "out there" and from what's right in front of us? Those
thought patterns and processes of co-learning and collaborative
self-reliance will stand us in good stead when the winds blow
and the power goes out.[25] Creating solutions together generates
ways of thinking (mindsets) and habits of action that embody
agency and efficacy. Use the money you have left over to be sure
full-systems implementation of locally generated solutions can
happen. It's widely accepted that in order to bring about transformative change, all you need is motivation, clear vision, and
actionable first steps.[26] I would humbly suggest that WHO is
setting that vision and crafting and assessing those first steps
matters. Everyone can help cultivate cultures of change.

To cultivate anything, we need to start from the ground (ahem,
soil) up. In other words, to imagine a new learning ecosystem, it's
sometimes easiest to start at zero. No grading, no curriculum
standards, no schedule, no building, no walls (metaphorical or
otherwise) between students and everyone else. Just what the
community and the kids dream about.[27] Whether or not it will fit
the state or federal system or even in a physical classroom is beside
the point right now. This is a moment of liberated thinking in a
culture of change, which could lead to adaptation or replacement
of the old systems if we do our thinking well and stay together.

Settle on the scale. Imagine that you are building your
learning community with only the people and other beings with
whom you currently share this place. Is the learning community

going to be limited to a k-12 school? A university? Rooted in a partnership? Can it reach beyond existing walls and be the heart and soul of an interconnected cohort of beings, a community of learners?

Settle on participation. Make sure that the voices usually drowned out or marginalized are not only heard in the listening circles but *in the decision circle*. That includes youth and elders and other quiet or ignored people. Study community-building, as in Peter Block's book *Community: The Structure of Belonging* (2008) and Susie Wise's *Design for Belonging* (2022). Explore co-governance models, from Indigenous wisdom circles to New America's Collaborative Governance workshops with many stops in between.[28] The way we make decisions has everything to do with how we relate to each other. Everyone deserves to participate in decisions that affect their lives, right? Pam Moran led the transformation of Albemarle County Schools in Virginia this way and has helped Hopewell City Schools do the same thing. Ask, as you set up early surveys and events—how can we root all five of the elements of safety in our learning community so that everyone can participate fully? How can we invite people in such a way that they choose to belong? How can we receive and give our gifts to the whole? We must learn to listen and think/feel instead of responding—how to disagree agreeably and humbly, because how could we possibly know it all?

Start With Your Visions of a Good Life

To learn openly and freely you need to have a vision of what a good life could mean to you, the communities you're in, and the biocollective of our home planet . We don't all have to feel the same way about things—indeed our different perspectives open up more possibilities. And keep the possibilities open! A vision should not be a fixed and static thing—it should be living, too. How can our learning communities come together to shape such a vision and make space for young people to design theirs? What kind of commitments are we willing to make to them? To function as a single large and evolving organism even when we are very different and unique cells? Do we have a process to guide us? (see Chapter 8 for community co-design thinking, if you do not already have a process you trust). Those who use processes like community co-design thinking are the stem cells, the imaginal cells, of our learning community.

Ask Big Questions

Here are some big "design lab" questions for your community of change makers, using principles of life and love to move beyond futurephobia. If you are already thinking seriously about these questions, you are on your way:

1. When was the last time you felt welcome and empowered in school?
2. How can we recognize our participation in systems of harm and spiral them into systems of care?
3. How might we envision learning communities that honor and facilitate our interrelationship with the other remarkable beings with whom we share this incredible planet?
4. How can our learning communities help us and help each other to live whole, meaningful, and evolving lives? This might include exploring both personal and civic identities and how they evolve and are expressed. It also calls for close attention to adaptable life skills and efficacy over time. It will mean cultivating a strong sense of belonging and safety while learning together.
5. How can we use processes like community design thinking to create a living curriculum that adds a sense of purpose to learning and keeps us focused and working together on the challenges we face?
6. How can we liberate ourselves from the tyranny of being right (and the fear of being wrong)? To learn and live fully you also have to embrace uncertainty, ambiguity, not knowing. Does that mean a new idea of success? To do this we need to remain open to other ways of thinking and being, and to let other practices and understandings inform our pathways to achieving our vision and redefining success. Don't forget to look around!! Lots of other schools worldwide are asking

the same questions. What are the beneficial actions that are taking place all around us (globally, regionally, locally) and right here, that we might participate in, expand, or learn from?

7. How can we empower and unite all the elements of our being—mind, heart, body, and spirit to deepen our understanding and to make learning coherent by bringing together the fractured parts into a coherent whole? (see also Chapter 3)[29]

In asking these questions we open up to the potential of others and magnify possibilities. We can open ourselves to the knowledge and lessons of our ancestors and the communities of beings around us. We can open ourselves to wonder and awe, and a consciousness of the gifts with which Nature has provided us. Pulling together lots of perspectives and considering these questions together, with empathy and humility and without blaming or judging or defending any point of view, are the beginning steps of community design thinking and set the seeds of agency and resilience, too.

When Students Are Asking the Questions and Co-designing Solutions

All of it works when all of it is working together. I don't know of many communities other than Indigenous ones that habitually grant children and youth a voice in decision-making circles. There's a lot of lip-service in that direction, and "feedback" and "input" is more and more frequently sought, but both of those terms advertise to the young people whose opinions are being sought that they are actually external to the civic process. Maybe this preventing youth from influencing their own lives comes from an overabundance of a desire to protect, or from a desire to preserve the illusion of innocence (degenerative love), or from a plain old "what do they know anyway" ageist bias (degenerative power), but most of the time we make children and youths dependent rather than allowing them to learn citizenship by being responsible members of a community. This creates a kind of frustrating tokenism, or a "learned helplessness" that causes them to give up easily,[30] or a "colonizing of the mind and spirit," any of which creates a sense of powerlessness that prevents many youth from developing adult alliances or even full civic identities and the adult-feeling confidence (efficacy) to be responsible and independent participants in their world.[31] We can stop doing that today.

Many of the kids sitting right in front of you *have* taken on real responsibility. They take care of their siblings or their grandparents or the ancient neighbors or they babysit. They work to raise food for their families or to contribute money to the family till. During "natural" disasters, they've constructed systems for making sure abuela on the 16th floor has water and food, gotten supplies across a raging river, packed the go bag that includes pet food, and in many, many cases, kept a clear head while the adults around them froze in panic. In *Children of Katrina*, we find one such example. One of the young people studied over the 10 years after Katrina struck New Orleans, Louisiana and the region around it full force, saw his mother hesitate to go into the rising floodwaters carrying his infant sister. Just 8 years old, he quickly understood the situation, grabbed a bedsheet, and tied his sister tightly to their mother. Only then could she venture out through the floodwaters to safety.[32] During COVID-19 too kids took on vital family and community responsibilities, from cooking to caregiving to organizing community events, protest marches, and food drives. Remember, resilience depends on the way the people around you react, and we adults can have a positive effect on both well-being and academic development if we prioritize and validate youthful capacities to influence the world around them. If we deny the civic and relational importance of their learning and doing in our quest to regain mechanistic "lost learning," if we exclude them from decision-making and institutional change-making because they are "too young," we invalidate all they have learned and accomplished, we invalidate them, and return them to a vulnerable and dependent condition.[33]

Here are three ways kids can be excellent leaders and citizens of learning communities. They are experts in their own experience and speak to it like no one else can, not even their parents or their teachers. The younger they are, the more fresh and "outside the box" their ideas are likely to be. They love systems and change processes and can quickly become excellent facilitators of change using a process like community design thinking. When they facilitate, the adults tend to play along to please the kids until they find themselves hooked. Sometimes even the cynics are more polite "in front of the children." In the end, the efficacy and agency that comes with authentic involvement in vision- and decision-making gives the children and youth civic courage for life. There are many different versions of Listening Circles (see Resource 2 for some ideas.). All can be facilitated by youths, with appropriate support. The point is that they are circles, and that there is no explaining or defending. People can dissent freely.

If you have done a lot of Listening Circles, the patterns that surface will help tremendously in the "what do we need to leave behind and what do we need to keep" discussion. Take your time and let them emerge. Your institution can acknowledge and validate all the valuable work that is already taking place in your arenas of well-being, climate learning, and change-making, and begin the process of looking at all school practices through the critical lens shaped by student experience.

Once you have your soil examined and ready (you know what people care about, what's working and what's troubling them), you can begin the process of "If only … ." and "What if … " brainstorming that will help to liberate our imaginations and shape vision. Look for allies inside and outside of your own district. Keep young people in the decision-making group and offer students authentic roles in holding the school system accountable—to them. Who else should schools and universities be accountable to, if not the students and the communities they inhabit? Keep the momentum going.

What the Regenerative Power of Love in Learning Looks Like: A Garden

If teachers AND community AND kids AND Nature's regenerative principles of life met up with the power of love, what kind of learning community would they devise together? In the age of climate crisis, it might look a lot like a garden. Regenerative School/Community Gardens are the embodiment of eco-literate schooling for power(full) and loving learning in the age of climate crisis. Growing something you can eat (whether you are doing it on a rooftop, vertically, or on the ground) changes the way young people think about themselves, and restores their relationships with each other and the interconnecting systems of life. (Figure 2.2)

FIGURE 2.2 Collective self-empowerment: marching to the garden

There's a small community in the mountainous rural south-west of Puerto Rico, in the Quebradilla sector of Peñuelas. It's called Barrio Rucio, and it has a dynamic history of hiding those escaping from plantation enslavement and colonialism, as well as providing workers today for commercial farming. It is a stunningly beautiful place that also struggles with environmental pollution from the coal ash spewed by the coal-powered energy plants near the ocean that rolls up the hills and sits. And they need consistent access to school. The families in the community have, in collaboration with some University of Puerto Rico-Mayagüez students (Impacto Juventud) and faculty, created their own Saturday-morning school, called Aula en la Montaña, "Classroom in the mountains."[34] It is both an educational and social justice project that fosters youth and community agency. (See Case Study, p. 211)

Here is how one of the professors, Dra. Sandra Soto Santiago, tells the story of a day in the garden:

"Throughout the curriculum children are encouraged to make decisions, to collaborate, to create and to lead. Aula is a learning space focused on the children's overall well-being and where they are respected and valued. As a result, we often experience beautiful moments that validate our pedagogical beliefs and practices. Facilitating, stepping back, and giving children room to be and do leads to critical thinking and empowerment. One of the components of Aula is the agroecology class, where the children and the community learn about sustainable practices to grow food and protect their natural resources. This is particularly important for a community that has been so severely impacted by natural disasters such as Hurricane María in 2017 [after which they were cut off from access to food or clean water].

One day, after we worked with the children to build signs/labels for the garden, the girls suggested we 'march' the quarter mile or so to the garden down the hill.

We had not been able to visit the garden for a couple of weeks and I noticed that the corn we planted did not do well. The husks were small and the plants were drying out. My initial reaction was that we had failed at our first attempt to grow corn here and was sad that the children would not get to enjoy eating fresh corn grown in their garden. We started collecting green beans that were ready and while doing that someone called my attention to Fabián, age 6, who had decided to collect the corn anyway. He opened the husks and quite skillfully started rubbing his tiny hands around them and applying the right amount of pressure to remove the now dried kernels. His eyes glistened and although he was wearing a mask, as part of our COVID safety protocol, I could tell he was smiling. "I have SEEEEDS!" he declared. "What are you going to do with those?" I asked, to which he replied "I am going to plant some, feed some to my chickens so I'll have eggs, and I am going to store the rest." He then started filling his pocket with the kernels and proudly showed us how packed it was. What a lesson was that moment for me! What I had initially perceived as a garden fail, the children turned into a big win. (Figure 2.3)

(a)   (b)

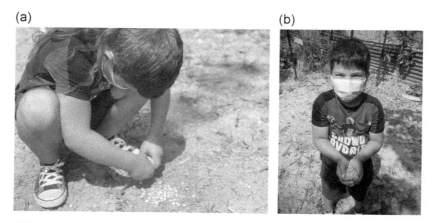

FIGURE 2.3 (a) and (b) Regenerative power in the garden: I have SEEDS!

Some weeks prior, the children had learned about the importance of seed preservation and of creating a seed bank, for both food security and food sovereignty. They took home their seeds to store and care for. Months earlier we had also talked about connectivity in nature and how the garden helps sustain life in a cyclical manner. In that moment we saw Fabián, making his own decisions, using information from previous classes and drawing from his community practices. He even thought about feeding his chickens with it, which had not occurred to us. I then understood that although they could not eat the corn, it was still valuable to them. Everything happening in that garden was of value to them.

On that same day Fabián's older sister showed us a video of him dressed as Isaac Newton for a school assignment. They were looking for a place where they could record the video and ended up going to the garden and recording by the marigolds and the passion fruit plant. Of every possible place in that community they chose their garden. It was a place that they considered beautiful, important and where they felt welcomed. So much so that it was worthy of showing his teacher in a school assignment. That is a level of ownership that engages students and ensures well-being and learning in ways that traditional classrooms often cannot." –Dra. Sandra Soto Santiago

Nature Is Continuously Changing and Resilient—Growing, Adapting, Evolving

Life is regenerative because it is always changing so as to create the conditions for more life. Regenerative learning recognizes that learning in a changing state is learning to live. One of the ways humans have been so adaptable and prolific as an "invasive" species (those which move into an ecosystem and knock it off balance) is because humans are continuously learning. Animals and plants learn, too, albeit differently. Nature enables us to go even further and to learn about learning, reflect on that, and creatively imagine other ways of being and growing. True learning is by definition regenerative change. When you have learned something, you have engaged with it until you can apply what you know in other situations and understand how it fits into the whole. Regenerative learning brings about continuous growth, development, and evolution.[35] The balance of *educare* and *educere* the teacher cultivates in teaching-learning reciprocity is regenerative.

The great Brazilian pedagogue Paolo Freire asserted, "The teacher is of course an artist, but being an artist does not mean that he or she can make the profile, can shape the students. What the educator does in teaching is to make it possible for the students to become themselves."[36] A tree might be able to survive in a limited way in a pot, but it is only superficially a tree. Its roots are cut off from all of the "right relationships" of the authentic world. A root-bound child might even get straight A's and at some point in 12th grade realize she has absolutely no idea who she is, what she might be interested in, what it means to feel internally motivated or to do something that matters in the "real world." Sound familiar?

As an educator trying to engage young people in the world, I have encountered a reluctance, even a fear of breaking free of the constraining pot in order to grow into well-being. It feels very risky—the letting go of the status quo, the self-decolonization. There is some comfort in the determination to master the master's measures and so prove to everyone their capacity to comply—what they might call their "high performance" in the game of school. This is the way the world is, students and their families say, and we must play the game in order to succeed. Teachers too, even though they want what works for their students in the long term, are reluctant to leave the short-term predictability of the system they know. Letting go is hard, writes Kyle Wagner, deep project-based learning (PBL) expert and international podcaster on education innovation. In a LinkedIn post, he asked, "Do you have a hard time 'letting go' of control in the classroom? I did. What if students don't learn anything? What if I can't cover my curriculum? What if the principal walks in? Letting go isn't easy. It requires trust in our students to lead learning, while we take a backstage role. But when we do, we unlock UNLIMITED learner potential."[37] Embracing freedom and agency (and therefore uncertainty) is a relational and reciprocal process that liberates us together or not at all. It won't happen without love. And it's love and solidarity that can bring us together so we can step out of the status quo with confidence. Empowered love unlocks regenerative possibility.

As such, teaching is also a civic responsibility. It always has been (think democracy needs an educated citizenry), but now especially. In the Preface, I referred to the fact that UNESCO (United Nations Educational, Scientific, and Cultural Organization) is calling on education systems globally to shift their focus to the four existential global challenges (Climate change, Democracy in Peril, Inequality, and Fragmentation).[38] In their words, the future of humanity and life on this planet depends on it, and they've identified education as the sector where love can lead. In countries like Finland, where schools are adapting well to the modern world and preparing young people for a flexible future, it is teachers and students who are trusted to design and implement the system.[39] Teacher preparation is extensive, ongoing, and reciprocal, in the sense of putting theory into practice and also learning from students to inform both. Indeed, all over the world new programs for teacher learning (professional development) led by youths are shifting the top-down paradigm and expanding the reciprocal re-generative properties of balanced *educare* and *educere*, teach-learning and learn-teaching.[40] And in some parts of the world, teachers are paid like they are enacting one of the most im-portant civic roles a person can accept. It's easy for communities to commit to the community's teachers (and their kids!), espe-cially when kids are involved in the process.

The regenerative properties of Nature make our ecosystems resilient, just as regenerative learning can empower commu-nities with vitality and love. People often say that disasters open up opportunities for change. That's true, to some extent, but mainly because of two things: "hidden" injustices are revealed for all to see, and the old systems' weaknesses cause a break-down that sometimes leaves space for new systems to emerge. In communities that thrive with power and love, new visions like Aula en la Montaña have been seeded and are ready to thrive. We are now at the painful stage of recognition that the old system is obsolete and the newer, more widely distributed, regenerative models are ready to step in with a little care and cultivation, a bit like decomposition creates the fertile soil for new growth. We know how to rethink schools to make them more safe and more just. There are great examples on just about every continent, demonstrating hearts beating with authenticity and integrity, power and love and creativity, nested in com-munities: deep problem-, project-, or challenge-based learning, place-based schools, forest and farm schools and Design for Change-style global networks, and school-based community programs. There are a growing number of organizations primed and ready to partner with schools. We know how to build belonging and tap into the genius of our historical identities to motivate, empower and engage. Great researchers, thinkers, writers, educators, our ancestors, and Nature herself have shown us the way.

What if school was a place of joy and well-being, where students and teachers felt coherence, connectedness, and care? Where learning was driven deeper by compassion, purpose, and relevance?

Where young people could feel the power of all kinds of knowledge flowing through them, and could deploy the love and wisdom of their ancestry and their communities to restore justice in the present and design an abundant future?

The rest of this book will help support you as you plant more seeds of thriving. It will make you feel right about what you're doing already and give you some new ways of tapping into our humanity and the vitality and the integrities of life to build regenerative, loving, learning communities.

Seeds for Planting

Love is the unifying force in the universe, just as gravity holds everything to Earth.

Love is a teacher's superpower. Teachers' well-being and agency come first so that they can be fully present with their students.

Everything/everyone is mutually related. The individualized competition model of industrial schooling is unnecessary and undermines trust and collaborative companionship. No one exists outside of relationships.

Coherence means that living systems are whole and nothing is superfluous. Fragmentation and biases against youth and elders make society weaker and raise the potential for disposing of people and other beings.

Biodiversity calls on people to lean together in safety and unity, not uniformity. Communities that have integrated decision-making, clarity around purpose, and trust built into their communication do much better during and after disasters.

Regenerative learning creates the conditions for more and deeper learning and with it, change. The teacher facilitates this as gardeners facilitate life in the garden.

Listening circles and rituals of belonging are very important to developing a shared understanding of the purpose of school.

If at all possible, including indoors or on the roof, engage young people in growing food.

Notes

1 Kahane 2010.
2 Paul Tillich (1886–1965) was one of the most influential existential philosophers and theologians of the 20th century. Influenced by Buber, Kierkegaard, Heidegger, and others, he, in turn, influenced Dr. Martin Luther King, Cornel West, and H. Richard Niebuhr, among others.
3 King, Jr. 1967. He asserted then that we have it within our means to achieve it. Well worth a read in the current conversation regarding poverty and climate justice.
4 King, Jr. 1967.
5 Benyus 2002.
6 Costanza-Chock 2020.
7 https://www.dfcworld.org/SITE/dfcstory DfC now has chapters in many countries around the world. Spend some time on their site, seek out the chapter site from your country, and if it's not there, start one! https://www.dfcworld.org/SITE
8 Kelly 2009.
9 O'Brien and Tabb 2020.
10 Fothergill and Peek. 2015.
11 Marc Freedman's article "What Happens When Old and Young Connect" (April 22, 2019) in *Greater Good Magazine* provides an excellent summary of the benefits for both groups, as well as providing links to many well-researched articles. Access: https://greatergood.berkeley.edu/article/item/what_happens_when_old_and_young_connect For research about the importance of a sense of purpose for older generations, see Musich, Shirley, et al. "Purpose in Life and Positive Health Outcomes." *Population Health Management,* 2018 Apr 1; 21(2): 139–147. Published online in PMC (US Nat'l Library of Medicine, NIH), 2018 Apr 1. doi: 10.1089/pop.2017.0063. https://www.ncbi.nlm.nih.gov/pmc/articles/PMC5906725/
12 King, Jr. 1967.

13 Hattie 2008.
14 For a thorough analysis of the teacher shortage as it looked in 2019, see García and Weiss 2019.
15 A 2006 report by a similar name also found that teacher empowerment was the number one factor in determining whether teachers would stick with teaching. Hirsch and Scott 2006.
16 In the US, United States, the unique problem of school shootings doubled in the fall of 2021, resulting in the death of 9nine people between August and mid-December. Threats made on social media and verbal and physical assaults in school and in the community against teachers terrorized school communities. In October, the Justice Department launched a special investigation of violent threats against teachers and school officials. https://www.justice.gov/opa/pr/justice-department-addresses-violent-threats-against-school-officials-and-teachers
17 Modan 2021.
18 Substance Abuse and Mental Health Services administration (SAMSHA). In their 2015 "Understanding Child Trauma" Report, SAMSHA listed traumatic experiences affecting more than two-thirds of our children as: Psychological, physical, or sexual abuse; Community or school violence; Witnessing or experiencing domestic violence; National disasters or terrorism; Commercial sexual exploitation; Sudden or violent loss of a loved one; Refugee or war experiences; Military family-related stressors (e.g., deployment, parental loss or injury); Physical or sexual assault; Neglect; Serious accidents or life-threatening illness. Accessed: https://www.samhsa.gov/child-trauma/understanding-child-trauma
19 Taylor 2020.
20 Behrendt and Favretti 2022.
21 Kahane 2010.
22 For a group of exciting case studies from the Green Schools Network, which supports schools trying to create environmental safety through school https://greenschoolsnationalnetwork.org/, see Seydel, Jennifer et al. *Trailblazers fro Whole School Sustainability: Case Studies of Educators In Action*. Routledge, Eye On Education Series, 2022.
23 Jackson et al., 2020. Dr. Jackson quoted in Youki Terada, Stephen Merrill, Sarah Gonser. 2021. "The 10 Most Significant Education Studies of 2021." *Edutopia*, 9 December 2021 https://www.edutopia.org/article/10-most-significant-education-studies-2021
24 Robinson 2021. Ishmael Robinson tells the story of how they had a million dollars to buy a math curriculum and instead built their own.
25 Nieves Rodriguez 2020. Take a moment and read about the power of what's right in front of us in Christine E. Nieves Rodriguez's beautiful essay "Community Is Our Best Chance," in *All We Can Save*. One World, 2020. Full of essays relevant to climate change and hope that you can use with your students, including essays written by students.
26 I believe this could be attributed to Ed Schein, MIT Sloan School of Management, but it is widely held to be common sense today. In education, it is easy to find the motivation and hard to shape the vision.
27 A great book about transformational leadership for school change is Socol, Moran and Ratliff 2018.
28 Here's one, from New America, December 15, 2021. https://www.youtube.com/watch?v=lz7SnwWtQCk

29 One area where most cosmologies, Indigenous, Western, Eastern, agree is on holistic coherence. The universe has a unified integrity, a coherence that it continuously converges toward and that humans exist within. Humans thrive in coherent conditions, in the loving embrace of life, where beings fit together and change makes sense. Fragmentation causes stress, conflict, and illness. In many belief systems, the fracturing of the whole represents an opportunity for imbalance and moral darkness to hold sway, but the whole never entirely disappears–its presence is always pulling back to the unified state of coherence. We see this reflected in such marvels in Nature as the life growing on the garbage island in the Pacific.

30 All teachers and school leaders should see this 7-minute video. https://www.youtube.com/watch?v=gFmFOmprTt0 Your students will be able to relate. Adults will recognize this feeling, too. Notice how soon they get discouraged and give up. You might also want to read Martin Seligman's "Learned Optimism." Vintage, 2006 edition. Seligman coined both terms, learned helplessness and learned optimism, and has written books about both.

31 For a detailed account of the meaning of the UN Convention on the Rights of the Child doctrine, and the ways in which children are and can be citizens of the world, see Liebel 2020.

32 Fothergill and Peek 2015. Follows 7 children over the 10 years after the disaster in New Orleans upended their lives. This is a scholarly research project that identifies important elements of recovery, including participating in helping others.

33 Berger 2021.

34 Rico 2021.

35 Myriad indigenous schools have fought to sustain their regenerative principles throughout the impact of settler colonialism on many continents. To go deeper into Indigenous scholarship on regenerative learning, see Hopkins, John P. Indian *Education for All: Decolonizing Indigenous Education in Public Schools.* (Columbia University, Teacher's College, 2021); Tomlins-Jahnke, Huia, et al., Editors. *Indigenous Education: New Directions in Theory and Practice.* (U of Alberta Press, 2019); and Linda Tuwiwai Smith, Eve Tuck, K. Wayne Yang, Editors. *Indigenous and Decolonizing Studies in Education: Mapping the Long View.* (Routledge, 2018), especially Newberry, Teresa, and Octavia Trujillo's "Decolonizing Education Through a Transdisciplinary Approach to Climate Change Education." To go deeper into regenerative concepts as understood by White scholars, see Wahl, Daniel Christian. *Designing Regenerative Cultures.* (Triarchy Press, 2016); Hutchins, Giles, and Laura Storm. *Regenerative Leadership: The DNA of Life-Affirming 21st century Organizations.* (Wordzworth, 2019); and Sanford, Carol. *The Regenerative Life.* (Nicholas Brealey Pub, 2020). All have been used in educational change management at the institutional level, but for a tighter focus on regenerative principles at work in education, see Kumar, Satish, and Pavel Cenkl. *Transformative Learning: Reflections on 30 Years of Head, Heart, and Hands at Schumacher College.* (New Society Pub, 2021) and Hannon, Valerie, and Amelia Peterson. *Thrive: The Purpose of Schools in a Changing World.* (Cambridge University Press, 2021). A new school entirely built on regenerative principles (which also offers sessions for teachers) as interpreted by a White woman in the US is Springhouse School, founded by Jenny Finn. https://springhouse.org/.

36 Bell et al., eds. 1990.

37 Wagner 2021.
38 Find the full report here. https://en.unesco.org/futuresofeducation/sites/
default/files/2021-10/UNESCO%20Reimagining%20our%20futures
%20together%20EMBARGOED%20COPY.pdf
39 Sahlberg, 2021.
40 Just a few examples: Big Picture Learning and participating schools (all
types of schools) https://www.bigpicture.org/, Onestone in Idaho (free
private) https://onestone.org/, Thomas Alva Edison School in Caguas, PR
(private) https://www.taespr.org/, Hopewell City High School (public,
Virginia), American International Schools, IB schools around the globe.
Here's a book, WestEd. *Teachers Who Learn, Kids Who Achieve*.
WestEd, 2000.

3 Cultivating (Re)generative Power

How did disempowering fragmentation come about and how is it reflected in schooling?
How can power audits help students and families to make sense of power?
How can our regenerative powers help us to resist and revitalize our learning and our world?

A healthy ecosystem functions "without inputs" or outside agents because it is autonomously co-empowered. Instead of one-to-many, it is an interrelated many-to-many. Because our human systems have fractured and "verticalized" power, we are significantly more vulnerable, because everything depends on the few. Futurephobia is a crisis of agency. The strong emotions people feel about climate change, like loss, fear, guilt, mistrust, and anger, are matched by the sense that we are collectively powerless to do anything about it. Many of those in power, especially those benefitting from the status quo, encourage us to take responsibility individually and change our personal activities, while not dramatically changing policies or corporate activities Although it is important for everyday individuals to do what they can, we will have to act collectively and systemically to reach our goals by 2030. The lack of agency we feel, resulting in the disengagement, fatalism, exhaustion (burnout), and depression

DOI: 10.4324/9781003215806-4

characteristic of futurephobia, is a scathing critique of social injustice and top-down undemocratic policymaking. As teen activist Amelia Kearney wrote in Chapter 1, it is tough to be optimistic when some people, the ones holding decision-making power and consuming the most, the 90 companies responsible for 60% of the greenhouse gas emissions, are committing moral and physical violence against others—undermining their well-being in the present and stealing their future, too. One student in Puerto Rico wrote, "In Life Lab, I realized how hard I was working to avoid thinking about my future. It just seemed so dark." Some of the elites are doing their best to invest in change, and to recruit their peers to invest in the planet, and we want to encourage that. Many who *could* be acting powerfully might recognize what needs to be done but can't seem to overcome the old logic in the rationalizing narratives of separation and extraction. It seems to these people that the way things are is the way they've always been, and so there are no other ways to be. Not so.

Hierarchical Fragmentations and Degenerative Power

Theologian and philosopher Paul Tillich, Dr. Martin Luther King, Jr., and many others have noted that power in the universe can be either generative or degenerative. Degenerative power breaks up coherence, not only by creating unhealthy and painful separations that affect our everyday lives, but also by creating unstable vertical hierarchies (Power Over) which can breed exclusion, mistrust, and suffering. Indigenous elders in the western hemisphere and wisdom traditions from the East share the view with many in the so-called Global South that everything in the universe including life itself is part of a single whole. Fracturing it into disconnected parts, especially when hierarchically arranged, defines unwellness and spells disaster.

Domestication = Man Over Nature and Man Over Woman

Eco-historically speaking, these binaries and the resulting top-down, patriarchal hierarchies are very new. If you were to think of the history of the earth as a year, humans only showed up at one minute before midnight on the last day. The hierarchical binaries I'm speaking of emerged with the advent of agriculture, about eight or ten thousand years ago, or about three seconds before midnight. By comparison with Mother Earth's lifetime, all of human civilization is like one quick breath in. Take a moment and explore the Climate Museum's "In Human Time" exhibitions, including the Arctic Timeline.[1] When viewed alongside Peggy Weil's "88 Cores" film experience, a four-and-a-half hour tour two miles through the (disappearing) Greenland Ice Sheet, it will slow and expand your thinking about time, even if you only see a section of it. Watch 30 minutes of it or scroll very slowly through the Timeline and then step out into the busy corridor or onto a busy sidewalk, and feel what happens in your body.

Even though humans have spread quickly around the world, they only came into the scene in the Fertile Crescent, Egypt, and China with agriculture, which eventually involved the domestication of animals. How much fertile land a man and his beasts could plow determined his family's well-being, and the notion of private ownership of property emerged, controlled and regulated by the men who controlled the animals. Women, who had been the keepers of life, chiefly by being the most reliable providers of food and by producing and feeding the next generation from their own miraculous bodies, lost their divine status and became legally domesticated themselves. These are the first two significant hierarchical fragmentations that dominate the story of civilization's destruction of the Earth to this day. "Civilized" men began to view Nature as something other than themselves which, once owned and domesticated, would submissively surrender its bounty to him as long as he made the right obeisances to the gods. Similarly, women's vital role in the natural order of being was gradually subverted to male regulation and ownership. Once colonization spread around the world, the male-female hierarchical binary was imposed on many societies and on most continents. The attention of the community on the success of the whole shifted to the success of one's own family which could also be "owned" (usually by men), and wealth could be transmitted from generation to generation. Conflict and war over land and re-sources grew. Karina Gonzalez asks us to consider the outcomes of the commodification of Earth's bounty, in Figure 3.1.

FIGURE 3.1 The Earth has to pay the price
Karina Gonzalez, 10th grade, Puerto Rico

The man-over-Nature divide is felt explicitly in today's ty-pically deNatured schools. Many buildings disregard children's need for natural light and fresh air to stimulate learning and health. Children rarely learn outside, though some schools are changing this. Most school systems are not ecologically sus-tainable, although some, such as those in the Green Schools Network (see Chapter 2), are changing this, too. Many colleges and universities are leading the way. Similarly, the man-over-woman split is reflected in the school hierarchy itself: the vast majority (close to 4:5) of teachers are female, while the vast majority of school superintendents (close to 4:5) are male.[2] Many societies have resisted these binaries and loving men, women, and non-binary people all over the world are seeking ways to tell a revitalizing, healing story, proving that these hierarchical binaries and the fear and hatred they spawned are by no means inevitable.

At the global level, for example, among the Elders and at the UN and in many bioregions, the importance of restoring women to their positions of leadership in planetary care and restoration is undisputed. In venues where long-term thinking, leadership in community, circular and caring climate-sensitive economics are a priority, women are sought out to take the helm. According to Project Drawdown, one of the best things we can do for the planet is to educate more women, and this movement is also beginning to gain momentum.[3]

Cognitive Over Emotional Knowing

Civilization also brought hierarchical fragmentations when knowledge and expertise stratified. Because the cognitive activity of the mind could bring you closer to the top of the patriarchal hierarchy, this kind of thinking was highly prized, and other kinds of knowing was suppressed in its favor. In Europe, once the Roman Catholic Church solidified its doctrine and its hold on socio-political hierarchy, classical rationalism was suppressed, but the patriarchy grew even stronger by directing antagonism toward wise women and Nature. The Body and its urges needed to be suppressed. Women who were such as herbalists, midwives, and healers could easily be blamed for meeting Satan in the woods, his natural habitat. Similarly, when Europeans encountered people on other continents, they generally assumed that they were both far from God and "savage" without the interventions of church and schooling, and viewed them in a feminized and therefore deficient stature.

The cognitive mind became associated with male superiority and moral purity, in constant struggle against the moon-linked, animalistic urges connected to emotions that made women impure. We still see this significant hierarchical fragmentation in Western notions of the self, which conjure the idea that the cognitive brain should be *in control* of the "heart," body, and spirit, and that the totality of a person can be rationally known, measured, and compared. There is no room for emotional displays in school, and indeed schooling has been so effectively severed from "real" life and emotional well-being that new add-on programs in both emotional awareness and "real world" engagement have emerged and are in demand after the worst of the COVID-19 pandemic, and as mental illness soars. Educators have always led with the heart, but it seems that this natural interaction gets tougher to do (even as it is more intensively needed) as the children get older and the system absorbs them into mechanistic measuring up.

Rationalism and Hierarchies of Knowledge

The European Enlightenment's rationalism drove the "cognitive over emotional knowing" imbalance even further into our heads and cut us off from holistic health. The patriarchal fascination with measurement and the possibility of using rational thought mechanisms to demystify the natural world further elevated the role of science and by situating it in the head, separated it from the coherent reality of life. As such, Western thinkers bestowed upon it a kind of "outside of us" reality, so that mechanistic "hard data" could be thought to be objective. Of course, it is anything but. Western thinkers broke apart natural and human systems to see and study the parts, particularizing knowledge discovery into specific discourses and specialized disciplines that need not mix. While science has helped us to know much more, and even to understand more deeply, and it can certainly help us to live as better partners with the natural world, the excessive focus on the parts instead of the relationships has led us to ineffectual systems thinking, or none at all. It should come as no surprise, then, that western societies such as the United States would have difficulties with multi-disciplinary complexity, possess a bias toward short-term over long-term thinking, and suffer from a shortage of critical and systems thinking in general. Competitive measuring has made us mistrustful of each other and unsure of our relationships, but ironically gullible where algorithmic manipulation, social media, and outright lies are concerned.

The rationalist hierarchy was built into schools too in the way time is distributed, the way children are sorted, the division of learning into subjects and disciplines, and the way young people are measured to see if they have been sufficiently standardized. These mechanisms not only reflect rationalist biases, but industrialist ones. The scientific efficiencies of factory standardization envisioned by the Committee of Ten in 1892[4] became the main drivers for decision-making about school practice in many typical school systems, resulting not only in disciplinary "seat time," but in outcomes like lunch at 10:23, bus schedules that have older kids in Physics at 7:20, standardized measurement, little time for resting or play, and separations of children by age and abilities.

Originally an effort to ensure that anyone graduating from high school would receive an education that prepared them well for life, over time school funding and certification tended to depend more on these efficiency factors, such as how many minutes a week a given student is in each discipline, and whether or not a student remembers the right iotas on the official day, than it does on the development of healthy lives and life skills, caring and kindness, internally motivated deep learning, or civic agency and responsible decision making. *This gap leaves students feeling that school is contributing to pointlessness and powerlessness.* And if you possess genius other than what the state expects, if your way of learning does not fit the mold, if your cultural approach is unique, if your language is not the state's language, if your perspective on history is not the one that's in the state-approved textbook, you will be deemed deficient, unlikely to be "successful" without help, and many times more likely to be punished. Fortunately, many schools and educators (and communities!) are pushing back, and providing plenty of examples of co-empowering learning, only a few of which are presented in this book. For regular infusions of examples of schools and programs that are busy telling new and more just stories, join platforms like *Getting Smart*, or follow educators such as Gholdy Muhammad, Chris Emdin, Shane Safir, and Jenny Finn. Explore Canada's First Nations pedagogy and Empowering the Spirit websites. Check out Justice by Design (and Agency By Design!) and the d-school's k12lab for plenty of free materials. Ask why. Imagine. Create.

White Supremacy

The European colonial project of expansion, first into Africa and Asia and then into the Americas brought White versus White brutalities and the inherited traumas of the era of the Crusades into the Western hemisphere, so that European men were expected to subdue people and Nature alike, enforcing domination to extract what wealth they could, all the while afraid of and rationalizing away what moral harm they had done (the root of "toxic masculinity"). Investors demanded profits, after all. Great wealth and fame was "out there" for the taking. People who had lived with and loved the land for millennia were expected to submit, by force or threat of force, to the greedy hands of "civilization." Indigenous people began to believe that these Whites were witchcraft, a kind of test foretold. Genocide by war, dislocation, deculturing, enslavement, and deliberate destruction of habitats and food sources proved the prophecies.

After Africans were dragged to the Americas, they sought allies and found some sympathy and empathy with Indigenous people and with oppressed Whites, and so White landowners, merchants, and colonial legislators feared they would join forces and upend their unstable minority rule. In fact, elite Whites proved the old adage true: you will fear what you oppress. At first, punishments for Black runaways far exceeded those for White ones. Eventually, laws mandating lifelong, race-based, and, by the 1660s, perpetual slavery by determining the status of a baby based on the status of its mother established the roots of systemic racism still with us long after race-based slavery ended. But the purpose had been achieved. Oppressed Whites still felt better off than oppressed Blacks, an imbalanced formula rationalized by the unstable logic of civilizational/cultural/intellectual superiority supported by pseudo-science. In some states today, the fear held by White supremacists is on full display. Taking over school boards and banning books, banning history, fleeing to White suburbs, it is clear that we need some serious relearning and healing reconciliation if we are to move forward together to preserve the best of what we have learned.

White supremacy also translated back into the other fragmentations. Separating Indigenous people and Africans from the land that was inseparable from their lives, "domesticating" Black men and women by force, belittling their greater emotional coherence as unintellectual, transcribed itself into school through segregation, "scientific" measurement, and by writing their brilliance out of school curricula.

I have oversimplified and painted with a broad brush. History is much more complex than this. In each era, there was debate, advocacy, decision-making. And that is my point. None of it was inevitable. And so it can and is being changed, unlearned, and redesigned, continuously.

We are always able to ask, what is the best of the learnings we wish to keep? What is no longer serving us in this life?

Degenerative Power Degenerates

Top-down, hierarchical structures are not stable because they break down agency and trust. If everything has to go through the "head," changes are slower, less agile, more dependent on that overworked, overinvested, overpaid small group of people at the top making "the right decisions" on behalf of everyone else. While at first some may feel a sense of security and relief ("I'm glad I don't have to make that decision," or "Papa will take care of me"), in the long run the safety is false. For one thing, what is actually best for you may not be a priority for the deciders at the top; for another, that false security is self-colonizing—learned helplessness erodes the agency and well-being that comes from sharing responsibility and being trusted to decide. With mistrust comes fear. The ones at the top fear they will lose their status one day, and the majority at the bottom fears the next betrayal from the top. It is said that a triangle is the strongest shape, but when we are talking about the power to drive change, that does not seem to be the case. Stop reading for a moment and imagine … what shape WOULD be the most stable and resilient? This is an easy one for most Indigenous peoples to answer. Like living systems, circles represent a community of distributed power, a unity of diverse beings in endless belonging.

Stable Shapes of Shared Power

Circles connect us with older and enable new, more "horizontal" and regenerative architectures of power. Co-governance, circular and caring economies, and success defined as contributions to life and well-being—all come from our circle of belonging, encompassing generative Powers With and Within, and giving ourselves the collective Power to change the world. When we belong, we have the power and the courage to dissent. As Arundathi Roy said elsewhere in the "Confronting Empire" speech she delivered 20 years ago, we don't have to believe the stories that the "corporate revolution" is "selling—their ideas, their version of history, their wars, their weapons, their notion of inevitability … ."[5] Instead of a narrative of separation and verticality, we can tell a different, deeply rooted story of a different shape.

 Mending News!

Co-governance Takes Root

According to the International Congress on Co-governance, we are entering an era of intensive collaboration, in which urban governance in particular is beginning to mimic the biosphere and also small towns by creating integrated participatory networks of experience, knowledge, and decision-making. As of 2019, existing examples in New Zealand, Africa, and more intensively in South America demonstrate that collaboration across sectors and silos creates greater resilience and stability, as well as smoother operations. https://www.co-governance.org/ In schools, OneStone co-governs with students, as does public University High School in San Juan, Puerto Rico, and many others. Participatory budgeting is one way that urban communities and also schools have widened civic participation.

We are in a non-linear and distributed "intensive transformation" phase of human evolution. More and more, people are reaching back and in and toward each other to find and reconnect with deep-rooted and regenerative narratives of life and change based on *relational* (not *separational*) principles—the logic found in the circular, loving interdependence of Nature. More than 20 years ago (2002), the late Sagkeeng Anishinaabe elder Dr. Dave Courchene, Jr. founded the internationally acclaimed Turtle Lodge Centre of Excellence in Indigenous Education and Wellness. It is a gathering place of unity and kindness, whose mission is to share intergenerational Indigenous learning with all people, revitalize Indigenous languages, and to join youth leaders together with the earth to find solutions to climate change. Visited by many from around the world including some of the Elders and the Dalai Lama, Canada's Governor General Mary May Simon observed, "Your work and the teachings and values you have given us are more and more being heard and heeded."[6] More people every day are stepping off the extractive, dominance, and growth-profits-oriented acceleration toward the cliff edge and focusing on our interrelationship.

There are thousands of promising examples from around the world, seen especially clearly in the domains of regenerative agriculture, "living" architecture, biomimicry, and community co-empowering economics. Educators, too, are planting and cultivating the seeds. It is becoming ever more apparent that generative power is a loving form of interconnected creativity and resilience as communities of care ease our relatively young species into a more mature, equitable, and long-lasting evolutionary stance. When generative power is connected with the essential characteristics of life we learned about in Chapter 1, in other words, as life creates the conditions for more life, so can generative power create the conditions for more life. This is what makes it regenerative.

There has never been a more important time to be an educator who is power literate and can help students learn from, redesign, and enact regenerative power and caring systems. Where do we begin?

Power Literacy

Power literacy awakens a deeper understanding of power, by looking critically at sources of power, power-impact flows, and the implications of words.

Unsettling Settler Colonialism With Coherence

Coherence is the opposite of fragmentation. Colonial structures have taken hold as firmly as they have because they provide an illusion of comfort and safety. You know what the boundaries are and what you need to do to survive or "get ahead" within those boundaries. But they work because of division and separation, which keeps most people from gathering together and accessing the powers that Nature has given us. When we find our way (or re-member our way back) to coherence in our lives and learning, we liberate our regenerative powers. One of my students called this process "defragging."

Most people think of power as domination or control *over* something or someone, within vertical or top-down structures, and with good reason. We've already delved deeply into why they would. But how many *other* ways can we use the word power? Power with, powered by, power of, empower, co-empower ... all of them have to do with bringing about change of some kind, together. And so we could view shared efficacy and agency as the collective power to dissent and redesign, a kind of "empowered resistance" form of resilience that moves toward justice through horizontality and networked communities of care and interrelated well-being. Futurist and regenerative culture expert Daniel Christian Wahl writes in *Designing Regenerative Cultures*[7] that we need to let go of "our obsession with command and control," and collectively embrace ambiguity and change. Arturo Escobar frames a future that can only exist through pluralism.[8] They are contributors to cohorts of regenerative culture theorists whose thinking parallels Indigenous wisdom keepers and posits that when we collectively envision (or remember) a just and peaceful future, it is a shared, plural, and opening out vision, or "foresight,"[9] combined with holistic coherence and a sense of belonging that gives us the power to move beyond futurephobia and its main cause, degenerative, fracturing, hierarchical power. White Europeans and Settler colonials (for the most part my own heritage) claiming authorial rights to "regenerative culture" requires a critical look, too.

Hundreds of years ago, Indigenous leaders and wisdom keepers from all over the colonized world began predicting that Whites' ignorance, greed, and incivility would come close to destroying life—the land, water, and each other. Then, at the last moment, some would turn to their Indigenous neighbors, the survivors of the genocides, the keepers of life-giving and evolutionary holistic ways, and ask, "how can we become whole again, and live as one with all beings?" Many Indigenous prophecies turn out this way, sometimes called the Prophecy of the Rainbow Warriors, or the Whirling Rainbow, with people of all kinds coming together in peace to co-create the coherent worlds in which all worlds fit. I am respectfully asking to learn from those who know, how might we relearn to thrive from our *many* roots and relations?

We don't have time in the age of climate disasters to be satisfied with just getting better at managing the destruction wrought by harmful systems (what some might call resilience), and we don't want to be in the middle of a "natural" disaster and just starting out to create a vision of coherence. Our role as educators is to intentionally build on our love and use the essential guidance of life to actively teach the tools of "the power to unsettle." We can show our students how power can be regenerative, when it is used together with others to create coherent, life-based cultures of change continuously and collectively evolving toward justice and well-being *all the time*. Graham Leicester writes that we should think of ourselves as simultaneously "hospice workers for the dying culture and midwives to the new,"[10] making sure that well-being is attended to as we educators, with our students, disrupt and move beyond the *status quo*.

Do the Power Audit

"Empowerment" seems like such an accurate word to describe what I'm talking about here, but there is a vertical power structure built into it. It implies that if I, the teacher, set about to empower my students, I have all the power and they have none. To be honest, I probably always will have more power in a room full of children, because I DO know more about the world and education than my students do. I DO have peda-gogical expertise and experience that they do not have, and which they need, for their own security, to believe in. What matters is our shared awareness of how that power is working, and how I can use it to be sure that I remain ac-countable to my students and their need for efficacy and agency. I cannot be the sole curator or evaluator of our learning experiences, or the students would not be empow-ered at all. So I propose one small change, with a big potential impact. Let's call it **co-empowerment**. Here's why. Using that word continually reminds me to lean toward a reciprocity of *relational* power flowing back and forth in our learning spaces. How are they empowering me? Is it the right kind of power they are yielding to me? How much of my ego is in the room and how might my assumptions be interrupting CO-empowerment? The discussions you can have with your stu-dents that question this word are an exercise in power literacy 101, the implications of the words we choose. And we can all hold each other accountable.

To see which direction power-impact is flowing in your learning system and your participation in it, take a moment and do a simple power audit of your classroom. Seriously, this opened my eyes. Have your students answer these questions, too, and keep track of your collective progress to disrupt top-down patterns.

1. Is your classroom indoors and rectangular? Does it have a front and back? Who owns the front? How is the furniture arranged? Do you have a desk? Where and how do the students sit?
2. Who owns the learning? Who makes the decisions about resources, and content, and chooses the tasks? Who gives the directions and settles on the format? Who controls the timing? Who picks the language and cultural framework of learning? Who decides what is acceptable and ranks success?
3. In a typical class, how often is your voice speaking to the whole class, and for how much of the time? In an open discussion, do you speak between students? How much time do you give to student-student talk? Ask a student to map the discussion.

I *had* thought of myself as a teacher committed to empowering my students. We had talked about different ways of thinking about power (over, to, with, by, co-) and identified contextual examples. But what I found by my simple audit led to my conclusion that I needed to make bigger changes if I was serious about co-empowerment, and one small thing I could do right away was to shift my thinking. I began considering my students as CO-designers, as accomplices in transforming the way power was flowing in "my" learning space. That led to more language changes and a shift in agency. If you did the audit and found yourself at the center of it all as I did, ask yourself the following three critical questions: why is it that way, does it really *need* to be that way, and what are the implications for your students? They can help you with these.

I wondered, did I need to be in control because *I was afraid* of what might happen if I wasn't? How could I prove to the authorities (including the students and their families) that my students were learning, if I didn't tell students exactly what was expected and then grade them according to how closely they complied? Also, how could *my voice* be heard if I was not standing at the front of the room, or at least standing while the students were seated? Would my students lose respect for me if I didn't know the answers to their questions? When I really looked at it, I was making their learning experience all about me. How must that look to them? I began to inquire and was surprised again by their responses. I did not take a giant leap.

It was more like walking carefully into a lake when you don't know what's on the bottom. The first thing we did was to get rid of the teacher's desk, the static symbol of a teacher's power, and the single object in the classroom that took up the most space. Fortunately, other teachers who used the room adapted. On the first day of class, the 11th-grade students entered the empty room to a jumble of desks in the center, and a cheery greeting on the whiteboard asking them to arrange the desks in a way that suited their desires for how the class could work best for them. Over the years, one of two things happened with revelatory consistency. Can you predict it? Option A: In 8–10 minutes ... nothing happened. Students stood around until I got there to tell them what to do. **OR**, Option B: the desks would be arranged in rows or U's, facing the "front" of the room. "You know, where the teacher is supposed to stand." I'd come in and sit down, in "the back." "I see what you're doing here," noted one student. "You want us to know you're different." It was still about me, in their eyes. They knew where the power was. One student drew this (Figure 3.2), during a reflection:

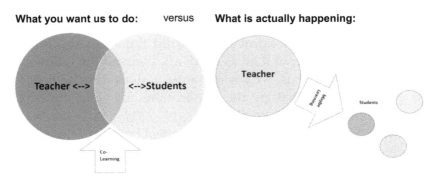

FIGURE 3.2 A Student reflects on power structure in class

Student Comment

"And that's ok with a lot of us. I know I am more comfortable that way. When you give us too much say, it makes me nervous because I get unclear about what you want."

Lesson Learned

It can be scary and feel unsafe for students or teachers to disrupt the now internalized vertical hierarchy of power (see also Chapter 10). Just as I had to acknowledge the security for me that came with doing what I was expected to do by my authorities, I was asking them to take on an unaccustomed agency. We needed to move forward *together*, step-by-step, into **co**-empowerment, unlearning the old and redesigning a new and living architecture of relationships. In spite of or perhaps especially because of the realities of power outside of my classroom that were always breathing down our necks, our relationship needed to be rooted in love, belonging, safety and trust, or we could not go anywhere together.

What did that look like? Over the course of my career in learning, my students have led me to understand a great deal about power—theirs and mine, and how we can lift each other up. We've co-designed culture shifts and relationships with our 5-point safety framework (see Chapters 2 and 4), identified what makes us feel well (Chapter 9), and named the sources of our shared power as well as those unique to ourselves. Together, we've enhanced our power literacy, our understanding of mutuality, positionality and criticality, bias and oppression, liberation and design, by doing regular power audits and reflecting on them, co-creating learning and regenerative power goals, and being intentional about relationships, language, and "messaging." Since my teaching work is situated at the nexus of cultural history, community climate resilience, public policy, and civic engagement, there are plenty of opportunities to enact our learning in the school and community. I probably took too long to change and still make a lot of mistakes, but I keep learning. I have supportive colleagues and trusting students and families, who "go there" with me. In team-teaching, my preferred mode, we regularly reflect on our power in our relationships and our actions. In every type of learning community I've experienced, I've met pro-actively resilient students and families who exercise their agency toward justice. I've learned the most about power, the power to inherit and create knowledge and the power to drive change, from them.

Parents, "Try this at home"

Is your family struggling with separation and fragmentation? Create a safe space for holding a family listening circle. Adults, ask/invite genuinely, from the heart, and don't defend or accuse. Saying no has to be allowed. Be prepared to just listen. Make the space as safe and comfortable for everyone as possible. No devices to distract. Share food, a smudge, a poem, a song, a joke ... something to bring you all into alignment with each other. Once you are present and sharing the space and it feels safe and energizing to everyone, ask.

What are the factors driving us (or, which COULD drive us) apart? Schedules, devices, imbalances in chores, no time, hierarchy inside the family (given that parents have a very important role to play to do their level best to provide love, security, guidance, and also space for growth), oppressions from outside the family (pollution, drugs, violence, racism, school, poverty, etc.)... .

What if we redistribute power? Are the young people being asked to take on too many responsibilities or too few? Are parents (or grandparents) doing things, like maintaining the family budget, planning meals, keeping the living spaces clean, holding people accountable, that kids could do? Can we all co-create together around specific barriers to coherence? For example, phones are a common dividing factor. We don't just want to "take them away." What can we replace phone time with that will add something lively and regenerative and "recharging" to our time? Music? Art? Movement? Play? Cooking? Adventures? Reading together? Sitting outside? Shared projects, or not? The value of unscheduled time is incalculable for its health benefits, especially because it liberates the mind, heart, body and spirit for imagination, depth of thought, reflection, play, and maturational growth. How will we hold ourselves accountable to each other and our goals? When is our next family circle? Who will be responsible for it? A large group (whole elementary schools-full) of parents in Heidelberg, Germany made a pact when they read about the impact of screens on the brain and saw what phones were doing to families in the US. No screens until age 12, and then a shared-with-family phone that does not travel to private spaces like bedrooms and is used during community-wide, agreed-upon times. Many families do this in Silicon Valley, too. They recognize that phones provide important ways to learn, connect, and co-create. So it's not just the time, but also how the phones are used that makes the difference.

A note about raising responsible, self-confident (empowered) children. Your intention has to be authentic. Starting from the beginning as soon as a child says "let me do it!" children need to be expected to care for someone or something (even small chores are caring for the family), in order to tap into their creativity, problem solving, and agency. Let them be accountable to whomever they care for, and if they have siblings, to the team of carers. Stepping in and doing it for them because it wasn't done right (or at all), nagging beyond the occasional reminder, signals that you do not trust them to become responsible and the situation shifts to being about your power over them. When they are very small, there might have to be some revision while they are asleep. Celebrate initiative, but please don't pay them in money or gifts to care and be responsible. Caring in the family and among neighbors is love and solidarity, not an economic transaction. There might be some big jobs to aspire to for pay in the family, but that is more about teaching job skills and financial literacy, different from family dependability and coherence. Children become trustworthy by being trusted, and confident because of the confidence placed in them. They become responsible, caring citizens when they learn how good it feels to contribute to the well-being of a group larger than themselves. That's regenerative power in action.

Regenerative Power in Puerto Rico

In the fall of 2017, two devastating hurricanes struck Puerto Rico in the span of two weeks. Most people had not gotten their power restored from Irma (Category 4) when Maria (Category 5) struck in the middle of the night with winds of 175 mph and enormous quantities of rain. Everyone and everything was affected. When the School Superintendents' Association (AASA) sent me there 10 days later to see if I could do anything to help teachers, the entire plane full of people burst into tears as a painfully brown Puerto Rico came into view. I held hands with a stranger as we lowered over broken trees, smashed homes and livelihoods, and tangled power lines. I had been using co-design thinking to contribute to community resilience, but the scale of this was a first for me. Trust the process, I kept saying to myself and the small team of educators with me as we fought off being overwhelmed, trust the co-design process. Talk to teachers. See what strengths, concerns, and priorities emerge. See what we can do together.[11]

In a "natural" disaster situation, hierarchical power flows are on full, brutal display. Urgency and crisis-rescue thinking on the part of government and other agencies simultaneously helps to respond to the emergency and marginalizes youth/community voices, undermining existing strengths. I could see this happening and also felt powerless to change it, so I concentrated on co-creating with teachers and school leaders ways to support other teachers and by extension kids and communities Follow through to note 11 to share in the iterations of what we made. And all around me, there were also communities activating their deeply integrated networks to stand up outdoor kitchens,[12] rebuild schools, and traverse flooding rivers with food and water. In the building where I was staying, young people organized a system for making sure elders living on upper floors had water: at each landing, there were cloth shopping bags with empty cooking pots in them and people carried one down with their own and filled it, carrying them both back up. Puerto Ricans rising up from devastation on a tide of artistic and political expression to unseat their governor less than two years later teaches that empowered resilience is the power to drive change. What are the sources of power, connected to life, that enable people to bring about change? If we name and know them, then we can continue to cultivate regenerative power in the midst of climate disasters. (Figure 3.3)

The Six P's, the Seeds of Regenerative Power

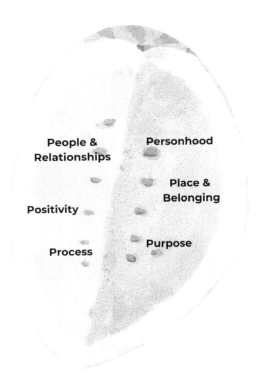

People & Relationships

Personhood

Place & Belonging

Positivity

Process

Purpose

FIGURE 3.3 "Six P" regenerative powers

Personhood

Personhood, or the power within. In English, the words *health* and *holistic* share a root with the word *whole*. In Indigenous and ancient ways of knowing and being from around the world, there is general consensus that well-being comes from being whole, and that the holistic coherence of the self deepens our understanding and empowers us to engage with and take our place in the world. Holistic learning and development balance the Mind, Heart, Spirit, and Body. The relationship and balance among these four elements are interrelated with seasons, maturation, and representative of the balance between feminine and masculine, Yin and Yang, Earth and Sky. When people are healthy and whole, they have a great deal of power from within. They readily shape their identities and "take up their space" in a world of relationships and systems.

Science also supports a holistic view of health. Our brains are incredible. The much older inner genius of our emotional limbic system functions as our secret security, faster and more potent than our logical brain, influencing our reactions to the world and the decisions we make no matter how we might wish to override it. Emotions can be confusing at best, and sometimes we feel truly awful and don't have the words to say why. We are taught to behave in a certain way, consistent with the fragmentations listed above, both at home and in school, and come to think of ourselves as broken if we can't. We learn we should be in control instead of in listening alliance with our emotions, and that upsets the balance right there. The regenerative power to move beyond futurephobia will not come from the outside in. Our wholeness is already there.

Join me in Chapter 4 (The Powers Within) to delve deeper into coming home to the coherence in our personhood. We will observe the gifts built in by Nature into our personhood, passed down for millennia, across generations and migrations, and discuss how to accept, integrate and grow with all parts of our being. Educators are already engaged in asking, how can we do the inner work together so we can help students re-member their wholeness and tend their inner power?

People and Relationships

People are the unique and ever-changing expression of their relationships with all living beings. We really *are* in this together. From the cellular level to the level of the infinite universe, we are interrelated. The elements that make up our bodies, the systems that make us live, are all linked up and reflected in each other. Everything we do, every word we utter, every decision we make, everything we feel ... to be alive is to be in relation. The systems within us are nested in and interconnected with the systems around us in mutual support. What happens if something is removed or changed? The way we participate in our relationships and the systems they are part of can ripple far beyond our own witnessing. Climate change is a good example of how interconnected systems do not fail to respond to impacts made years ago and far away. Yet it is too easy to choose ignorance of the moral violence committed against vulnerable people by doing nothing other than "business as usual." A growing number of people know how to heal the separation between Man and Nature and shift from extractive to regenerative activities. We know we are never alone in our calling to be a good neighbor in our natural ecosystems, and this matters—our lives depend on it. We feel empowered by turning toward each other, a rainbow of warriors for life on our home planet.

Have you ever witnessed a child, learning to walk, fall down, and immediately look at their parent to gauge their re- sponse? Or felt the downshift in a student's distress when a teacher connects with them? Have you felt your own mood lift the more you smiled at strangers on the way to work? We saw what happened to people during the COVID-19 separation. We need direct contact with other humans and our wider living communities in order to live, and the quality of our relation- ships determines whether or not we will thrive. We will in- vestigate connectedness and collective well-being more deeply Chapter 5 (The Power of Our Relationships), but for now, consider this question. How can we reconnect with ancient human fundamentals of interpersonal and interbeing mutua- lities and collaborations as a source of regenerative power?[13]

Learning is relational, too. To learn deeply, people need to have both internal and external coherence. We can't learn if we are rejected or distressed, and so a reconnecting to the fun- damentals of collaboration and conversation is needed in this time of healing. Our kids watch the adults and mimic the shouting, the pulling away, the confrontational postures, and the silo-seeking. Many people of all ages seek the pseudo-connectedness of the phone and social media (whose algorithms push us apart even further), shying away from the potentially awkward situations and everyday disagreements that define the natural progression of human relationships. To learn is to embrace change, but risking making a mistake or wondering out loud or changing one's mind in an uncertain social setting can make learning in any other than the most superficial way, impossible.

And so we will have to disconnect from the anti-social practices found in typical schools and replace them with pro-social, healing ones. From the perspective of many youth, school begins to lose its attractiveness around the time the state testing and official sorting begins. At this point is when the web of social connectedness many 2nd or 3rd graders are just starting to build starts to get snipped. They are young enough to internalize the sorting and competition, and old enough to understand that it matters what category (or quintile) they are in. For some, school ceases to be safe at this point. For others, later. By the time they finish high school, IF they stay that long, the majority of our youth are disengaged.[14] Why? Trusting inter-relationship with oneself and others has been ruined by highly individualized competition and "measuring up." For a few students, those who excel on those kinds of head-only assessments and at playing the game of school,[15] reality sets in much later, when they realize that no one cares what grade they got in AP, it didn't really matter what college they went to,[16] that standardized test-taking is not actually a useful life skill, and the only people they can really count as friends are not their high school or college classmates.

Human beings are naturally collaborative and derive a great deal of regenerative power and well-being from it. Think how energized you feel after your team has played well together, after being part of a symphony or a band that brings people to their feet, after you have worked together to serve 300 meals a day from an outdoor kitchen in the weeks following a disaster. After one power audit, a student returned to class the next day with a funny drawing. It looked something like Figure 3.4:

FIGURE 3.4 No power = No energy[17]

They said, "When I left here, I had 'power audit' in my head, but as I went through the rest of my schedule, I kept hearing 'energy audit.' I looked around and realized that *no power equals no energy.*"

A learning space where students have power, agency, and purpose is charged up with energy. It looks and feels different. Students will be standing, sitting, moving, leaning in. It will be loud. They will be talking and listening to each other and making eye contact.[18] Human beings understand at a deep level that we rely on others for everything from our humanness to our health and happiness. Most children enjoy playing with others and seek out that sense of shared challenge and experience that might come from anywhere—playing hide and seek at dusk in a cemetery, tunneling through a snowbank, dancing *bomba* in the street, or playing basketball in a schoolyard. They sing, dance, make music, videos, and art. It runs counter to life and the nurturing of relational power to take away arts, recess, and the unscheduled time to simply learn how to be and reflect on being in relation to each other. All of this "play" involves communication, problem solving, learning, and creating something together. During and after a crisis, the agency and shared efficacy that comes from collaborative play and problem-solving enables restorative healing and civic creativity. Join me in Chapter 7 (The Power of Purpose) to explore how doing something that matters in school validates and builds up students' civic courage and collaborative creativity. And tune in to Chapter 5 for consideration of how educators and youth can co-create a space where different people bring different inspirations and assets to the circle and are valued for it because the outcome has shared and authentic meaning. We can teach full and embodied listening.[19] We can redefine collaboration as the dance of giving and receiving, shared trying and growth, listening and telling, and, when rooted in context and belonging, see that it builds trust in oneself and others and empowers us to move beyond futurephobia, together.

The Power of Place

The power of place is rooted in history, culture, and belonging. People are powerful when their histories and collective wisdom consistently energize their essence and their becoming, in school and out of it. All people need coherence and authenticity in order to feel healthy and whole, but everyday typical schools ask young people who are still shaping their sense of self to dissociate—to leave some or all of their interests and drive, their emotions, and their lived contextual and historical realities outside the door. Ideas and language lose their meaning when they are taken out of context. What happens to people?

"One size fits all" curricula and assessment exacerbates this fracturing displacement problem. sam seidel of Stanford d-school's k12 Lab refers to this as "solutionitis," where districts spend a lot of money on curriculum developed in a far away place instead of co-designing it in the living context where it belongs.[20] Imagine that the system selects your clothes for you, depending on reliable "hard data" about the sizes and needs of certain demographic groups, broken down by age. No matter whether or not it fits comfortably or suits your sense of style, no matter whether it may be inappropriate or even cause you problems, you wear it in order to "succeed."[21] After all, you are not going to step out into the world naked.

Here is an important empathy exercise for educators and community members: follow a student (or a teacher!) for a day in a typical school and I guarantee you will experience this alienating and disorienting feeling of un-belonging, being out of place (you will also feel the impact of the spaces and places in which we ask students to be comfortable and open to learning). School is designed for what most people "your age" should be able to do, and you have no say in it. You might be tracked into a socially segregated class. Your schedule is further split into time and subject confetti, which do not at all reflect the ways in which real people experience real life.

In its own bubble of reality, typical standardized schooling is caught up in actions that affirm the social inequities of the "real world," and at the same time does not enjoin youth and teacher strengths to encourage collective co-creative change. The very fact that educators have to refer to our actual lives "out there" as the "real world" with which youth will engage "someday" ought to be a warning pointing to the scope of much-needed unlearning. Instead school should be an invitation to re-root learning in our sense of place.

Our identities and our living realities come from our past, our families and communities, and the natural environment we are growing in. Like trees, people and communities thrive on the wisdom they have in their roots, breathing the air of their ancestors. Think of the power in that. The thousands of generations of living nourishment from Nature and people and love that brought you here. Our learning spaces should be living spaces of nourishment, too.

What if we thought of our educator role as cultivators and mentors facilitating access to holistic nutrients so that our students, in the fullness of their whole humanity, can thrive?

A living school flourishes with the power of place.[22] Join me in Chapter 6 (The Power of Place) where we ask, What if we thought of schools as learning ecosystems, flourishing *because* of their sense of interdependent community and their cultural habitats? What might happen if students feel that they matter? If learning was framed by rooted wisdom and celebrated cultures? What if students felt that the school was *their* place? A liberating sense of aliveness and belonging will emerge. As John A. Powell, director of the Othering and Belonging Institute at UC Berkeley once wrote, "Belonging means more than just being seen. Belonging entails having a meaningful voice and the opportunity to participate in the design of social and cultural structures. Belonging means having the right to make demands on society and political institutions."[23] What if learning was driven deeper by students' curiosity, charged by their agency, motivated by authentic local needs and challenges?

The Power of Purpose to Create Change

<u>Purpose</u> **energizes the regenerative power to create change.** When we have *a reason* to act, especially when it is for something greater than ourselves alone, we are much more likely to dig deeper and connect with others to make a positive difference. Purpose draws out our inner resources, such as intrinsic motivation, compassion, creativity, genius, and our other unique strengths. Purpose joins with passion to drive learning deep.

Most teachers feel a strong sense of purpose in working with kids. They love it when "their kids" do well. This motivates them to work long hours, expend a tremendous amount of energy, and to keep learning more. And these same teachers are in typical schools, where they and their students confront a lot of static and external, complex pressures clouding their clarity around their own sense of purpose, or their sense of "why." The external motivators of grades and test scores, even when these motivators are internalized (a voluntary subversion of the self), are not enough to engage students in deep learning. Have you ever heard students call homework "busy work," or say they don't understand how they will ever use math, or that they forget everything as soon as they take the test? You are probably working very hard (and in many cases succeeding!) to make a "one-size-fits-all" curriculum engaging (entertaining?) for students whose main motivation is to get a good grade or just to get it over with.

In a typical school, seniors slump. If the purpose of school was transactional, to collect the grades needed to go on to college, for example, then what is the purpose of it once admission has been achieved? For most, college-bound or not, Senior Slump is a sign of burnout. At least half of your seniors haven't been engaged with school for years, and what would be the point of engaging now, with graduation just around the corner? Senior Slump is often an identity crisis, too. Now that I am about to go out on my own, what is it that I would like to pursue? What does it feel like to be motivated from within? Am I prepared to direct my own life in this world? For many, this is when futurephobia strikes hardest. Educators do not expect their students to share their sense of purpose about being educators, but if we are serious about teaching to strengthen change-making power, our schools will move in the direction of engaging students k12 and beyond in work that is meaningful to them and to their living communities. That will ensure that young adults continue to act from internal motivation and with civic courage in living contexts.

Purpose-driven curriculum co-empowers community and youth, enabling them to build transformative resilience and efficacy together.[24] We'll take a deeper dive into youth as community designers enacting their power with purpose in Chapter 7. When a resilient community confronts a sudden shock or a slow threat, it pulls together its resources. Neighbors ignore their differences and reach out to help each other. Together, they gain strength around a shared purpose. Young people are no different. Research tells us that children have much deeper reserves and stronger drive than they are acknowledged for, and when there is a challenge that matters, they not only *can* tap into those resources, but it also helps them to do so. (See Génesis Ramos interview) Without a sense of purpose, youth can feel irrelevant, useless, lost (in the sense of directionless), or worthless, all among the several potential causes for powerlessness, futurephobia, and depression. There is belonging in helping out, a validating trust, and empowering shared responsibility. There is creative confidence and self- and shared efficacy. There is honoring of place and identity. A comforting feeling of "we got this."

When students are driven by passion, compassion, and curiosity, they have a reason to pursue learning. In the context of belonging and connectedness, with their sense of place and the people around them, youth can become co-creators of their own learning experiences, civic leaders, and difference makers. Which would motivate you to go deeper? Making a difference or getting a grade? Go back to your original motivation reflection in the Introduction. Which matters more to you?

Here are a couple of vital questions to consider as you put this book down and think:

What if diplomas were not based on Carnegie units, or the number of minutes spent warming a chair followed by a minimum score on a test, but on your actual capabilities and contributions?

What if our k12 curricula were built around local-to-global challenge strands, such as food security, water, home, Nature, energy, leadership and governance, identities, culture, and student lives?

The Power of Process

If the regenerative power of purpose is the "why," the power of process is the "how." A problem-solving process like community co-design thinking (see Chapter 8, Figure 8.4) and the toolbox of skills and mindsets that go with it, give the power of purpose traction. A trusted process allows people to collaborate across and even heal fragmentations, separations, and divides. A process can provide the multi-disciplinary and convergent means to unleash ingenuity and achieve change.[25] A reliable process engenders a sense of security and confidence. Knowing HOW to drive change, how to challenge our own assumptions and biases, how to create vision and consensus, how to surface the right problems at the right scale, how to tap into our own historical knowledge and inner drive, how to create the alliances needed to enact our ideas, enables us to disrupt oppressive power-impact flows and build agency through transformative action. The power of process, especially one viewed with a critical lens, unlocks the doors to a life of belonging, collaborative problem solving, shared restoration, renewal, and joy.

One cautionary note about design thinking. First, it has a history of its own, which we will visit in Chapter 8, and which you will want to know in order to unsettle the top-down and extractive posture some have given it. Educators and youth alike will need to keep asking, who holds the power of design? And another potential misstep: once you see how it can work, it is tempting to become very attached to "the process." You might become so attached to teaching The Process, that you lose sight of the designers, the challenges, and the living solutions, and so the power-impact flows can replicate oppressive ones or skew counter-cultural. Without constant critical reflection and adaptation, the process (any process, really) can accidentally become the goal instead of an open toolbox to facilitate place-based and youth/community empowered change making.

Educators around the world have picked up on the potential of design thinking processes and mindsets to teach creative problem solving and to foster positive growth around transformation—of school, community, and life. In some countries and regions, it is built into centralized curricula, and fosters civic, collaborative, and positive engagement from the beginning of school, involving children in issues they care about. With the support of the k12lab at Stanford (and its spin-off work in belonging, liberatory design, school space design, and life design), teachers and students can be part of a community of thought leaders continuing to research, apply, and critique design thinking, even as they are using it to transform.[26]

Process as a co-empowering principle of living systems leads directly to regenerative systems thinking. Regenerative solutions are never permanent, but "living," because they are iterative: continuously changing, emerging, and evolving. The process (whichever one rings true in your context of design) itself and the implementation of the results generates an interrelated ecosystem of support and the ecosystem in turn iterates the process. The process itself is both rooted in and generates a strong sense of place and purpose. Not only does one step follow upon another in reassuring fashion, community-led change through co-design thinking fosters trust, communication, empathy, and equity-minded, life-affirming advocacy and leadership. A process like co-design thinking not only unleashes another regenerative power, it also forms the living bridge between the powers of people, place and purpose, and the positivity that results from them.

What if youth and their community ecosystems got to enact, celebrate, and iterate their community-and-research-based, innovative ideas?

The Power of Positive Action

<u>Positivity</u> flourishes where the roots of co-empowerment thrive. What does that feel like, to belong in an integrated community of care, to be collaboratively applying Process to Purpose from a position of deeply rooted trust and connectedness? To feel that sense of efficacy, the knowledge that "Yes, we can," and exercise the agency to bring about changes that affect our lives and our planet for the better? Students who have built out their own integrated systems of power keep influencing and creating change as adults.

You can feel the positive energy in student Génesis Ramos's description of how Impacto Juventud grew out of the devastation of Maria, and how it keeps deepening and expanding its impact on its members and their communities today. You can also join José Obregón's interview or Sena Wazer's or Javier Moscoso's journeys (pages 262 and 270) to hopefulness and co-empowerment. As "Generation Z" Jordan Salama wrote in his beautiful essay "A Letter to My Generation,"

> ... A movement is beginning, and in my circles, at least, it's no longer acceptable to stay silent. Ironically, it took months of social distancing to help spark this remarkable level of engagement in society, especially among young people. [After what we've seen], how could we *not* seek change? ... It's only natural to think of ourselves as Generation Screwed--but I want to think that we're shaping up to be Generation Renewed. We will not go down without a fight. And what will define us far more than our struggles in this moment is what we'll do when we come out the other side.[27]

Indeed. An uplifting spirit of awe, belonging, and interconnected, empowered resilience embodies the positive and healing feelings of hopefulness, creative confidence, self- and shared agency, and civic and emotional well-being that comes from the individual and collective power to effect real and living change. Our regenerative habits, relationships, and collective actions, guided by the intrinsic logic and principles of life, move us beyond future-phobia with the knowledge that together we will be okay. Beyond physical health and safety, what makes up a person's feeling of positivity about their future, and their role in shaping the opportunities within it?? In Chapter 9, we'll take a closer look (Figure 3.5).

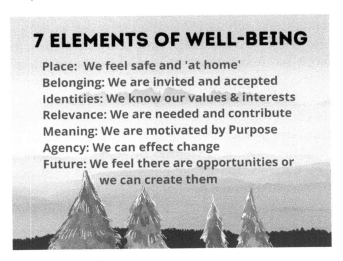

FIGURE 3.5 Elements of well-being

People Are Resilient When They Have the Power to Drive Change

People, even young ones, are experts in their own experiences. We know when something is wrong, and we usually have some sense of what we need in order for things to work better for us. A significant source of overwhelm and futurephobia stems from the low self- and shared efficacy and agency of not being able to make things happen in order to meet our needs. This power-lessness is particularly common in disasters, both fast and slow, when so much is out of our control. The less socio-economic-political power we have, the more vulnerable and less resilient we frequently are. When most people think of resilience, they think of some personal characteristic, and something like quickly recovering from setbacks, and indeed this kind of personal confidence is important. But it is very difficult to generate by oneself. Resilience scholar and researcher Michael Ungar identifies 12 factors that need to be present in order for people to be and to feel resilient.[28] Not one of them relies solely on individual capabilities—all exist in relation to others and our environment, and *all add up to addressing challenges by changing some aspect of our world to enable our well-being.* Thus, people are resilient when *collectively* they have the power to drive change. They are even more resilient when the changes they call for transform systems so that the power to act for the well-being of themselves and others grows and evolves as they do. The good news is that we can teach this, and in teaching this kind of resilience we find energy and co-empowerment, and contribute to the well-being of both teachers and learners and the living communities and nested systems we inhabit.

Much of the time, governing systems expect people to be resilient in such a way that we get "back to normal" quickly after a disaster. Resilience "training" and preparation often emphasize the risk reduction measures, the emergency kits and response workshops, the patches and bandaids, and quick fixes that can be applied and *should be.* Integrated and multi-disciplinary community- and youth-led innovations in disaster risk reduction, however, need space and support to evolve. Learning ecosystems based on continuously seeking and solving climate challenges can be excellent leverage points for students to engage creatively in civic roles, tapping into their courage and bringing a powerful measure of agency to youth. By assisting their communities in this way, they can (and many are already!) make a significant difference in their own and others' well-being.

Resilience as Resistance

Much of what passes for resilience in education never questions the systems making us vulnerable in the first place. As educators in the age of climate disasters, we have to ask ourselves, whose interests is this serving? Of course we should engage in the short-term emergency prep trainings and practice response and recovery in the age of climate disasters. But let's keep asking, How can we support and ally with our students' vitality, their wholeness, to co-empower them for real and forever? How can we curate learning spaces and experiences that liberate? To do that, we need to expand our power literacy and demand the freedom to co-create. Expand and demand, to energize the regenerative powers we already have to move beyond futurephobia and restore our connection with the beauty of our living and infinitely related universe.

Seeds for Planting

Futurephobia is the predictable outcome of centuries of fragmentations, but these fragmentations are not inevitable or immutable.

The hierarchical fragmentations of most concern are Man over Nature, Man over Woman, Cognitive over Emotional Minds, and White Supremacy. These fractures are the underpinnings of the narratives of separation and degenerative power structures troubling Earth and threatening us with ill health extinction today.

Power Literacy grows with the practice of "power audits," raising awareness among all participants of how power is enacted in the classroom first—parents may find this lesson comes home—it definitely spreads out into critical civic consciousness. Go slowly and stay together.

We can resist the fragmentations by using what ancient wisdoms and Mother Earth gives us—coherence, interrelatedness, imagination, love, and the (Re)Generative Powers that are rooted in her rich soils:

Personhood, coming home to the coherent self. People, the strength and empowered resilience of interrelationship. Place, the sense of rooted culture and belonging that gives us the power to say no, we are doing it our way. Purpose, that motivates and energizes us and gives our lives meaning. Processes that co-empower, and the Positivity and well-being that arises from our individual and collective actions for the good of the whole.

Notes

1 The Climate Museum, Arctic Timeline. https://arctictimeline.org/
2 Glass 2021.
3 If you are not already familiar with Project Drawdown, go to this site and click on Solutions. https://drawdown.org/ There you will find hundreds of examples of the good news we need to be realistically hopeful. It will also give you lots of ways to involve your students in the real work of co-creating their future, based on their own compassions and interests, as well as meeting the learning goals you may hold for them.
4 The Committee of 10 was appointed by the National Education Association to make recommendations about a nationwide set of acceptable methods, standards, and programs. Their recommendations will seem familiar–5-day school week, 8 years of elementary school (smaller in scale) feeding into four years of high school (bigger), with summer break for agrarian life. They split the teaching of traditional academic subjects into separate disciplines taught in separate periods of the day. A summative examination could be given in the academic subjects for the purposes of College Entrance Requirements (set in 1895).
5 Roy 2003.
6 Hobson 2021.
7 Wahl 2016.
8 Escobar 2017.
9 Wahl 2017.
10 Graham Leicester is the Director of the International Futures Forum. This quote is from his Forward to the Daniel Christian Wahl (2016) book, *Designing Regenerative Cultures*.
11 In the end we created foundational relationships and a small guide for teachers and a library of activities as they rebuilt learning, often outside and without materials, but with a lot of community support. We then doubled the library of activities when the RISE Network-PR, an alliance of university professors interested in equity and "constructive resilience," brought me again during the worst of the earthquakes in early 2020, connecting and co-creating with 100 professionals and students in six locations. During COVID-19, Design Ed 4 Resilience converted the activities to "virtual'"and "socially distanced" versions, in two languages, thanks to translation help from Pamela Silva Díaz. They are now in use across the Puerto Rican archipelago, the Bahamas, and the United States, not to mention the United Arab Emirates, India, and Kenya. Access for free by signing up here: https://www.designed4resilience.org/tools-for-school-and-life
12 Climent Belda 2019.
13 More depth and breadth later, but I wanted to note roots and influences here in Indigenous ways of thinking, such as Robin Wall Kimmerer, *Braiding Sweetgrass*, secular Buddhism-influenced thinking such as that found in the work of Margaret J. Wheatley, *Turning to One Another*, Nature-based feminism such as found in *All We Can Save*, and a host of educators writing about youth agency and liberatory literacies, led by Paolo Friere

and bell hooks, and the new generation, Bettina Love and Gholdy Muhammad.

14 In fact only about a third of the thousands of students Gallup has surveyed over the years still say they are engaged in school by the time they are in high school. Hodges 2018.

15 Fried 2005.

16 Bruni 2015. A controversial book about a crisis that mainly affects the 3% ... but then those are the parents expending a tremendous amount of energy, time and money on the game of school, and in the process (and very likely unwittingly) compromising the health of their children by overemphasizing external and inauthentic measures, that is, counting what doesn't count.

17 Pndrawing. "How to Draw 3 Bored Students At School in Anime [Slow Tutorial]." nd. 25:08 min. Educational Video. https://www.youtube.com/watch?v=dVQXDhi7Y0s

18 It amused my colleagues and sometimes frustrated my supervisors when they would have to scan the room, sometimes for a few minutes, to locate me. Earlier in my career, older colleagues would ask me to "keep it down," because they could hear us "right through the walls." Fortunately, my first boss liked it when kids got so excited they would stand on a chair during a debate, or get up to act out something they were trying to explain. So I never actually had to comply with the request to deaden the vitality and joy of learning, and eventually, they stopped asking. Administrators, take note of the important role you play in unleashing joy and creativity.

19 We will take a closer look at this in the next chapters. See also 4 levels of listening, from Otto Scharmer's *Theory U* (2016) (here's an 8+ minute video of him presenting it: https://vimeo.com/199593914), and Thomas Hübl, *Healing Collective Trauma*. 2020.

20 Getting Smart Staff. 2018.

21 Favretti 2021.

22 There is a beautiful collection of essays on what makes a living school pulse with vitality and well-being, edited by Catharine O'Brien and Patrick Howard, *Living Schools: Transforming Education*. It can be downloaded, along with other valuable free resources, from https://www.livingschools.world/publications-and-resources Schools enacting living school principles can be found all over the world, especially among Indigenous and marginalized communities, such as the public Farm School's earth pedagogy in Orocovis, Puerto Rico, Aula en la montaña in Barrio Rucio Peñuelas (PR), or Vista Innovation & Design Academy (VIDA) in San Diego. Springhouse, a regenerative private school in North Carolina offers professional development opportunities and tools to transform your school by letting vitality and wholeness be the core.

23 Grant-Thomas nd.

24 There is a great deal written about this remarkable consensus among educators, and we will dive deeper into it later. Here are some starting resources: Tom Vander Ark and Emily Liebtag, *Difference Making at the Heart of Learning: Students, Schools, and Communities Alive With Possibility*. Corwin, 2021. Stephen Zemelman. *From Inquiry to Action: Civic Engagement with PBL in All Content Areas*. Heinemann, 2016. Dayna Laur. *Authentic Learning Experiences: A Real-World Approach to PBL*. Routledge, 2013. All of these authors (and many more) are working hard on various platforms (Getting Smart, ARC Learning, What School Could Be, K20, Stanford's

d-school k12 lab, Teachers' Guild x School Retool, Harvard's Project Zero) to build on what's good and transform education systems to add meaning, purpose, equity, and belonging so as to deepen engagement and learning.

25 In recognition of the multi-disciplinary complexity of the challenges that confront us in our actual lives, more colleges, and universities, and now k12 schools as well, are developing programs and curricula that connect various disciplines (convergence) to focus on a complex issue.

26 K12lab access: https://dschool.stanford.edu/programs/k12-lab-network Transformation: https://www.teachersguild.org/toolkit-resources Liberatory Design: https://dschool.stanford.edu/resources-collections/liberatory-design Design for Belonging: https://dschool.stanford.edu/resources/design-for-belonging School Safety: https://dschool.stanford.edu/k12-lab-network/safety Life Design: https://lifedesignlab.stanford.edu/

27 Salama 2020.

28 Ungar 2018.

4 Personhood and the Power Within: Coming Home to Ourselves

How can we connect ancient understandings of wholeness to modern brain science in order to come home to our interrelated and coherent selves?

How might we address futurephobia by creating the conditions for holistic coherence to nourish our important roots of regenerative power?

> "Most of the time I don't come to school. I feel like it is not helping me or the situation. School should make sense. It's frustrating. I'm just waiting for it to be over because it's just not for me."
>
> –Alanís, 16

School should make sense. Think how much better we learn when we feel known, loved, and motivated, and how much more deeply we understand when all of our being is engaged. When school "makes sense," teachers and learners together can be in a "state of flow."[1] We are "in the zone," with passion, purpose, past, and future flowing right through us. It feels like being in the

DOI: 10.4324/9781003215806-5

right place at the right time. Time schedules recede in importance and deep, memorable, even spiritual heart-knowing happens. When this experience is shared, we might call it "bonding." We feel more *alive* than ever. Full of focus and willingness. Full of coherence, of things just fitting together and making sense in relation to each other. A power-full feeling of well-being and contentment is with us, too. Now school is not like this every day, certainly not for every person, but the project of school should be to support the conditions so that coherence is present and the potential for flow is always available. Educators, including the majority who are carrying their own emotional loads, navigate this shifting landscape with skill and grace, times however many students (usually more than a hundred) they see in a day. Mostly, they do it with their own heart-thinking, motivated by what some describe as a calling. Teaching just makes sense. What doesn't make sense, in many cases, is the system that fosters incoherence and the frustration and disengagement Alanís and hundreds of thousands like her feel. For increasing numbers of teachers, too, the fragmentation, disconnection, and struggle to achieve co-herence and flow have become overwhelming.

Degenerative systems of harm (colonialism, racism, sexism, extractive consumer capitalism) and their rationalizing narratives have resulted in fractured and isolated selves, and have left most of us with some vital healing to do, and soon, if we are to function in and reach beyond futurephobia to resist. In the context of our shared situation here, brought to the edge of the existential cliff by the forces of destruction, healing is not only necessary, it is revolutionary.

Revolutionary, But Not New

Educators of all kinds can turn to Indigenous, ancient, or the more newly healing "global South" for guidance and full un-derstanding of the regenerative power of coherence. In their seminal work (1997) on re-engaging youth and teachers with school and life, *Sentipensar*, Saturnino de la Torre, and María Candida Moraes wrote,

"Sentipensar es la fusión de dos formas de percibir y interpretar la realidad a partir de la reflexión y el impacto emocional, hasta converger en un mismo acto de conocimiento y acción. Sentipensar es el encuentro intensamente consciente entre sentimiento y razón."[2]

"*Sentipensar* [literally feeling-thinking, or heart-thinking] is the fusion of two ways of perceiving and interpreting reality based on reflection and emotional impact until they converge in the same act of knowledge and action. *Sentipensar* is the intensely conscious encounter between feeling and reason." A living principle in both Colombian coastal Indigenous communities and Andean mountain ones, the mind-body-heart-spirit connection and the living connectedness of worlds is not only a guiding cultural belief, it is at the very core of personhood, relationships, and healing for Indigenous people in the so-called Americas going back thousands of years. When people ask Joe Rice (Choctaw), Executive Director of the Nawayee Center School in Minneapolis, if there is research, data attesting to the power of coherence and of Indigenous relational values, he is fond of saying, "We have 100,000 years of keeping what works and discarding what doesn't. The fact that we're doing it this way today means that it has worked—and in many instances, has worked for a really long time."[3]

One might say that this holistic approach to knowing and being is "more Western than Western," native as it is to the Western Hemisphere, North and South. But similar holistic coherences, that join together Mind, Heart, Body, and Spirit and move together with the rhythms of Earth and the infinite interrelatedness of love as the essence of health can be found in the eastern hemisphere, too: Africa (e.g., the Yoruba concept of *ori*),[4] South Asia (Buddhist interbeing), and the Pacific Islands and Australasia. It was controversial for the Sufi poets, Hafez, Kabir, and Rumi, for example, to embody the whole self. They felt that the mainstream dogmatic versions of their Western monotheisms had split existence into dualisms that ought to have remained whole, and that "reason" further split us off from ourselves. Kabir, revered also by Hindus, wrote: "Inside love there is more joy than we know of … / Those who hope to be reasonable about it fail./ The arrogance of reason has separated us from that love./ With the word 'reason,' you already feel miles away."[5] It is no surprise that people yearning for coherence find Sufi poetry appealing. It seems so fitting for the present fractured, urgent moment, like this oft-quoted gift from Rumi: "Sit down and be quiet./ You are drunk, and this is the edge of the roof."

It is difficult to write about spirituality in relational coherence without being reductionist or generalizing, and it is impossible to encapsulate either its mysteries or unique differences in a few words, but one commonality emerges: a spiritual unity connects lands, seas, and all beings in infinite and dynamic interrelationship across time. Earth is seen as the loving mother of all, home of the ancestors, and creator of life itself, and humans return that love by being guardians or stewards of living systems and each other within them. Importantly, people are not separable from the land. Another spiritual commonality seems to be awe and reverence regarding intricately and infinitely intertwined dynamic living systems where nothing is superfluous and there is no beginning nor end. For monotheisms in the West, this immutable and also unknowable fact is seen as proof of the existence of God. For many Jewish, Christian, and Islamic climate activists and regenerative farmers today, this felt connection to the Earth and all of Creation energizes their spiritual commitment to care for it.

 Mending News!

Youth-Led Zumwalt Acres Raises Food, Lowers Carbon, and Builds Spiritual Coherence

Two sisters, Remi and Gabi Welbel want to raise "food we can believe in." Their approach combines Jewish spiritual beliefs relating to caring for creation and community, with regenerative farming and agroforestry practices and horticultural research on the Zumwalt family farm in Illinois. The Welbels and their team are generating a positive cycle of coherence, embodying head, heart, body, and spirit in interconnected community, which then generates more community and holistic well-being. https://www.zumwaltacres.org/

The ethical idea of social justice has its roots in spiritual coherence. Concepts of human coherence through interrelationship, such as Ubuntu in Africa, "I exist because you exist," demand an ethical consideration—"Is my life better because yours is worse?" And a spiritual commitment to well-being and coherence with the environment as well does not allow for hypocrisy. In Pope Francis's 2015 Encyclical, he postulates that ecology and social justice are inseparable. "A true ecological approach always becomes a social approach; it must integrate questions of justice in debates on the environment."[6] Caring for our home and ourselves means caring for others. Caring for others is one of the most fundamental spiritually based ethical principles across the world and can unite many behind circular and caring, that is, revolutionary but not new, economic systems,[7] and re-graft humans to their regenerative roots in all endeavors, from agriculture to governance to education. More about interrelationship is presented in the next chapter. Many people today who describe themselves as "not religious" still feel a healing connection with Earth that fills them with awe and soothing and a calling to social and environmental justice that "just feels like the right thing." Feeling coherence and wholeness in their lives empowers them to think well enough of themselves to act with civic courage.

Healing as an Act of Resistance

Coherence is one of life's most important healing powers. With an awareness of the healing power of coherence, we can disrupt the encrusted and harmful systems, and open up to new and old ways of knowing and being. We can begin to restore ourselves to ourselves by focusing on it, looking for opportunities to bring the intellect and emotion, mind and body, brain and soul, spirit and head and heart and environment together to create a foundation of wholeness. Returning to embodied wholeness is an act of resistance in itself. A leading voice in education justice, the late bell hooks wrote,

> "I think that one of the unspoken discomforts surrounding the way a discourse of race and gender, and sexual practice has disrupted the academy is precisely that mind/body split. Once we start talking in the classroom about the body and about how we live in our bodies, we're automatically challenging the way power has orchestrated itself in that particular institutionalized space."[8]

In a fragmented world, coherence is a form of resistance. Once you reclaim your body and start approaching it with reverence and curiosity, many transformations become available, including deep acceptance of oneself. There is power in that. As Joe Rice put it, "Defiance is always something young people are attracted to. And, if loving oneself and being happy is an act of defiance, then so be it. Young people will see they have a lot of work to do, but they also know it's very doable."[9] Helga Maldonado, a community psychologist in Puerto Rico, wrote this about the children she knows best.[10]

> *The children of the community where I work have all the excuses in the world to be "bad" and they aren't. In fact, they are wonderful.*
>
> *The children of the community with whom I work have every reason in the world to hate education. But they don't. They love it and are eager to learn … .*
>
> *The children of the community with whom I work deserve healthy, worthy, safe and appropriate living [and learning] conditions. But they don't have them.*
>
> *The children I work beside choose to be good, warm, kind, and loving all the days of their lives … . How brave they are!*
>
> *But please! Don't ask them to be resilient anymore when every day they are faced with so much violence and injustice.*

Helga's students are alive and well, learning and healing and growing as an act of defiance. Students who are healing are not "bouncing back" to strengthen the systems that harm them. They are not deficient or lost. Joe Rice puts it this way. "Healing is not about fixing anything that is broken. It's about re-membering the wholeness that has always been inside of us." Imagine what flourishing could emerge if every child could find their way home to themselves, or stay home in the first place! For help in understanding what this kind of self-discovery could mean in the context of school, I asked Joe what it looks like in Nawayee Center School, and he generously gave us his thoughts. I did not change them but put them here in their entirety so we can take some time with them and consider them deeply. After she read his words, Alanís said she wished her school could be more like the Center School. Do you feel any resonance? Can you relate?

Indigenous Learning, Direct From Joseph C. Rice, Executive Director, Nawayee Center School, Minneapolis, MN

Indigenous alternative schools have always arisen as a response to the lack of education for Indigenous students and their Families that is appropriate to their needs and cultural perspectives.

The truth is that American schools and the American educational system were not created for Indigenous children, but rather, in spite of them.

*Historically, mainstream American schools, rooted in a worldview of colonized peoples with little or no connection to the land, utilized a pedagogy emphasizing rote memorization and regurgitation of "facts" and typically provided very little time for **movement, self-discovery, or relational thinking**, three essential ingredients of Indigenous cultures or lifeways. The result has been that "educational institutions" have served often times as an anathema to learning for Indigenous children. In fact, the mission of the earliest schools for Indigenous children (government-run boarding schools) was "Kill the Indian, Save the Man,"*

The resulting high levels of disengagement for Indigenous children have demanded a response, which for most of the Indigenous alternative schools has been to use cultural content and pedagogy to create culturally contextualized learning environments.

An elder once said to me that "For thousands of years we have spent ninety percent of our lives outdoors and perhaps ten percent indoors, so it makes no sense to spend most of our learning time indoors."

Immediately I saw the truth of this and began to consider the implication of this simple statement: our kids are active, relational learners not passive recipients of "knowledge." (to be received from 'teachers" with little or no experiences relevant to the lives of the young learners they propose to teach)

I began working at Nawayee twenty years ago and we have been working quite earnestly at **re-shaping our students' educational experiences so that they understand that they are safe and welcomed here, and that they are, in fact, brilliant, powerful and insightful learners capable of unlimited success.**

The primary methodology for doing this has been to try and incorporate Indigenous lifeways into every facet of our programming.

A little about Indigenous lifeways:

> Indigenous lifeways are rooted in a coherent understanding of the universe and how to live on this world. They are at once practical, pragmatic, prosaic and magical. We understand that this planet is our oldest living relative and that she provides everything we need to live as well as all of the important information about how to do so. For example: nothing here lives solely for itself but everything is a relative with a role to play just as in any family.

To understand Indigenous cultures in general, know these four things: Indigenous cultures are autochthonous (they arise from the land), relationships and relatedness are what informs them and holds them together, they are ancient and part of an infinite universe and all that infinity implies. They are continuously evolving as are all living things.

In developing culturally relevant learning environments for our students we have identified several **"Best Practices"** which have been the source of much of our success:

1. *Teaching and learning happen co-creatively and within the context of culturally appropriate relationships,*
2. *Learning experiences are much richer in potential when they are multi-sensory and draw from Indigenous cultural wisdom,*
3. *Learning needs to encourage the growth of mind, body, spirit, and soul,*
4. *Learning endeavors should address issues important to both learner and teacher,*
5. *Teachers must be good listeners.*

The above Best Practices have led us to continually evolve as a school and develop partnerships to work co-creatively with community partners to develop solutions to our community's problems.

One such problem has been the intense levels of trauma experienced by Indigenous peoples in North America, and specifically our children. To that end, we developed our Medicine Wheel Health program to address the historical, inter-generational, and on-going trauma that our kids are living with. To make a long story short, Trauma became an academic subject that was ultimately integrated with all other areas of study using a multi-disciplinary approach. While we have stand-alone health classes or groups to address Health, we also address it in all areas of study. For example, History can teach about/explore Colonization and Genocide in North America, while Science can investigate the effects it has had on the environment, including the people whose homeland this is. Language Arts classes can read narratives of Boarding School survivors, while Math classes can look at the relevant statistics and consider the implications of such horrific numbers.

The students' response to this has been to become more engaged in learning about these issues to help put today's experiences in their proper context and to begin to work on taking responsibility for finding solutions. In a country where intellectuals are revered and respected, many of our students would be well-positioned to help us move forward as a people.

At Nawayee, student engagement, attendance, and graduation have steadily improved, but more importantly, the quiet, respectful ambience here tells us that students value being here and that they feel safe and welcomed. The staff as well as visitors often remark on the uniquely peaceful feeling of this place as opposed to the feeling of cold aloofness or disinterest they report feeling at many of our mainstream schools.

The most difficult aspect of the COVID lockdown has been that we are not able to offer many of the aspects of our learning place that our students like and need the most. They miss the one-to-one conversation, the calm atmosphere of 65 people in a small building co-existing peacefully (and even gratefully), the sound and feel of friendly voices, and the feel and spirit of a living culture.

Indigenous cultures in general and Indigenous schools in particular, have and practice much of the wisdom that has been lost over the years due to colonization. Where once the entire world was Indigenous, it is now mostly colonized save for a few small pockets of Indigenous culture remaining around the world that hold on to the ancient wisdom of how to live in and care for this world. In the United States, for example, Indigenous peoples are roughly 1% of the population, making coherent thinking about the realities of life on Planet Earth a rarity for sure.

> *"And every time the Takers stamp out a Leaver culture, a wisdom ultimately tested since the birth of mankind disappears from the world beyond recall."*
> – Daniel Quinn

Mainstream American education is in a similar position.

Its greatest flaw is its desire to train rather than to educate. As Albert Einstein once said, "Education is not the learning of facts. It is the training of the mind to think." Indigenous understandings of learning and the relation of the human mind, body, spirit and soul to the world are missing in the current science (if it is that) of education. We cannot "train the mind to think" if we are asking children to sit passively and be receptacles for information that they are not interested in and cannot connect to. Students must become learners by their own volition, choose what they want to learn and be mentored in the art of learning by identifying their strengths and developing those strengths (assets) to their greatest advantage. It takes wise persons to do this with children. They must be both patient and insightful. They need to learn how to identify the spark of interest and insight in a child and be creative enough to encourage the growth of that spark in as many different children as they can relate to. This is not a pedagogy that can readily be translated into a number of steps as in a cookbook, but above all requires that a teacher ("Cook") be willing to adjust their recipe as required by circumstance.

In a 2020 conversation with *Education Reimagined*, Joe went further. "How we look at learning, life, community, and healing sets us free. It encourages kids to become truly brilliant, rather than just well-trained." Yes! You could be forgiven if, as a parent, teacher, administrator, or state ed leader you jumped up and said, "We want this for our kids, too! We are making it official. The whole state is going to do this, starting tomorrow." But wait. If you do that, it will not only be appropriating a culturally coherent approach and taking it out of context, it will be like pinning a tail on a donkey (because every donkey needs a tail) and expecting it to wag. Adding good programs onto a bad system makes incoherence even more overwhelming. Besides, top-down command and uniformity in education *cause* fragmentation, because in many cases, the program just doesn't fit. Read Joe Rice's words again. Especially the cookbook sentence. Metaphorically speaking, every learning community needs to make its own Medicine Wheel.

Yet your excitement about coherence and well-being and health in school signifies something very important to slow down and notice. We are all yearning to be whole. Aside from all the data about youth unhappiness, anxiety, and futurephobia in the Introduction, Alanís and so many like her know/feel right away they want to go to a school "like that." Every parent wants their children to be healthy and to grow into healthy adults. When parents talk to parents of kids in a school like this, or like Aula en la Montaña (see pp. 251–255), they sense right away that the kids like being there. They feel safe. They are welcomed. They belong. They exercise creative agency in the life of the school and community. Those of us who are part of Daniel Quinn's "Taker" society,[11] who are living better because someone else is living worse, feel the pull strongly. We have lost ourselves in the Taking. The yearning, the pull to be whole, is our Mother Earth, the essential love, the unifying force in the infinite interrelationships and coherence of life, drawing us in like gravity and like gravity, keeping us from flying apart.

Medicine Wheels for Healing and Health

When June Kaminski (Métis) was looking to support healing practices as a health practitioner and educator in western Canada, she created a Medicine Wheel (she calls it the Four Directions) that looks something like Figure 4.1.

FIGURE 4.1 First nations medicine wheel
Source: Adapted with permission from June Kaminsky

The original version she made many years ago is found on the website Dr. Kaminsky and her colleagues put together called First Nations Pedagogy.[12] About it she writes,

> *This holistic view is just one example of the incredible knowledge and healing practices that were rejected during colonization ... . In contemporary times, renewed interest in the ancient teachings of Canada's First Nations peoples is emerging. Tried and true methods of maintaining and restoring holistic balance of body, mind, heart, and spirit are resurfacing across the nation, even in mainstream health care. It is up to each teacher to gain understanding and openness to these teachings to provide cultural safety to all First Nations people but to also care for **all learners** in a more aware, sensitive, competent, and insightful manner ... .*[13]

When Joe Rice's students created their Medicine Wheel, with attention to mind, body, soul, and spirit, they painted it on the outside of their school. How's that for a mission statement? See the photograph of it, in Figure 4.2.

FIGURE 4.2 Nawayee Center School Medicine Wheel
Source: Photo Courtesy of Joe Rice. Artwork: Students of Nawayee Center School

I asked him why all the Medicine Wheels I've seen are somewhat different from each other. "When I look at it," he said, "I feel infinite possibilities for understanding and well-being."

Basic Life Principles Found in the Medicine Wheels

There is not a one-size-fits-all formula for achieving a learning environment that is holistic and healing. That would miss the point. But the basic principles of life should guide us in our thinking as we consider where we are as an educational institution and how we would like to keep growing. Let's keep these in mind:

1. Everything in the universe is part of an interrelated, infinite, living (changing) whole. Science establishes this, and common sense dictates it when we humans share DNA and our very breath with plants and animals and elements with rocks and stars and return our beloveds' bodies to Earth when they die. The self is the self only in relation to every aspect of itself (mind, heart, soul, body, spirit) and in relation to everyone around us (and they to those around them and so on infinitely). How are we contributing to the well-being of the self AND the whole? Once we begin to appreciate that every Earth-mate is also connected to the land and to each other as relatives, it is not difficult to rethink our education system in accordance with life.

2. Learning is not only necessary, but it is also a function of being alive. The adults in the community and the school, the space itself, the curricula, and young people themselves are teaching all the time, even in hidden and unintentional ways. We must be intentional.

3. Separation is traumatic. Fragmentation of the self as well as the other separations endemic in typical schools are disruptive to healthy development and stressful at best, triggering and terrifying at worst. Given this and the amount of trauma coming at young people from many sources, every school needs to be built on trust and be trauma-safe.

4. Wholeness and well-being is not a destination but a journey. Joe Rice describes the Medicine Wheel as a

source of infinite possibilities, a mnemonic device to help us both connect, clarify, and express our intentions as we grow.

In a Life Lab, DE4R (my org, Design Ed 4 Resilience) and colleagues in Puerto Rico asked students to draw a personal version of a Medicine Wheel, where they added to the symbols with collective meaning those that represented historical events of change, inspirations, wonderings, and those aspirations shaping their becoming. They returned to it many times for sustenance, and reflected on how it interconnected with the shared version, and also on what was getting in the way and throwing things out of balance. Our role as "cooks" to borrow Joe Rice's term, was simply to listen, to think and act with our hearts, and to help young people clear away as much of the static as we could in their process of self-discovery. Their agency to act in their lives came both from learning to identify, integrate, and balance (more than to "regulate") their emotions, and to become aware and intentional about the interactions between themselves and their kin in the outer world from a position of harmony and inner strength. This kind of balancing awareness of coherence (a type of health literacy, or mindfulness) is the basis of transformation, as it enables us to tune in to where we might be getting stuck or knocked off balance by repeating biases or fragmenting patterns or negative "self-talk." Learners sometimes identify with adrienne maree brown's description of herself as a "'cell-sized unit' who can leverage a shift of the whole organism as much by HOW I AM as the things I do."[14]

Self-respect grows with the relational sense that we are never alone and that how we are and who we are becoming is something that affects all of us. One student wrote, "Every part of us is part of something bigger. We matter." In a highly racialized society such as the United States, the intersectionality of race(s), gender(s), abilities, class, ethnicities, religions, etc. is one aspect of inviting coherence in identities (or not) that strongly influences a child's sense of opportunity and potential or futurephobia and oppression. One thing we know is that we cannot consider ourselves as only one thing and be whole. In her 1984 essay collection, *Sister Outsider*, Audre Lorde wrote, "My fullest concentration of energy is available to me only when I integrate all parts of who I am, openly, allowing power from particular sources of my living to flow back and forth through all my different selves, without restrictions of externally imposed definition." (120–21) Lorde's self-awareness reminded me of Bettina Love's recollection of her own turning point: "Loving my Blackness was the first step in my politicization, mattering, and wanting to thrive."[15] *Loving my Blackness. Wanting to thrive.* Self-discovery, honoring, and loving the self is an important root of agency and regenerative power.

Reviving Life in School

Re-membering the coherence of the self and the importance of safety and trust might cause you to question everything about your school system. What might start with, "this can't work here—our school is too big" soon becomes (perhaps with the urging of students and parents) "how might we co-create smaller scale learning within the school?" What might start with, "but we have to comply with the state rules about no discussion of racism, colonialism, sexism or the environment," might result in a movement for access to historical genius rooted in truth, or youth-elder-led actions within the community that reveal and heal. What might start with, "our school looks and feels like a prison" might result in community collaborations and outdoor and distributed learning that does not demand students enter that triggering space at all. Maybe we can replace fear of climate disaster with the love provided by Nature—the comfort and sustenance in the gift of a cool breeze on our necks, a droplet reflecting our appreciation as it rests on a fond green leaf, and yes, the miracle of life in a garden and a bounty of delicious food to sustain us. When a child is not safe at home, the role of the school as a safe home place grows in importance, making the difference for some between surviving and thriving, and in other cases making the difference between life and death. The teacher works with students and families to co-create the day-to-day learning experiences which provide both belonging and opportunities for risk and growth. You can see where I am going with this. Our intention must match our goals, and if health and well-being is a key goal (IF???!!!) then these changes need to be priority one. Our children deserve to thrive. Every. Single. One.

A Life-Learning Teacher

I had a progressive science teacher in Middle School (1970s) who combined natural sciences instruction with what he called, "life learning." Mr. Lawrence was the embodiment of his "CDC" (Challenge, Discovery, Confidence) approach. We all knew about his efforts to work with his stutter so that he could teach, the one thing he told us he had ever wanted to do. He taught human anatomy and physiology to us 6th graders through First Aid and CPR (cardio-pulmonary resuscitation). On a given Saturday, after we had studied and practiced and *understood* every page of the Red Cross First Aid Handbook, there were students lying around, in and out of the building in all stages of pretend ex-igency. It was our job to respond appropriately, to the satisfaction of the older, already certified kids, the local EMT (Emergency Medical Technician), and the Red Cross observers. We all got certified, and we were powerfully motivated to learn even more deeply about the marvels of the human body, and to mentor the next class! On other days, we learned earth science, geology, and plant science while we learned orienteering, rock climbing, and wilderness survival (we even went winter camping). We studied actual earthquakes (and built shake tables), volcanoes, floods, and hurricanes and created "what if" emergency plans for the school and the town. We tested and observed the soil and the forest, noting and drawing the species that grew there and the conditions that made them thrive. We did increment borer samples and learned how trees grow and support entire eco-systems. We studied the geologic history of the area (as we scrambled and climbed over it), learned about the symbiosis of moss, lichen, and rock (who knew that soils and rocks are alive, too!). When Mr. Lawrence melted his championship ring trying to dry it out in the soil sterilizer, we consoled him and then turned our empathy for him (we could relate to making mis-takes!) into an unscheduled series of experiments concerning the relationships between heat, solids, liquids, and gasses.

Together, Mr. Lawrence and I and the other "CDC kids" designed and built (physics, math, proto-engineering, carpentry, and knot tying!) a high and low ropes course, so we could have fun while learning to work together and to conquer our fears. Mr. Lawrence wanted us to go deeper into ourselves, to come to know "what makes us tick." He was very spiritual (I have to use past tense, as he passed away a few years ago), and, while he never shared his religious views with us directly, he felt strongly that every person is here for a reason, and contributes in some significant way to the world around us. I'm not sure he ever articulated this to us, but that he held to this conviction with spiritual force was as plain as day to the 12-year-old me. It was our shared joy to find and develop that inner motivation and confidence, to seek our role and our contribution to the interdependent whole, to live fully and well. I felt understood, loved, and connected. I felt his delight and comfort in teaching us science through "life." I felt the wonder and mystery of the unexplained. I decided to teach the day I overheard someone ask Mr. Lawrence what he taught. He responded, "I am in the science department, but I teach kids." To this day, nearly 50 years later, I remember the content of those lessons with remarkable clarity, but most importantly, his sense of wholeness and coherence in teaching and learning, his prioritizing well-being and "learning through life," his ability to embrace all kinds of learning and his capacity to listen to and love all of us. What I learned first was love and trust. After that, I could learn anything.

Toward Coherence With Educators First

School should make sense. We have a yearning for our true humanity, humming with life and belonging. We long to know and care for our inner selves and our neighbors, and we need to know that they care for us. We have lived through thousands of years of the slow and traumatic separations outlined in Chapter 3,[16] and our learning systems and spaces reflect those dualistic splits and fragmentations. Our minds vs. our bodies. Our natural environment "out there" vs. "in here." Schools vs. the "real world." Our individual success vs. collective well-being. Our past vs. our present ... and thus our future. Most schools and universities are very effective representations, in both systems and structures, of the degenerative hierarchies we inherited. Our own bodies and our students' reflect the pain and trauma associated with these separations.

Educators, both formal and informal (parents, youth clubs, community centers), know that scientifically and experientially, people learn best when they are emotionally present, inspired, and safe. Inspiration, belonging, awe, engagement, motivation, self-esteem ... all are *emotional (as well as relational)*. And if we are aiming for learning that is holistic in the authentic meaning of that word, then we need to build coherence by reintegrating and healing those splits--with educators, first. You are not deficient in any way, or broken and in need of fixing. Instead, I want to acknowledge the reality that our academic institutions, as representations of westernized culture, have typically not created space for emotion and connectedness, and these are your superpowers!

Teachers often close off their own feelings as "unprofessional." Self-care (often a return to Nature) is needed just to recover from the stress of school. Without it, exhaustion (burnout) takes hold. That's a red flag warning that the system isn't right. Relational, coherent learning is energizing! But...

"Isn't it safer for everyone if we just don't acknowledge the presence of our bodies and attendant emotions in the room?"

"I am afraid to open that can of worms."

"I don't do that touchy-feely stuff. I'm a teacher, not a therapist." [Translation: I feel unprepared to address the varied yet collected emotional needs of my students in class.]

"There isn't time."

These often-expressed sentiments throughout education (including higher ed—indeed, the older the youth, the less attention is paid to well-being) are intertwined with understandable confusion and anxiety about how to join the three powerful kinds of intelligence Nature gave us—our body, our emotions (heart or soul), and our cognitive mind.

As educators in the 21st century, we are heavily invested in cognitive development and rational thought. Most of us have internalized (because we grew up in it and understood how to swim in it) the narrative that emotion clouds judgment and rational thought, and therefore it has no place in school. A gendered notion of reason (masculine) vs. emotion (feminine) adds to the weight of this narrative. A quick look at the percentages of women in the most "fact-based," "objective," "hard" fields as opposed to those in "soft," or more "subjective" ones (calling out the gender-associated language that often accompanies the descriptions of these academic areas of study) indicates the impact of this gendered narrative still today.[17]

Educators have also been trained to take things apart and boil them down to their simplest formulae. Mostly, as a society, we have become so adept at the admittedly useful praxis of taking things apart to study them that we have started seeing even complex, beautiful, interrelated phenomena *like learning* as discrete, measurable, interchangeable parts that somehow enable those who are measuring to claim objectivity. In the commercialized world we inhabit, education leaders then find themselves spending heaps of money to buy separate programs (with consultants) representing what never should have been separated out in the first place. Kind of like taking vitamins and supplements instead of eating food, learning can't be achieved by sticking together discrete parts if we hope to achieve depth, beauty, coherence, and meaning.

But science is important and necessary, too. It helps us to understand what is really going on in there! If we hope to draw on all of our roots of knowing and being, so as to empower ourselves through futurephobia with all of the tools available, science and the latest technologies play a vital role. In both *Gathering Moss* and *Braiding Sweetgrass*, Indigenous botanical scientist Robin Wall Kimmerer (Potawatomi) reminds us that, "In Indigenous ways of knowing, we say a thing cannot be understood until it is known by all four aspects of our being: mind, body, emotion, and spirit."[18] In order to tell the mosses' story, she needed both western science and Indigenous ways of knowing, and in order to help our students tell theirs, the same applies.

The guiding adults (not just teachers) need time to be steeped in relational and regenerative coherence, to acknowledge their fears and futurephobia, to sit with their grief and guilt, to pack up and put away old systems and unlearn their internalized assumptions, until they are *comfortable* enough with themselves as whole people that they are confident in teaching whole people instead of "brains on a stick." They need a process they can rely on and enough information and support so that they will not shy away from seeing and knowing real students in all their developmental struggles, and raw, revolutionary emotional power. There is no special formula for this, but time and trust are essential. To our holistic approach, let's mix in some "brain science" of the self.

Body and Emotion Work Together to Keep Us Safe and Well

Nature equipped humans to survive and to thrive. Have you ever jumped at a loud noise? Flinched and pulled away from something hot? Sensed when someone wasn't telling you the truth, or what another person was feeling? Found yourself swept away by impractical attraction? Cried at a sad spot in a film or burst into tears at bad news or felt confused during an argument? Steered clear of someone who gave off a "bad vibe?" Found yourself transported to a different time and place by a certain song or even a smell? Felt a sense of awe at something very beautiful or extraordinary? Started rocking, foot-tapping, or humming without realizing it? We humans have a brilliant limbic neurological system. It is the combination of body and emotion—our feelings are almost always accompanied by a physiological reaction. And because this limbic system is directly connected to our spinal cord, decisions are made and our reactions happen so fast that our cognitive brain, moving slowly through rational logic, doubt, weighing options, questioning our biases, can't keep up.

Our limbic system does way more deciding on action than our cognitive brain does, even though sometimes we might wish that our reason was in control. Our limbic system is our Secret

Service and Central Intelligence Agency, acting and reacting, flexing and soothing, very swiftly taking in and sending out information and messages to our body and cognitive brain, both. In his book, *The Happiness Hypothesis: Finding Modern Truth in Ancient Wisdom*, Jonathan Haidt (2006) describes the relationship between the limbic brain (emotion and physical reaction to it) and the cognitive brain as an elephant and a rider, with the body and emotional centers as the elephant, and the rider, the cognitive brain, as the much smaller entity who must be very clever indeed to control the elephant if the elephant doesn't want to be controlled.[19] Scholar and thought leader Brené Brown once wrote, "It's a huge part of the mythology around emotion that if we look it in the eye, it gives it power … the reality is that if we look it in the eye and name it, it gives US power."[20] Understanding the biological interrelatedness of our feelings, our bodies, and our minds helps us to gain insight into the full integration of the self for coherent well-being—the rider and the elephant learning to slow down and work together for the well-being of both.

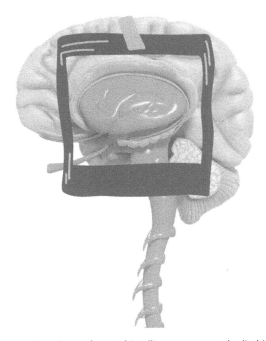

FIGURE 4.3 Your secret service and central intelligence agency: the limbic system

Meet our "body brain" in Figure 4.3. Some call it the soul[21] or heart brain—my Puerto Rican students call it the "coqui" brain—the coqui is a tree frog who is very tiny, very hidden, very fast, very loud (it says *coquí! coquí!* all night long), and a superior survivor. The limbic system is not just metaphorically your *central* intelligence agency and secret service. The parts of our brain that emit the chemicals that result in all the emotions and "gut reactions" we have is literally in the center of our head, in the most secure and protected part of our cranium. Sometimes referred to as the lizard brain, most people would think of it as instinct, or 6th sense, or intuition. It is the home of the quickest, most alert, most certain part of the brain, and it has but one single purpose: keeping us safe. Just like the Secret Service, our body (and soul) brain is programmed to constantly scan for potential and actual threats and to act instantly, without any time lost to cogitation. Fortunately, we don't have to decide to jam on the brakes or jump out of the way. We just do. Athletes rely on this "physical memory" and quick reaction time. But it's not all fight, flight, or freeze. We also rely on our body brain for our happiness, love, awe, playfulness, contentment, appreciation of beauty, art, and music. Our body brain decides whom to trust, and when to open up to them. It's our body brain that falls in love. In a universe of interrelationships, how fortunate we are to be so well equipped!

Of course it's not always smooth sailing. Sometimes our "gut feeling" is biased, or flat out wrong. That body brain's where we find confirmation bias and fears about other people that might be based on false information, and both are very difficult and take a long time and effort spent on unlearning in order to overcome. The body brain is how White police who do not think they are racist jump to the gun, and how White teachers who think they are not racist or sexist overly discipline Black girls. It is also how White physicians under-treat or mistreat Black patients.[22]

Futurephobia (and the powerless feeling of fatalism that goes with it) also resides primarily in our limbic system or body brain. Usually, you can feel your body's reaction to heightened stress, either good stress, or threatening—your gut clenches or flutters, or you sweat, your heart beats faster, or you breathe more. You may feel confused or euphoric or expansive, depending. Certain organ functions slow down while there is a crisis, and others speed up. Once the crisis is past, you probably feel tired, or shaky, or that you need to shout or sing or laugh or go for a walk to release the extra energy still charging around in your body. Normal levels of stress are a good thing. If we are in an important interview, we want that heightened alertness and increased blood flow to the brain. On a first date with someone we want to impress, we benefit from being especially aware and charming. What does either have to do with the "safety first" job description of our limbic system? Potential social and cultural threats (can we say fear of rejection?) are just as important to our body brain as physical threats. But what about what I call "futurephobia?" That kind of stress seems to encompass lots of different complex feelings, including the sense of powerlessness and overwhelm.

Trauma—When the Body Is Powerless

Trauma is usually the result of not being able to stop threatening people or events from doing damage to ourselves or someone else. Our body brain tries to protect us from that moment or that period of complete powerlessness by treating the memory of it like a "third rail," an internal threat—suppressing the memory, or creating a blockage so that later we might not be able to feel any emotion relating to the threatening person, or the incident, or that time in our lives. We might actively dissociate from the event, "putting it on the shelf," avoiding it or anything that might trigger it, to the extent of ignoring emotions and our bodies as much as we can. But even if we have thick mental armor protecting us from our most powerful emotions, the trauma doesn't go away, at least not readily. We might not be able to see it clearly with our cognitive brain, like looking into a cracked mirror, but the feelings and associative "tracks" are still there in our body brain. They may eventually resolve by themselves, or we might adapt to life with blanks and walled-off areas, or they could emerge as

Traumatic Stress Syndrome, also known as PTSD, with generalized chronic stress or anxiety or low self-esteem/self-trust, waking eruptions of emotion that feel like "flashbacks," and nightmares, any of which can result in lashing out, addictions or other self-destructive behaviors. We metabolize trauma in our bodies, and not only can chronic stress and unintegrated or unresolved trauma arrest the development of the part of the brain affected, but it can also cause an epigenetic effect. In this way, the results of historical traumatic stress can be inherited through DNA, and expressed physiologically, in the lived context of family relationships, and in the way we relate to our environment.[23]

Trauma and chronic stress (people in disaster situations often suffer both at once) can cause severe illnesses. Many types of crises can stress humans out. Our body even reacts to threatening events that haven't happened yet (anticipatory stress), or things that happened to us in the distant past. It reacts to collective threats like racism or colonialism with the same potency, which is why so many people living within those oppressions feel chronically stressed, too. Our body brain reacts as well to events that have occurred, are occurring, or might occur to someone else. Dread, fear, anger, and anxiety all elicit a full-body, immediate response. All three, or a single or ongoing traumatic situation, can cause the body brain to go on hyper-alert. This hypervigilance, or chronic stress, can cause both mental and physical illness and certainly distracts from and potentially interferes with everyday activities and relationships. Futurephobia is a kind of complex, chronic, collective stress. It feeds on and contributes to fragmentation and incoherence, and the powerlessness and sense of betrayal within it can develop into full-blown trauma. In this sense, it compares to the historical, and intergenerational collective traumas such as the systemic racism and colonialism experienced by the young people at Joe Rice's Center School, and so their approach to coherence and health, their best practices, are worth spending some time with. Trauma affects educators and learners and members of the larger community equally, but not equitably, just as climate change impacts are felt much more strongly by those who have done the least to contribute to it.

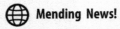 **Mending News!**

Nuestra Escuela Is a Safe Place

Nuestra Escuela, in Caguas, Puerto Rico, provides a safe place for those who have been out of school for a while, often having been pushed out. Justo and Ana Yris lost their daughter to a car accident when she was 15, and she became the inspiration for the school, which begins with a 3-day healing retreat to Orocovis and assigns a social worker to each student. A specialist in biopsychosocial approaches to learning, Ana Yris Guzman has created a holistic experience where students integrate their "vital essence," set personal goals for learning and becoming, engage in social initiatives through their circles, connect with holistic programs from India and Kenya, and reflect on teamwork, creativity, and citizenship. For a moving video and more about the school, watch this 15-minute film. https://futureforlearning.org/media/nuestra/

Another area of trauma that is relevant to teachers is vicarious, or secondary trauma (or even tertiary), in which the teacher, as emotional first-responder, absorbs in sympathy or empathy the traumatic stress of another person. Similarly, young people who are not directly affected by climate impacts might see images on social media or the news, and experience symptoms of trauma. Symptoms can include exhaustion, over- or under-eating, sleep issues, sadness about or even anger at kids in crisis, and bone and joint pain. Since traumatic threats to safety can also be social (think harassment and abuse), cultural (think slavery, racism, and genocide), and environmental (think natural disasters, pollution, and climate change), we also need to take into account collective and historical trauma when we are focusing on safety and trust at the core of well-being in school. Since *accumulated* adverse effects can lead to longer recovery periods and a greater risk of PTSD, teachers are even more likely than children to exhibit signs of traumatic exhaustion, chronic stress, and PTSD than their students. It is essential to make sure that there are enough counselors present in schools and universities so that adults are tended to as well, so that in turn they will be able to tend to themselves, their own families, and our children, and that healthful coherence is baked into everything we do.

What Can We Do About It?

As institutions of learning, our schools need to focus on coherence, trust, and safety, and on creating a little extra room in the nervous system for growth and possibility. The institution needs to clearly prioritize holistic well-being and work to be sure that every decision is guided by its vision joining head, heart, hands, and spirit. Ask, how is this decision going to contribute to the *integrated* healing and *relational* development of the whole person who is in turn integrated with their living community (and may well be living through trauma)? Every decision. Every learning space needs to be trauma safe.

Play, people, play! We can design together for flow and fun. Play, especially outdoors, is healing (and educational!). According to the Environmental Protection Agency, in the United States, as much as 90% of our lives are spent indoors. Children spend less than 30 minutes *a week* playing outside. Considering that a lot of the indoor time now is spent in front of a screen (between five and seven *thousand* hours before kindergarten!), and possibly there is not a safe place to play at home, outdoor spontaneous playtime becomes that much more important. Children (and teenagers and, may I please put in a plug for adults needing to play, too?) need play to learn how to relate to others and their environment, to learn collaboration and sharing, creativity and problem-solving. They need play to create some space to grow into their independent selves and to take on responsibility for their time. Most of all, we need movement and we need to be outside. Let's design together for that!

When work feels like play you might be in a state of "flow." To know how good that feels, you have to play, have unscheduled time to wonder and think and reflect, and time to engage deeply in something of interest, purpose and meaning. What can your school do to maximize opportunities for the healing power of play and flow? How can playfulness, making things, growing things, learning how things work be part of your curricula? At least 17 recent research studies agree that guided play is significantly more effective for deepening learning than direct instruction.[24] Let's do more of that! How about game design with older students designing with younger ones? Good games teach logic, cooperation, structure, and systems. A good book to consider for "systems thinking" activities and to get kids moving is Linda Booth Sweeney and Dennis Meadows' *The Systems Thinking Playbook*. And let's make ourselves useful citizens in our communities, too. Could the school be a resource for local community elders? Could it engage in the design of more resilient living coastlines? Figure out how to improve salmon spawning runs? Could it become a community repair and restore station? What moves your students?

The body brain is the oldest and most universally felt part of the brain. We have different ways of thinking in different cultures around the world, and different ways of describing and managing our emotions, but the feelings themselves are pretty much a condition of being human. Creative expression, especially in making music, singing and dancing, but also in design and making visual arts seems to be just as old and just as interrelated. Is there a culture that does not have music and dance? For coherent lives we need plenty of opportunities for creative expression. It's an indication of the hyper-rationalist and mechanistic view of school that so many schools have taken away the arts as a "frill," or something unnecessary to invest in. It should come as no surprise that removing the one thing that helps most to directly connect with emotion—through movement, music (music is what emotions sound like), art, theater, etc. results in greater mental health distress. I visited a school in central Harlem where budget cuts had ruined their theater, dance, and music programs, the cultural heartbeat of the school. Then they were forced to squeeze into one floor from three to make way for a charter school. Cut off from access to it, the betrayed and heartbroken children destroyed their piano.

Arts can bring people together, too. As protest, the arts can take on powerful systems and shift mindsets. One of my favorite examples combining play and protest came in the form of see-saws put on the Mexico-US border fence. I heard even some of the agents went for a ride! Music and dance are often shared collectively, and they represent the relatedness of the holistic bond between mind-body-heart-spirit that is at the heart of being human. Music seems to connect directly to our emotions and also to connect us unconditionally to each other in liberating ways. We can be unapologetically individual and also be unified in an uplifting experience at the same time. Jon Batiste's award-winning song and dance video "Freedom" (20224 min.) is the embodiment of the holistic meaning of its title. During the anti-corruption protests in Puerto Rico against ex-governor Rosselló in the summer of 2019, the arts motivated, energized, and as community psychologist Dr. Eduardo Lugo says, "freed people to be unified by love and solidarity."

There needs to be plenty of opportunities for civic participation and authentic work. We will address this more later on in the book, but wholeness and healing also come from mattering. If powerlessness and un-health are the results of fragmentation and incoherence, then authentic agency, responsibilities, and meaningful activity are a vital pathway toward healing. We feel safe when we belong, and we belong when we are trusted, when we are trusted we can trust ourselves, and so on in a joyous cycle of coherence and civic action. Have we truly enlisted our students to be our full partners in transformation? Having a process at our fingertips to do this helps (see Chapter 8). Are we working with students to uncover their perspectives and act on them? Do we make room for feelings and reflection?

As advocates for the power of personhood, we need to give ourselves and the kids time. Control over flexible time enables the time to listen, time to feel and think, time to heal, time to imagine, time to relate gracefully to the others in our living communities. Ask, do we really need to do this thing we do with bells every 43 minutes? Are we giving students time to get in the zone? To pursue their interests and go deeper into challenges and opportunities that matter?

Make sure language and praxis follow suit. You can't have some teachers shifting to non-binary pronouns and not others. You can't have some teachers who are safe and not others. Life is relational, and trust comes with coherence and consistency. Walk the walk. Don't just say the words to signal that you care—anti-racism, resilience, agency—if you don't plan to work with the kids to change the system that's harming them. Otherwise, it's a betrayal and a hidden (but strongly felt!) curriculum of disempowerment and oppression. Our kids (remember Alanís?) know when they're being strung along, and they deserve better.

Remember, prioritizing holistic coherence, healing, and an integrated and relational self is not the same thing as "SEL (Social-Emotional-Learning)," classes or advisories, though one can inform the other. That said, mindfulness, soothing, and harmonizing are important elements of both. I suggest that what you call it is less important than how you consistently and intentionally enable young people and their teachers to remember the wholeness of their being and reconnect the fullness of it with the rest of our living community at the same time.

Before Anything Else, Safety

Trust is at the center of all well-being, because well-being is relational. We will explore more in the next chapter about the nature of those relationships, but when we think about safety in school, before, during, and after disasters, we can turn to the 5-Point Safety framework, in Figure 4.4. Before diving into emotions, we need to be sure we are in a safe space and in a trusting frame of mind and being. People can't be open to change, and won't be able to acknowledge emotion or engage with deep learning if we forge ahead in an unsafe way. Every learning space needs to be trauma-safe. What you can do to co-create safe spaces is a great design challenge (See Chapter 8). You might want to refer to the excellent (and free) new book, *Changing the Conversation About School Safety*, (https://dschool.stanford.edu/resources/changingtheconvo). As a school, commit to using the 5-Points (Figure 4.4) as opportunities to design systemic and classroom steps toward improving students' and teachers' feelings of safety, trust, fun, and belonging.

As administrators: you could think together with teachers about how to create safe spaces for teachers, and how best to establish trusting relationships. Perhaps a trip to the woods. Observation games (listening, watching), thinking time, reading poetry together, working on a project together that is not schoolwork (like helping to build a local playground or working in the community garden), or even on something that is school-related. Learning the basics of meditation and harmonizing (see Resource 3). Noticing the impact of putting the phones away for a while. Reflecting together on the experiences and how you could put what you've learned to work in your classes or ideate together about how to center the children in the redesign of your school schedule, curriculum, and so on.

Enlist the students in addressing these challenges as opportunities to plan together and act with collective agency to interrelate on the basis of trust. Be sure to reflect, and to keep all options open. Maybe the safest space is outside, but some might have concerns about that. What can we do to address those concerns? How can we do our best to hear and respect and relate to all voices? How can we keep the students authentically engaged in the ongoing learning and development of the school? From the students' perspective:

5-Point Safety

FIGURE 4.4 5-Point Safety is Physical, Emotional, Social, Cultural, and Environmental

1. **Physical Safety:** I need to know that the school building is well,[25] and that no harm will befall me because I went to school. My belongings will not be stolen or ruined, either. My journey to and from school is not dangerous to my health.
2. **Emotional Safety:** I need to feel supported, interconnected, and whole, to help me balance stress and prioritize well-being.
3. **Social Safety:** I need to belong. I need to feel welcome, seen, heard, and valued.
4. **Cultural Safety:** I need to know that my language, my ethnicity, my race, my identities are welcome, seen, heard, and valued. I can claim my justly due space in history, the present, and the future.
5. **Environmental Safety:** I need secure food, water, shelter, and protection from pollution and climate impacts now, and to engage with my school and community in preparing for, adapting to, and mitigating the effects of climate change overall. Aware of the likelihood that I will live into the next century, I need to see and feel my school system's commitment to me and my future by actively seeking opportunities to engage with me in sustainable and regenerative practices that will enable life on our home planet.[26]

Not much deep learning can happen if 5-Point Safety is not valued and enacted, because our emotional, body brain will do its job. It will protect us. And because it is protecting us, our brain will keep us feeling stressed, on edge, and exhausted. We will be distracted in class or at meetings and sick a lot. We might overly focus on external measures instead of internal ones. We might burst into tears at a B+ or a professional criticism. It will be hard to concentrate and mostly we might decide school is not making sense and we just have to get through it or wait until it is over.

Tips for Teachers:

◆ **Always put love before learning.** It doesn't work any other way. Slow down. Listen, listen, listen in a heart-close and ego-distant way (no defending or explaining or fixing) and be sure to suspend judgment while listening. Build harmonizing and mindfulness into your daily routines.

◆ **Make time to learn.** Learn as much as you can about your students, both contextually and individually, and how they see themselves. Each one of them. Visit home and home communities if culturally appropriate and with permission. Shadow. Reflect. Share. Repeat.

◆ **Enlist students in studying your own habits and theirs.** Gather their "Street Data,"[27] analyze it together, and co-create solutions. Do power audits. Design the optimal learning environment together. Is it outdoors? In circles? On a work site? In the mangrove swamp? On the floor? In a garden? How can we adapt the space we are in to make it better? Studies show that images of Nature have an impact, too.

◆ **Believe your students and believe in them.** They are experts in their own experience. If a student tells you his house is on fire (actually or metaphorically), don't say, "gee that's too bad. Now can we turn to page 6?" I may never have done exactly that, but I'm pretty sure I came across this way at least once. I am still trying to pay that emotional debt.

◆ **Co-create your classes with your students (and their parents) wherever it is possible.** Think of them as architects of their own learning experiences, with you as the main guide, resource, and "matchmaker." Be sure that coherence is part of all that you do. Reach for depth in personhood and growth as well as knowledge. If they are motivated by compassion or passion or purpose or some combination of the three, it will not be difficult to nudge them to set and stick to rigorous learning goals and keep them looking for ways to go deeper into personhood as a source of power. This will help them to feel your trust and their agency, and will help them to accept and trust themselves in all their wholeness. Doing something *together* that matters will emphasize the relatedness aspect of the integrated self. More on that later. Do something together that matters.

◆ **Become familiar and comfortable with the stages of grief and what they look like** in children, young adults, yourself and your colleagues, and community elders. As climate psychologist Leslie Davenport wrote, "Grief is a form of love. [We are facing] the loss of what made us feel most deeply connected."[28] Denial, for example, might look like hiding. Trying not to think about the future at all. Anger: Why is this happening to me?! Why aren't you protecting me? Why can't I do anything about it? Bargaining: Maybe it won't be so bad, or if I just teach climate science, isn't that enough? Depression can show up in anyone, no matter how young. Your science teaching colleagues may be the first to hit this wall, but if you are reading this book, you aren't far behind. With Acceptance, you may be able to, as Sarah Jaquette Ray puts it, move past your fears and choose to stride toward love and joy. Remember, fluctuation is normal—and so in a class, all of these stages of grief may be present at the same time, and kids may be moving back and forth. The key is not to get stuck.

◆ **Do not lie to children.** Don't even try to hide the truth. If a student tells you his house is on fire, avoid saying something meant to be reassuring, such as, "No it isn't, and nobody's house ever really burned down." I know this sounds ridiculous in a literal context, but this kind of denial, gaslighting, and outright lying about injustices and racist/sexist/ableist/ethnophobic incidents and systems goes on all the time, especially but not limited to White-washed history lessons. Indeed, current legislation in a number of states would mandate that teachers lie in exactly this way. We will address culture-murdering in the next chapters, but you may have heard some of your colleagues say this: "My elementary school students are too young to understand racism (xenophobia, sexism, ableism, etc.)". The American Psychological Association says that age five may already be too late to begin.[29] *Unpack Your Impact* is a book packed with ideas for teaching little kids about big issues.[30] Being honest has to start early, because oppression is quick out of the blocks.

◆ **Learn about trauma.** As of 2017, before the magnitude of natural disasters reached the levels of today, before COVID, over a third of our students (nationally—there are concentrations in underserved and disaster-affected areas) had experienced more than one potentially traumatic event. More than half had exposure to at least one.[31] Advocate for and secure trauma and mental health care for yourselves first. Remember you might not feel either primary or secondary trauma right away. Know the signs and create preventive strategies and mutually support your and your colleagues' well-being. Know what trauma looks like in your students. It can be very difficult to spot. Some mask it very well. Some exhibit symptoms, like not speaking, zoning out, or acting out. Unfortunately, those could also be symptoms of something else. You have to know your students.

◆ **Become comfortable practicing holistic healing techniques relating to mindfulness, guided imagery, and connectedness with the natural world.** One of the first things I do with learners is breathing. Also, teach them to feel their heartbeats. Also to feel the way they are connecting (through gravity as it acts on their nerve endings, muscles, and bones) with the Earth, and connecting Earth and Sky. There are lots of breathing and movement exercises you can do, and some are borrowed from Tai Chi and Qigong (from ancient Buddhist roots), which also emphasize body awareness and its integration into Earth and Sky. In Resource 3, you will find a few specific examples and some helpful resources. Sometimes, depending on age, audience, and location, I don't bother saying we are meditating. We might be "playing sensory observation games," when we go outside to listen, smell, feel, see, and welcome all that we can know about our environment through our senses. These games can evolve into silent walking, or closing our eyes and letting someone move us to a different spot, and without opening our eyes try to tell where the biggest tree is nearby. Or studying a scene intently and then closing our eyes and trying to describe what we saw, felt, heard, etc. The most important thing is to deepen our awareness of our thoughts, feelings, and bodily sensations without judgment of any kind, just noticing with curiosity. It's a kind of deep listening to oneself and other beings that will be mirrored in the way we live our lives.

◆ **In a disaster of the sudden shock variety, an earthquake or fire or tornado or hurricane or flood or pandemic school closing, you also need to be honest.** Students need to know they are safe physically, of course, but they can't be safe emotionally unless you give them clear information and truthful assurances. Do not say, "it's going to be alright, don't worry," as tempting as those kinds of superficial assurances might be. Better to say you will find out the correct information (and follow through) than shrug your shoulders in answer to their questions, or worse, say what you *think* it *should* be and then have to give correct but conflicting information. Better to ask, "would you like to stay here with me or go to our quiet space or see the counselor?" or "would you like me to help you to call someone?" or "I am here for you. Would you like to talk, draw, run around, listen to music, etc.?"

◆ **Work with your school counselor or a climate disaster specialist if you live in a zone where sudden shock disasters could happen.** What kinds of additional activities could you do to cultivate (before the disaster) and activate their inner strengths? This is when the breathing and noticing work you have been doing comes to the fore. Leslie Davenport provides some wonderful body exercises for those crisis moments—her description of the doggy shake and butterfly hug are summarized in Resource 3. Also, there you can find a link to the agency-building activities starting with questions to ask to help normalize and vent feelings, and activities to build back self-trust and efficacy, that I developed with Puerto Rican educators and therapists in the months and years since the double hurricanes and earthquakes. And yes, they've been modified for COVID-19.

◆ **Don't forget that there is a growing body of research that shows that the more separated from Nature we become, the more stressed, depressed, and anxious we feel.** Holistic coherence happens in the relational context of the natural world, and our health depends on its connectedness to our mind, soul, body, and spirit. An "ecoharmonious" life is the best path to health, and it helps us to think of everything we do according to regenerative (life) principles.

The Power in Becoming: Continuous Change

The regenerative power of personhood comes from the fact we are continually becoming. As educational theorist Benjamin Freud is fond of saying, we should be called "human becomings instead of human beings. We are not nouns; we are verbs." Identities are confusing sometimes because they overlap and intersect. They make us strong and put us at risk. They evolve and weigh in differently at different times. And they really do generate and regenerate in the relational in-between. But coming to know ourselves as we are growing, putting together that puzzle as we are becoming (a life-long learning), is essential to well-being. If the first step of tapping into the power within is understanding and teaming up with the genius of our emotions and our body brain, the second step is getting to know and honor the growth of the identities that make up ourselves. This is not easy to do, and is intertwined with other risks. How my identities intersect and are perceived by others shapes me as much as anything. We are who we are because of our experiences and our intra- and inter-group relationships (which we will visit more closely in the next chapters), and this is always changing just as our inner self grows. Many children feel "pinned" down by test scores or grades, an identity, a trauma, an ability, or an interest expressed at age seven. They feel trapped like a butterfly pinned to a board in the middle of its transformative life cycle, as if people around them expect them to always stay the same.

In fact, many educators are already pulling the levers of disruption and working toward coherence and making space for holistic growth. Some are teaching in Indigenous schools, creating new schools, or working in the middle of large public systems. In recognition of the need for a course correction to holistic well-being in school, many learning communities (the whole nest around the school) were already demanding and producing new realities prior to COVID-19, and are resisting a "return to normal." Black and Brown and Native youth, LGBTQ + youth, differently abled people and their families have taken up the reins of change. Students have begun speaking out on their own about the importance of taking up the lenses of emotional intelligence and anti-racism and coherence and critically analyzing the whole school day. In Maximilian Park's case, he found his way to a course online, which he credits with saving his life. He tells two main growth stories—all his own, the first one about a student who does terribly on a test and the emotions snowball into anxiety, and then a student who uses gratitude thoughts and other coping strategies to put things into perspective. He never learned anything about emotions in school, and that fact nearly killed him. Azhane Pollard takes on racism and liberation in her award-winning poem, "Generations."[32] Her strong voice resonates with many her age, from all around the world. They are not backing down.

We are honing our disruption. COVID-19 blew the lid off the already startling increases in anxiety and depression among youth, and the ways in which inequitable systems are harming them. More and more, educators are turning to regenerative change leadership best practices, anti-racist and decolonial methodologies, mindfulness, trauma healing, and systemic social and emotional learning and the brain. Healing the self and healing nature are becoming synonymous. Most importantly, educators not already living in it are opening up to ancient holistic thinking and Indigenous learning about pedagogy—in other words, seeking all kinds of wisdom to heal the fragmented self and liberate ourselves to be both healthy and whole, and this gives us a chance to be better kin to our planetary relatives. Let's let the powerful voice of an 11-year-old from Hisar, India, remind us that we can choose interrelated wholeness. (Figure 4.5)

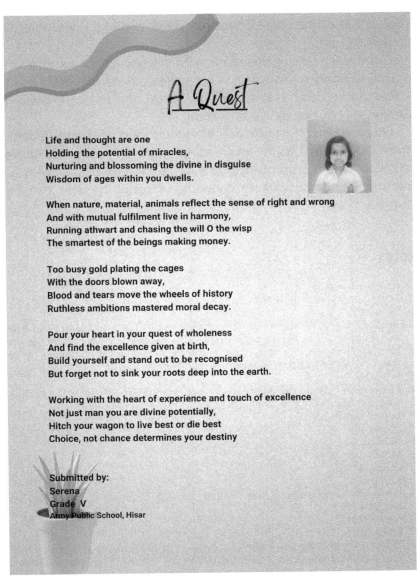

FIGURE 4.5 "A Quest," by Serena, 5th grade, Hisar, India

Seeds for Planting

Coherence is revolutionary when held up against fragmentation, but it is not new. Indigenous wisdom tells us that coherence is the natural healthy state that combines the head, heart, body, and spirit in intra- and interrelated wholeness within the infinite whole of the universe. Educators need healing invitations to wholeness first.

Combining ancient wisdom with science opens more doors to coming home to ourselves. Our emotional, limbic, body brain is also our security system and the oldest and most universally human part of our nervous system.

Our nervous systems are interconnected and can become overwhelmed by trauma and futurephobia. Educators, learners, and the wider community can all play important roles in creating safe conditions for coherence through holistic learning and practices.

Notes

1 Czikszentmihalyi 1990.
2 De la Torre y Moraes 1997.
3 Rice 2020.
4 Adefarakan nd. In this essay, the author shares the Yoruba story of how two youths chose the wrong heads, and the third, who considered the internal character of being, chose correctly. " ... A good character, or *iwa pele*, is regarded as the essence of a beautiful person."
5 Bly 2004.
6 Read more about the Economics of Care in Van Osch 2013. Also in Singer 2015.
7 Pope Francis 2015.
8 hooks 1994.
9 Rice 2020.
10 Maldonado 2022.
11 Quinn 1995.
12 Kaminsky.
13 For more information about healing through Indigenous pedagogy, see McCabe 2008.
14 brown 2017.
15 Love 2019.
16 These fragmentations are also clearly laid out in Hutchins and Storm 2019.
17 The AAUW (American Assoc. Of University Women) has put together a powerful set of data reports and tools called "The STEM Gap: Women and

Girls in Science, Technology, Engineering and Math." https://www.aauw.org/resources/research/the-stem-gap/

18 Kimmerer 2003.

19 Haidt 2006.

20 Brown 2021.

21 Menakem 2017.

22 Morris 2018.

23 Van Der Kolk 2014.

24 Skene et al 2022.

25 The International Well Building Institute has created standards to ensure that the building your child is learning in (and you are teaching in) will not make them or you sick. Well Buildings save millions of dollars in lost productivity due to sick employees and save children's health in myriad ways, from improving focus to reducing asthma. Is your child's school a Well Building? Is the place where you teach? https://www.wellcertified.com/

26 Ray 2020.

27 Safir 2021. Required reading for school transformation.

28 Davenport 2017. Required reading for activities you can use for trauma healing and everyday health.

29 Sullivan 2020.

30 O'Brien and Tabb 2020.

31 Minero 2017.

32 Pollard 2021. "Azhane Pollard, Virginia's 2021 Poetry Out Loud Champion, is the 2021 Poetry Ourselves spoken poetry winner for the poem "Generations." https://www.youtube.com/watch?v=0GP5_QhSElk

5 The Power of "People": Kinship With the Whole of Life

How might we sustain children's natural sense of interrelatedness and expand their affinities as they grow older?

How can school and community gardens become embodiments of the power of our relationships?

What steps can we take to build thriving communities of change and learning in our schools and universities?

From Apart to a Part

"I bet you don't know this one," said the elbow-high kid at the County Fair. I was in the 4-H[1] hall, filled with youth exhibits. He was practically hopping from one foot to another with excitement. "Which one is that?" I asked. I like riddles. "What is it that we can't see but we can't live without?" I was all in now. "Air!" I declared, mentally patting myself on the back. "Nope," he said with a huge grin that covered his eyes. He leaned in. I leaned in. He was getting ready to tell me a secret punch line. "Air is what everybody says. But what I'm thinking of is," he paused and leaned in further,

DOI: 10.4324/9781003215806-6

speaking carefully around his big new front teeth, "the rhi-zo-sphere!" I was hooked. As we walked over to his booth, he was reassuring me that everyone guesses air first, before they learn about how the "soil is alive. Can you believe some people think it's just dirt? The rhizosphere's a thin layer, kind of like the skin of the earth, just full of roots and microscopic things like good bacteria and animals like worms and insects like bugs and fungus that connects all of it together and did you know that the fungus and those bacteria are even older than the plants and did I tell you that it's all connected under there and all of this is going on all the time and we don't even see it?" He stopped to take a breath. "And it's all *communicating* somehow, with the chemicals that some plants have that the other ones need and the fungi are helping to move all that along like our pipes and telephone wires. If something bad happens, like a flood or a fire, all of the rest of it just steps in, to help it recover and if it's healthy soil to begin with the whole area might come back even stronger. And did you know? Every time something dies it fertilizes the rest of it. The fungi grow all over it and the bacteria, worms, and bugs break it down—that's called decomposition (he said that one carefully, too)—and all of the good stuff in there gets to be food for something else. Nothing goes to waste, not even poop. Everybody's poop is somebody's food, I guess" He stopped to giggle, so I jumped in with a question. "So what does all this have to do with me and you?" He sighed and took a deep breath. "Where do you want me to start? The air you breathe? Water? Food? Cooling the planet? Controlling flooding? Or how we have the same chemicals and good bacteria inside us as the soil does? How about what happens to you after you die?" Fifteen minutes later, after he'd schooled me in the integrated systems he had illustrated in his booth, he finished with a flourish. "See? That's why air is only part of the answer."

That's why WE are only part of the answer, I thought. That little boy had touched on so much. He made me feel like he was letting me into the secret of life—into the infinity of relationships and networks, into the wood-wide-web that pre-existed humans by billions of years, into one of the oldest friendly collaborations there is, between rocks, fungi, and plants. Fungi and mosses gather nutrients from rocks and feed them to other plants. Plants give nutrients to fungi. This is the friendship that oxygenated the atmosphere and began the global network of interconnected living systems that create the conditions for all species to thrive. This young 4-Her's excitement about his "secret" made me think of how he was drawing some *powerful* energy from tapping into his understanding of the most fundamental principle of life. The way organizational theorist Meg Wheatley puts it, "Relationships are all there is. Everything in the universe only exists because it is in relationship to everything else."[2] The energy he was generating filled the whole booth he occupied and then some.

One aspect of the 4-Her's presentation struck me. Here was a child, maybe seven or so, who already thought in systems and networks. I began to consider other children I've known, and the ways in which they, too, seem to display a kind of natural predisposition for systemic awareness. Perhaps it's because they haven't been schooled to think of things in parts and siloes, and to think of themselves as outsiders to the very systems they inhabit, that young children naturally do what adults are just beginning to relearn. Like Serena, whose poem ended Chapter 4, they see the world with eyes of wholeness and relationality. Kinship with the living world just makes sense. When I asked a 5-year-old to draw me a picture of anything, Annabelle Clark drew not just a flower, but a flower in the rain. When her Mom asked her what she would say about the picture, she offered, "a flower needs rain to bloom." (Figure 5.1)

FIGURE 5.1 A flower needs rain to bloom
Annabelle Clark, age 5

The systemic awareness that Annabelle and the kid at the fair shared shows an appreciation of the energy, the dynamics, the rhythms, the flow of life moving this way and that over time among complex systemic relationships. In a very deep place, they know that nothing lives solely for itself. We are never alone because we are always part of something, a glittering web, an extended family, larger than ourselves. For organizational theorist Otto Scharmer, the kid's excitement and awe, the joy in sharing "the secret" embodies an "open heart."[3] For regenerative leadership theorists Hutchins and Storm, the children are naturally demonstrating the most complex awareness humans can aspire to: "ecosystemic awareness."[4]

When the 4-Her asked me which system I wanted him to start with, and made me hear them all because "you can't just hear a part of this," I realized that this child with only four (could it have been just two?) adult teeth in the top of his mouth understood that these interlocking and nested systems within systems were all part of a single living, changing and all-encompassing whole. It just would not do to only hear part of his story. When he began telling me about how our body chemistry is made up of the same compounds and even hosts many of the same organisms as a healthy rhizosphere, I thought, to this child, complexity is simple. I can't resist thinking that his conspiratorial glee was perhaps an expression of his sense that his ecological awareness is the best and most promising way out of our predicament. The more connections he makes, the more connected we are. As climate psychologist Leslie Davenport writes, "recognizing the living connections between ourselves and other life forms, we begin to discover our role within the larger reparative movement." We discover our role as humans in our larger family of being.

If anything, it is a sharp-edged discovery for some children that not everyone understands. When she was about Annabelle's age (five years), Sena Wazer learned about whales in a children's book, cheering for the one who gets stuck in a giant fishing net to get freed. Read her short essay (pp. 262–264) to discover why she became a very young environmental activist. Sena, and others like her, are not just advocating for their favorite animals and their own lives. They are fighting for all of life and the interrelationships that sustain it. My childhood friend and now teacher-colleague Jamie Harper recently found some graffiti in the 4th-grade bathroom. It said, simply, "animal rights." (Figure 5.2)

FIGURE 5.2 "Animal rights" in 4th-grade bathroom

Kids these days. Unless older people have made them actively afraid of and cut them off from the natural world, interrelationship seems to come naturally to kids, and interbeing doesn't seem strange at all. If you ask a kid to draw any picture, they almost always draw kin—human or otherwise. It might be something of an amazement for children to learn of adult's efforts to reconnect, through regenerative leadership efforts like Scharmer's *Theory U*, Hutchins and Storm's brilliant *Regenerative Leadership*, and Hutchins' latest, *Leading By Nature*. Indigenous scholars and parents might ask, why did you break it all apart in the first place? Educators might ask, what are we doing that is facilitating interrelationship with our whole community of being? What are we doing that is breaking it up?

In *Braiding Sweetgrass*,[5] Robin Wall Kimmerer tells her new academic advisor about her desire to learn why purple and yellow asters look so good together. He tells her that's not botany or even science. She is in the wrong school altogether. Maybe she, Robin Wall, who grew up thriving alongside her companions in the web of life and who wanted nothing more than to appreciate its wisdom more deeply, maybe she, he said, should be somewhere else, "like art." Kimmerer presents us with a cautionary tale that demonstrates what can happen when a closed mind and an open mind/heart meet up in an academic power structure that thrives on separation. In typical schooling, separateness is the norm. Not only is learning divided into silos called "disciplines," but testing and sorting and individual competitiveness begin officially in grades 2 and 3. The message is already there. A school is a building with a threshold that must be crossed. Closed doors behind and in front and individualized measuring up in between. Who is going to win? The accumulating mechanistic fragmentations of that space stymie full coherent and relational learning and create vulnerabilities for all beings. This brings me to another thing that struck me about the kid's presentation—"if something bad happens, like a flood or a fire," he said, the interwoven systems nourished by the healthy relationships among the rhizosphere, come back even stronger. Healthy relationships interweaving and evolving within healthy systems create resilience and collective power.

Many adults I know share affinities for other beings, too. My husband is a photographer, and we live on the edge of a tidal river. The peeping sound the ospreys make calls him outside many times a day. He'll stand watching, camera cradled in his arm, for minutes that can roll easily into hours, only sometimes taking a picture. He wonders about their lives, and they let him in. I have a friend near here whose heart beats faster when she is near cormorants. When snorkeling with her children, one actually dove near her, swimming around her and the kids. That moment, that spirit-bird, has become part of her identity. A friend whose husband passed away believes he is present in her kinship with the red-tailed hawk who watches over her, and our school garden. In Puerto Rico, I know teachers who crave the time they'll join with waterfalls in the mountains or find waves kissing the shore or drumming in hollowed-out rocks. Water soothes and restores the spirit, they say. I'm sure you have felt this, too. There's Elizabeth Tova Bailey's famous memoir called "The Sound of a Wild Snail Eating" (very teachable) about how her relationship with a snail helped her to heal from a long and isolating illness.[6]

A former student of mine pets bees. "Look!" she'll say, "they LOVE it! I wish I was a bee." Affinity and kinship. Kinship and affinity. We stick up for what we love. Elliott Clark, 8 years old, drew a picture of his favorite lizard, a gecko (Figure 5.3). When we asked him why the gecko is his favorite, he said, "because he likes to climb trees just like I do, only his special feet make him much better at it!"

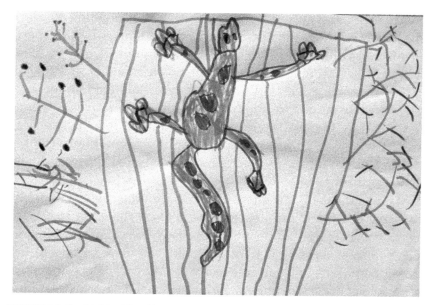

FIGURE 5.3 "I wish I had feet like a gecko!"
Elliott Clark, Tree Climber, age 8

Phil Young, jazz and blues drummer well-known from his role at the historic Apollo Theater, inherited his love for flowers. Flowers are the way we connect at the most emotional times, he says. They help us overcome awkwardness and to say that we care. They brighten our lives and help connect our spirit to the divine. Robin Wall Kimmerer might choose to be part of Maple Nation, or her moss family. I have an affinity for trees (Chapter 6), but I also find myself drawn to moss and weeping in the presence of whales. What about you? Is there a flower or an animal you love? Eighteen-year old Isabel Colón shares hers. (Figure 5.4)

From "The Flowers of the Sun"

My lovely yellows,
You look so fragile today.
All the wrongs in the meadow
I can't seem to repair.

My lovely sunflowers
Tall as a tree,
Bright as October
You bring happiness to me.

...My dear flowers,
The compassion I feel
Doesn't compare to your
prowess.
Even in my best, I can't
compare to thee.

FIGURE 5.4 From "The Flowers of the Sun" Isabel Colón, Caguas, Puerto Rico

What other special beings cause us to feel and wonder? This might be a good starting place with kids. What we love, we pay attention to. When we are paying attention, we are building a relationship. We want to learn more about and to protect the beings we love, and in reciprocity, they receive and teach us. As Joe Rice wrote in Chapter 4, "Earth is our oldest living relative.

She gives us everything we need and information about how to live together." What do we learn about life's foundational relationships, *when we pay attention?*

We learn that mosses, the first green relations to live out of the ocean, survive in all kinds of conditions (there are thousands of species!) and have lived through five mass extinctions already, simply by depending on interrelationship and collaboration.

We learn that ants tell each other where the food is instead of hoarding it, operating on the principle that the more of them that gather the food, the more they will have as a community.

We learn that flying geese take turns doing the hard work of flying in front, and starling murmurations engage in deep trust and clear and consistent communication, with each bird focused on its seven closest neighbors in order to create total synchronicity and flock cohesiveness.

We learn that plants and trees do compete, but also thrive through mutuality. Where oaks live in grasslands, together they create "islands of fertility" up to 60 times more fertile than open grasslands. The trees block wind, hold soil, lift water, and boost nutrients all around. "In fact, the more stressful the environment, the more likely you are to see plants working together to ensure mutual survival."[7]

We learn that, in the wood-wide web of forests, paper birch and Douglas fir exchange different types of carbon that one has aplenty and the other needs, through the mycorrhizal/fungal networks. Totally, 80% of the world's plants thrive in relation to these networks, as opposed to surviving in agricultural fields. In fact, trees do their best in forests of hundreds to thousands of acres.[8]

We learn that desert plants collect more water from condensation than they do from rain. Humans, too, are excellent humidistats. Most people, like desert plants, can tell if there's a slight change in the amount of moisture in the air.[9]

We learn that "every plant is a solar-powered factory, producing the organic material on which all life depends. Every plant is also a pump, which is constantly raising water from the ground to keep the factory running."[10] Plants also cool the planet directly and indirectly, and play an essential role in the water cycle through their transpiration above ground (ever wonder why dew appears overnight?), and holding carbon and water below.

We learn that willows are one of the most useful trees to humans—and to fish. And that they are the first to produce pollen in colder climates, helping the bees to make it through the long, lean months.[11]

We learn that all is connected through land and sea relationships, recognizing that salinity is essential to our survival as well, and acknowledging that forests slow erosion and filter water emptying into the ocean, while leaf decomposition makes iron available to phytoplankton at the base of the ocean food chain.

We learn that humans can assist in ecological restoration in many ways, not only by ceasing to destroy our home habitat but also by restoring land and water ecosystems through regenerative practices. We can protect our own existence and enliven our spirits, through our understanding of equitable relationships with other beings.

 Mending News!

On Every Continent, Efforts to Create Biodiversity Corridors

A biodiversity corridor is an area that is conserved or restored to a natural condition that enables ecosystem habitats and migration and pollination to occur, and which connects other "wild" spaces so animals can travel safely between them. Trees and plants also can connect underground with a thriving rhizosphere, providing the foundation for the ecosystem and capably restoring carbon sequestration, erosion control, and water filtration capacity to the soils. In some states, "greenways" are biodiverse parklands that allow for human recreation, too. Is there a state or NGO organization in your bioregion that is working on biodiversity corridors?

More Mending News! In Every Ocean, Efforts to Restore and Conserve

#oceanoptimism began in 2014 and has since reached over 60 million people through Twitter. This is not empty cheering. Ayana Elizabeth Johnson's project amplifies the conservation work and charts the progress in moving toward ocean health. Join the network and see what organizations are working in your area!

Bren Smith founded GreenWave to teach regenerative ocean farming as a way to heal ocean ecosystems. GreenWave works with oysterers, crabbers, fishing communities, and educational institutions to reach his goal of 10,000 regenerative ocean farmers by 2030. Is your learning community near the shore? Teacher Trevor Soponis worked with GreenWave to connect his students with their community adults and co-created a regenerative ocean farming project in Alaska. Reach out to him on LinkedIn and ask how they did it!

Scientist James Lovelock writes that life regenerates life on earth because "the entire planet is one complex, self-regulating web of interconnecting systems, all of which contribute to a whole that displays the ability to adapt and evolve through continuous change."[12] In Buddhism and Taoism, there is a name for this: **Interbeing**. In Hinduism, there is the story of Indra's web of stars, infinitely glistening with the reflection of all the others. No one being can be expected to thrive on its own, let alone to push back against the slow threats of poverty, colonialism and racism, and the sudden shocks of climate disaster.

Ecoliteracy helps us as educators to learn from, and find meaning in the relationships we see all around us, the relationships that define our living and changing existence. The applications of Ecoliterate, regenerative learning based on the above observations of our kin in the natural world might look something like this: (Table 5.1)

TABLE 5.1 Making regenerative, ecoliterate meaning in school.

Observation	Meaning	Application in Schools
Ants tell each other … , geese share … , trees share …	We are only as strong as our communities are The harder life is, the more collaboration happens No one exists alone	Lifelong learning from age 0 focused on building caring, collaborative communities based on abundance (of love and regenerative power) rather than on competition and scarcity. Redefine success.
Starling murmurations	Deep trust and continuous communication leads to unity of purpose and cohesion	School/uni can be a hub for trust, 5-point safety, well-being, good multi-age conversation, shared efficacy, and purpose
Rhizosphere extends indefinitely in a continuously adapting web where nothing is wasted	Extractive, linear consumerism and waste will eventually lead to extinction and in the short term is already causing disasters, gross inequities, and hardship	Study relationships more than parts. Combine subjects more than dividing them. Circular economics and true cost accounting taught in school along with other natural laws. Zero waste schools, and other restorative and regenerative "sustainability" habits Participatory civic role for youth in adapting human behaviors and culture. Encourage continuous adaptation and change, reflecting on getting stuck and unstuck, elevating human creativity
Plants are solar-powered factories …	Our human infrastructures and systems should mimic natural ones	Green our infrastructures, beginning with the schoolyard.

(Cont.)

TABLE 5.1 (Cont.)

Observation	Meaning	Application in Schools
"If we had to pay for the services trees provide, we couldn't afford them."[13]	Forest and ocean restoration corridors connecting healthy forests and protecting ocean regrowth are infrastructures for life	Invest in Living and WELL schools and learning spaces, civic role for youth in reforestation, ocean restoration, renewable energy, regenerative food systems Consider the importance of a school garden/outdoor learning spaces
Fragmentation of forests and habitats causes separation and extinction Species survive when they migrate freely	The logic of separation and hyperindividualism are unnatural and will cause anxiety, depression, and possibly death Humans have survived on planet Earth by migrating, too. Rigid borders and boundaries are dangerous	Coherence, collaboration, and love should be the heart of learning Include perspectives from around the world and study migratory species in both direct and metaphorical wonder. Question and heal restrictive attitudes and us/them mindsets.
Biodiversity connotes thriving Diversity is the "magical elixir for healthy soils--> plants-->food→ soil"[14]	It is difference AND commonality that makes us thrive in relationships	See students and families as unique, not groups or titles, but interconnected Teach appreciation for difference, nuance, complexity. Promote regenerative and restorative practices based on life and love such as anti-racism and democratic class systems.
No species are discarded; all have a role to play	We all exist in relation to each other, and everybody has something to contribute	Teach true collaboration and seek full participation from all. Every person, no matter how young or old, is an expert in their own experience.

Critical ecoliteracy not only asks learners to learn from and apply natural principles to our relationships, but also calls on us to explore where those relationships are broken or where systems driven by competitive, extractive consumerism, and neoliberal markets have created environmental and social injustice. We are morally bound to ask, how might the wounds of those injustices be healed by restoring relationships of abundance, collaboration, and life?

 Mending News!

Indigenomics Takes a Seat at the Table

In 2021, Carol Anne Hilton released *Indigenomics: Taking a Seat at the Economic Table*. This book does more than take a seat at the table—it builds its own table and sets a place for the rest of the world to share a meal. It demonstrates that billion-dollar economies can be built on relationships, multi-generational stewardship, and care for all. It smashes myths of Indigenous dependence, points to the pathways that are already being opened through the barriers of neoliberalism and extractive "free-market growthism," and leads the way through the Great Transition based on economic regenerativity. If you have students who are interested in planetary well-being through economics and law, this book is for them.

Growth Mindsets or, Why Every School Needs a Garden

Regenerative School Gardens are the embodiment of ecoliterate schooling for power(full) learning in the age of climate desperation. Growing something you can eat changes the way young people think about themselves, and restores their relationship to each other and the interlocking systems of life. As former President Jimmy Carter and lifelong gardener pointed out, "Like music and art, love of nature is a common language that can transcend political or social boundaries."[15] Like gravity and love, a garden pulls people together in the project of life.

In the garden, young people and their teachers come alive with possibility. Working together, choosing what to grow and where to put it (What plants help other plants? What do people need? What do plants need? What brings me joy?), sustaining a cultivating, facilitating relationship with the soil, plants, and the rhythms of natural systems over time, learning by doing (and letting Nature teach us what's what), and the sense of security that comes from growing your own food (and someone else's) restores confidence and makes us whole. There is nothing like the awe and feeling of celebration when we share the first sun-warmed strawberries or the first tomatoes straight off the vine (these taste SO much sweeter than the ones from the store!) ... or when we take home collards and beans or share them with the folks down the street, or better yet invite them into the garden. We always remember to thank the sun and the rain, and to give back the parts of the plants we don't need to our healthy soil, in gratitude for our reciprocal giving relationship with Nature. We always leave some unharvested to make the seeds for next season which, if we observe and tend them carefully, are like resilience in our pocket. If we live in a system that keeps us vulnerable, using just what Nature gives us—sun, soil, water, and seeds to grow our own food brings the self- and shared efficacy to believe in our own power to cultivate change, and the agency and skills to go ahead and do it.

A garden is the best possible classroom. It is said that parents are the First Teachers, Teachers are the Second, and the learning space is the Third. In a garden, we realize how our interrelationship with the Earth (our mother, our teacher, our learning space) contributes to all three. For teachers, in particular, the garden is not only a way to see your students engage as they maybe couldn't before, it serves as a metaphor for regenerative teaching. In the words of the late Sir Ken Robinson, "A gardener does not make plants grow. The job of a gardener is to create the optimal conditions."[16]

How might we create the optimal conditions for empowered regenerative learning?

Some people have learned to fear Nature. When they think of the natural world, bugs, dirt, and possibly a traumatic history (like disaster or displacement or enslavement) comes to mind. In a garden, whether on land or sea, the wonder of the connections between us and our food, between our food and nature, between nature and our histories and ourselves grows. The knowledge our ancestors had about these connections, the love that they gave, these are the reasons why we are here. In African ways of knowing, our ancestors persist in the Earth. They are there to transmit guidance and encouragement.[17] What will be our legacy? It is hard to be afraid of something once we know it as a relative. Instead, we begin to see how to cultivate those relationships with mutuality and reciprocity.

From roots in the garden, critical ecoliteracy, or clarity around the intersections of climate and social justice emerge. If we accept that "Earth is a relative, not a commodity,"[18] it changes how we think about ourselves and our participation in extractive and exploitive one-way materialist systems. Instead, we may demand access to our Mother's gifts for all beings: air that won't make us sick, healthy soil and food, clean water, and the promise of abundance in our future as fundamental rights of life. We may shift our thinking "from egosystem to ecosystem," and begin asking questions like, What are the human relationships that need to change in order to guarantee the fundamental building blocks of life? What would it mean to develop a personal and collective practice of interbeing? To go from feeling apart from each other to being a part of something immense and interconnected for the sole purpose of propagating and supporting life for ourselves and others? We will clearly need a better word than "school" to encompass this.

 **Mending News!**

Equal Rights for Pachamama

Pachamama is the Andean Indigenous name for Mother Earth. Bolivia led the world in establishing her rights under the law. These rights include the following: the right to be alive, the right to continue without human alteration (including at the cellular level), access to clean water and air, freedom from pollution, and the right to ecosystemic balance. Several countries have followed suit, naming rivers and river basins as legal entities who can be guaranteed similar rights. Ecuador, Colombia, New Zealand, Australia, and Bangladesh are currently figuring out how to enforce the rights of their rivers, while India and several municipalities in the United States which have also given rivers, lakes, and other natural areas rights are seeing cases through the courts. Is there any environmental law or policy interest among your students? Are there environmental attorneys nearby who could use some research or paralegal help? Politicians who could be persuaded by young people to get behind policy changes that would strengthen these laws?

Coming to see oneself as a participant, a teammate, a partner, a neighbor, an equal with other beings in the great web of life makes it untenable to treat others as less. Sharing the knowledge Earth provides facilitates her processes by participating in her design—all this is an incredibly simple and co-empowering act of love. As systems thinker Megan Swoboda puts it, "I may not be important, but what I do, and don't do, matters. My actions and inactions affect everyone around me. Our survival depends on the relationships we build."[19] We matter.

Communities of Trust and Care

Few strengths (if any!) rival the resilience of such a tightly woven web of interbeing. In disaster-affected areas, the most vital action toward power-full and proactive resilience, the kind that widens the circle of care and weakens unnatural systems of harm, has come from frontline communities. Christine Nieves Rodriguez, widely known for her belief in the power of relationship (see her TedMed talk) and a main catalyst for unified action that saved her town after Hurricane Maria, said this:

"When everything collapses, the life-saving infrastructure is our knowledge of one another's skills, our trust of one another, our capacity to forgive our neighbor, work with our neighbor, and mobilize ... we understood: the times we will be facing are going to require us to recognize that the most important thing around us is community."[20]

The communities that have taken the lead, if you will, charting the path for the others, are the ones that had a clear identity and strong social networks to begin with. These "communitarian entanglements," as Mexican sociologist Raquel Gutierrez Aguilar calls them[21] remind me of the rhizosphere described by my young friend at the fair. "You can't knock down 100 oak trees bound beneath the soil! How do we survive the unnatural disasters of climate change, environmental injustice, over-policing, mass-imprisonment, militarization, economic inequality, corporate globalization, and displacement? We must connect in the underground, my people!" wrote poet and Soul Fire Farm co-founder Naima Penniman[22] Given the predicament we find ourselves in, turning toward each other, with roots firmly planted in the biology of love and life on our only home planet, connecting being to being, community to community, converging discipline to discipline, linking relationship by regenerative and natural relationship, seems to me the best way to leverage the turning of whole systems, and will certainly be the most important resistance work of this century.

In the midst of the global pandemic disaster, we are seeing a new awareness of the need for human connectedness. Isolation is toxic to humans. Our national mental health problem, accelerating as it was pre-COVID, has become a full-blown crisis. Said US Surgeon General Dr. Vivek Murthy, "If ever there was a time to build meaningful relationships, it is now." As I am writing this book, we are appreciating a return to reconnecting, and recognizing the basic human need for understanding ourselves in ongoing actual relationships with others, as well as what happens when we are disconnected for a time. We feel strongest and most capable when we are part of an interdependent network, connected "underground" (soul to soul, body brains responding to body brains) like oaks. We are capable of our best thinking when we are among trusted creative companions. We know that familial warmth in our professional relationships helps us with feelings of anxiety and loss. After a disaster, when there are multiple layers of complexity and powerful emotions, communities need to come together to grieve, to heal, to co-create pathways connected to life. To tell our stories, hear truth resonating among us, and feel the strength of our regenerative power to create. We need to be relevant to others and feel a sense of purpose and contribution to others in order to make our lives worthwhile. Our sense of related belonging enables us to ask for and receive what we need.

"As a classroom community, our capacity to generate excitement is deeply affected by our interest in one another, in hearing one another's voices, in recognizing one another's presence," wrote bell hooks, in *Teaching To Transgress*.[23] And there's great power in it when we do. Our relationships help us to conquer our fears, to heal from disaster, to co-create resilience by making change happen. Christine Nieves Rodriguez tells about how, after the disorienting shock of Hurricane María, after they started feeding people in their home, "we realized that neighbors had become our family. People knew what to do and brought what they had." After 10 days, Proyecto de Apoyo Mutuo (Mutual Support Project) was born. They had gotten a community gathering center set up around an outdoor kitchen, and they were producing and serving 300 meals a day. "Everyone contributed their whole selves—full of respect and solidarity. Through this process of DOING, we were able to heal instead of despair."[24] Adults and children react to catastrophic disasters significantly better when they can act to improve the situation of others. Through our relationships, we become leader-full and exercise civic muscle. The sense of agency and resilience we feel when we are actively and collectively engaged in making things better, whether it's caring for neighbors, or planting a garden, or advocating for justice, or even electing a school board that believes in learning through play and experiences, rests directly on our relationships with others. Our relationships, local and global, give us reason to hope. We are capable of great things when we turn toward each other in relation, with open hearts and minds.

The evidence is plentiful. Belonging to a community of trust with shared aspirations has a staggeringly positive effect on health, resilience, happiness, focus, energy, and a sense of fulfillment. The now-famous 75-year-long Harvard study found that in addition, people lived years longer when they were in trusting relationships.[25] One thing COVID-19 and online school taught us is how significant a role school plays as a nexxus for interconnectedness. Children returning to school realized, maybe for the first time in their lives, not only how important it is to be together for the development of their closest relationships, but also how important it is to be surrounded by those looser connections, those smiles or open glances or friendly hellos. To feel the strength of community, like the rhizosphere, lifting you up. To feel the heart-stirring potential of making new friends. How good it feels to be known. Our bodies yearn to belong, to be held and lifted up by love, and we are our bodies. For many, returning to "normal" did not hold out very much relational promise.

How can schools and universities and communities cultivate the most fertile conditions for love, the basis of life, to grow?

Other-Wise: Teaching Interpersonal and Community Relationships

Do a "relationships inventory" of your teaching (your students can help with this) and your school system's organization. How much time is spent renewing our connectedness with our non-human family? Are we actually connecting with each other and the communities we live in? The health of any organization is determined by the quality and depth of those relationships. In your classes and in your professional workday, how much time, structured and unstructured, is given for physically and emotionally present listening, empathy, and real conversations? How much trust is shared? Do the students care about each other? Do the adults?

There are some who might object that school is not the place to be teaching things like relationships. I posit that school has always been precisely that, for better and for worse. In schools and universities where little to no intention is applied to relationship-building, there is often a pervasive feeling of mistrust and of being "stuck." As educators, we have no less need to be seen, to be appreciated, to be included, to trust, and to be trusted. If intentional caring for each other and creating the time and space to build trust is important for the students to thrive in our learning community and beyond, the first and best thing we can do as adults is to build our interconnectedness with each other. In India's Dream a Dream program, founder Vishal Tareja demonstrated after 20 years of research into well-being and life skills that empathy was only learned when children witnessed it in adults. They needed to see adults respecting, listening deeply to, and caring for one another. Only then could they rely on teachers to be a place of safety for them.[26] Shane Safir, co-founder of June Jordan School for Equity & Justice, recommends "symmetry," mirroring and practicing the kind of trusting and collaborative relationships educators hope to develop among their students. How well is your school succeeding in this? What is getting in the way?

The adults in our learning communities need to be sure that structures and practices are building toward co-governance, mutuality, growth through shared change making, and creative companionship. Walkabout[27] takes adults (not just the teachers, but all adults in the learning community) to the woods, often together with the students and administrators. They reconnect with nature, "survive in the wilderness" together, share structured reflections, complete projects together, and essentially prepare and practice what they will be doing "at school." The fact that school may feel more like a wilderness and learning is energized most in the woods is not lost on them as they reflect. They learn how important relationships and shared purpose are to our sense of agency and collective efficacy, and to be intentional about curating the in-school and out-of-school experiences that will honor and activate positive relationships. When the adults return to school and mix the relationship/community-building techniques and reflections on collaboration into their everyday work, student behavior and engagement improve and students report an eagerness to learn. Teachers and students and other adults in the community are working together to co-create the school. In some cases, parents report that prescribed medications for focus and anxiety are no longer needed.

As a kid with teachers I trusted, I could discuss all kinds of matters I could not discuss with my parents. There's an emotional freight in all families, and so students *should* seek out other adults they can confide in and lean on. Is there time and space for this in your school? Can a student find and access an adult during the school day for academic support? And then there's the informal connectedness. One reason the teachers I know went into mourning during COVID-19 was the loss of those incidental contacts, the informal check-in reading body language, and the quick, eye-to-eye emotional connections that simply could not happen online. And then the cameras and mikes went off. How many people you know credit their success, the turn they made, their very self-esteem and abilities to thrive to the teachers who knew them best? Students don't really learn from someone who doesn't authentically see, hear, and know them. In fact, the education system as it is set up right now is a good example of what columnist Charles M. Blow meant when he wrote, "You don't have to operate with great malice to do great harm. The absence of empathy and understanding are sufficient."[28] Teachers and students both are feeling overwhelmed, and afraid for our future. How might we work with young people and their adults to support meaningful relationships?

Trust, Again. The Foundation of All Relationships

Why does trust matter? It is the starting point for emotional, social, and cultural safety, which is the starting point for all meaningful relationships as well as for openness to learning. Trust is the starting point for real conversation, collaboration, and eventually individual and collective thriving. Taking the time to establish trust saves time and creates opportunities for collective change. "… perhaps most important, there is a re-cognition that building community is a requisite foundation for building a better world. It is important to take the necessary time, make the necessary space, invest in the weft and the weave between us."[29] In the age of futurephobia and disaster, our students need to feel less alone.

Educators feel the scarcity of time. Overcoming our con-ditioning to the curriculum (we "know where we are supposed to be by now") and setting aside our sense of urgency to make time for trust-building can be a challenge. One colleague said to me with a touch of irony, "maybe someday AI and robots will do enough of our paperwork that we can just focus on re-lationships." If you lead with love, if you are attuned to the people right in front of you, together you can make changes faster than the system can stop you. From the beginning of school, trust and safety can be intentional in all things you do. Focusing on belonging, listening, conversation, and con-spiratorial collaboration on issues that matter creates an environment conducive to trust, creative and intellectual risk-taking, and growth. As Kim Ondrick, Principal of the Mill Bay Nature School said, "When people feel that you really love them, even adults, they will try things that they didn't think they could do." *With fewer stops for discipline, regaining wandering attention, and compliance demanding, you'll actually save time that can be reinvested in learning.* There is no feeling for a teacher as powerful as walking into a classroom late and seeing that the kids are already engaged in their meaningful work.

The first step in re-establishing trust is on us as adults. Remembering that you can teach your students to do the same kind of internal work you do, and once they know you are really listening to them, prepare to be discomforted by what the students will say. Take the time to rein in your own instinct to explain. This is so hard for me that I have to train my brain to focus on breathing when I am tempted to interrupt and explain. The kind of ego-distant humility that it takes to absorb without defending, to inquire further without seeming to debate or needing to explain, to pursue with a curious mind and open heart will take some effort. It is hard to tamp down your desire to enthuse, to join in, or to be the hero. But it is precisely breaking through this tension, sitting with frustration and anguish and grief and fear that will form a creative companionship based on truth. It was not easy for Hopewell City school leaders to hear what the students had to say, but it gave them the basis for co-creating, with the community, a new vision, and to design, with the students, a whole new school.

As the kids tell it, the high school in Hopewell City, VA, used to be a horrible place. From an early state survey on school culture, they found that nearly half of their students had been bullied because of their sexual orientation and nearly 60% because of their race. What was also true is that over a third felt that no one cared.[30] There were serious attendance and discipline problems. Academic results were predictably low, and self-confidence even lower. The "hidden curriculum," or what students carried away from school every day, was that the system was not set up for them and had no interest in expanding their opportunities. New Superintendent Dr. Melody Hackney, who describes herself as "ridiculously conscious of change-leadership," made a liberating proposal: what if we made school about the kids? She told the school board, "we are going to hold ourselves accountable to the students in our care. Not test scores and one-size-fits-all metrics. Student voice will be our North Star, because the Kids. Deserve. Better." Every day and in every way, they keep asking, "whose school is this?" and modeling real talk. "All we need to do is listen to them, and they will tell us what they need," says Greg Burlin. "And you can't get defensive, no matter what they say. You can't solve what you're unwilling to talk about."

Over the last five years, Hopewell City High School has been asking the hard questions and holding themselves accountable to the kids. They are developing a culture of courageous creativity, asking "what if" instead of saying, "yes, but," and then following up. They are working with young people to invest in their communities, building community partnerships and mentorships through two-week challenge/design intersessions. These are followed up by a "block party," where the community shares in celebrating their successes and solidifies a shared vision around "what we want for our kids." The school staff keeps asking, "if you didn't have to, why would you want to come back to school?" Together they have co-created curricula in all disciplines (and across them) around self-awareness, identity, and self-worth. There is a large and loud makerspace, where kids are continually asked, "what do you want to create?" Students and teachers co-create activities and projects that drive learning deeper because it has purpose and meaning. In the words of Sommer Jones, Hopewell's Innovation Coach, "we want to help kids find their inner genius and unleash it. And that means knowing how to take up your space *and how to show up for each other*. We ask them what problems in the world are troubling them and help them do something that matters. We make sure that hope is part of everything we do." At Hopewell City schools, by following the lead of students doing what matters, they are healing other kinds of oppressive fragmentations introduced by western thinking habits and factory-style efficiencies. Any challenge complex enough to be worth investigating is likely to be multi-faceted and multi-disciplinary.

A Pluralistic Stance Honors and Celebrates Uniqueness (and Biodiversity)

"Hard data," standardized curricula, and typical school processes label and obscure students, all the while creating the illusion that through these shorthand labels we know them. Instead, we are "othering" them by making them all feel categorized or pathologized or dehumanized (or all of the above). I remember how frustrating it was for me as an adult to hear, "well, of course. You are an ENTJ (I don't actually remember what my classification was)." We are so much more than our labels. If we want our students to turn toward each other (and other beings) with open hearts and curiosity, we need to cultivate a desire to know each other, from a pluralistic stance, where there is an understanding that Nature (and therefore life) loves diversity.

We know that in Nature, and therefore in life, diversity leads to thriving. Pluralism among humans replicates the notion—we exist in interrelationship with others, and those individuals who surround themselves with others of different hues and perspectives and histories and contexts in openness and curiosity are more likely to be resilient and to be able to adapt. Our typical education systems were created by someone else (mostly White and male) other than present-day mostly White teachers and administrators, but that means all educators have a special responsibility to view the system and our parti- cipation in it through a critical lens.

Color-Blindness Is Monocultural

In typical schools where there is a fetishizing of "neutral" data and meeting "outside" expectations, there is a temptation for educators to assert, "I don't see color (or shape, class, or sexual orientation, or disabilities)--I treat all my students the same, regardless." Usually, it is White teachers who use that frame with regard to race and, to put the best face on it, are trying to say that they care about all their students and try to treat them fairly. But stop and pay attention to that language for a moment. From a student perspective: if you don't see color, and my skin color is part of my identity, then you are blind to my wholeness, my Blackness, my history. You might also assume certain things about me but are blinding yourself to your own subjectivity there. Are you uncomfortable talking about race? Then maybe you are uncomfortable accepting me. And are you suggesting that in order to accept me you have to accept me "in spite of" my Blackness? Am I not to be seen fully until I make myself like you?

Teachers and professors and administrators remember: you don't have to articulate that statement out loud in order for students to feel it.[31] Double award-winning young poet Azhane Pollard of VA said, "If you don't see color, you don't see me." The number one job description of an educator (and I mean any adult associated with learning) is to co-create a world of safety, where students can be loved because of who they are, not in spite of it, and can be known and loved for *all of themselves* and not as a representation of a category. In the age of climate disasters, we cannot afford to be neutral about this. *The Niceties*, a play by Eleanor Burgess, explores the relationship between a liberal White female college professor/historian and her Black female activist student, in all of its intricate and multi-layered detail.[32] A terrific exploration with older students and colleagues and informal educators, it will surely get you talking. We can't learn together until we can relate to each other with curiosity, humility, and love.

"Don't Say Gay" legislation is dangerous. It is signaling to all children, including the cisgender and heterosexual ones, that LGBTQI+ identities and fluidity are so threatening to society that they can't even be mentioned. How can we as educators be trusted adults in that context? Ayana Verdi has created a safe space in Florida. Every single function of her school has been thoughtfully considered, making sure it is both based on and cultivating relational principles of life. She says, "If you don't listen, they won't come back. We have to give them a *reason* to come back." Using her school as an example, what caring relationships can you bring into yours?

Verdi Eco School

Each day here starts with standing and breathing together, listening to shared music (maybe dancing), culturally appropriate food, inviting ancestors, clapping, rocking, playing a simple name game, reading a poem, expressions of gratitude—any or all of these kinds of harmonizing activities that join the students in fun and belonging.

The Verdi Eco-School is a safe place. Founded by Ayana Verdi to reflect the African-American communitarian values she grew up with, she wanted her school to be in a garden in an urban residential neighborhood. In Melbourne, FL, she located a community doctor who was retiring and moving away. The office was in an old house, updated for ADA (Americans with

Disabilities Act) requirements, and full of community spirit. It was already viewed as a place of comfort. The ten different gardens are also the classrooms—nearly all of the students' time is spent outside, working in teams, taking on responsibilities, studying transformation and life and growth. With weekly field trips to community and federal agencies, the ocean, inland waterways, and NASA, and with invitations to pick fruit and write poetry on chalkboards hanging on the school fence, the school is inseparable from its neighborhood and surrounding community. Its ecosystem is theirs. And it's not just an act. Agencies at all levels consider the students, who range in age from kindergarten to 10th grade (adding more soon) to be a valuable resource, finding living solutions to ocean erosion, wastewater and waste management, carbon sequestration, aging, community well-being, and the older students using their expertise with plants to help NASA to discover which plants might thrive in the Space Station and beyond. The community keeps these kids safe and valued.

Eco-school students keep all of their community friends and relations safe. They built a butterfly house so that they could study metamorphosis, but realized that their numbering system for the chrysalis "apartments" was too impersonal, so they gave them names and "stories of change." These children are learning a relational kind of science, receiving lessons in transformation from butterflies that lead them to trust that there is something special inside them just waiting to emerge. They've created and posted reminders and inspirations and have important responsibilities—to each other, primarily, but also to the Earth. Verdi EcoSchool provides a safe haven for kids who have been bullied, LGBTQ+ kids, and simply kids who are seeking a place where they can reconnect, be themselves, be whole, be trusted, and learn deeply. Approximately 50% of students attend using a state-sponsored scholarship. They are proud of their place, their community, and their garden. While I was there, a student offered me a small container of mulberries from their tree. As Ms. Verdi says, "the puzzle pieces may seem to be all over the place, but we are making pictures." A sense of peace, confidence, and freedom to think and be, to grow, and to

celebrate infused the learning spaces. We should never underestimate the power of acceptance and love. These kids are
thriving.

From the beginning, our students can become active in a
flourishing of care for each other, recognizing each others' unique perspectives, contributions, and growth. The youngest
students are not at all too young to infuse them with the sense
that who they are and what they do matters to everyone else.
Involving them (and their parents) from the youngest ages in
projects like El Valor (Chapter 6), studying and assisting in
monarch migration, and the Mau Forest Native Species
Reforestation project (Kenya) connects them to each other, their
communities, and the kin all around them. For the youngest,
using language they can understand but being honest with
them about complex issues like climate justice and how they can
contribute positively enables them to act power-fully and calms
both their fear of disaster and their potential mistrust of adults.

Carla Marschall and Elizabeth O. Crawford's excellent book,
Worldwise Learning, is full of activities and resources for teaching
holistically, and importantly roots all of its suggestions in not
only what we DO in school, but in building mindsets and
mental models that are conducive to relational citizenship. They
point out that understanding others in our world is a practice of
looking inward and outward at the same time. Just as the coherence of the self and the integrity of interrelationship is inseparable, being self-aware plays an important role in our
ability to recognize our own biases and how they might be influencing how we see others. As educators, we will want to be
aware of the fact of our own biases as well. I have often been in
situations where a group leader asks people to "imagine what
trauma x must be like," even though there are people in the
room who have experienced or are experiencing it. Our learning
experiences have to be spaces of kindness and consent. Don't
ever ask a student to share personal experiences, even if others
are, unless they explicitly tell you they are ready. It is often
better to bring a person or people into the class who can speak
for particular perspectives. Gathering a lot of perspectives also
allows young people to break up stereotypes, and pull back the

lens to look for patterns in the larger web of relationships beyond themselves.

You might find in high school that competition and "getting
ahead" seems to matter to your students more than kindness. In
fact, Richard Weissbourd's study showed that for most adolescents, even though they thought their parents wanted them
to be kind, the message that came through from parents and
school was that the most important thing was getting ahead,
gaining an individual advantage.[33] Kindness could come later,
or other, nicer people could take care of that in the collective. If
they were showing kindness or joining community-oriented
activities, it was sometimes simply to impress or to be more
attractive to colleges.

Your students could help you look critically at this too and
co-create new options. It may be difficult to prioritize relationships at first, particularly to lift up true collaboration and
co-creative mindsets when "the system" seems increasingly
intensely individualized, competitive, and mechanistic. The
message that gets through is that in order to succeed, you have
to master playing the game, but even that, when looked at
critically, emphasizes that it is not natural. Our moves need to
be intentionally trustworthy, restorative, regenerative and
whole, retelling the narrative of separation as a narrative of
connectedness.

Harmonizing and Listening Deeply

Human beings are social creatures. We only feel fully safe when
our nervous systems are in proximity and feel reciprocity.
Perhaps you have felt the calming presence of another person,
whose trusted attention helped to soothe your emotional state.
We are bodies. In the narrative of separation, we "have" bodies.
But the reality is that we ARE bodies. We are wired to connect.
Our nervous systems are interconnected and communicating,
like the rhizosphere just beneath the forest floor. We harmonize
with each other. Have you ever felt yourself relax when
laughing with someone? Do you know someone who sings or

hums, sometimes without even realizing it? And then there's rocking chairs. Do you or your culture have certain songs, dances, drumming rhythms, chants, or certain comfort foods that are always shared? Culture is how our body draws on its past and integrates it with the present. The coherence of life that is felt when repeating these actions (which are frequently repetitive or rhythmic in and of themselves) is healing and energizing and compels hope. When these actions take place in harmony among others, we feel a certain flow of collective power—of shared joyful exuberance and rootedness.

Global collective trauma expert Thomas Hübl emphasizes beginning each group session by not only tuning in to yourself, but to the others in your space. My students giggled the first time we did an "I feel you feeling me" exercise, and then they wanted to do it again. We began calling it harmonizing, and sometimes they would clap together or sing. (Resource 3) Because our nervous systems are connected, our brains release way more feel-good hormones (oxytocin, serotonin) when we are actually together than they do when we are together through a screen. As much as our society valorizes individualism and competitiveness, as awkward as we may feel coming together again after long periods of pandemic isolation or screen-filtered (mis)communication, the heart of being human is love. Human hatreds are often the result of fear, unrequited love, of violence (or fear of violence), of neglect or alienation. Propagandists have to press hard on these in order to get people to hate. For most humans, it's hard to harm the people you have shared a song or a clap and response game with.

It is certainly possible to upset each other, too. Have you ever been in a stressful situation where one person's panicky reaction causes others to panic? Maybe there's a test coming up and the anxiety spreads throughout the classroom, even to the students who are not normally prone to it. Or, when a prediction of a storm in your area comes in and one person's fear triggers another and another and another until a whole room of children (and maybe the teacher) are feeling anxious and overwhelmed.

What if we could help our whole class to feel a sense of belonging and well-being through harmonizing our bodies?

We could breathe together, drum together, sing together, clap and dance together. I taught my students some basic breathing and meditation techniques ... and invited them to do it if they felt stressed. (Resource 3) "Can we all do it *together*?" they asked. "Please? Every day?" One of the things about harmonizing activities is that they make us slow down and connect ourselves with our selves, linking mind, body, and spirit (see Chapter 4). That's important. But they also connect us with each other, intentionally building a healthy mutuality and reciprocity. I feel me. I feel you. I feel you feeling me. This lifelong practice of connectedness leads to a compassionate citizenry, is more likely to support healthy integration of trauma, and helps us know, at a visceral level, that we are not alone.

Listening Fully Means Listening Slowly

How do you want to be heard? How do you want to show up to listen? adrienne maree brown wrote, "To a certain degree, our entire future may depend on learning to listen, listen without assumptions or defenses ... listen closely to all that is within and beyond our human ways of knowing." The rushed and accelerating pace of life, the urgency of crisis-to-crisis decision-making at school, in government, at home, politics, surviving, competing—none of it seems to allow for listening of the kind brown is calling for. Our current definitions of individualized success seem to rule out full listening—so we listen only for information or agreement, shoring up our own sense of our world AND the isolation and vulnerability we suffer because no one is listening to us. Echo chambers and sub-cultures form, full of fear of the others and a siege mentality of loneliness and hostility. In our noisy, speedy era, only the loudest get the attention we all need.[34] Teenagers and children, in general, have reason to feel unheard. Typical school systems are really run by policies made far from the hallways and classrooms and playgrounds resounding with the voices of youth. When young people are involved, in school student councils, or as a non-voting rep on a school board, their participation is frequently tokenized. People pay full attention to what we love. It makes sense that their takeaway (as it was at Hopewell City) is that no one is listening, and that that means the adults don't care.

How do you listen? How do you want to be heard? Does your school give you enough time and space to really listen to each other? Do children and young people have the chance to really talk to each other in structured and unstructured ways? Think of a time when you got some good listening. I had a high school music teacher who showed me how to listen. Mr. Wallace said it was because music had taught him how we were all connected at the heart, and so he always thought of listening as if there were guitar strings connecting us, and the real "happening" was the vibration between. He never tried to fix me or intervene in any way. He always invited me into a reciprocal space. It wasn't until I read Meg Wheatley's translation from English back into Shona that I learned the source of his greeting when I'd pop up in his office or classroom at lunchtime. In Zimbabwe, they say, Makadii? (How are you?) Response: Ndiripo makadiwo (I am here if you are here) Response: Ndiripo. (I am here).[35] I usually burst in with, "Hey. You got a minute?" Without fail, he would say, "I have a minute if you have a minute." I'd say, "I brought my lunch." He'd say, "If you're having lunch, I'm having lunch." In the process of this exchange, he'd stop what he was doing. Then he'd say, "First we breathe. Then we can eat and you can tell me how's life." Two cleansing breaths later and I was sharing everything and absorbed in his stories, too. Sometimes I forgot to eat.

The temptation to intervene, to explain, to make things better, to coach or advise is very great for teachers. After all, like parents, we want to protect! We want to help! But the seed of all relationships, the seed of trust, is listening. Listening is harmonizing, feeling the vibration, hearing the music between two beings in the web of life. Healthy relationships require whole listening. Slow down and ready yourself. Breathe. Be present to sit with their suffering and overwhelm, if that's what's required. Breathe more instead of jumping in or distancing yourself (our own histories and overwhelm might draw our attention away). Listen with your whole body—your eyes and your heart especially, to bear witness to your student's experience, even their pain, without turning away. Usually, that's what people need most. Make it clear before they start what your reporting responsibilities are in your context. Never ever try to make it better by saying it's alright or saying things that sound like you are minimizing the impact this is having on them or that you know what they are feeling. Just make sure they know that you hear them, you are noticing how much strength they have, that you appreciate their trusting you, and that you are and will be with them. Later, you can find out more. Do some research into the context of their lives to help you listen better, and perhaps find or seek together some possible pathways forward. Paolo Freire called teacher—listeners practitioners of a liberating "pedagogy of love."

Then teach your students to do this with each other. Story-listening is even more important than storytelling, from a relational standpoint. I love combining the harmonizing practices and heart-listening here with listening outdoors. Sitting in a circle comfortably, who or what do we hear? Who's sounding from up close? Far away? What's out of the ordinary? What's missing? What inferences can we make about the beings and the context based on what we hear? Don't forget that this is heart-listening, so students with hearing challenges can do it with their eyes. What is the real story going on here? What are the feelings present? What could it all mean? Now we are ready to listen to each other. Turn to Resource 2 for more information about Listening Circles.

Curiosity Drives Conversation

Margaret Wheatley says that a good conversation is one in which there is some tension. "We don't have to agree with each other in order to think well together. There is no need for us to be joined at the head. We are joined by our human hearts."[36] When care-full listening becomes a habit, it calms down our egos and opens up our minds. Our desire to know more about how others think unfolds, and we can disagree without being disagreeable. How can we fear someone with whom we have shared truths? When we allow ourselves to open up with humility and curiosity, we can love more of the world, and there's a regenerative power in that. I remember my father taking me along with him while he delivered eggs to the old people. I was young and fidgety, I'm sure. I vastly preferred it when the old folks had something sweet set aside for me. I soon realized, however, that this was about so much more than sitting still and listening to dusty old people telling stories about their past. The more I listened, the more they made me wonder. They instilled in me without even my being aware of it a curiosity about others, about other ways of thinking, about what it means to be human in a different time and place. As I listened with my eyes open I could imagine the place, and when I opened my heart I could grasp the way it felt—to them. How can we cultivate this cross-generational connection in our learning experiences?

I think we are often too rushed today to allow for full conversations. We want to know if we agree with that person, and if we don't, we move on to find someone who echoes our own views to confirm our sense of reality, like the reflections seen in Plato's Allegory of the Cave. Maybe we avoid people we think might not share our own perspectives. But this can lead to fear and hatred at worst, and siloing, mistrust, and loneliness at best. Add into that mix the need to talk about climate change and the inequities in it and the disparate impacts of disasters, and what changes we need to make in our lives and organizations and systems, and things get even stickier.

Thriving requires community, and community requires good conversation. Good conversations move slowly and are full of what Meg Wheatley calls "surprises." Those are the moments that allow for our natural curiosity to make us wonder, ask for more, respectfully disagree, and possibly change our minds. They cause us to reflect back on and highlight the assumptions we might have been making in those interiors hidden from our awareness. Smithsonian's StoryCorps has started a program called One Small Step.[37] People who are bound to disagree can sign up. They get some main goals and some questions to ask. The scaffolded conversation not only enables them to connect, it gives them ideas about how to converse with each other after the session is over. Check it out and try it with your students and their families! It will give them a valuable civic relationship-building tool. At the Teachers College Reading and Writing Reunion, Cynthia Satterlee shared a Progression of Talk conversation scaffold that might help students who are really struggling. Based on the work of Katy Wishow, Shana Frazin, Donna Santman, and Gaby Layden, it goes something like this. Say Anything, Say Something Relevant ("something you just said," "that just made me wonder"), Say Something Back ("I … too," "I feel differently"), Say Something to Clarify ("Did you mean," "So I think what you are saying") Say Something to Revise ("Let me try that in a clearer way," "As I'm listening to you I'm realizing"), Say Something to Provoke ("I'm not following-say more about," "convince me of"), Say Something to Extend ("to go deeper," "to illustrate my/your point"). I have found this helpful with adults, too, but especially with young people as they are interacting with each other and facilitating conversations around civic issues.[38]

We can connect at the heart—there's no need to agree on everything to acquire a fuller understanding and to think well and design well together. It is important to remember that students may never have been invited to share their ideas or opinions, or to question the way things are, and for some this would be culturally challenging. In general, however, they've picked up on all the signals that playing the game of success in typical schools means not asking too many questions or making too many waves. In her book, *Raising Your Hand*, Komal Shah writes about how stifling it was to be the model student.[39] She learned to suppress her natural curiosity (as well as her authentic self). What is more, without opportunities to show up with love to have good conversations with others who hold differing perspectives, how can young people imagine collective action on a global scale?

But How Do We Talk About Climate?

In this loud, speedy world, we are craving to be heard. To be able to tell our truths to people who will listen. To trust and be trusted in return. Some people feel the need to shout. But good conversation is a give and take among equals—equally human or equally be-ing and becoming. I think of this all the time as I watch my husband run out of the house to stand in perfect stillness watching the osprey, listening with his whole body. To teach the ancient practice of conversation, it might help to envision what a good conversation looks like. In this, I am inspired by Indigenous knowledge keepers, people like Carol Sanford who writes in the Regenerative Life,[40] that Good conversation usually begins with something meaningful that we care about. A powerful question that draws us to a commonality. In my neighborhood, I can easily talk with people who aren't sure about all this climate change stuff if we start with our children and grandchildren and our hopes for their future. It puts us on the same level, as peers, real people, and not cut-outs of roles we play. We wonder together. We ask "what if …" We do not make statements, because wondering and what-iffing is curiosity and openness. Statements are closed. We ask each other questions respectfully and listen without judgment. Everyone has something to teach me, and it is easier to share our own truths when curiosity and humility is present. Each question and each answer is a gift. We do not interrupt, check our watch, or make it all about ourselves. We give each other time. We wait before we answer. To listen more. To breathe. To think. To avoid rushing past each other's meaning. To say thank you for sharing that. We don't try to speak for anyone but ourselves, and we don't try to connect other people's ideas together too soon. That might cut off people who suddenly feel the conversation has gone beyond them. We help each other to listen better, to not hurt, even though we aren't perfect and sometimes it doesn't go smoothly. There is no scarcity of attention, even if there hasn't been any mind-changing or convincing or "productivity" in the conversation. That doesn't matter, because the relationship has deepened and grown. Taking the time now saves time later. The next step will be easier when we ask, *how can we change this together?*

Power of Interrelationship in Communities

When focusing on a project that matters, such as advocating for changes needed to mitigate or adapt to climate change pressures, getting the school or the community ready for disaster, or welcoming and resettling displaced families, petty differences fall away and the focus can shift to the joy in shared effort, especially if you have a process you can trust (Chapter 8). Interrelated and integrated communities involve everyone, including children and youth, in decision-making about shared protective actions. Sharing the responsibility and putting all shoulders to the wheel is a protective action in and of itself—research shows that self- and shared efficacy and agency is critical to recovery after a shock like a hurricane, tornado, sudden freeze, or fire. What we also know is that agency and efficacy play a significant role in well-being and civic belonging overall. Too often in the urgency of emergency, and in the urgency of rushed and mechanistic schooling, only certain voices are attended to, resulting in imbalanced, potentially dangerous inappropriate responses. Those most affected, including children and youth, are least heard. Typical schools, racing from one crisis to another, and adhering to one-size-fits-all demands, can fall into a similar pattern.

What if we engaged people of all ages in collective community conversation and vision for change making? What if youth facilitated those conversations?

"**The presence and quality of our relationships** may have more impact on learning and development than any other factor," wrote education scholar Linda-Darling Hammond in a recent research report.[41] Study after study demonstrates that cognition and emotion are inextricably linked. If a student is trusted and engaged in making contributions that matter, their sense of belonging and safety is enhanced. If students feel that they are important to the teacher, the brain sends signals to relax and open up, and they can learn well. Most of us can recall the excitement of being in class with a teacher who we felt cared about us. We learned much more and more deeply, were free to question, inspired to do more even after the class ended.

What if we can deepen those connections further by collaborating on school and community challenges together?

"Oak trees don't set an intention to listen to each other better or agree to hold tight to one another when the next storm comes. Under the earth, always, they reach for each other, they grow such that their roots are intertwined and create a system of strength that is as resilient on a sunny day as it is in a hurricane."[42] When we consider ourselves as part of the coherent interrelated whole of the universe, we can never be alone. There's power in that.

Seeds for Planting

Young children are naturally interrelated and in affinity with Nature. They understand living systems at a visceral level. How can we sustain those relationships through the "school years" and lifelong?

Making meaning together from lessons of Nature and doing so in a garden enables an appreciation of our embedded relationships and an appreciation of ourselves. As bell hooks wrote in her beautiful book *belonging: a culture of place* (2009), "When we love the earth, we are able to love ourselves more fully."[43]

Habits for Harmonizing, Listening, and Good Conversation can be taught. Here's how. Every day, together.

Notes

1 4-H is a US-based non-profit organization dedicated to holistic (Head, Heart, Hands, and Health) youth development. It not only has strong roots in rural and agricultural areas but it also serves urban counties as well. Its inclusive policies extend to encouraging young folks of all kinds to join or co-create any club that fits their interests, and to take on leadership roles at the club, regional, and national levels. There is usually a community-oriented emphasis, including civic skills such as public speaking and

community improvement. All clubs are expected to demonstrate their commitment and accomplishments. 4-H also sponsors inexpensive camps for outdoor summer experiences.

2 Wheatley 2009.
3 Scharmer 2016.
4 Hutchins and Storm 2019.
5 Kimmerer 2020.
6 Bailey 2016.
7 Benyus 2020.
8 Robbins 2015.
9 Schwartz 2020.
10 Andrews 2015.
11 Robbins 2015.
12 In the book, this is referred to as the Gaia Theory. Alternatively, these are the foundational principles of life. Hutchins and Storm 2019.
13 Robbins 2015.
14 Zelikova 2020.
15 Carter 1988 and 1994.
16 Robinson 2010.
17 Penniman 2020.
18 brown 2017.
19 Escobar 2017.
20 Nieves Rodriguez 2020.
21 Escobar 2017.
22 Penniman 2020.
23 hooks 1994.
24 Nieves Rodriguez 2020.
25 Gregoire 2013. There are hundreds of articles about this study, since it has been going on for so long and has revealed so much about the developing human psyche. Don't hesitate to snoop on the study's own site, https://www.adultdevelopmentstudy.org/news and stay tuned for the Second Generation Study!
26 Explore Dream a Dream, whose mission is to put thriving at the center of education. Their Arc of Transformation is very helpful, as are the other approaches you will find here. https://dreamadream.org/ Quoted in Hannon and Peterson 2021.
27 Cioffi 2022.
28 Blow 2012.
29 Johnson and Wilkinson 2020.
30 Dr. Melody Hackney, Sommer Jones, Greg Burlin and other staff generously shared stories and data from their ongoing school transformation. They were the main presenters in Moran and Socol 2019. Moran and Socol (and Ratliff) have also published *Timeless Learning: How Imagination, Observation, and Zero-Based Thinking Change Schools*. San Francisco: Jossey-Bass. 2018. Moran and Socol consult on community-centered school transformation.
31 Marschall and Crawford 2022.
32 Burgess 2019.
33 Weissbourd 2016.
34 Wheatley 2001.
35 Wheatley 2001.

36 Wheatley 2001.
37 Explore both StoryCorps and OneSmallStep here. https://storycorps.org/discover/onesmallstep/ both would be good projects for your students and could produce great elder-youth connectivity.
38 Satterlee 2022.
39 Shah 2021.
40 Sanford 2020.
41 Cantor, et al., 2020.
42 brown in Johnson and Wilkinson 2020.
43 hooks 2009.

6 The Power of Place: Belonging in Contexts

What would happen if we allowed the place we learn in to inscribe its curriculum on our learning, too?
What happens when people are decontextualized, or dis-placed?
How can experiential local projects re-root us and build belonging and regenerative power?

A Name

When Eve walked among
the animals and named them—
nightingale, red-shouldered hawk,
fiddler crab, fallow deer—
I wonder if she ever wanted
them to speak back, looked into
their wide wonderful eyes and
whispered, *Name me, name me.*

–Ada Limón, "A Name:" from *The Carrying.*
–Copyright © 2018 by Ada Limón.
–Reprinted with the permission of The Permissions Company LLC
on behalf of Milkweed Editions, milkweed.org[1]

DOI: 10.4324/9781003215806-7

I grew up in the embrace of two trees in a forest of many. Grandfather tree (both of my human grandfathers died before I could know them) was a White Oak hundreds of years old that still stands partway down the hill to the swamp, beyond the foot of the main pasture, and very importantly just far enough out of sight of the house. He had a beautiful thick branch reaching almost straight out from his side, about 12 or 15 feet above the ground. An invitation. I built a rope ladder and climbed up. I felt welcomed, comfortable, held, leaning my back against his trunk. Time slowed down. I felt completely accepted, and my mind opened up in connection with my heart. I could feel the stories Oak had witnessed, and imagined Nipmuck men and women, walking in conversation or running silently past on their main trail, and wondered who their grandfather trees were (perhaps this one) and what they called them. I re-named myself and considered my own ancestors. I composed music and poetry. Stories. Then I built a little platform, so I could stay longer before my legs fell asleep, and went there to think and watch. Sometimes I read books, but most of the time I just let my mind and heart go freely where Grandfather tree took me. Did he notice me taking in the life among his branches, and under his bark? Detect my awe at his age, the breadth of his strong shape, and the flourishing of activity on and under the ground? Maybe I was just a brief appreciative shadow, like the breeze and the leaves uplifting, patterns reflected on my skin. I walked home through the tall grass in the golden light of the setting sun. No one else felt the love "my" grandfather tree gave me, and I never dared tell anyone at school.

Another tree loved me, too, but hers was a different and more motherly embrace. Hemlock's tresses gracefully brushed the edges of the stream that fed the swamp. She did not challenge me to climb and perch. Instead, she invited me to rest, softly, on her apron of cool mosses, in the sweet and enclosing shade by the soothing stream. I went there when I was upset. And soon enough the sound of the water, the flickering light reflected there, the golden cowslips and the cantankerous crayfish (not a fish at all), and the game of picking out all the different kinds of moss and lichen in that one spot would restore my spirit. Hers was a different perspective from Grandfather tree's, but it also felt like love. They were my secret.

My daughter has my mother's gift for remembering names. Both are botanists, and my daughter's specialty is trees. Recently, she wrote this:

> Black Gum, *Nyssa sylvatica*, is my favorite tree. … When taking field dendrology at Cornell, "it" was described as "not looking normal." I could relate to that! "If you see a tree and have no idea what it is, but can rule out everything else, it's a Black Gum." And sure enough, every time I was stumped (no pun intended) by a tree, it was always Black Gum! After moving to Arkansas for a winter to study trees, the same thing happened. Except the Black Gum were everywhere! And the first time I recognized one on his own merits - and not by ruling out what he was *not* - I felt such a sense of acceptance! Not even accomplishment, but acceptance, as if he finally recognized me back. As if he was grateful to have been identified! I started seeing them everywhere I went - and not as leftovers. I have a twig of one tattooed on my foot![2]

How would society be different if all humans felt that Earth, mother of all, knew us and loved us?

If we felt that a tree appreciated being called by name and recognized us, even named us, in return?

If those of us who have culturally cut ourselves off restored our relationships?

If we could remember that ALL living things share the same four amino acids that make up our DNA?

My daughter shares the same DNA as Black Gum, the tree who recognized her. The visual reminder is inked under her skin. We are all known by our place and its inhabitants. We are named, by nightingale, red-shouldered hawk, grandparent trees, and *Nyssa sylvatica*, though we might not be able to hear that through all the static. Maybe we just need to ask.

What would happen if we allowed the place we learn in to inscribe its curriculum on our learning, too?

In *Braiding Sweetgrass*, Robin Wall Kimmerer writes, "When we call a place by name it is transformed from a wilderness to a homeland. I imagined that this beloved place knew my name as well, even when I myself did not."[3] People are powerful when we feel like we belong in much the same way that we are powerful when we feel loved. For millennia, and among many people still, there was no separation between Mother Earth and her family. And then, quite recently in fact, some of us left home to colonize other places, patching over the wounded dysfunction by retreating to our heads and creating rationalizations of dominance to explain it. Education systems were created to perpetuate the myths. In many cases, children were and still are required to leave home to go to school, one purpose of "cells and bells" schooling seeming to deprogram human beings from their sense of self (autonomy) *and* their sense of place. Those of us who were uprooted are trying to find our way home, now, in the hope that it won't be too late, wondering how to become part of a place again, looking around and asking, who else lives here? Turning to Indigenous neighbors and asking, "we got lost—how can we learn what it means to be human again?"

Human beings are capable of learning, creating, gathering their regenerative power, and using it to repair the world around them and to make the worlds called "home." If they feel out of place, they can't thrive. A tree, too, needs certain conditions. You won't find many Black Gum trees in northern New England, at least not yet. For humans, a sense of place is a very personal thing, and it doesn't necessarily happen in predictable ways, but there are some patterns. One is a sense of emotional and physical attachment to the environment of a place, natural or not. Beauty, awe, comfort, sensory perceptions (a friend said she missed the smell of cooked nuts from the food truck outside her building in New York City) all count. An affinity for the forest, or a tree, the beach or a waterfall, a particular playground or park, all of that counts, too. Reciprocally, we need the place to know us. Are we wanted and needed there? Do we feel we belong? Are we stewards of Black Gum trees or Salamanders or Mangroves? Are we carefully keeping our favorite buildings from coming down and going in the dumpster? Of course our relationships with people play a part, too. Do we belong in the plurality of cultures in this place? Are we accepted and needed and loved? Are we working to keep our community whole? Are we claimed and named and is our way of learning guided by the place?

There are differences in how we feel our sense of place, too. For example, a person might not feel that any particular location is their "at home" place because their sense of belonging comes from other people and not a specific location. Or they call plural places home. Some may be deeply affected by dislocation and others re-root easily. For some, the power of place is all about a sense of belonging to a community's shared identity. In Caguas, Puerto Rico, home of Major League Baseball Hall of Fame catcher Iván "Pudge" Rodriguez, they say the place "tastes like baseball."[4] Can you taste it? Then Caguas has claimed you as its own. For others, it's about deep culture, how people ARE in the world, that maybe they can't even describe. Deep culture turns up in more visible things, too, like favorite foods, or music. Place is personal, emotional, and relational.

I want to consider my older-than-human relatives, too. They are also given to favor a specific place, having adapted over millennia of millennia to its specific character. What will happen to them if the environment changes faster than they can adapt? Can they (or we) survive out of context?? What can we do as educators (formal and informal) to contribute to the place-based well-being of all at this time of ecosystemic crises?

Displaced While at Home

As you may have noticed in the last chapter, I like to look at what small children do in order to learn about human nature and how to realign with it. They are the champions of Biophilia, which literally means "love of life." They can watch leaves for hours, crawl around in the grass chasing crickets, gasp with surprise and awe at fireflies, and play in water until they are shivering. They pat the flowers and some learn to pat the bees, too. Small children usually have a deep connection with place, and their interrelationships within it define them. There are specific trees that Elliott climbs in. If he moved away, he would have to reset. It would feel like a loss. There are specific neighbors Annabelle greets. What would Fabián do without his garden and his seeds, his hens, and the abuelos who are teaching him how to make medicine? We all watch over the kids. If they moved away, we would all feel the loss.

School is usually the first step away from a sense of place. For one thing, the classroom spaces are usually not filled with very much other life than human, and even that is constrained—by thick walls, long straight corridors, and uniform furniture. In my elementary school, we were forbidden from going into the woods during recess. My first and last experience with forgery took place because I broke that rule, probably to climb a tree, another punishable offense, and I put my parents' signature on the letter of apology the school made me write. I assumed that my parents would think the whole thing as ridiculous as I did—I climbed trees and played in the woods all the time. They were not happy about my choosing to become a child-felon over it, though. In typical schools like mine was, students are passively taught to disregard Earth and those who work with her, to detach from the rhythms of life in favor of bell-driven schedules.[5] Those who are aligned with the curves and flourishes and diversities of life are condescended to and discriminated against as odd, other, and deficient. In order to "succeed," one has to decontextualize at the schoolhouse door, "perform" at a specific pace and with a specific formality in language (set by White men long ago) and excel at playing an incoherent game in an unreal world.

There is little awareness of the wider world while in school. Most students are not thinking about where their energy comes from, for example. In Middlebury, Vermont, it took a student to apply his own systems awareness and do the math. Vermont is one of the greenest states, partly because half of its power comes from "clean" hydropower from Quebec. But student Will Ebby, a conservation biology major, followed the chain. He found that the "clean hydropower" calculation does not take into account how much CO_2 and methane is released into the atmosphere from the nearly six million acres of flooded and decaying forests in Canada, or the moral cost of the destruction of Indigenous food sources and displacement of First Nations peoples.[6] Ebby is working to identify energy sources and advocate for practices that are actually "clean."

 **Mending News!**

Living School Building Excels at the Three E's

There's a school in Gladstone, NJ that prides itself on its ethics-based education. Interrelationship with Nature seemed like a good way to teach ethical principles. When they added their first two buildings, they made sure they were LEED Silver certified, and planned for a lot of time outdoors. School co-founder Mark Biedron personally oversaw the construction of their third, the "living" building. Living Buildings are regenerative. They give back to the ecosystem more than they take out. At the Willow School, elementary-school-aged children are managing all of the building's systems. When they enter, they pass a tower cistern that collects rainwater to use for the toilets and for watering the plants. A large screen monitors energy and water use, and how much compost and waste they have produced. Kids decide when to dim the lights, open the windows and doors to the outside, and cut back on water use and waste for the day. They aim to have only one bag of trash at the end of *the week*. Biedron says, "not only are we learning all the time from Nature, the big E (for education), but we are also helping the Environment (Ethically) and our Economic bottom line is stellar. The living building covers the expenses that the LEED ones don't."

In schools that are aligned with life, such as the Verdi EcoSchool described in the last chapter, being present there feels coherent and whole, and like being "at home." What can we do as educators to explicitly encourage students to think contextually and act in relation to whole systems? Students who have been educated in place-based schools, and especially in living schools such as The Willow School in Gladstone, NJ, are far more likely to wonder about the sources of their energy and water, and what is happening with their food and waste. They are participating in life as partners, and in civic systems with a sense of responsibility and agency. Students like Will Ebby are much more likely to conspire with Indigenous people and fight for the rights of Nature. When the school is embedded in the wider living community, civic engagement is natural.

Displacement When Community Schools Close

Community schools are often the heart of communities, and they help to define it as a place. Austerity-level fiscal policies to meet the predatory debt crisis in Puerto Rico have also resulted in mass childhood displacement. From 2017 to 2019, just over a third (34%) of the schools in Puerto Rico were closed and their students scattered to other schools.[7] The mythology around school consolidation is that it is an effective cost-cutting strategy, and efficiency-minded Americans who look at everything in terms of "bulk pricing" and "scale" agree. However, there are considerable costs associated with consolidation, including infrastructure adaptations, transportation equipment, staff, fuel, and most importantly, child well-being. The quality of teacher-learner relationships suffers in larger schools and larger classes as each child gets less attention and less personalized learning. The larger school is more likely to rely on top-down efficiencies to keep everything "running smoothly." Many of the children in consolidated schools do not feel that they belong. Consolidation- and disaster-displaced kids, even from nearby schools, report being bullied by the ones who now have to share their teacher's time. Last-minute teacher reassignments disrupt nurturing relationships. The disaster mental health challenge that this whole picture poses is exacerbated by long commutes. Consolidation is not in any way better for the kids, unless they are able to get special services they need in their new schools that were not available in their old one. In Puerto Rico, there was a significant drop in attendance following the mass short-notice school closures in 2018, and many families described the impact on communities as being "worse than María."

In many US districts, consolidation in rural areas and charter and magnet schools in urban ones have for a while now affected children's sense of belonging in their communities. In *Between the World and Me*, Ta-Nehisi Coates explains that the school was not at all welcoming or responsive to him. "The streets were not my only problem. If the streets shackled my right leg, the schools shackled my left. Fail to comprehend the streets and you gave up your body now. But fail to comprehend the schools and you gave up your body later. Suffered at the hands of both, but I resented the schools more."[8] The push to get children out of their community schools and across town contributes to their sense that their own community is not adequate. Failed. The only way to succeed is to leave. What if we made community schools into the restorative hubs of well-being, intergenerational learning, innovation, and repair culture that they could be?

When US President George W. Bush and his Education Secretary Rod Paige set out to use standardized testing to "close the achievement gap," they couched the scheme in civil rights terms. As a thinly veiled push to close and privatize public schools, the tests themselves, matched with vouchers and "school choice," became the main weapon of cultural and physical displacement in the mostly urban United States. Instead of investing more heavily in schools that were struggling, "No Child Left Behind" (NCLB) and Race To The Top test results penalized and then closed or "reformed" schools that were "failing." Blaming teachers and emphasizing deficits, the majority of schools labeled "failing" or "underperforming" held students of color, and students just learning English. The sense of community and place built around the school was layered over with shame. Parents entered lotteries and prayed to have their child accepted to a charter school with better equipment and smaller classes. Many walked away in tears as their child was doomed to stay "at home," a place that they now believed was intrinsically incapable of offering what a commute across town on a train and a bus could do. They may have been right, but only because place- and cultural belonging and brilliance as a source of strength were deliberately undermined and devalued. Those schools were struggling because of systemic and historical underinvestment in the schools and the communities, not because of deficient teachers or less bright students.

Displaced Ways of Knowing and Being

Curricula and methodologies that are rooted in place and culture are more likely to thrive, like plants in their home conditions. Universal curricula generated far away usually doesn't fit well. It aspires to being "neutral," which means that it is not culturally responsive and shifts to the default narratives, which in the United States are White male dominant. It also feeds the shaming assumption that the most reliable knowledge only exists outside the community itself. The western industrial model of education with which we are so familiar today prioritized monocultural uniformity and set out to assimilate or eliminate other ways of knowing and being, using both physical and cultural/social displacement as key strategies (Figure 6.1).

In 1872, John Gast created this painting for engravings in western travel guides. Called "American Progress," it shows displaced bison and Indigenous people fleeing before a tide of White settlers in wagons, stagecoaches, plows, ships, telegraph wires, and trains.[9] Above it all hovers a spirit representing Progress, White of course, and wearing the star of empire on her forehead, in a White shift implying innocence. In her hand she holds a book with the only word in the painting: "Schoolbook." She embodies the power of schooling to uproot, in the name of "progress." Early frontier schools and reservation schools were run by missionaries, who were infamous for their wide-ranging and violent strategies to convince Indigenous peoples that their own spiritual beliefs and holistic worldviews were merely superstitions and that there was only one morally good way to live, dress, speak, and think. By the end of the 1870s, the Carlisle School had opened to become the template for hundreds more schools that

FIGURE 6.1 John Gast, American Progress, 1872
Source: Reprinted with permission from Autry Museum, Los Angeles; 92.126.1

forcibly removed thousands of children from their families, separated them from the land, and sent them across states to live suffer, work, learn, and conform to the European-American monocultural ideal.

Similarly, students in territories outside of the United States gripped by American colonialism found themselves displaced at home, forced to attend schools that required them to leave their own cultures at the door, and encouraged to feel contempt for themselves and their own families. The original caption to Dalrymple's cartoon (Figure 6.2) states, "School Begins. Uncle Sam (to his new class in Civilization): Now, children, you've got to learn these lessons whether you want to or not! But just take a look at the class ahead of you, and remember that, in a little while, you will feel as glad to be here as they are!" Local teachers had to be "re-trained," usually by White, English-only educators shipped in (literally) to do the job.

FIGURE 6.2 Louis Dalrymple January 1899 "School Begins"[10]

It didn't always go as planned, however. In Puerto Rico, local teachers were at first required to learn and then to teach in English, but that proved to be impossible without their consent. You have to want to learn a second language, and in addition, the scheme was difficult to enforce. Within a few decades, instruction officially returned to Spanish, although today English is a required course at all levels, even for students for whom any form of linguistic communication is a challenge. While Puerto Rico funds most of its education itself, it still must follow federal law and, like the States, continues to follow the typical western hierarchical methods of teaching, testing, and fragmented curriculum structure consistent with "Carnegie units," a unit of time corresponding to a "credit" in a specific discipline.[11]

When "Home" Is Complicated: Environmental Racism, Displacement, and Migration in the Age of Climate Disasters

Environmental racism demarcates certain areas and zones as "sacrifice zones," where polluters congregate with relatively unregulated ease. Government neglect, "necropolitics," and outright disrespect results in humanitarian crises related to "slow" environmental disasters, such as undrinkable water in Flint, Michigan, and Peñuelas, Puerto Rico, repeated and ongoing oil spills in the Gulf of Mexico, fracking "accidents" in Pennsylvania, coal ash poisoning in Puerto Rico, and the poisoning of fishes and marshes Indigenous lives and cultures depend on around the Great Lakes.[12] A slow or inequitable response to a sudden disaster can have a similar effect. These populations experience the loss of their place while they are still living there. For David Warren and the rest of the Ogiek people in the Mau Forest near Nairobi, commercial deforestation of the old-growth cedar ruined their coherent way of life. Nothing the Ogiek could do could stop it, until they succeeded in convincing the government to make it a conservation zone. What happened next was brutal. The law banned people, any people, from inhabiting the forest. The Ogiek had to leave their ancestral land. What was familiar and culturally defining became illegal and even dangerous, and without both financial and emotional support, there were no options. Today, Mau's remaining trees are still stolen. David wrote this: (English translation follows)

INGEPWAAT INGUPUUT AG CHOMIET-AP GONETUTIIIG CHEGEGERCHINIGEY!

Ginataagte imbareniig chelopoen ainyon, ag goriso-on wirireniy! Gokwoyote-ey gartasisieg solo-otey! Gopotey puywet en ng'asianet neeooow …

Orogenenyo-õn; Opote apwaat genyisieg taman ag gey chigipaa, imbarenichu lopoeen go ginyitoti getiig, sotiendos toritiig, gipkataisieg gopõldoos en isawanit nenegit ag iyu …

Emuroo!

Woi gising'oy gay emey, 'gugo ag gogo' en iyeloo …

Omune! Omune!

Omune somogigetu ge-giyuu, mawõ otoamech rupeet, momi pesiet negiyãm emet geserpenech …

Ongemin getigaap gipkaa, omu gigegeer gosê-ey, ogemin en MUGULELWE-ÊG.

English translation

RETHINKING POWER AND LOVE ON NATURE'S REGENERATIVE TEACHINGS

I was staring at a bare land, wind whirling along, picking pieces of plastic bags and hanging on its way towards the upper part, small particles of soil disrupting my awe …

My awe; I am trying to think of fifteen to twenty years back, when the same open land was densely populated with trees, birds chirping, frogs in the nearby swamp croaking …

Whoops!

How beautiful it was, the rainbow view in the background …

Why! Why!

Why can't we put back the forest the way it was, we never starved, we never went dry when we were young …

Let's plant indigenous trees, the ones we saw diminishing; let's do it from our HEARTS.

By David Warren, Youth from Ogiek community, living alongside Mau forest in Kenya.

FIGURE 6.3 David Warren (at left) teaching children about planting indigenous trees

Today Warren is working hard to create a nursery for indigenous trees, so that big reforestation NGO's don't just install vast quantities of fast-growing plants from some other place (Figure 6.3). He uses his journalism and speaking skills to advocate for a just return to his home in the Mau Forest and his role as a forest steward. Even if it happens slowly, this kind of moral betrayal and violent displacement, with all the grief and anger and futurephobia that goes with it, is no less traumatic. Your classes are likely to be filling up with students who have been displaced by climate impacts and land hoarding that they did not cause. Do they share resonant experiences with others, maybe adults, elders, or other youth, in the community? How can you connect them to authentic work in their new communities and old? How can you engage with your students in community activism in safe but authentic ways? They need to know that the school or university is doing what it can to keep them environmentally safe.

 Mending News!

Compensation for Residents of Flint

The state of Michigan eventually settled the $626 million-dollar class-action lawsuit on behalf of the residents of Flint, Michigan. Over 50% of the residents are Black, and 40% live below the poverty line. The KWA pipeline, a cheap replacement for a defunct water system, poisoned them with lead, while the state repeatedly ignored warnings and complaints. Now, every child, everyone who paid a water bill, certain businesses, and adults who can show harm will have access to compensation. Since attorneys are claiming close to a third of those funds, residents are setting their sights on the banks that underwrote the deal in the first place.

Jeremy Williams's book is called *Climate Change is Racist*,[13] and he provides plenty of evidence to make the point. Climate change affects everyone, but definitely some more than others.

While wealthy, mostly northern, mostly White countries are contributing the most to increasing global warming and pollution as they acquire greater wealth and consume more of the Earth's resources, they remain generally "climate privileged," or the least vulnerable to the impacts of climate change and degraded home environments. But that privilege is held by a small percentage within the polluting countries, too. Within the United States, one of the largest polluters, the vast majority of people displaced by climate change impacts are poor Whites and people from marginalized or colonized communities, many of them Indigenous, Black, and Latinx, counting hundreds of thousands of Puerto Ricans. African-American member of his school's Green Team, Raymond Woolery from coastal Brooklyn asks, am I next? "My Mother grew up here and never experienced the unrelenting summer heat and mild winters, ash from wildfires, flooding which seem "normal" to my brother and me ... . I am on the frontlines of this climate emergency—at the mercy of those melting ice caps and rising sea levels. I truly hope it's not too late." Wealthier, mostly White Americans have the resources to take up residence elsewhere, and often can choose when and where they go, buying up multiple "investment properties" and creating housing crises in the process. Other people may have such a strong cultural and social attachment to the place, an abiding interrelationship with the land, that they stay, even as the home they love becomes uninhabitable. When they DO have to leave, it is often in disaster crisis mode, where their living situations are untenable. It is up to all communities today to innovate ways to support migration—in consideration of the basic rights of all people to have a home place. The concept of home and away could be a k-12 curriculum and design strand, another "naming," a gift to you from your community.

Crossing Borders

Migration is how species survive on Earth. In many places the human-built fences and borders and highways and mist screens, the walls and fragmentations disrupting necessary biospheric migration are starting to change, in recognition of the importance of movement for animal survival. Historically, humans have been mobile, too. Most people know that human migration populated the planet from Africa over tens of thousands of years. Within bioregions, human migration and nomadism, even semi-settled life followed seasonal patterns and occasionally permanently abandoned ecosystems that became unlivable. Humans today are even more mobile, and generally for the old reasons—either they pull up roots and move on to seek work or because their home is inhospitable.

One day soon we will acknowledge that impenetrable borders will do the same thing to humans that they do to animal migrations—they ultimately result in massive suffering and death. Some significant innovation is needed here, to address the problem of the nation-state and the nationalist borders that go along with it. Climate citizenship calls on us to be pluralistic planetary citizens as well as citizens of our own nations and bioregions. In her essay, "Becoming a Climate Citizen," Kate Knuth writes that the very concept of climate citizenship implies belonging to a community and protecting the "sacred trust between the individual and the collective." The climate crisis calls on us to exercise the right (and responsibility!) to hold the collective accountable through "a dynamic process of consent and dissent. Climate citizenship involves taking on the work of ensuring that mass human migration does not lead to mass human rights abuses."[14]

The sense of choice, as well as transportation and communication technologies, allows for a certain kind of long-distance sustenance, but un-belonging, "I be longing," as one friend put it, separation trauma, homesickness, and a feeling of loss at being uprooted and divided still occurs. The new land may represent new and safer opportunities, but the traumas remain. In *My Grandmother's Hands*, Resmaa Menakem reminds readers that "we've been trained to think of the past in terms of a written historical record. But events don't just get written down; they get recorded and passed on in human bodies." The separation from place can even track in our epigenetic code. "Our bodies retain and re-enact history."[15] Officially, the United States has a history of violence against others' sense of place. Is this an enactment of their own traumas of dislocation? Displacement lives in our bodies and has the potential to override all cognitive thinking. How can educators build place-based healing into the curriculum, too?

How Educators Can Invite Students Home

All over the world, all communities have life in common. We are all expressions of our interrelated ecosystems and the community cultures within them. Our community ecosystems, while they look and feel and smell and sound different everywhere, just like life itself are made up of connected, nesting communities within communities. An educators' job, truly their expertise in this time of climate disasters, is in cultivating "befriending and tending," and citizenship at all of those layers at once. Groups or teams, classes, schools, neighborhoods, ecosystems, and Earth. Belonging and citizenship at all of these levels generates power-full agency, energizing and empowering generations of humans to continue the Great Transition away from the narratives of separation and extraction and toward justice no matter where they are. The stakes are high, but educators are expert community builders, and so we can start there. If we are going to teach students to be good citizens, of their community, their ecosystems, and their planet, we might slow down a bit and be explicit and intentional about what that means in the age of climate disasters.

Let's look at just one example, of a Head Start program (never too early to begin with place-based regenerative learning) in Chicago, called El Valor. This place-based environmental project in Chicago combines safety, parent involvement, migration, civic action, and early childhood learning. El Valor, organized and facilitated by Mike Rizo of the US Forest Service, engages mostly Mexican-American, often recently immigrated kids in observing butterfly-friendly plants and trees and learning about seeds and pollination in pre-school and Head Start programs. With their parents in tow, they seek different species, look for butterfly larvae, and make culturally celebrated monarchs in paper and papier maché. Soon they graduate to making and monitoring monarch butterfly habitats, learning all about migration, seeking and finding monarch eggs, and caring for them until they are ready to fly back to Mexico. They gather expertise, and perspective on their own migratory paths. I asked what they do with their learning once they go to school. One student responded, "I am an expert on how to raise the monarchs. Since I already know how to do it, I can help my teacher." The sense of belonging, efficacy, and agency he had gained empowered him into a position of expertise and leadership among his teachers, and made him feel needed and relevant in his new community.[16]

A community is simply a group with a common purpose, and often that purpose is connected to a sense of place. People become attached and attuned to the well-being of their communities—the ones where they live and the ones they've left behind. When María hit Puerto Rico, many Puerto Ricans living in the states came home to help out, including Hall of Fame baseball players Jorge Posada, Iván "Pudge" Rodriguez, and Carlos Delgado to name just three. The children involved in the community of care with the monarchs in El Valor are totally attuned to the monarchs now, as well as to the urban ecology that supports their migration. Like the kids at Verdi Eco School making the chrysalis experience more personal, they can relate. Butterflies are powerful symbols of transformation and strength. How can educators build a sense of community out of the shared purpose of citizenship, or caring for community? We can let the community tell us.

When the Place Generates the Curriculum

What would happen if, like El Valor, teams of learners and educators "read" their curriculum (as well as themselves) as an expression of the place? South Side Chicago is home to many immigrants as well as being on the monarch migratory path. It is also a food desert and after generations of redlining and other discriminatory practices, home to some of the worst air and water pollution in the region. What environmental/social issues do people care about where you live? Themes such as food, water, air, shelter, energy, health, and concepts like expression, leadership, cultures, and flourishing identities would emerge, in which depths of scientific and societal knowledge could be achieved, and through which health and regenerative agency leading to social justice could be energized.

Climate change is not something happening "out there" in the environment, safely squared away as the subject of environmental science classes and the "NextGen" science standards alone. It's about humans and relationships, and what it means to thrive in communities/ecosystems of care and change. Every "subject" needs to converge holistically around the issues the place is naming. In this, climate change is no different from any other complex problem. It needs to be viewed from many perspectives, and citizens in the age of climate disaster need to be able to think coherently at both local and global scale. Rebecca Solnit writes about the "communities that arise in disaster." They are communities with a strong sense of purpose holding them together across all kinds of fragmentation.[17] Many of them dissolve as the disaster recedes in memory, sometimes snapping back to a situation even more inequitable than before. What if we could capture that unifying energy (love), connect it to our sense of place, and join with our students and community allies in ongoing and regenerative place-based climate justice action?

One thing you could do immediately is this little exercise. Go outside. Get comfortable (dress appropriately), under a tree or in a sheltered sunny spot. Begin to think about your area of interest, and what your students seem to be interested in. How could you use what you see before you to teach what you teach? To connect it with what your students would like to learn? Maybe use some co-design thinking for this. Ask them to tell you about a time when they really felt like they learned something. Where did it happen? Under what conditions? When did they feel like they were really part of a team? Brainstorm learning experience and learning space possibilities with kids, parents, colleagues, and other local friends. How can the natural environment teach social and life lessons you want the students to experience? Who are the allies in the community who could help? How can the students co-create the project and own the power of design within it? What are your learning goals for the students within it? What are theirs? How will confronting surmountable roadblocks and barriers create generative struggles resulting in growth? How will you know about the depth and shape of that growth? How much space is there for students to lean in their own directions and nourish each other as well?

Your Class as a Safe Contact Zone

The elements of belonging and place fit tightly together. As educators and parents, our Power of Place driving question is this:

How can we create a sense of togetherness and vitality in a trusted community and environment, building on varied cultural backgrounds and experiences and on life itself? What if we thought of "school" not as a building but as a safe contact zone?

In bioregional and anthropological/sociological thinking, there are zones of accelerated change and dynamism called contact zones, where diversities stimulate active growth and feed potential for change. In *To Know the World*, Mitchell Thomashow describes a "contact zone" as "any place where you encounter difference, and these will inevitably be places for both cooperation and tension."[18] School is kind of like that already, in the sense that it is an opportunity to bring lots of different perspectives together. Highly individualistic competitiveness in schools rears its ugly head at about the same time that the state testing begins, and kids want to know if they are "measuring up." They'll soon want to acquire individual grades on group projects, because they don't want to be "held back" by that new kid over there, instead of seeking ways to include and incorporate that "other" kid's unique potential in order to succeed. Relationship-building activities are devalued because they "don't count," and frequently students find camaraderie and belonging in teamwork only in activities outside of class. My students admitted that they had trouble listening to their "new" and "different" peers, and definitely had trouble learning from them.

The Hofstede Scale[19] of national/cultural individualism and collectivism is important to think about here, as climate migration will bring many more cultures together in our contact zones. While of course we want to avoid stereotyping and flattening out complex cultures with oversimplification, it is still revealing to note that the top five countries leading the pack for collectivism (group-orientation and relationships essential to both business and learning, collaboration over competition) are all Latin American countries (Guatemala, Ecuador, Panama, Venezuela, and Colombia). Imagine how out-of-place a student from any one of these places might feel plopped down into a regular classroom in the United States, the leader in individualistic tendencies? The other four of the top five individualistic countries are Australia, the United Kingdom, Netherlands, and New Zealand. Notice a trend? And the next NINE are all European countries as well. All just to say that cultural trust does not just happen, and students will not be able to access the power of place and belonging unless their educators proactively create a trusting community in class.

Many societies value welcoming strangers very warmly. It would be unthinkable to ignore someone because they were new. But this is not all on you, educators! Enlist students in the effort! If students are young, enlist their parents, too! Belonging is built with civic responsibility and relevance. What if your students rotated through important jobs like Welcomer, or Carer in Chief, or English language helper, as Susie Wise's book *Design for Belonging* (2022) suggests? How could opening rituals and closing ones, with breathing, harmonizing, reflecting, and sharing activities led by kids help to make people feel welcome and connected through life to the whole community? Author Ralph Ellison wrote, "If you can show me how I can cling to that which is real to me, while teaching me a way into the larger society, then and only then will I drop my defenses and hostility, and I will sing your praises and help you to make the desert bear fruit."[20]

We can begin with our stories. We are all experts in our own experiences, and our experiences shape our identities. Deep listening and noticing require time and space and guided practice, though children seem predisposed to empathy (fellow feeling) and compassion (the drive to act on it). Storytelling and "storylistening" build trust, but some people aren't ready to share even part of their stories until there is even deeper trust, particularly if there is pain and displacement in their past. How can we cultivate a culture of caring and make sure our community is a trusting one? What would happen if every child had at least one adult or older kid champion besides the teacher?

 Mending News!

"Community Faces: Humanizing the Immigrant Label"

Stories can be gathered throughout the community, utilizing photography and other art to illustrate or reflect or show connectedness. Exhibits can be guided by students AND their subjects, such as the project at New London, Connecticut's Interdistrict School for Arts and Communication (also an EL School) 6th grade exhibit "Community Faces: Humanizing the Immigrant Label" in 2018.[21] Visitors to the exhibit included those interested in learning about new populations, and the immigrants themselves. Music, food, and children facilitated the conversations. Humanizing mission accomplished! Spend a few minutes on the website watching the video, and don't forget to read the transcript of some of the comments.

Connecting With Communities of Knowledge and Wisdom

Meeting students where they are, connecting love and stories with belonging and place, joins all students with curiosity, mutuality, and understanding. They come to understand how to find the roots we share and value the different perspectives we bring as sources of knowledge and insight. Together, students are better able to pursue collaborative creative strategies to redefine success based on their common interests in life. Further, they are more likely to collectively pursue changes to enhance life and co-create a strong sense of place and rootedness wherever they go.

Why is it important to see communities important funds of knowledge, equally as important (if not more so) as outside agencies? For psychologist and educational theorist Lev Vygotsky (1896–1934), learning is a "socio-cultural process."[22] In other words, it doesn't happen in a vacuum, or because of a place-neutral school curriculum. Instead, the family and community context is what assists the child in making sense out of learning. For Vygotsky, social context is inseparable from cognition and meaning. For the teacher, his research is crucial, because it elevates the importance of place and culture in the learning process. If the educator is going to facilitate a positive learning environment, it has to be place based. Puerto Rican scholar Luis Moll took Vygotsky's thinking a step further. He viewed the students' communities as "Funds of Knowledge,"[23] that not only serve as filters for how the young people make meaning out of learning, but also as repositories of knowledge in and of themselves. Funds of knowledge are everywhere. Older-younger, intern-mentor, or just the guy at the corner shop—an educator can play an important role in vetting and nourishing community caring. This is not a new concept, but the importance of social networks in collectivity, community-building, and resilience cannot be overstated.

What if the students were viewed by the community as valued resources and contributors?

Try this critical first step in listening to the nested communities in and around the school. Learn more about the context and culture of the place, even if it is your own, from a stance of curiosity, respect, and with your "deer ears" open. Get a large paper map you can write all over, and learn your way around, even if it IS your community. Humans are a bit like cows … they follow the same paths that outline their daily routines all the time. If this is your community, find the corners you have never been to and talk to the people you never meet. Go to open spaces—parklike and not. Bodies of water. Map potential allies in learning—a zoo, library, park, gov't offices, senior and community centers, small businesses, and non-profits interested in the environment … as a starting place for building on the funds of knowledge right there in place. Notice environmental and economic threats and also areas that are thriving. At the end of the chapter, you can get another glimpse into what communities might do if they could create their own learning experiences named by the place itself, at Aula en la Montaña, in Puerto Rico.

Black Genius; Black Joy

Hundreds of schools and thousands of teachers who are moving in the direction of culturally restorative and sustaining practices do exist, although they are pushing upstream against historical oppressions, internalized shame, institutionalized political hierarchies, and little access to funding. Importantly, these educators have not given up creating ways to connect young people to their sense of place and cultural wealth. Is your classroom full of the joyful curiosity and intensity of multiple perspectives and is your curriculum holistic, historically wise, flexible, culturally welcoming, and sustaining? Does your classroom invest in creating its own culture of care and celebration of plurality?

In *Cultivating Genius*, scholar Gholdy Muhammad tells the story of hundreds of years of Black scholarship and literary genius, creativity, intellectualism, civic leadership, and virtue.[24] She makes the essential point that "history from Black communities tells us that educators don't need to empower youth or give them brilliance or genius. Instead, the power and genius is already within them." It is on educators as well as parents to help them come to deeply know and inhabit this ancestry and to facilitate their ability to draw power from their own cultural wealth. While *Brown v Bd of Ed* was a significant step forward in access to opportunity, it came at the cost of a certain kind of cultural safety. Black schools were closed, and most Black teachers lost their jobs. Some relocated and were hired elsewhere, but a significant cultural displacement took effect. Black students were sent away to schools where they were frequently un-welcome, and where mostly White teachers delivered a curri-culum that was, well, mostly White. Every teacher should read Dr. Muhammad's book, and with it Dr. Zaretta Hammond's *Culturally Responsive Teaching and The Brain*,[25] Rethinking Schools' anthology *Teaching for Black Lives*,[26] and Shane Safir and Jamila Dugan's *Street Data*.[27] It is definitely okay to put this book down while you absorb those. The sense of place and belonging as a regenerative power relies on trust, at the deepest, cultural level, and so knowing how to establish cultural safety, expand cultural competence, and sustain cultures is a prerequisite. The cultivation of cultural genius and the embodiment of ancestral wisdom is an essential taproot feeding the power of place. Conspiring together to connect and correct harm, befriending and tending, deep listening, telling our stories, standing up to-gether arm in arm, and finding our way to our universal Mother Earth as the ultimate fund of knowledge and wisdom—this is what makes us the powerful expressions of place.

In her own beautiful reflection on place, bell hooks writes that in her youth in Appalachian Kentucky, "Nature was the place where one could escape the world of manmade constructions of race and identity ... . Nature was the place of victory. In the natural environment, everything had its place, including hu-mans."[28] Enslaved African-Americans, whose ancestors were ripped from their own home places and transported to com-pletely new ecosystems, sustained their interrelationship with Earth, who kept them alive, and within that love created new communities among themselves and alongside Indigenous people who shared their understanding of their interbeing with the land. This was how they survived. hooks continues, "Certainly it must have been a profound blow to the collective psyche of black people to find themselves struggling to make a living in the industrial north away from the land. Industrial ca-pitalism was not simply changing the nature of black work life, it altered the communal practices that were so central to survival in the agrarian south. And it fundamentally altered black people's relationship to the body ... . Estrangement from nature and en-gagement in mind/body splits made it all the more possible for black people to internalize white supremacist assumptions about black identity." Healing these fragmentations demands a return home, a re-rooted naturalizing of human bodies. From a social justice standpoint, stopping violence against Mother Earth's body might begin to heal the man over woman binary, too.

Coming Home to Earth

bell hooks recommends, "Wherever black folks live, we can restore our relationship to the natural world ... ."[29] There is the history, for example, of members of the Great Migration carrying seeds with them, sometimes sewn into their dresses for safekeeping, after the manner of their ancestors, who had woven seeds into their hair as they said good-bye to their homelands. Of growing persistent window-boxes of herbs and greens and flowers, and of course today with thriving and nourishing community gardens emerging in lands deemed "unproductive."

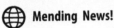 **Mending News!**

Soul Fire Farm Offers Soul-Mending Reconnection in Upstate New York

Grown from Afro-Indigenous roots such as honoring relatives (the land), uprooting racism, and seeding sovereignty in the food system, Soul Fire Farm "works to reclaim our collective right to belong to the earth and to have agency in the food system. We bring diverse communities together on this healing land to share skills on sustainable agriculture, natural building, spiritual activism, health, and environmental justice. Our food sovereignty programs reach over 160,000 people each year, including farmer training for Black and Brown growers, reparations and land return initiatives for northeast farmers, food justice workshops for urban youth, home gardens for city-dwellers living under food apartheid, doorstep harvest delivery for food insecure households, and systems and policy education for public decision-makers." https://www.soulfirefarm.org/

We humans draw strength from our belonging to Earth and sharing in her wisdom, and show it in the ways in which we take up our responsibilities as neighbors in a living community of beings. Our thriving in the long term may ultimately rest on the ways we can combine the best of the community and cultural knowledge we have access to—learning from the violence of the past still haunting our present to listen curiously and humbly, and to re-root ourselves where we belong.

Earth-Linked Well-Being

COVID-19 got many people outside more, and news about climate change spurred transformative and life-oriented conversations, encouraging more denatured people to find their way back. This beginning is already helping them to redefine health and success. "If we think of life and health as a dynamic and co-evolving mutuality that links cellular health to individuals→family→community→ecosystem→bioregions→planet, we come to see that systemic health and well-being might be a much more appropriate indicator of success [than any material measure beyond security]," wrote Daniel Christian Wahl[30] in *Designing Regenerative Cultures*. Forest bathing, nature therapy, walks in the park, team wilderness challenges, bioregionalism, biophilic architecture (of schools, too!), circular economics, re-indigenizing, relocalizing, and renaturing (rewilding) are just a few of the unlearning and relearning movements taking hold in the world. Those humans are learning that our Mother Earth still loves us in spite of it all.

In the first decades of the 20th century, there have been at least 14 scientific studies of the benefits of connecting with our full, natural living communities. These include many different aspects of health benefits, from improved immune response and lowered cortisol to better blood pressure and cancer resistance; from improved concentration and unleashed creativity to sharper cognition. People report feeling more contentment, happiness, and openness to others, among other indicators of wellness such as a renewed sense of agency and purpose in one's life.[31] Books like Florence Williams's *The Nature Fix: Why Nature Makes Us Happier, Healthier, and More Creative* and Wallace Nichols' *Blue Mind: How Water Makes You Happier, More Connected, and Better At What You Do*[32] must seem very basic to the mostly Indigenous authors represented in the five-volume anthology *Kinship: Belonging In a World of Relations*,[33] but the good news is that sales of books such as the latter, as well as hits on websites and blogs about Indigenous education, are escalating rapidly. There is more collaboration going on between federal agencies and First Nations and more and more academic institutions and communities are seeking to learn from them in climate/social justice and resilience work, and to advocate for the land, land return, and land rights.

Make Room for Awe and Wonder

I always thought teaching ecology to young kids would be the most fun ever. I came close, in the garden, but high school kids have had more time to be acculturated to life in the head, and are less demonstrative of their awe. Young kids are still able to be amazed. Let's see if we can hold onto that. Awe fills us with beauty, joy, and wonder. Wonder opens up curiosity and expands our sense of possibility and our place in it. It can bring gratitude and moments to savor and share. I make a practice of challenging kids of all ages (yes, elders can be kids in this way!) to find one thing that moved them each day and make a record of it somehow. Take a few moments to dive in to wonder: https://www.youtube.com/watch?v=ZxmDC4XynA4 Research shows that experiencing natural beauty and awe makes us happy, and sharing it makes us even happier. Why IS that, I wonder?

There is surely an emotional or spiritual connection (love?) to Earth that draws humans beyond ourselves and also deeper into ourselves in these moments. We feel it in our bodies. Our body brain loves these deeply connected times, so many people crave them, and don't feel well without them. Robin Wall Kimmerer tells a wonderful story about a moment in her field ecology class when she finally got the opportunity to take her students outside. After a long day spent observing and recording and discussing what they were seeing, she felt like a failure. She thought she had failed to teach them the "science deeper than data. I'd told them all about how it works and nothing of what it meant. How will people ever care for the fate of the moss spiders if we don't teach students to recognize and respond to the world as a gift?" As they hiked down the mountain in the dusk, the students spontaneously and softly sang "Amazing Grace," harmonizing verse after verse. She wrote, "I came to know that it wasn't naming the source of wonder that mattered, it was wonder itself."[34] Connection came at a level much deeper than data.

When our sense of place is associated with a specific location and with the awe and wonder and love and security we may feel there, it becomes an important part of the story we want to co-create with our students. We might say that an educator's role will be to create the conditions for wonder and connectedness outside the classroom walls, in a garden (in the ground or on the roof), a park, an aviary, the stream, the woods, and that is absolutely essential. When we think about community-building and the power that comes from our connectedness to the Earth, it helps to generate energy and creativity for ecosystem-based learning in all of our classes and interdisciplinary collaborations. At the deeper level, though, we are really building a sense of community, of interdependent civic engagement and responsibility with all beings.

Shared Experience and Purpose Builds a Sense of Place and Community

Sometimes a community is entirely built around shared experiences. In the case of Science Moms,[35] Dr. Rosimar Rio-Berrios brings her experiences in Puerto Rico to the table. "Rosi" and the Science Moms use humor and wit, along with common sense and good storytelling to help other moms and children to understand and talk about climate change, storms, drought, and other disasters. She is a professor of atmospheric science, and so she knows how bad things could get—but she finds strength and power among the 80% of moms in the United States who want action to mitigate climate change … for their kids. What if you had a chapter in your community, and allied with them to co-create caring-community-building efforts like El Valor?

After the double hurricanes in Puerto Rico, the Mariana community, on the mountain hit first in both cases, stood up and stayed standing. Their identity (based on place and history) and social networks were strong. Family ties make a web over the map. Christine Nieves Rodriguez demonstrates what we can learn about place and community from those in the center of the storm. She writes,

> The state will likely fail to protect its people—the way the US and Puerto Rican governments have repeatedly disappointed us. But communities like mine have always been tending to the root, telling the history erased from books, doing the most radical thing, especially for a colony: building a foundation based on dignity, abundance, and self-love. These are the examples we need to be looking toward. This is the infrastructure to invest in.[36]

Dignity, abundance, self-love, the love of Earth, from our ancestors and our fundamental love for others. Look at your students and your children. Do they feel this in school? Biophilia is innate, as is human fellow-feeling. Children feel affinities for animals and plants and other children. They are excited to be in a community in school. They look forward to meeting people from other places and cultures. Schools are "contact zones," where differences meet and overlap. Our job as educators is to be sure that it is a safe place to be, no matter where you are "coming from." The power of place begins with belonging. The 6th graders Kelsey Gualberto, Laura Hallisey, Zoe Kargl, and Jamie Ahrens at the Myrtle Philips School in Whistler, British Columbia belong to their place (See Figures 6.4–6.7). They took it upon themselves to create banners protecting their home, and are working together to advocate for climate justice, protecting Earth and the animals because she is inseparable from us. They are eco-citizens, helping others to thrive—all of this builds community and energizes the regenerative power of our sense of place.

FIGURE 6.4 Western Pine Elfin Butterfly. Protect our wilderness

FIGURE 6.5 Grizzly Bear. Protect our alpine meadows

FIGURE 6.6 Bull Trout. Protect our wetlands

FIGURE 6.7 Wolverine. Protect our glaciers

The Power of Place in the Age of Climate Disasters

Acknowledging the power of place as cultural as well as environmental helps us to understand that the climate crisis is not just an assault on the natural world, but also an assault on people, and this fact needs to underscore all climate education. According to mainstream news media, children will know *at least* three times the number of "sudden shock" climate change disasters during the next few years as their grandparents knew. If they don't have to evacuate and relocate once in their young lifetime, they will be fortunate indeed. According to the language of the Green New Deal,

> Climate change, pollution, and environmental destruction have exacerbated systemic racial, regional, social, environmental, and economic injustices, disproportionately affecting Indigenous peoples, communities of colour, migrant communities, deindustrialized communities, depopulated rural communities, the poor, low income workers, women, the elderly, the unhoused, people with disabilities, and youth.[37]

Look at our communities and classrooms. How can understanding and cultivating their sense of place (both cultural and environmental) and belonging help them? They can experience "physical" displacement without leaving home, by witnessing the environmental degradation of their neighborhoods and feeling the encroaching environmental impacts on their physical and mental health. When sudden shocks happen, psychologists and sociologists who specialize in disaster recovery identify six keys to emotional stability: safety, routine, accurate information, social connectedness, cultural sustenance, and self-efficacy. Social connectedness, cultural sustenance, and agency. All three come from the power of place.

So far, this book has focused on the agency that comes from integrating power and love, integrating the elements of the self, and understanding our role in creating good relations with all beings and in belonging, to Earth, to our communities, and each other. The regenerative Power of Place arises from the "optimization of the whole community as a crucial lesson in how life creates the conditions conducive to life."[38] For this, young people need to feel the strength of biocitizenship. I'm not talking about papers and numbers and passports. I mean how we participate in the formation of what Mitchell Thomashow calls "constructive connectedness" within the greater biocollective.

Here's a simple community project to get started, which supports municipal place-making efforts, and so will likely be supported by the municipality. Municipal communities intentionally set up "place-making" experiences and events to help residents feel more connected, more like this is "their place," more like they want to belong here. Music and the arts rarely fail to energize and reconnect to life through the most basic, emotionally human sense of place. The universal power of the arts to heal, to protect, to defy, to lead, to express what it means to be human, to be connected, to be seen and heard and essential to a place and its cultural communities is well researched and understood. Music especially provides opportunities for a diverse group to share and bond. Similarly, the opportunity to retreat, to "hole up," to just be silent for a while to think, to slow down, to reflect, to recharge, is also a universal need. Both contribute to safe, trauma-informed settings and provide opportunities to harmonize together (see Chapter 5). A simple cleaning-up project, accompanied by a neighborhood music and art weekend event, can help to create a shared sense of place, and belonging through purpose. When our place looks like no one cares, people won't care, writes Dubar Smalls, Jr., from Brooklyn. "People don't realize that we ARE our environment. How we are *for* it shows what we think of ourselves. There are some neighborhoods where there is a lot of trash around. This not only makes people feel bad about the neighborhood, it encourages a stereotype about them ... . We could change how we feel about our neighborhood and dispel those stereotypes by taking better care of our neighborhood environments. People often say you are what you eat, and the people you hang out with make up who you are. I would argue that you are your environment as well." Youth of all ages can team up as climate citizens and stewards of the environment in their home place. I agree with Dubar. I think it will make everyone feel a little bit better.

Imagine ...

Dream a little. Imagine your existing school building as mostly empty, as teams of adults and students are out and directly engaged in sustaining life through place and community learning. Some are working with officials and other allies to monitor and reduce waste at school, or monitor and reduce energy use in public buildings. Some are with the planning department, helping to determine whether or not the water treatment plant will need to be moved and where, or how best to improve public access to open space. Another team is meeting with an architect about a new senior center, doing soil testing and traffic studies, as well as interviewing elders about intergenerational activities that could take place there. Some are monitoring the wastewater and helping their community comply with state and federal regulations, as well as testing for lead and other contaminants. Others are studying the migration patterns of butterflies and birds and designing appropriate habitats. Some are developing new circular business strategies with local businesses, while others are running their Culture of Repair shop.

 Mending News!

Culture of Repair—It's Just What You Do

My parents were guided by the wartime adage, "Use it up, wear it out, make it do or do without." Post-war, Americans prided themselves on being consumers, and being able to consume a LOT. Shopping malls became the key attraction. Expectations for bigger and more and especially newer things grew. And grew. Now, we waste millions of tons of useful items, each of which comes at a cost to Earth. Culture of Repair provides teaching tools to encourage makerspaces, libraries, tech schools, and everyday schools to become community hubs of repair, restoration, and reuse. Learn how things work and circular entrepreneurship at the same time! https://www.cultureofrepair.org/

Some are co-creating a living culture center that will celebrate the stories of all who live here and be engaging for both kids and adults. Others are developing local histories with elders and co-creating adaptive parks and playgrounds. There are some teams at school, some in the computer lab investigating the best ways to build and sustain community and sense of place in a digital setting, some using the tools in the makerspace, and others doing research. Some are working with teachers to understand the biochemistry of water or the history of the Black literary conference that took place there or the languages of the first people in the area. Some teams are communicating with their partners in other parts of the world. Others are experiencing "firsthand" through virtual reality an exploration of the ocean floor. Teams are working with teachers on their plans for a public art project or honing their presentation for the school board advocating for more inclusive learning opportunities. Imagine that the schedule is set by the learning experiences and not the other way around. Imagine that the technology is used to support the learning and not the other way around.

Imagine an 11-year-old, her snappy brown eyes lit up as she explains how her "school in a coffee shop" works and how awesome it was to create the best-selling flavor EVER, and how much she learned about history through the spice trade and ecology from where cardamom could grow and how important it was to certain cuisines and cultures, who did the growing and processing of it and what their lives were like in our current food system, how the food system would need to work to supply that and the other (secret) ingredients, the economics and social dynamics of it all … Wait. This is not a dream. The kid is real. She's part of an Embark learning experience (not called a School) in Denver, CO.[39] She collaborated with her learning guide to create those learning goals. And she will reflect on the other skills and dispositions she is gaining in her coffee shop school. This kind of regenerative learning is happening all around us. It needs to be normalized.

Engaging students in deep place-based learning like this is not in addition to the curriculum. It IS the curriculum. This is the curriculum named by the place itself. Learning about the world we live in happens best when we are in it. What are the opportunities in your place? Collect examples of where you see it working in lots of environments so that you can get ideas. They won't transplant and replicate directly but might help shed some light on your own possibilities. Check out Workspace Education

(100 Roads), Springhouse, and Operation Breakthrough[40] for three very different examples. There are also books full of examples, especially *Trailblazers for Whole School Sustainability*,[41] Sobel's *Place-Based Education: The Power of Place*, and at the elementary grades, *Worldwise Learning*.

The place- and community-based learning I am talking about is not without structure, constraints, and critical evaluation. It has (co-created) frameworks and protocols and even (co-created) rubrics. It defines depth. One of my favorites of the latter comes from OneStone (a free private design thinking school in Boise, Idaho). They call it the Disruption BLOB, Bold Learning Objectives.[42] You might also wish to consult Resource 5. It grows and changes with experience and co-creation. But all of the iteration happens in the living context of Places.

What could begin at home as age-appropriate chores which bear real consequences, emerges in school as a willingness to take on civic and cultural responsibility as well. Young people are essential to the "social capital" of any community or ecosystem they are in. Being essential and relevant is what makes a person WANT to belong. Students disengage from or act out against a monoculture that displaces them. Conversely, most students are excited by learning experiences that enable them to act on their passions *and* do something that matters to the community at large. If they are new to the community, what better way to join and learn about their new place? The school/university and all of the students associated with it can be valuable community contributors, bringing all of their expertise and varied perspectives to bear on shared challenges. How does it feel, when you're young, to be a trusted resource in your community? This is the power of place, and what brings meaning to their lives, allowing their whole beautiful selves to flourish in "dignity, abundance, and self-love."

The power of place, that feeling of belonging and rootedness that enables a person or people to stand up together and make demands, to drive change, and to be resilient, not only comes from having an authentic role to play in the real community. *It comes from having the sense that you are indispensable to it.* Your presence is not only valued, it is *named and needed*. Being relevant and responsible and relied on is the taproot of citizenship. It is also the essence of regenerative eco-citizenship. Nothing is wasted; every part is needed, and all is focused on creating the conditions for more life.

Seeds for Planting

Places claim and name us because we belong to Earth. Why not listen to what our place is asking us to teach? Instead of disciplinary "subjects," why not engage with community challenges such as food, water, air, land, and community identities?

"Place" is nesting and interrelated communities within communities, along with cultural and relational belonging. The effect of western education has been widespread displacement in both the literal and metaphorical sense. Make your learning space a safe contact zone.

Eco-citizenship projects are shared restorative experiences that can start at the youngest ages (El Valor) and can re-root people who have had to migrate. In this way, we become inseparable from our roots and indispensable to our communities and ecosystems. We belong.

Learning to co-create communities of care and connection, restoring our relationships to each other and the land, practicing agency through engaged citizenship—all this is the healing power of place.

Notes

1 Limón 2018.
2 Myers 2022.
3 Kimmerer 2020.
4 Bridges and Martin 2022.
5 Bigelow 1996.
6 Ebby 2022.
7 Caraballo-Cueto 2021.
8 Coates 2015.
9 Gast 1872.
10 Dalrymple 1899.
11 In 1992, The Carnegie Foundation for the Advancement of Teaching found the fragmentation of disciplines and the emphasis on seat time to be harmful and declared them obsolete. They are still prevalent in most typical schools and colleges.

12 Riley 2022.
13 Williams 2021.
14 Knuth 2020.
15 Menakem 2017.
16 Rizo 2022.
17 Solnit 2009.
18 Thomashow 2020.
19 Hofstede et al 2010.
20 Ellison 1995.
21 Learn more about the ISAAC program here. https://eleducation.org/resources/community-faces-humanizing-the-immigrant-label-a-better-world-project
22 Lev Vygotsky (1896-1934), a cognitive psychologist, is also known for his identification of the "Zone of Proximal Development," or the area between existing development and what a child is actually capable of with guidance or collaboration with more advanced peers.
23 Puerto Rico-born Luis Moll is Emeritus from the University of Arizona. The *Funds of Knowledge Toolkit* based on his work is essential for thinking about community- or place-based learning projects. https://www.k12.wa.us/sites/default/files/public/migrantbilingual/pubdocs/Funds_of_Knowledge_Toolkit.pdf
24 Muhammad 2020.
25 Hammond 2015.
26 Watson, et al Eds. 2018.
27 Safir and Dugan 2021.
28 hooks 2009.
29 hooks 2009.
30 Wahl 2016.
31 Thompson 2018.
32 Williams 2017 and Nichols 2014.
33 Van Horn et al 2021.
34 Kimmerer 2020.
35 https://sciencemoms.com/
36 Nieves Rodriguez 2020.
37 Green New Deal: https://www.congress.gov/116/bills/hres109/BILLS-116hres109ih.pdf
38 Wahl 2016.
39 Learn more about coffee and bike shop learning experiences here: https://www.embarkeducation.org/
40 Springhouse Community School https://springhouse.org/ and Operation Breakthrough https://operationbreakthrough.org/ For more information on Operation Breakthrough, see https://www.gettingsmart.com/2022/01/12/operation-breakthrough-changing-life-trajectories-from-birth-to-citizenship/?utm_campaign=coschedule&utm_source=linkedin_company&utm_medium=Getting%20Smart&utm_content=Operation%20Breakthrough%3A%20Changing%20Life%20Trajectories%20From%20Birth%20to%20Citizenship
41 Seydel, ed 2022.
42 https://onestone.org/

Batey, Bomba, and the Regenerative Power of Place-Based Learning in Puerto Rico

Dr. Lugo, a co-conspirator on a research project to study youth agency and well-being in the teeth of climate change (and co-founder of Aula en la Montaña) texted early one morning. "What if we call our listening and wisdom circles *el batey*? I want to reclaim strength from our Black ancestors, who found there a space of solidarity, resistance, and reimagination of possibilities." *El Batey* is indeed a Taíno word, indicating inseparably the physical, emotional, and spiritual aspects of an outdoor gathering place and of gathering itself—to play freely, to talk, sing, dance, and laugh, for ball games and ceremonies, storytelling, giving thanks to and celebrating the Earth and Life. *Batey* was one deeply rooted concept the Spanish conquistadors and missionaries could not erase. Caribbean history scholar Luís Martínez-Fernández said to me in the spring of 2022,

> "*Batey* is one of my favorite words. It not only sounds beautiful, it was the powerful beating heart of Taíno societies and later, of the maroon societies of people who had freed themselves from enslavement–the *cimarronaje*. Into those spaces of self-liberated freedom and wholeness, Afro-Puerto Ricans brought their African languages of message-drumming and dance–and Bomba was born. Bomba drumming echoed in the hills far away from the low-land sugar plantations, where plantation masters feared the drumming that communicated messages they couldn't understand. There, it was banned by law and punished. In the hills it not only flourished as networked encoded communication among *cimarronaje*, it symbolized solidarity and resistance."

DOI: 10.4324/9781003215806-8

Much later, when the time came to resist American colonization, Bomba took on yet another life, connecting mountain communities of the interior in rebellion, when other forms of communication were easily intercepted and dangerous. In perhaps the most clearly articulated "power of place" significance, co-design thinking conspirator and engineer Pamela Silva Díaz, herself a bomba drummer, says that there is an indescribable mutuality and connection between Dancer and Drummer, Dancer and Drum, Drum and the Mountains, the Mountains and Beauty, Dancer and Drummer and Mountains and Beauty, Past and Present, in totality creating a powerful sense of solidarity for what is right and resistance to what is wrong with the world.

Bomba is not taught in colonial public schools. It was the *first* thing taught in Aula en la Montaña. Older residents appeared from off hillside porches to show the kids that they still had the moves. Aula's possibilities, shared through *bomba en el batey*, became the whole community's possibilities—a Learning Community in solidarity, energized by the power of place.

It is worthwhile mentioning that the COVID-19 pandemic in the archipelago was preceded and has been accompanied by a series of earthquakes that damaged a substantial number of schools, especially in southwest PR. The effects on those with lack of adequate resources for online education and high levels of special education needs has been severe. These communities have experienced limitations with the consistency of the electric grid and WiFi access which made connecting with teachers throughout the pandemic a challenge. A primary concern of this situation is children's access to quality education and the consequences of these challenges and repeated traumas on their socioemotional well-being. In the town of Peñuelas, 69% of children and youth under the age of 18 live under the poverty line, 58% of children live in single-headed households and 51% of households receive nutritional assistance (Instituto de Desarrollo de la Juventud, 2021). Overall educational levels are low, particularly for children's grandparents and women. Coal-ash air (and consequently water) pollution levels from the coal-powered energy plants near the shore are very high. All these risk factors set a concerning scenario for children's current educational progress and future prospects. Yet the sense of community identity, their excitement about their garden (Chapter 2) and reclaiming their connection to the land remains strong.

Aula en la Montaña (Classroom in the Mountains)

This section is by Dr. Eduardo Lugo-Hernández and Dra. Sandra Soto-Santiago

Amid this context, we developed the Aula en la Montaña project in collaboration with the community of Barrio Rucio, Quebradilla sector. Quebradilla is a beautiful sector that has a wealth of natural blessings and its people are kind, welcoming, hardworking, and tight-knit. This project brings together Non-Governmental Agencies (NGOs), the community, universities, and other volunteers to provide educational and socioemotional support for children. Aula is based on the Declaration of the Rights of the Child with a primary emphasis on promoting children's voice and participation. It also promotes deco-loniality, feminism, and anti-racism as core values of our pedagogy and community action.

Aula el la montaña consists of four-hour sessions every Saturday in the community to provide support and educational activities. It brings together professionals from diverse disciplines such as school psychology, clinical and community psychology, kinesiology, agroecology, solar energy, forest ecology, education, social workers, and speech pathology. We have been able to evaluate them with the aid of school psychologists and speech pathologists to design their educational experiences and draw from their strengths. We have also linked them with other services that should enhance learning and development.

Our teaching model (1) focuses on children's needs and interests, (2) promotes collective learning (Vygostky, 1978), and (3) uses a dialogic process necessary for praxis. Critical thinking is necessary to challenge the conditions that affect children's well-being, while empowerment allows children to have agency in their own destinies and creates the conditions for short- and long-term change.

We have partnered with Afrolegado, a Bomba group that provides historical and cultural education about Bomba in Puerto Rico (https://www.facebook.com/AFROlegado). *We also partnered*

with *Proyecto Agroecológico Tres Caminos* to implement an agroecology component with the children. This is consistent with our intervention model in the community which promotes food and energy
sustainability, connection to nature, and to our history. *Aula en la
Montaña* also places great value on physical activity as it enhances
physical and emotional development and potentiates learning.

Socio-emotional support has been a central aspect of our work.
With the collaboration of clinical psychologists, we have implemented
an approach to clinical intervention that takes into consideration
children's voices, cultural aspects of mental health and has situated
intervention in the community, making it more meaningful and per-
tinent. These children have suffered multiple traumas, including
hurricanes and earthquakes resulting in elevated levels of anxiety.
Children have learned strategies to identify triggers and manage anxiety related to climate change. This has helped them cope with
memories of these disasters. Older children have used their acquired
skills to teach younger children in the community. This was evident
one day when it was raining and a six-year-old boy with speech difficulties experienced anxiety. His sister, who previously had panic
attacks every time it rained, took the lead in teaching him breathing
exercises to calm down. These skills have also transferred for them to
manage other types of anxiety-provoking situations. As Paulina
stated: "One Saturday we practiced inhaling and exhaling with bub-
bles. Now I am doing it in my classroom when I have a test and that
calms me down".

The outcomes of this project have been positive and significant.
Children's voices and participation have been articulated through
purposeful in-person activities where they are included in the decision-
making process, project design, and evaluation. These experiences
included in the development of a children's COVID-19 prevention
guide with the Puerto Rico Public Health Trust that has been distributed in PR public schools. Two girls in the community met with a
Senator to express their views on child poverty. Also, some of them
have participated in TV interviews and written newspaper columns.
They have begun documenting their own experience in the community
and with Aula, using donated cameras. The message is clear: "Your
voice matters and can lead to concrete actions and change!" Children's
learning and academic progress have also been an achievement. Last

year all of the participants in the project were promoted to the next grade and they were able to maintain or improve their academic progress.

Overall, Aula en la Montaña has been a space for decoloniality, learning, and socio-emotional development. It has been developed in a backdrop where there is a dire need to achieve social justice and equity for children who have been severely impacted, not only by the pandemic but by other natural disasters and an economic crisis. The collaboration with the community, inclusion of children's voices and participation and the offering of services in the community (for children and adults) are key educational strategies that we must promote in the midst of the climate crisis. These will be vital moving forward to support children and youth who can become agents of change and who help us work towards equity and social justice in Puerto Rico.

References

Brusi, R. and I. Godreau. 2021. "Public Higher Education in Puerto Rico: Disaster, Austerity, and Resistance." *AAUP Journal of Academic Freedom*, 12. https://www.aaup.org/sites/default/files/Brusi_Godreau_.pdf

Caraballo-Cueto, J. 2021. "Aprovechamiento académico y el cierre de ecsuelas en Puerto Rico." Technical Report. https://www.researchgate.net/publication/343636485_APROVECHAMIENTO_ACADEMICO_Y_EL_CIERRE_DE_ESCUELAS_EN_PUERTO_RICO

Eckstein, D., V. Künzel, L. Schäfer, and M. Winges. 2020. "Global Climate Risk Indez 2020: Who Suffers Most from Extreme Weather Events? Weather-Related Loss Events in 2018 and 1999 to 2018." Briefing Report. Germanwatch. https://germanwatch.org/sites/germanwatch.org/files/20-2-01e%20Global%20Climate%20Risk%20Index%202020_10.pdf

Freire, P. 1970. *Pedagogy of the Oppressed*. New York: Seabury Press.

Instituto de Desarrollo de la Juventud. 2021. "Indice de bienestar de la niñez y juventud de Puerto Rico." https://www.juventudpr.org/idj/indice-de-bienestar-de-la-ninez-y-juventud-de-puerto-rico

Vygotsky, L. S. 1978. *Mind in Society: The Development of Higher Psychological Processes*. Massachusetts: Harvard University Press.

7 The Power of Purpose: Motivation, Flow, Depth, and Meaning

How does our "why" (our compelling sense of purpose) motivate depth and persistence as well as belonging?
How can we create the conditions for purpose-driven learning?
As educators, parents, policy makers, how can we think of learning spaces as infrastructures of meaning?

Community-Led Resilience in Puerto Rico

Trigger Alert: What follows is the story of a community flooded during Hurricane Maria, in Toa Baja, PR. I am not using anyone's real names, to protect their identities.

After an extremely loud and windy night, Paola gave up on sleep early. She swung her feet over the edge of her bed and onto the floor. Suddenly she was fully awake. Her feet were in six inches of water. On the second floor. There had not been any power in her village in two weeks, ever since Hurricane Irma had wiped out much of the unstable power grid. She knew from word of mouth that Maria was coming, but there had been other storms.

DOI: 10.4324/9781003215806-9

They had weathered Irma, right? Besides, where would she go? She thought of her neighbors. Above the howling of the wind and the banging of debris, she thought she could make out screaming that sounded like it was coming from an animal. Out on her balcony, she could just make out her neighbors' horses, exhausted, thrashing and fighting to keep their noses above water. She looked down the street to her cousin's house. It was completely gone. Most of the other roofs were missing or torn back.

Paola's neighbor had left a fishing boat tied to his shed that he sometimes let her use. Most of the shed was gone, but the boat was just floating there, tied to the remains, like a message. She swam to it and pulled herself in. Even though it was day now, Paola still calls what happened the longest night of her life. After the gas ran out, she rowed and paddled from house to house, yelling and banging on the walls and on the little metal boat itself. Is anybody in there?? Eduardo y Yasmina-a! Mina-a, están aquí?!? Silvia, dónde estás?!? Papí, papí, dónde está mamí!! She knew some houses were empty from after Irma, but then some just *seemed* empty now. She desperately wanted to find everyone. The muddy water on the second-floor balconies was up over the railings. Paola's elderly neighbors were taking care of their grandson while the child's mother had gone to take care of his other grandmother. He was five. They had put him on top of the refrigerator under the last of the roof and held him there, their arms up, clutching the note they had written to his mother while the water rose to, and then above their waists. "Lo sentimos. Te amamos." We are sorry. We love you.

The boat full of people was hard to row, but everyone helped, bailing out water and paddling with their hands. They knew their only chance was to go to the school, the highest spot in town. It was only 19 feet above sea level, but it was several feet higher than their homes and it had two floors and bathrooms. Schools are usually shelters, too. They fought to get there, promising others out on their balconies and rooftops that they would come back for them. Paola's cousin Silvia could not stop shaking. Her parents were in the old wooden house that had floated away. When the school came into view, somebody started screaming, "no no no it's locked, it's locked, the gate is locked!" Another boat full of people had already arrived, making the grim discovery. They looked around. Someone saw a fragment of a wooden gate with a metal bar on it floating by. Paola said later, "we would have pulled that bar off with our teeth." They pried open the lock and went in. Paola and Eduardo went out to get more of their neighbors.

Community Resilience Design Lab students from neighboring Bayamón listened intently. Interviews were sometimes tearful and always followed by hugs. It was over a year later, and still there was debris and many homes that had not been repaired. You could see the flood line high up on the walls. By walking around the neighborhood and talking to people who were at home, Paola introduced the students to many of her neighbors, who each told about their experiences during and after the storms. One opened a community kitchen in her yard and her neighbors pitched in to cook what food they had. Another, a church leader, hosted a play space for children so their parents could "clean up" and "manage getting food and water and batteries." Paola and her friends cleaned out the community center. Today she serves her community every single day. Long, exhausting days. When I asked her why she does that, she said it feels like it was what she was called to do. She said she might "fly apart" if she did not follow through, even when she was beyond tired. She said it was her life.

The design lab students used co-design thinking to work with Paola and her neighbors to generate community-designed resilience solutions. They dug into the history of the place and learned about their strong community identity and cohesion. They explored climate science together and worked with a geoscientist to assess and map the risk level of various threats. They questioned the US Coast Guard[1] about search and rescue practices, how heavy the helicopters are, and why they couldn't land one on the school roof (and don't actually need to). The students returned to the village to ask the harder questions and confer about what they had learned and share ideas. They sought out other community leaders known for their community-led activism, like Christine Nieves, from Mariana.[2] They generated ideas reflecting their commitment to listening closely and their willingness to find opportunities for change. These ranged from securing a promise from the PR Department of Education that the school would remain open in the event of an emergency, to mapping a more efficient evacuation and rescue plan. They included ideas for flood-proof houses, and in some cases, earthquake proof, too. One, called "Casa Calma," looked a lot like a big boat in a hammock. And they discussed with a local university's health department how to set up a mobile fun station that would double as a stigma-free mental health clinic. As they presented their ideas together with their community partners, they realized they had grown together. Some of the students returned regularly to mentor and play and work in the garden with the kids.

During the two-weeks' intersession for design lab there was perfect attendance and not a single "behavioral issue." There was always music, because some students said they "needed music to think." There was one moment when we really needed a pep talk—as the prototyping made the ideas take shape, there was a hiccup, a hesitation in the momentum. When we reflected on their collective reluctance to keep going, we realized that they were wondering if their ideas would match the depth of feeling, the sense of purpose and the meaning behind their every move. They were having a crisis of efficacy. Can we actually do this? Will anything change? Three adults stepped up and called in that day (with a video chat made possible by a student standing on a chair in the corner holding up a hotspot) to remind them that they are loved and trusted. That they are part of something bigger than themselves, yes bigger, and that meant it was holding them up, too. That they matter and their ideas matter, too. "Why can't school always be like this?" one asked. Another shared, "Now I know what I am here to do. I am going to be an attorney who can help people move to safer ground." A third reflected, "I never thought learning about climate change was important. Now I see that it is." And this was when Ayana, one of the main inspirations for this book said, "After the storm, I couldn't speak. All I could do was draw. I just drew and drew. Design Lab has given me my voice back. Now I know I have ideas that can help."

Jane Goodall is often quoted as saying, "You cannot get through a single day without having an impact on the world around you. What you do makes a difference, and you have to decide what kind of difference you want to make." In the age of climate disasters, education needs to move purposefully if it is going to co-empower students and educators to find their purpose through futurephobia and what psychologist Bob Doppelt calls "the Traumacene." At the most basic level, education systems need to have purposeful, explainable, and actionable reasons to do what they do. These reasons need to be relevant and rooted. With more teachers leaving than entering the profession, with young teachers staying an average of 2.5 years, with absentee rates of all school participants skyrocketing, a reframing of purpose and a redesign of practice is needed posthaste. If your school or university has not chosen what kind of difference it wants to make yet, now would be a good time to join the global movement, the Great Transition, while there still is a chance to recruit teachers to do it, and to join kids and communities together in purpose and change making. Young people have asked their institutions to advocate for their environmental safety. Meg Wheatley has said that there is no greater force for changing the world than when a community decides what it wants to do. When we DO listen closely and deeply to hear the heartbeat, the music behind why a sense of purpose adds so greatly to our regenerative powers, we find that there is a strong positive force motivating purpose: and that is "meaning."

There is a lot of talk about "purpose," these days. It is a word with many definitions, and none of them entirely fulfilling, but we do have a sense of it. Education innovators like Tom Vander Ark and Emily Liebtag took a gratifying swipe at it with the overview and compendium of "purpose in action" examples called *Difference Making at the Heart of Learning*.[3] It is subtitled *Students, Schools and Communities Alive with Possibility*. Alive with possibility. **Alive.** Jeremy Lent's *The Web of Meaning*[4] lays out clearly why "our why" is the embodiment of our chance to weave our thread into the web of life, and so now we will pick up some of his threads to guide our thinking in this book, too. Educators know what Purpose is not: it's not short answers to narrow questions, it's not "is this going to be on the test?," and it's not the ages-old answer, "because you might need this someday." The dispiriting frequency of those moments is what makes educators and students alike feel that school systems today are purposeless, and for many, destructive of hope. For those reasons alone, we should dig into it—with a purpose.

What Is Purpose?

Let's start with the most basic elements of "purpose" and spiral into its powerful center: nothing other than the regenerative and vital meaning of life, or as one dear friend puts it, the "radical joy" of being alive.

Purpose signifies intent. It describes an action that is not accidental. If you do something "on purpose," you *mean* to do it.

Purpose signifies presence. If you do something "on purpose" or "with purpose," you not only intend to do it, you are paying attention to it as well. Combining intent and attentiveness can express a mindful practice of the power of purpose, according to Hutchins and Storm in *Regenerative Leadership*, the Power of Purpose might come from helping us see "beyond what might be holding us back and focus not so much on what we do but the way we do it." This can set us on a path of growth and giving, according to Leider's Power of Purpose.[5] "How do I choose to grow today? How do I choose to give?"

Purpose indicates some level of persistence. If you say you are doing something "with purpose," it suggests that you are determined to see it through. Such as our project here, unpacking purpose "with purpose." Stay with me. Sena Wazer's purpose-full story could shed some light on persistence, even to the point of having to change the way she engages with her purpose in order to keep at it. Now, at 18, she is graduating from college as a Truman Scholar and is also leading the Connecticut chapter of the Sunrise Movement. What can we do to support and sustain the creative sense of purpose of youths like Sena Wazer (read on) and Javier Moscoso (pp 270–272) and David Warren and the others who have contributed to this book and beyond? As you will see, a purposeful and passionate journey is often not an easy journey. What nourishment can we provide as educators? To you, from Sena Wazer:

The catalyst for my environmental activism was a book my parents read to me when I was five years old. It was a book called Ibis, based on a true story, in which a whale got caught in a fishing net, but was lucky and got rescued. I loved the story, so I asked my parents to read me the author's note. The author's note said that most whales don't get freed; they die. At five that really upset me, so I started crying and whining. I continued to cry and whine for three days, until my dad couldn't take it anymore, and said "If you don't like something, then do something about it." And so I did: I started to take action to protect whales and the ocean.

At six, I did a Public Service Announcement on the local radio station, and started going to the local farmers market to hand out information about how people could help protect whales and the ocean. Although I took some breaks, I generally continued with some form of activism focused on whales and the ocean until the age of 14.

By that point, I had already started to become more interested in broader environmental activism, as well as focusing more explicitly on how environmental degradation affects people (for example, I talked about microplastics and their effects on both sea life and humans). Then, I read about the UN Intergovernmental Panel Climate Change. While I had always known that climate change was a thing, and that it was concerning, this report laid out a timeline for how long we have to prevent the worst consequences of the climate crisis. The timeline shocked and scared me. Similar to when I was five, it also propelled me to act.

Within a few months, I had joined Sunrise Movement Connecticut (CT), a statewide hub of the national Sunrise Movement. I soon became involved with organizing climate strikes, and in early 2020 lobbying for bold climate legislation in CT. Over the next two or so years I learned a lot about climate activism, environmental justice, and political change. That growth was really positive and something that I'm extremely grateful for, but I also learned about some of the less positive aspects of being a youth activist.

During that period of time, I was driven mostly by fear and anger. I was afraid of what climate change meant for me, my sister, my

friends, and really our generation as a whole. I was angry at politicians, corporations, and others with immense amounts of power and
privilege who sat by and did nothing while the climate crisis accelerated and began destroying communities. While I am still afraid
and angry, being driven primarily by those two emotions was not good
for me, and I would hazard a guess that it's not good for other people
either—especially young people. Being driven primarily by those two
emotions propelled me to a place where I was constantly overwhelmed,
fearful of the future, and burned out—struggling to stay on top of the
work that was required of me in my position with Sunrise CT.

That period of time was really challenging, and there are moments
when I relapse to that place of panic and burnout, which I've come to
associate with that form of climate activism. However, what I've also
come to understand over the past few years is that climate change will
not be solved overnight and so if I want to be in this fight for the long
haul, to continue fighting for what I believe is right, then I'm going to
have to be intentional about the way I fight, and what drives me.

I know that this might seem kind of obvious, but when the narrative around climate change is always one of dire urgency, it can be
hard to take the time to consider how you want to fight. However, I
would argue that considering how you want to fight is absolutely
critical precisely because of the urgency, scope, and sometimes,
seeming insurmountability of the climate crisis.

As such, over the past year, I've taken time to re-evaluate how I
want to fight. I've taken time to consider what I want to be my main
motivator. Although I'm still angry, and I'm still afraid, I don't want
that to be my main motivator anymore. I also can't do this work
sustainably if that is my main motivator. Instead, I'm choosing to be
grounded in community, in love, and in hope.

As a young activist, I'm often surrounded by many other people
who care about the same things I do. While some activist spaces and
organizations are really negative—only ever focusing on how much
more work there is to do without acknowledging the wins, some spaces
are really beautiful and caring. There are certain activist communities
that are able to both acknowledge how much more work there is to do,
while also celebrating our wins and keeping faith in something better.
They chose to continue believing that we can create a safer and more
just world, even when the present moment might not feel hopeful.

Those are the communities and spaces that I'm choosing to be a part of and surround myself with.

That's part of what being grounded in community and hope means to me. Another part of it is understanding the communities and people that I come from, and drawing strength from those. I, like many others, am first generation American. My mom's family fled to Canada during the communist regime in Romania, and then later she moved to the United States. While the circumstances that forced my family to leave Romania were extremely difficult and caused my family and many others a lot of harm, I have been lucky to grow up with a connection to many beautiful parts of Romanian culture. By leaning more into where I come from I've found another way to ground myself in community, love and hope. Not only through doing traditional activities, such as cross stitching, but also by re-membering that I am not the first woman in my family to fight for what I believe in, and it is because of the strength of those who came before that I am where I am today.

Finally, I am grounding myself in the place and community that I grew up in. While CT might not normally be thought of as a farming state, I was lucky enough to grow up on a small farm in CT, surrounded by a community of other small farmers. For many of these farmers sustainability was one of their main focuses, and so without even trying I had the chance to learn from them what it looks like to farm in a way that is beneficial to both people and the en-vironment. By remembering my connection to the farming commu-nity that I was and am a part of, it is a way to stay connected to the place I grew up, to fight for climate action from a place of care and love for the land and those around me, and to stay hopeful, because these are real people putting sustainable methods into practice every single day.

By grounding myself in these communities, and fighting from a place of love and hope, I am finding a way to continue fighting for what I believe in, in a way that is both authentic and sustainable. While each of us have a different story and background, I hope that by sharing this part of my story I can encourage other people, and especially other young people, to consider how to fight for what they believe in, but in a way that is sustainable and positive for them and the climate movement. Sena

"To consider how" to engage with purpose is something that educators can guide. Connection with place and community, land and purpose can feed the bold hearts of the activists.

Purpose can also be a means to an end, gratifying need and satisfying desire. The task orientation of this sense of purpose can easily become self-serving or linearly transactional. Jeremy Lent would call this kind of purpose "hedonistic," as it fades as soon as the need is gratified and then the person is left purposeless until the next desire needs to be gratified.[6] The majority of my high school students felt that their purpose was "more about the grade than the learning." They had internalized, already by 9th grade, that the purpose of school was to get them into "the right" college. For them, "everything counts now," so schooling had become transactional, their relationships with educators and each other performative, their extracurricular activities just the necessary cards to gather in the game. The joy in learning and even their sense of self gained through intrinsic motivation was drained away. They felt stressed and suspected that they would never be good enough. After college admissions, many had a severe crisis of being. They called it "senior slump" but it was plainly symptomatic of their loss of themselves and the exhaustion that this emptying out had caused. They had done what they were told, achieved what they set out to achieve, but could not answer the question, What is the purpose of ME?

If the praxis of learning has no clear (and meaningful!) purpose, it becomes frenetic but boring "busywork," both stressful and exhausting. The pressures of the system I taught in eclipsed students' awareness of their own interests, passions, or compassions. Even if they had gotten into the college they wanted, they felt bereft of being able to "do anything that matters." Rachel Wolfe began the research for her documentary *Losing Ourselves* as a junior, based on her awareness of herself and those around her. You can tell by the title what it is about.[7] (https://www.youtube.com/watch?v=D56fpXZw8cc) To them, it felt like a loss, not something they could come home to with recentering coherence and calm. And if this was happening among students whose privilege afforded them every opportunity to look forward to their future ... .

I noticed that those students who engaged fully in socially valued and heartfelt actions like resettling refugees or cultivating a giving garden, were much better off emotionally, no matter what happened with college admissions. In 2008, William Damon researched teenagers' attitudes while in the process of creating his book, *Path to Purpose*. Only about 20% of high schoolers felt that they were "purposeful and dedicated to something larger than themselves." The rest, [about eighty percent] reported feeling either "adrift, full of big dreams but lacking any plans," or overwhelmed by the frenetic pace of purposeless work.[8] "Why do they keep telling us to wait to use what we've learned?" one frustrated junior named Chris in our Student Caucus demanded to know. "I'm alive NOW!"

Kiran Bir Sethi, whose Design for Change movement also appears in Chapter 2, found herself frustrated by the shallow and lifeless education her children were receiving, and disappointed by the message that schools implied—you have to be rich and powerful to make change happen. In 2009, her now famous TEDTalk launched the Riverside School and Design for Change movement.[9] Today it's a global "We Can" phenomenon, engaging school-aged children in authentic change making using a simple Feel, Imagine, Do, Share empathy-based collaborative design process. They can share their work globally and connect with others. Here is a story about the impact Design for Change was having (https://www.youtube.com/watch?v=Et35L0pvyrw&t=3s) by 2014, not only on the emotional and cognitive development of the children involved but also on the attitudes and mindsets of the wider community. Children do not need to wait until they know everything to create positive change, and now their whole communities think of them as valuable resources. Their numbers are growing. Place-Based Learning and deep Project Based Learning also engage students in local action with purpose, such as Trevor Saponis' Metlakatla Annette Island regenerative ocean farming project described in Chapter 5, as well as the purpose-full work of community gardens and teaching farms in Puerto Rico and the United States, wilderness and river rights such as the 6th-grade advocacy in Whistler, clean-up projects in coastal

Brooklyn, and advocacy for climate change curriculum that also supports mental health in Connecticut. What do your students care about? That's what will keep them coming back and motivate them to persistent action.

Critically aware minds should also ask, *whose* purpose is a given action serving? How do we prevent saviorism in community service and competitive credit-taking? These aspects undermine trust in both civic and professional life. The fact that purpose can take on a hedonistic and performative element needs to be looked at critically in all civic relationships. Stating your purpose upfront as well as what you hope to give builds trust. Now that colleges and universities are seeking demonstrable and meaningful "service to community," beware of performative purpose. Performative purpose is an outgrowth of the emphasis on highly individualistic competition in schools. Whose interests is that "required community service" actually serving? What about the ethics involved in some extractive social entrepreneurship and research programs in universities? Purposes may be in conflict. The purposes of a dozen multi-billionaires who own half the world's wealth, and their narrative of continuous economic growth led by a network of virtually unregulated global corporations could destroy life on the earth. Which global narrative of purpose is your school system serving? A regenerative or a degenerative one?

Purpose calls out relevance. If something has no acceptable or valued purpose, it is often considered irrelevant and useless. We've seen that learning that has a clear and relevant purpose readily energizes and engages students, teachers, and communities. We should also think critically of this as "relevant to whom?" And what is the *nature* of its value in association with its relevance? For example, in colleges and universities in the second half of the 20th century in particular, STEM (Science, Technology, Engineering and Math) fields at first had money flowing in because of the Cold War arms and space race, and then because they could appeal to the purpose of "marketable" skills.

FIGURE 7.1 The Atomic Bomb, 1945: In the lab of human affairs
Source: D.R. Fitzpatrick, 1945 Reprinted with Permission from GRANGER 25 Chapel St.
Suite 605 Brooklyn

The apt 1945 cartoon in Figure 7.1 by D.R. Fitzpatrick predicts (in part) what happened: fields of study that explore the beauty of life and the meaning of being human (arts and humanities), and fields that explore coexistence and thriving (social sciences and education), have been underfunded, institutionally marginalized, and mocked as "soft." Today, there is considerable pressure in the United States (both cultural and economic) to study something like STEM that directly links to income, and then get a "real" job. Education departments are often "feminized" and placed at the edge of campus, viewed by most universities as little more than teacher training and certification centers. People in science-related and engineering fields typically have access to more funding than those engaged in social sciences and humanities. I'm not saying that science is bad or that people should all study the liberal arts.

What I am saying is that this market-driven, disconnected utilitarian view of purpose and relevance has not only robbed us of meaning and vitality, it has hobbled our ability to deal with a VUCA world of uncertainty. How will the de-emphasis on humanities and social sciences help us to address UNESCO's four greatest existential challenges confronting life on earth: climate change, inequality, breakdown of democracy, and fragmentation? Let's make it five if you believe, as Tom VanderArk, Emily Liebtag, and Jeremy Lent so ably establish, that artificial intelligence (AI) may soon be making decisions, taking actions, and replicating with very different purposes (algorithms) in mind than human kindness and global peace.[10] All five of these challenges require deep and meaningful consideration of complexity, aesthetics, ethics, interbeing, and systems of care that take into account what it means to be human in interconnectedness with all other beings, and our ability to reflect and change direction—to come back from the edge of the roof. How will we make sure that the metaverse isn't simply a repeat of everything that's wrong and that AI doesn't make injustice worse?? We have to make it purposefully relevant to change the narrative from global domination and continuous extraction for economic growth to an ecological and social narrative that reconnects our humanness to the purpose of life.

 **Mending News!**

Artificial Intelligence Helps, Too

For measuring and modeling, such as species biodiversity and migration monitoring, human-environment interaction and interest data, measuring leaks from pipelines, wells, and abandoned infrastructures, disease and heat and methane release mapping, disaster prediction and preparation, and for processing all that research data, artificial intelligence can't be beat. The question is always, who has access to the information and who can access the tools to get the information and solutions they need? Here's a related question to ponder. Will the metaverse allow humans to develop greater empathy for our older relatives? Could I be a tree for a day? Or a whale?

"Purpose" as a means to relevance is a distinctly linear way of looking at things, but it also makes sense. How can a student engage with learning when it seems disconnected from everything they need to know in order to engage with what they care about? Disconnection and irrelevance make learning purposeless. Students need to be able to answer the fair questions, "why does this matter to me?" and "do I matter to anyone else?" Javier Moscoso decided to study engineering as he saw his island home devastated by two huge hurricanes and then struggle to re-energize. In Figure 7.2, you can see him about to connect his very first solar nano-grid, completely independent of the privately owned and operated Unreliable and Exploitive Grid (electricity costs four times as much in Puerto Rico as it does in the United States). For him, having access to electrical power is synonymous (or at least analogous!) to being independent from colonial status. Access to power is, well, access to power. For Javier, electrical engineering is not separate from political power or the will to assist in co-empowered community resilience.

FIGURE 7.2 Javier Moscoso connects his first nano-grid

I was a senior in high school when Hurricane María hit Puerto Rico back in 2017. This event was for sure the key to my future decision toward heading to Mayagüez to study Electrical Engineering. Why? Because I viewed it as the only logical way for me to grow and experience the field of renewable and sustainable energy, particularly with solar photovoltaic (PV) systems. I am now in the last year of my bachelor's in electrical engineering at the University of Puerto Rico at Mayagüez. Having had the opportunity to understand what Puerto Rico is dealing with (needs, vulnerabilities, injustices, etc.) has really opened my mind. Ever since I started at the university, I've set myself to study and become involved in the discussion of alternatives that work and have an instant impact for the better of those who engage with them. From my point of view, the energy transition into more than renewable, sustainable sources of electricity should be complemented by a shift in our current patterns of how we consume. It should be accompanied by an energy awareness effort that is welcoming and interactive with those participating as to help assure why it is important and needed. It should be a process of understanding how we engage with energy systems today to rethink and set new and better ways for tomorrow.

I am very grateful and excited to be in conversations regarding Puerto Rico's energy future. I believe that a sustainable Puerto Rico is possible and it is the reason why I decided to become an engineer. I also am in favor of Puerto Rican independence and view the work I am doing as very political. For example, shifting away from fossil fuels and taking the bold step into guaranteeing accessible energy are both political actions. I consider that achieving energy security should be a pillar for Puerto Rican independence. I've recently become interested in plants and agriculture and see a combination of energy and food security as a vital part of any future sustainable development plans. In the end, electricity and food both provide us energy to keep us going. With this in mind, I consider there's a lot of potential for agri-voltaics as one of many alternatives to address the energy question.

I plan to help pave the way towards the energy transition that Puerto Rico needs to become sustainable and resilient in the face of vulnerabilities, crises, and disasters. Hurricane María showed us the fragility of our infrastructure as well as government responsiveness. Going to communities all around Puerto Rico makes you wonder how we're still here. Every time I leave a community (after a visit) makes me feel assured of who I am and why I'm in the spaces I am doing what I do. I've learned it is up to us to take initiative and make things happen. I am committed to work towards making Puerto Rico a more educated society in terms of energy systems to empower and lead the way towards the future we all want to enjoy. Through real-life experiences and education, we can analyze the past and rethink the present in order to imagine and create alternative and sustainable futures. Javier Moscoso, Mayagüez, 2022. While I was writing this chapter, the power went out again in Puerto Rico. For days. Javier's family was able to help their neighbors charge up their phones and laptops, as well as enjoy some light from his experimental mini-grid.

⊕ **Mending News!**

Culebra Plans to Go Solar

The small island off the east coast of Puerto Rico famous for its beaches was devastated by the hurricanes in 2017 and did not get electricity back for nearly *two years*. They have been busy rebuilding and redesigning their infrastructure so as to take advantage of the work of young electrical engineers such as Javier, high school students, and of community organizations such Mujeres de la Isla (Women of the Island) to create micro-grids around the island that will provide energy from the sun that powers all of life. A micro- or nano-grid system is much more resilient when it comes to storms and hurricanes because you can stow the panels safely away and put them back afterwards. Also, there are no massive solar fields where they could be growing food to eat. Culebra's goal is to be the first totally solar-powered island in the Caribbean by 2030.

Purpose Pushes Motivation and Learning Deeper

Having a good reason to do something can be called our "why." The closer the purpose is to our hearts, the more likely we are to engage, even when the going gets tough. We all know stories of people whose "lives were changed" by an experience or a person. I had a student whose baby sister had Type A diabetes. He knew from the time he was eight years old that he was going to study medicine. Similarly, the empathy and compassion in the air in the village as we shared stories of the hurricane motivated the design lab students to learn deeply, risk more, collaborate better, and gain a sense of future direction. The Oxford English Dictionary tells us that "courage" comes from the Old French word for heart, as the innermost seat of emotions.[11] As Meg Wheatley puts it, "we develop courage for those things that speak to our hearts.

Once our heart is engaged, it is easy to be brave."[12] Indeed, once the design lab students understood what mattered to them and they came to embrace this as a generative power, they could accept the trust of others (this can be very scary) and act. They were learning from the inside out, internally motivated, determined to make things better for all of them together. Without this motivation from the heart, without the clarity of direction it brings, without the assurances of a trusted team, we can become reactive and even fearful about change and uncertainty. We could become paralyzed by futurephobia.

When we engage students in work that matters and that they care about, they can achieve the flow that positive psychologist Mihaly Czikszentmihalyi studied. He found, that with internal motivation that came from the power of the heart, it is much more likely that a healthy sense of *flow* can be achieved, which is that moment of coherence when the spirit, body, mind, and heart are concentrated on something that carries meaning, and the result is an intensity of joy, creativity, and a feeling of total engagement with life.[13] To share this experience gives a powerful sense of belonging such as we saw emerge in the last chapter and will follow through the next ones. Think for a moment about the preschoolers who are now monarch experts who know they "will be able to help their teachers." They will not only democratize the power structure in their classroom, but they will also follow their curiosity deep. Purposeful, motivated curiosity leads to indelible learning. When purpose is driving learning, learners of any age will stop at nothing to learn more. Critics are concerned that place-and-purpose-based action learning might not prepare students well enough for the tests. Quite the contrary, Ayana Verdi (Verdi Eco-School) says that they don't do anything to prep for state tests, which they must take once a year to continue the scholarship support, and her students do better than they did in regular school. They look at them as a fun diversion. People who are used to the accountability of "real" life, of the high stakes of butterfly migration and the thriving of flying cousins, who love problem-solving challenges and feel they belong in the world—these are the ones who learn for real.

Purpose Fulfills Motivation With Agency and Belonging

Purpose can imbue motivation with agency—attaching purpose to social or civic value, or the desire to improve the situation or the lives of others around you, to "make a difference," adds to your capacity for taking action, for collaborating, and finding ways around barriers. Just knowing in your heart that you want to engage, that you see a shared path even though the end of it might not be visible, this feeds the momentum to keep at it over the long haul. Rosa Parks said, " … knowing what must be done does away with fear."[14] When we feel in our hearts that we are doing the right thing, we have a rush of efficacy. We feel a confident, eyes-open, "yes, we can," instead of a "let's wait for someone else." Efficacy is the feeling that you could make a difference. Agency is the mindsets and capabilities that make change happen. Both are energized by the power of purpose. Tom VanderArk and Emily Liebtag write, "difference-making is as much about problem-finding as it is about solving. It's about stepping forward, not as saviors but as emergent, relational change makers leading meaningful change. Everyone can make a difference, and everyone deserves the right to experience the agency of difference-making, and to be part of a community of difference makers."[15] Our sense of purpose from the heart, empowered by agency, this is what gives us the power to move beyond futurephobia.

Purpose can bring on belonging—if you know you have a purpose in life, you have the feeling that your actions matter. You matter. According to the Deloitte Millennial and Gen Z surveys, younger adults are searching for purpose—and seeking jobs in businesses that prioritize climate, equity, and community.[16] Humans long to be part of something bigger than themselves, no matter their situation in life. Without it, we are easily overwhelmed. With it, we can deal with uncertainty. I'm sure you can relate to a time in your own lives when joy and belonging came with a shared purpose, even if the situation was difficult overall. The camaraderie of sharing a goal, overcoming an obstacle, or making a difference *together* overcomes minor differences and disputes easily, and sometimes can overcome even bigger ones. As educators, we want to be sure to give students plenty of opportunities to collaborate on life-affirming challenges. Dr. Eric Williams of Loudon County Schools outside Washington DC says that student ownership of making a difference in their communities not only strengthens dispositions like autonomy, curiosity, and empathy, but it also builds a civic identity based on strength. The harder the work gets, the more persistent they get. "Ultimately, the learning will be deeper and longer lasting."[17] A civic identity that builds on strength and belonging overcomes boundaries. Such a collaboration is emerging among three schools in three very different places: Caguas, Puerto Rico, Hiras, India, and Sharjah, United Arab Emirates (UAE). Children and youth ranging in age from 10 to 17 are connected by a shared purpose: helping their communities address climate challenges using co-design thinking. The students have named their collaboration simply, "Collaborate." Students learn about each other and then about the climate challenges in each other's locales. Working together using design thinking, local knowledges and "school learning," they generate solutions to problems of waste management, agriculture and water scarcity, and air pollution, to name a few. Most of the students have already started building alliances with organizations in their communities to generate climate actions at home, but they will tell you that the most valuable alliances they are building now are with each other. The ancient wise ones from seemingly all traditions note how acting for the good of the community brings love and life into the world. It is a form of the interconnecting, interrelating citizenship that brings us all closer to the meaning of life.

 Mending News!

Sunrise Movement Provides Avenues for Advocacy and Action in the US; Earth Uprising Has Global Reach

Both organizations were founded by frustrated teens with a purpose. Both are youth led. Both provide training in advocacy and a unity of local networks. If you have students or children or grandchildren who would like to be part of something bigger than themselves and learn to act locally, meeting activists from all over the world, one or both of these organizations might be right for them. It's not only about marching—it's also about legislation and lobbying, lawsuits and civil disobedience. Looking for a way to get involved? There is no age limit. https://www.sunrisemovement.org/ https://earthuprising.org/

The Superpower of Purpose Is the Meaning of Life

What is it that made the design lab students' eyes shine with excitement when they shared their ideas for the village? Or made the little boy hop from foot to foot with eagerness to tell me about mycorrhizae? Why does connecting around a shared purpose make us feel so alive? Why is it that, once we've experienced a deeply connected moment of learning and action, we want to do that again and again? Jeremy Lent sums it up. *"Meaning is a function of connectedness: the more extensively we connect something with other aspects of our lives, the more meaningful it is to us."*[18]

Researchers already know about the health benefits of purpose, but there's also an ineffable (words don't touch it) feeling of well-being associated with purpose that we usually shorthand to "meaning." It represents much more than a self-serving kind of connectedness—instead, "our well-being is my well-being." What is it that draws us to yearn for lives of meaning? What is it that sparks our energy, makes us feel especially alive and increases our shared potential when we acknowledge our gifts and give them? Author Audre Lorde could see beyond her fears in this state of well-being and power: "When I dare to be powerful—to use my strength in the service of my vision—then it becomes less and less important whether I am afraid."[19] *When I dare.*

Inquiring into the purpose of life, into our purpose in life, in particular when we are living in a time of deep wounds and sudden shocks, can get complicated. Educational theorist and citizen of the world Paolo Freire warned that people "may discover that our present way of life is irreconcilable with our vocation to be fully human," revealing a liberating but not easily achieved purpose.[20] So those privileged to escape the worst of the impacts of climate change can, for a time, numb themselves to the woundedness of the world. Many students who are in the teeth of it seek to protect themselves by not engaging with life and their future at all. Fear holds us back from our truest purpose. The feeling of futurephobia is also a crisis of meaning.

Science can help us out here. Research shows that meaning is felt and heightened when students give help to another learner, and they learn much more than when they receive the help themselves.[21] Interrelatedness plays out in the brain chemistry of helping others, too. The endorphins and other "good feeling" chemicals released make us feel happy and content, lower our stress levels, and facilitate physical and cognitive health. People often describe feeling more "whole" when they are working and learning together for a purpose, especially a helping one. Laughter and joy and a sense of belonging comes back in. It is no surprise that the root of the word "health" is the same as the root of "whole." Coherence and flow have their roots in holistic well-being. People who have had experiences that have suppressed the cognitive "rider" in the brain, either through stroke or near death, frequently describe a sense of integrated oneness with all being, of total contentment, of infinite completeness. Scientists have been able to replicate what is happening at this time in the brain by using chemicals found in mushrooms, those used to treat severe depression and also to aid spiritual access to deeper states of consciousness. Activity and connections within the brain itself speed up, and parts of the brain that ordinarily pay only brief attention to each other are fully engaged.[22] This is the genius of our most ancient body brain, our "animate consciousness" generating "meaning." Being more fully present, more fully alive, more alive with interconnected purpose gives our lives meaning. Holding it all together is love.

 **Mending News!**

Climate Cardinals Translating Climate Documents

Sophia Kianni (see Chapter 9) was visiting her family in Iran when she noticed that the smog was so thick she couldn't see the stars. When she asked her family what they had heard about climate change, it was practically nothing. She began translating everything she could into Farsi, and her Iranian family started to change their habits and share the information with their friends. Sophia later realized that almost all of the UN documents, IPCC reports, and 80% of the research is written in English, but more than half of the world can't access that. Climate Cardinals was born. If you speak languages in addition to English, join some of the 8,000 volunteers globally working to make information accessible while there is still time to make a difference. https://www.climatecardinals.org/

Way before microscopes and telescopes, worldviews were shaped by spiritual cosmologies that came to the same understandings about meaning, coherence, and well-being in life that science has now confirmed. The African concept of Ubuntu, expressed in the Nguni/Ndebele phrase: *umuntu ngumuntu ngabantu*, or, a person is a person through other persons, rippled outward with waves of migration throughout the world. The definition of person or being is not limited to humans. Indigenous peoples around the world connect their identities and well-being to the well-being of the whole. The Buddhist story of the Jewel Net of Indra is a beautiful image to illustrate the concept of the original world wide web. Indra's heavenly dwelling is an infinite net. Every crossing of the net contains a shining eye, a highly polished multifaceted jewel that reflects every other one, infinitely. This image of infinitely reflecting relationships developed, in the wisdom of Neo-Confucian sages, into the consciousness of *li* as the principle of connectivity. Such a principle guides effortless action in Taoist *wu-wei* and travels directly to our generations in the teachings of Vietnamese Buddhist Thich Nhat Hanh, who wrote "We are waves of one sea," and challenged us to see all the universe of "interbeing" in a single piece of paper. Monotheistic mystics emphasized the unity of the Divine and through Judaic notions of *tikkun olam*, and elevated meaning through social justice and Islamic and Christian practices of charity and interrelatedness. Transcendentalists like Ralph Waldo Emerson wrote about his experience of interconnection in "The Transparent Eyeball," and scientists such as Einstein said that our sense of separateness was a "kind of optical delusion of consciousness."[23]

That delusion of separateness, that Euro-Western hyper-individualized dis-integration of the self, has led to the present crisis of meaning and the destabilization of life. As Iain McGilchrist puts it, once we lost our sense of wholeness, we became de-vitalized.[24] When our lives are fragmented and interrupted, betrayed or oppressed, when we are diverted from those purposes which connect us to life, we become unwell. In John Berger's words, "nothing flows through; everything interrupts. There is no continuity between actions ... no pattern, no past and no future. There is only the clamor of the fragmentary present."[25] Coherence and integration empower our spirit to create meaning in life. Life creates the conditions for life by pulling us toward those moments of belonging, joy and abundance experienced when we feel ourselves to be "part of something bigger than ourselves." Humans are the most adaptable creatures on earth because they are also the most cooperative. In fact, the science of emergence reveals that integrated whole life systems are more than the sum of their parts—they inspire beauty, thrum with rhythm, learning and change, and give reflected meaning to every jewel.

Carol Sanford talks about levels of "paradigm" that motivate the decisions we make and the actions we take. The lower three, Value Return, Arresting Disorder, and Doing Good are all necessary, and Doing Good (difference-making) begins to take on more layers of meaning because it brings us into love and contribution and belonging as motivations to act. For regenerative theorist Sanford, life creates the conditions for life, and so we have a shared true purpose: it is living a Regenerative Life that gives our agency and purpose meaning. Living out our vocation to be fully human, fully alive … that is when we are most interrelated, and that is when we become most fully ourselves. That is when we can begin to heal the wounds we are living and learning in.

Paola said that she felt called to work long hours with her community, and it was helping her to heal. But what does that mean? Many teachers say they are intrinsically or naturally teachers—they feel it is what they were born to do, or meant to do. It is their true purpose, and they are not sure they will ever be as happy doing anything else. They are heartbroken if they have to leave it. To borrow language from spiritual leaders, they are living a vocation. Does it feel like a vocation because it so plainly involves so much interrelatedness? Is that what makes teaching and learning with purpose "alive with possibility?"

What if the purpose of "school" aligned with the re-generative purposes of life? And we could co-create conditions for a flourishing of vital, fully integrated patterns of learning, coherence, and connectedness? It seems that "to live a life of purpose and meaning" might just be finding a way to help students weave their own thread into the fabric of the whole, and in doing so regenerate the infinite web of life.

Learning Ecosystems as Infrastructures of Meaning and Emergence

It is easy to spot the symptoms of dis-integrated fragmentation in our schooling: individualistic competition, siloed disciplines and decision making, standardization, initiative overload, and mental and emotional anxiety and exhaustion. The narratives of separation globally make phrases like "we're all in this to-gether" not only seem hollow but also downright dishonest. Clearly, some people are more "in this together" than others. We only have until 2030, based on the IPCC (Intergovernmental Panel on Climate Change) predictions from 2018 (as of 2022, we have until 2027), to make the systemic changes we need to make so as to avoid crossing the line from which we will no longer be

282 ◆ The Power of Purpose

able to protect the children in our schools now from experiencing massive suffering and dislocation, civilizational and species collapse. We need a new shared purpose, one that derives its meaning from life itself.

The good news is that one of the most important and beautiful intelligences of life is the concept of emergence. Like the imaginal change cells gathering up in a caterpillar, or the incredible shared consciousness of an ant colony, or abundant vitality and music of the forest underground by comparison with a few separated trees, change is already underway. We work in concert with those around us, and they work with those around them, until the systems holding us back in this transitional epoch are replaced. As Meg Wheatley wrote, "the beauty of the universe is that it expresses itself in simplicity." Pema Chödrön followed up: "We don't set out to save the world; we set out to wonder how others are doing and to reflect on how our actions affect others' hearts."[26] We need only to tap into the power of shared purpose to find the abundance of life right in front of us.

Education renewal is happening at an accelerating pace across the globe. Educators are allying, finding or creating space to act according to their sense of purpose. And their number is growing as they empower other educators, too. More and more, schools are asking the key questions: How might we focus on the interrelationships between things rather than on separating the things themselves? How might we create communities of belonging? What is integrated well-being, and how do we know when we are successfully co-creating infrastructures and experiences to foster it? How do we need to reimagine the governance structures of school systems? How can we design for bio-engagement and bio-citizenship? How can we design for flow? How might educators of all kinds bring together allies, including our Indigenous neighbors and our global ones and ask the question, what is success? And what skills, dispositions, and mindsets are needed to create thriving in a meaningful life?

In our thinking, "school" is a vibrant community "change studio" which functions according to regenerative principles of interrelationship and (r)evolutionary change. Students and educators join with community members and others to become part of a collective purpose and share in meaning making. In this, the educator's role, and the school/change studio's purpose is "purposeful meaning-making" by taking up and sharing the challenges of life. The first and ongoing project will always be the school itself, evolving, iterating, holding itself accountable to its participants. In this, school starts to feel like an invitation instead of an obligation. It starts to pick up a kind of purposeful momentum and collective attention as the positive changes take hold. There is a breathing kind of reciprocity: community drawn in; studio goes out, in a mutuality that eventually breaks down the barriers between life and school. If you were to map the movements of a community-held change studio from above, it might look a lot like the circulatory system, and would function to support life in a similarly interconnected way. It would most certainly look and be different in every ecosystem, every gathering concentration of life. But we could see education preserving the purpose, integrity, and meaning of learning itself. We could feel the liberation and joy surrounding a learning ecosystem that is about becoming fully oneself—fully human and fully alive.

What are the current manifestations of purpose and meaning in change studios, schools, and programs we could look at now? What do they look like? There isn't one model, though they all inhabit the principles of life (interrelatedness, coherence, change, meaning). In addition to the ones explored in depth in this book, one of the clearest examples of regenerative schooling in the United States is Jenny Finn's Springhouse Community School in Pilot, Virginia. Another example is free private OneStone, in Boise, Idaho, where youth create the school as they experience it. Or place- and learner-centered Teton Science, or Hudson Lab School, which uses the World Economic Forum's Education 4.0 imperatives. And we're not just talking about private schools. Living schools can be almost any school that builds learning around a giving garden, like most of the Green Schools Network, many of which operate with the support of organizations such as GrowNYC. Some schools spend much of their time outdoors, from San Francisco Unified to Five Towns Schools in Maine, sometimes supported by organizations such as Green Schoolyards, or Children's

Environmental Literacy Foundation (CELF). Regenerative principles surface in most of the Big Picture Learning network, and in schools for social justice, like June Jordan School for Equity, or in large school-community collaborations working toward more regenerative school goals and approaches, such as IowaBIG's ecosystem, Menlo Park City's (CA) Learning Framework, and Hopewell City, VA School District. A change studio school could be in a shared working space, like the big district collaborative concept in Fort Wayne, Indiana, or in a coffee cafe or a bike shop like micro-school Embark Education.[27] Often regenerative schools don't look like schools at all. You could walk in and think you are in a woodshop. Or a grove. Or a garage. You feel uplifted and inspired by the hum of life all around you, with no dark hallways with numbered ultra-vio-lit rooms and loud bells signifying marching orders. Biophilic design of the spaces for learning and change emphasize inter-connectedness and break down the separation walls and the "not-thinking" about nature, that thing out there that we need to command or protect ourselves from. There is no "de-vitalizing" distinction between school and the "real" world, school and the natural world, school and learning that matters.

School "change studios," rejoining learning at many levels and ages, might initiate transformation with institutionally soul-searching questions, or they might begin with exemplary projects. When people see the reluctance and boredom disappear, when they begin to understand that the young people in their midst are a valuable resource, when they see the gleaming excitement of belonging and meaning reflected in their eyes, they begin to say, yes, this is good. Let's do more of this. What do you need to make it happen? How can we clarify our purpose and support the values that bring schools alive? What do we want our goals to be? How will we know when we're reaching them? Some people might recoil from schools that are not driven by "hard data" and standardization. Regenerative, living schools defy standardization and scaling because they are alive with the in-terrelated diversity of talent and genius in their ecosystems.

Living schools have music in their veins. Music is the con-vergence of consciousness within us, it integrates the parts of ourselves most directly. Watching young people work together in a living school is like watching a dance, choreographed by the needs of the moment: standing, sitting, leaning over a table or a machine, humming, snapping fingers, rocking hips, lying down, humming, bursting into laughter or a shared song. Living schools, change studios, have community gardens, where people come alive with the reciprocating rhythms and patterns of life and feel the embrace of the food Mother Earth provides. They have big blocks of time and so you can make things to try and or go to a different space to collaborate with people or meet to create goals and benchmarks and ways to cultivate and demonstrate learning and change. They might happen in an open workspace, where parents and families (including elders) convene to learn together. With approval, anyone can offer or subscribe to any course. People of all ages do real work together, co-creating healthier marshland, advocating for and enacting social justice, reforesting with native trees, co-creating energy independence and food security, and exercising the right to an education that taps into everyone's potential for purposeful contribution to life.

Rituals and routines of connection and belonging are important, especially in the midst of the energy of change. Maybe every day begins and ends with El Batey,[28] a gathering and reflection, maybe with music, a dedication of the day's work to a person or another being or an issue of concern. The day closes with gratitude. As a learner, you are culturally and emotionally supported in a small but interconnected group you know well. Your living school or change studio might have created topical and locally framed multidisciplinary strands, such as Water, Air, Food, Identities, or Home, or maybe they used the United Nations's Sustainable Development Goals (SDGs) as a starting point. Maybe you are reading books like Zachary Jones's *Worldchanger's Handbook*[29] or Naomi Klein's *How To Change Everything*.[30] You are encouraged to stay informed, with a critical eye, searching for the opportunities and challenges to weave your sense of purpose into a larger web of meaning. You read in the news that the Yale School of Public Health has issued a warning: exposure to smog increases the likelihood of dementia in older adults, and this is expected to worsen over the next decade if we don't improve the air quality to significantly below the World Health Organization (WHO) guidelines.[31] Living in the city, you had one grandparent who died of "early onset," and another who is showing signs. You feel the resonance, the near-musical vibrations of connection. You meet with your changemaker educator, and together you create a team (which might include a college student or a doctor and an urban planner) and set your learning goals.

If you decide to go to college, you can select from a number of different purpose-oriented life-interconnected schools. Does it have to be Schumacher or Gaia? It could be, but it could also be College of the Atlantic, or Olin, or Mines, or, if you speak Spanish, UPR-Mayagüez, just to name a few. You notice there is a whole coalition of institutions investing in life, calling themselves KEEN [Kern Entrepreneurial (in the sense of problem-seeking) Engineering Network] members. You can help them stay true to their missions. You can join the American Society for Engineering Education (ASEE), which has specifically dedicated itself to using engineering for the well-being of the world, or you join Engineering for Change.[32] You sign up for economics classes using data and AI to solve interconnected economic and social problems. You might expand your artistic talent to encompass and lead whole movements. You might attend a university that was part of your change studio—which you already know believes in convergence: integration across disciplines and outward into the communities and ecosystems around. Or maybe you are already engaged in meaningful work with an agency or a business or a public service. Keep going! But keep your ears and eyes open for more moments that resonate with you and might give you more chances to use your collective powers to heal more of the wounds of the world.

On the day that I gathered all these examples from the United States about regenerative learning opportunities (and there are SO many more!) Olumide Idowu took on the responsibility for the African Youth Initiative on Climate Change, I was online when he posted the news. Within ten minutes, he had congratulations and offers to collaborate from similar organizations—from Abdullah Dreiat of the Arab Youth Climate Activists, from Karuna Singh and MyFutureMyVoice, and from dozens of other youth organizations from every continent and many whose citizenship is planetary. On that same day, I participated in a conversation launching a youth climate impact collaboration between three schools in three different parts of the world—Puerto Rico, the UAE, and India, and met to discuss youth-led climate resilience research connecting Puerto Rico with British Columbia. Later in the day, I heard from a jubilant Davey Warren (see Chapter 6), who had just led Indigenous Ogiek people and their allies in a conference to replant and Indigenize their home—the Mau Forest near Nairobi, and read about a new success in Ecuador to have a river basin declared a legal entity with its own natural rights. I finished the day by checking online again, and saw an article in *Nature* about the University of Okinawa, with no departments and "high-trust" research funding to work on "complex, multidisciplinary challenges." There is a Chinese Proverb that says, "Those who say it cannot be done should not interrupt those doing it." There was nothing in the way that day. I could feel the hopeful emergence of the power of purpose.

Seeds for Planting

Purpose (internal motivation, our "why") adds intention, persistence, depth, and relevance to learning.

Educators can guide purpose toward actions that bring about a greater sense of belonging and meaning—being a part of something bigger than ourselves that is acting in the interrelated interests of someone else or the whole.

Purpose and meaning , especially when shared, enable coherence, flow, and overall well-being.

Students, educators, parents ask, "why can't school always be like this?" Let's re-think the purpose and shape of school using these understandings about motivation, depth, and meaning.

Notes

1 The kindness and generosity of the Coast Guard Sector San Juan cannot be overstated. The approval of CAPT Eric King and the enthusiasm of LCDR Jesse Harms made it all possible.

2 Christine's efforts and the power of community are featured in the film *Mariana Pa'lante*, a 31-minute documentary directed by Xabier Climent Belda and Aaron Kudja (2019), in her TEDMed Talk (https://www. tedmed.com/speakers/show?id=730915), and in her essay "Community Is Our Best Chance." *All We Can Save* (2020)

3 Vander Ark and Liebtag 2021.

4 Lent 2021. I am indebted to this book and its author for deepening my understanding and confirming that those strange moments of inter-connectedness are real.

5 Hutchins and Storm 2019.

6 Lent 2021.

7 Wolfe 2014.

8 Damon 2008.

9 Bir Sethi 2009.

10 Vander Ark and Liebtag (2021) and Lent (2021).

11 Oxford English Dictionary.

12 Wheatley 2009.

13 Czikszentmihalyi 1991.

14 Parks and Read 1994.

15 Vander Ark and Liebtag 2021.

16 The Deloitte Surveys are huge and cover a wide swath of Millennial and Gen Z responders. Because people from these groups make up more than half of the world's population, I am encouraged to see their values and priorities. They release a new report each year. This one is from 2019. https://www2.deloitte.com/content/dam/Deloitte/global/Documents/ About-Deloitte/deloitte-2019-millennial-survey.pdf

17 VanderArk and Liebtag 2021.

18 Lent 2021.

19 Lorde 1977. First published in Sini. *Her Wisdom* 6 (1978) and *The Cancer Journals* (Spinsters, Ink, San Francisco, 1980).

20 Freire 2018.

21 Eskreis-Winkler et al., 2019.

22 Lent 2021.

23 Lent 2021.

24 McGilchrist 2021.

25 Wheatley 2001.

26 Chödrön, Pema quoted in Wheatley 2001.

27 Examples with links: Springhouse: https://springhouse.org/, OneStone: https://onestone.org/, Teton Science: https://www.tetonscience.org/, Hudson Lab School: https://www.hudsonlabschool.com/, Green Schools Network: https://greenschoolsnationalnetwork.org/, GrowNYC: https:// www.grownyc.org/, San Francisco Unified School District: https://www. sfusd.edu/, Five Town School District: https://www.fivetowns.net/, Green Schoolyards: https://www.greenschoolyards.org/, Children's Environmental Literacy Foundation (CELF): https://celfeducation.org/, Big Picture Learning: https://www.bigpicture.org/, June Jordan School

for Equity: https://www.jjse.org/, Menlo Park's Learning Framework: https://district.mpcsd.org/page/1303 (scroll to link), Hopewell City Schools: https://www.hopewell.k12.va.us/, Fort Wayne and AMP: https://www.fwcs.k12.in.us/AmpLab, https://education-reimagined. org/a-conversation-with-riley-johnson-amp-lab/, IowaBIG: https://iowabig.org/, Embark Education: https://www.embarkeducation.org/

28 ...**el batey** is a Taíno word describing both the communal gathering place and the sense of community generated there.

29 Jones 2017.

30 Klein 2021

31 Kristofferson 2022.

32 Find Engineering for Change here: https://engineeringunleashed.com/, https://www.engineeringforchange.org/ and "The Power of Borderless Research: The Okinawa Institute of Science and Technology" Nature Portfolio: Research. https://www.nature.com/articles/d42473-021-00382-2

8 Power-full Processes: Democratizing How We Change

Everybody designs. How does having a process of design give us power and agency in the age of climate disasters and futurephobia?

How can a critical awareness of design help us democratize our relationships and systems, shifting from human-centered to bio-centric design?

How does regenerative co-design work?

If Purpose is our "why," then Process is our "how" to learn and act and learn again in ways that are relevant and meaningful. The right combination of place, purpose, and process motivates and deepens learning and helps to bring those who share in our living worlds together in unique and shared becoming. The way I think of Process is not a linear or single pathway, but a tapestry of potential for transformation that emerges from relationships and collective knowledge and creativities, using tools and mindsets that are culturally rooted in design. To be alive is to be constantly changing, and so all living things are designers. We have to be, in order to stay alive. We are inseparably nested in living systems, so we have to keep redesigning our very existence to shape and adapt to change. What worldviews and change processes we choose can either

DOI: 10.4324/9781003215806-10

support or undermine our socio-ecological resilience, so it matters how we enact and critically shape those processes. Agency is the power to act on the world around us. The agency embodied in design results from the wise application of a whole constellation of (teachable!) mental models and tools, such as how to spark our imagination and reflect at multiple levels to bring about and sustain the life-affirming (r)evolutionary changes we envision.

We know we have to eat to survive, but deciding what to eat or adapting our life processes to access it or produce it is a matter of design. Humans often think of themselves as the only designers, assuming that animals and plants are acting on instinct or DNA "programming," but the domain of feeding invites us to look closer. Human-centered thinking might miss how some humpback whales have made feeding more efficient through collaboration, communicating with each other and working together to synchronize their swimming and breathing so as to create a bubble-net around a school of fish that confuses the fish and causes them to stop and huddle together. This maximizes the food source density for an animal that must ingest as much as 3,000 pounds a day. Local birds have observed and adapted to the whales' habits, alerting each other to the presence of the whales' bubble netting and diving from the top just as the whales are rushing up from the bottom. The birds have learned that the whales' baleen won't allow them to be swallowed along with the fish.

Domesticated animals also exert some design agency and process to influence their situations. My parents have a clever dog who quickly understood that if she received a treat for good behavior during training, she could *initiate* the treat process by behaving badly and then responding to correction and … *voi lá!* a treat came her way. When my parents began ignoring her performance, she began self-correcting her bad behavior in expectation of a treat. I believe researchers of canine reasoning call this process "backwards chaining." She was intentionally (and hilariously) training her humans to produce treats, and iterating her approach when needed. Intent and agency, by design.

Humans design in collaboration with *other* beings, too. Reading the behavior and attitudes of plants and animals has saved many a human community over time, and taught them how to be good stewards of their home ecosystems. Certain trees will only release their seeds when they are exposed to smoke, for example, but too much fire will kill them. Most Indigenous groups use frequent, controlled fire to facilitate the natural flourishing of Earth's nested ecosystems. Children create monarch habitats to assist in their migration. Animals notice subtle changes in energy fields and chemistry in humans, such that some dogs can discover and draw attention to cancer[1] and other pathologies. Animals feel and hear electricity in the air (storms) and draw humans' attention to potentially threatening or out-of-the-ordinary situations. Pets have been known to go get help from other humans nearby when necessary.

Beneath the surface of the soil, organisms actively generate the very conditions for their own thriving as well. They work together to not only respond to environmental changes but to initiate them. This happens in our own bodies, too, where even the shape of our cells can change and adapt according to the situations presented to them, communicating from cell to cell locally and long distance in order to work together to inhibit disease, grow, heal, react, feel, and think.

We could look at just about any adaptation in Nature as an iterative process of design that tells us that all living beings have the capacity to change themselves or the circumstances around them as needed. Plants that change the shape of their cells on one side of their stem so as to position leaves toward the sun. Pecan trees that only make nuts (all of them do this at once) when the squirrel population is low and the nuts are desperately needed and also guaranteed to be transported. Lichens that transform minerals from rocks to feed mosses. Those most adaptable are often the most successful from an evolutionary standpoint—just look at humans. Or ants. Have you ever seen an ant colony iterate? They are very persistent. If they can't get where they want to go the first route they try, they keep modifying the route and trying again. They could spend hours making a bridge out of their bodies for the rest of the colony to cross. If you accidentally scuff out the entrance to their colony, they soon redesign another not far away, but hardly ever in the same place. They are infinitely collaborative, and share all of their information about juicy picnic crumbs with each other. And they plan. Like many species, they anticipate need and plan ahead, in their case not eating all of their food at once. Nature is the best designer of all.

Design = Relationships + Intention + Agency => Transformation

By observing design in Nature, we can identify some important characteristics of design processes that might otherwise be overlooked or taken for granted by humans. In the continually changing context of life and becoming, design is the expression of *relationships*, *intention*, and *agency*. Design in Nature is continuously iterative (evolution) and inseparably interrelated. Transformation occurs *within* systems and patterns and simultaneously *shapes* them, creating a reciprocal and integrated "ripple effect." If we were to envision a shape for design, it would not be a linear, problem-solution, problem-solution series of steps working toward a static ideal. Instead, it would be ongoing and multidimensional, unfolding in all directions. Design adheres to evolutionary life principles and patterns of iteration and adaptation, which enacts intent in a way that creates conditions for more life and also fights against entropy and death. In this sense, design is a form of love in the universe. In the age of climate disasters, we humans are needed (all of us) to exercise our design capacities as if life depended on it, remembering with love a design culture of coherent and integrated alignment with life. When humans design while holding this awareness and critical consciousness of life, we could say that design is ecological, or bio-centered rather than human-centered. Because design is itself a function of being alive, it stands to reason that it functions best according to life's principles.

Principles of Bio-Centric Design

Whatever processes of design for change you use, we want to be sure that they arise from design values based on life—otherwise design can be degenerative or hedonistic, and entropic. Bio-centric (literally, "life" centric) design will result in regenerative and sustainable relationships and realizations of our shared and unique potentials, and will make the processes and tools we use power-full with life's teachings. (Figure 8.1)

Universal Principles of Life lead directly to	Biocentric Design Characteristics
Coherence	Systemic and holistic Rooted in place and culture
Interrelatedness	Multi-disciplinary Focused on relationships Integrated across sectors and silos
Regeneration	Grows and sustains without waste or additional inputs Autonomously motivated
Evolutionary Change	Dynamic and Iterative Reveals, Amplifies and Connects Emergent Adaptations
Biodiversity	Inclusive and fully participatory Community-building Collective strength through diversity

FIGURE 8.1 Bio-centric design characteristics

Design and the processes deployed in design are not philosophically or morally neutral. Certainly one could use design to exclude, to undermine and attack social and biological communities, to extract information and resources, and to destroy our home planet. We are suffocating under that morally and ethically bankrupt approach to design already. Thus the critical awareness of the values present in our design (embodied in learning experiences and spaces), as well as the design processes we enact, will help guide our work and keep it both liberating and life-affirming. Daniel Wahl calls these values and attitudes "dimensions" of design, which support life by being ethical, aesthetic, dynamic, socially and culturally rooted and sustaining, holistic, and ecological.[2] There are a handful of immutable natural laws governing these dimensions of biocentric design, and as we can see in Figure 8.1, they all come from life itself.

 Mending News!

The Growing Fields of Biomimicry and Biophilic Design Reconnect Humans With Nature

Some Biomimicking designers observe design at work in Nature and apply what they learn to solve and evolve in one area. Mechanical engineers at the University of Colorado at Boulder are studying how a stiff fish-fin with no muscles is able to flex quickly and smoothly to help the fish change direction. Watch for evolution in airplane wings and robotic surgical helpers. Biophilic designers aim to create whole spaces and systems that contribute to human well-being because they embody the principles and materials of healthy ecosystems. Buildings that help you to feel connected to the natural world, like Kroon Hall of Environmental Studies at Yale and Thorncrown Chapel in Eureka Springs, Arkansas, or regenerative farmers and educators like me, would land in the world of Biophilic (literally life-loving) designers.

Because of the interconnectedness in the web of life, any design will affect everything around it in a kind of multi-dimensional ripple effect. Most educators feel a strong moral and ethical drive (our motivating sense of purpose) to help make a difference in our students' lives, and we are happy to see when our best efforts are both internalized and spread outward and into the future. We can easily relate to the idea of making sure that the thousands of decisions we make every day will affect our students in life-affirming ways. The safe biocentric design cultures we create in our learning spaces emphasize that the realization of our ideas emerges from our relationships and attitudes and stances within this infinite web of life, among changing communities of living beings, and not so much from a linear process of solution seeking.

All designing we do has local impact, whether it is direct and transparent or indirect and "hidden." In this sense, like the arts and literature, design both expresses and influences culture. In *Designs for the Pluriverse*, Arturo Escobar cautions readers that design tools and processes are reciprocal—we design the tools and the tools design us back.[3] A critical consciousness not only demands we design for socio-ecological justice, it requires that we apply the same awareness to the processes and tools we are using. Safe design, or "just design" begins with belonging and equity. In Rob Fleming's *Design Education for a Sustainable Future*, he writes, "Design education is an essential tool in moving from superficial greening to transformative and re-generative ways of being,"[4] by shifting toward integrative and ethical values of cooperation and inclusion rather than compe-tition and exclusivity.

This does not mean that everyone will be living in some universal "greened up" monoculture, nor that design pro-cesses or their outcomes should "scale" in order to be valid. Indeed, design needs to be based on how change occurs in living systems, and local ecosystems are different everywhere. Change theorist Carol Sanford assures us that the energy for change is within all living beings, but that does not mean its expression in change systems and processes (its "essence") will look or be the same everywhere.[5] As educators, we are engaged in change design every day. We must be careful not to aim for a universalizing monoculture. In his seminal work *Design, When Everybody Designs* (2015), Ezio Manzini makes this clear.[6] The Great Transition the world is engaging in now, he writes, fosters collectivism at the local level with global resonance. His vision is instead a kind of "cosmopolitan loc-alism," where systems are held more accountable to life and biocentric design dimensions because the consumers and producers are closer together. The new localized culture of design, he writes, is one where design is happening at all le-vels with "distributed agency" to build collaborative and in-tegrated local systems that transform.

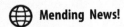 **Mending News!**

Buen Vivir Helps All to Envision a Better World

Futurists and design scholars like Ezio Manzini and Arturo Escobar have described this period of transition we are in as the shift toward a post-extractivist, post-development world characterized by *Buen vivir*, or "good living." This concept grew in the 'global South' from the intersection of Indigenous understandings with emergent Afrodescendant, environmentalist, women's and youth struggles, and demonstrates how economic growth can be subverted to social justice, ecology, and the dignity of all beings. Now part of the Ecuadoran (2008) and Bolivian (2009) Constitutions, it supports bio-centrism (and the rights of Nature), encourages pluralities of ways of knowing and being, and adopts an interrelational concept of all life. Since the early 1990s, the Bhutanese Constitution has embodied similar principles, which has redefined "progress" as ecological well-being and is famous for registering its "Gross National Happiness" in GDP and GNP (Gross Domestic and Gross National Product) indices.

When everyone commands civic and regenerative design literacies so that everyone knows how to bring about change (and isn't this a vital role school can play), the distributed agency Manzini references is likely to generate certain patterns of change toward fairness and well-being, albeit in very different contexts. Because regenerative design practice does not start with problems to solve but with individual and collective potential, Daniel Christian Wahl writes, "The potential of people and place to manifest their unique essence in ways that add value, meaning, and health to a greater whole" will emerge.[7] Indigenous commitments to life arising from natural environments, *Buen vivir*, and a dynamic sense of place in living communities will likely re-establish right relationships. The newly re-established mutual and horizontally oriented architectures of relationships (that might in fact be very old) will, as adrienne maree brown puts it, "relax into co-creativity."[8]

Everybody Designs?

Or, can a system that is set up to process students in an industrialized way become biocentric?

In living systems, the power to design is distributed, and there exists a dynamic balance around change. In most typical schools and communities, however, imbalances of power create design problems. The bias toward expertise and academic degrees paired up with negative myths about youth (and age! and race, gender, class, etc.), taken together with wobbly top-down power structures, leads to hierarchical decision-making, unsustainable and unsafe design. Two design process problems whose made-up names accurately describe them are "charismitis" and "solutionitis." All of us in education are familiar with what sam seidel of the d-School's k12 lab termed "solutionitis," or what I like to call "initiative overload." It generally arises from a top-down, linear problem-solution, problem-solution approach to school design that gradually expands the number of discrete and disconnected items to juggle. Unfortunately, this pattern becomes degenerative. Most of those solutions are not integrated with place-based or purpose-driven vision and change processes, so they break up life-affirming principles like coherence. They are created somewhere else to be a one-size-fits-all solution to be purchased and added on in order to "put out a fire." Everyone gets stressed by the incoherence—the parents who don't understand what it is, the students who have one more thing in their schedule that doesn't seem to connect, the teachers, who not only have one more thing to juggle, but have to figure out how the get it to fit their students, and the administrators, who seem to "always be putting out fires" and never able to step back and work toward developing and updating coherent shared goals and practices. In the end, the fragmentation in the system gets even stronger and potentially causes more harm.

"Charismitis" (adrienne maree brown's word) is what happens when we think of ourselves as the designer-hero, setting up learning FOR our students, doing a fair amount of the designing and discernment that they could do, and thus depriving them of the empowering benefits of design. In the excellent book *Empower*, authors and educators John Spencer and A.J. Juliani mirrored my own experience when they said that the only way they could break out of this mold was to keep asking themselves, "am I making a decision here that the kids could make? Am I doing work that they could do?"[9] Organizational change leader Carol Sanford says that this 'heroic do-gooder' mindset, especially when it comes to teaching, is often unexamined. After all, isn't the teacher *supposed* to be in charge of the learning design? The "heroic do-gooder" teacher is valorized by institutions and communities that hold up individual shining examples for special praise, often unfairly building up expectations for self-sacrificing behavior on the part of teachers, relying on them to do what is best for the kids without questioning harmful systems that are stretching and stressing them.

In my view, this charismatic change model leads to credit-seeking and credit-taking competitive mindsets and battles over time and space, instead of feeding collective opportunities to transform. It almost never results in long-lasting systemic change. As soon as the innovator is gone, their innovations go with them. In Sanford's words, the "heroic" changemaker "robs us of our responsibility to discover and choose ways of thinking and acting that might truly transform and make meaningful and lasting contributions to the world."[10] But all this capability in their hands might not be immediately apparent to young people. One student shared in a reflection that as most students don't feel that they can change complex systems, they find themselves desperately waiting or searching for the expert with the latest technology who is going to save the day. (Figure 8.2)

FIGURE 8.2 The knight in shining armor has arrived
By Xion Torres Luccas, Guayanilla PR 2022

Often the credit (and the funding) for "saving the day" goes to "the highly trained expert (or university)." This creates another hitch in the dynamic balance and distribution of the power of design. I am not suggesting that we do without experts or universities. Similarly, I want to emphasize that specialized, in-depth research and knowledge creation are absolutely necessary. What I mean is that the highly trained expert cannot be the only designer voice in the change-making community, urging or persuading "buy-in" from everybody else. Experts often don't have a lot of space in their mental models or time in their urgency-driven schedules for community wisdom, authentic youth engagement, or local expertise. And communities, educators, youth, elders … they need time to consider how ideas from afar might fit or not fit or potentially be adapted.

Frustration with all the community conversation and time-taking, particularly in the age of disasters, results in top-down decision-making and costly solutions-designed-for-others that don't fit well and won't last. From the perspective of many communities, these "take it from the experts, we know how to help the helpless" ways of thinking are mildly insulting at best and at worst create vulnerabilities and undermine youth and community agency to autonomously design for change. In fact, ignoring the community's need to create meaning from what matters to them can cause even greater harm. There is no trust established when "resilience education" is coming from the powerful, when designs for "community transformation" are coming from outside the community, when something as intimate and culturally rooted as Social-Emotional Learning (SEL), for example, is purchased off the shelf or zoomed in from afar. Some community leaders have used the phrase, "It's not about us without us." Stop for a moment and consider when was the last time you and your community (of any size) made a major change and felt that it fit and functioned well? What was your role in it?

Engineer Pamela Silva and I have been co-creating with communities in Puerto Rico. We've learned many important lessons, among them:

1. Design thinking processes are empowering based on who is doing the designing
2. Design is hard work and risk-taking, but doesn't feel like it when done collectively
3. Design empowerment without resources to implement ideas undermines agency

We mapped the moves toward democratizing change making in Figure 8.3, so you could see how the dynamic balance of power shifts.

Top-Down	Designed FOR	Designed WITH	Designed BY
'Old-School' Government & NGO's	User-centered Design thinking	Co-Design Thinking	Community Designers
We know what's best for you Constrained by disciplinarity	We design for you based on your stated needs	Community design partners invited into the process	Community teams invite facilitators and outside experts into their multi-disciplinary process
One size fits all is most efficient	Needs-based design is more contextual	Greater contextual and cultural accountability	Place-based and regenerative
Community feedback	Community Input	More Community engagement	Community-led

FIGURE 8.3 Who holds the power of design

"Designed WITH and Designed BY" is where you will find trusted design and local knowledge gathering, and those locally nourished roots are more likely to generate long-term transformation. We care for what we have designed. When we look at "vulnerable" communities, we see how, when Everybody Designs, great things happen. In her article "Design for Climate Resilience," engineer Pamela Silva Díaz discusses the importance of community-led design for long-term resilience in Puerto Rico. There is a lot of resilience design going on there, much of it from the outside, with well-meaning people coming in to leave, for example, solar-powered charging stations, for the community to be able to charge up after the next hurricane. "Everyone is excited!" Silva Díaz writes, "After two lucky years, the first major storm causes a community-wide blackout, and everyone rushes to the station – only to find dirty and damaged solar panels, families of pigeons who made it their home, and ultimately a useless device that will now become solid waste in the community."[11] If the community, especially young people, had designed this solution, they might have put it in or near the school, so that they could charge their phones every day. Then it would've been cared for. Silva Díaz also reminds us that local communities can design better to address inequities in their communities and also to sustain historically and culturally valued natural protections like mangrove swamps and coral reefs. Silva Díaz (UPR-Rio Piedras and MIT) mentors emerging engineers, such as Javier Moscoso Cabrera (UPR-Mayagüez), who is determined to connect everyone in Puerto Rico to their own solar nano-grid systems, and teach them how to install and maintain them. For Moscoso, energy security is an emancipatory act. (p. 270) That just doesn't happen with distant planners.

Knowledge Hierarchies

Knowledge hierarchy and fragmentation hobbles transformative change. Bio-centric design relies on three kinds of expertise, braided together: life or Nature herself, trained and certified academic or practical human expertise, and diffuse, experiential or historical "community" expertise. When all three emerge from the context and fullness of being, we might call this wisdom. Our best teachers will be the enablers who can connect all three without forcing or tokenizing or talking above or around anyone. To this end, our learning is rightfully guided by the Indigenous peoples whose lives on the land and sea represent relational principles established among human and non-human ancestors tens of thousands of years before the period of western extractivist colonialism. The growing movement toward convergence and coherence across disciplines and also connecting all kinds of knowledge and all kinds of designers can accelerate to connect all kinds of expertise and ways of being and learning.

The power audit enables us to look critically at research, knowledge creation, and design practices to make sure that the intended participants are receiving the co-benefits and exercising agency: the power of design. If you have not been in this position, imagine what happens when researchers descend on a disaster- or trauma-affected community, asking for time and commitment and sometimes other resources, and the community gets relatively little tangible or lasting positive change as a result. The following critical and ethical questions must be asked and answered. Who is benefitting from the research? What exactly IS the Nature of the long-term relationship between a research institution and the "participants?" Does it extend beyond the duration of the project? Who does the inviting (and how), and who participates in the design of the research? Does the community own and regenerate the outputs of the research? Will there be funds to implement solutions?

Participatory research sometimes makes strides in the right direction by building relationships in communities and engaging community learners in the knowledge and meaning creation, but then often the resulting articles and highly useful data are trapped behind paywalls and written in an academic language only a few can understand. For the academics, the esoteric language might be a hoop to jump through to establish professional credibility, but the consequences for communities, educators, and learners of this academic exclusivity are real.

If we engage each other in learning to do research, we co-empower to drive change. When university researchers and their community engagement labs support trusting, more-than-participatory, *community-co-created* research, they are in a much more equitable relationship with communities than when they are seeking communities who will support the scholars' agendas. There are universities that are moving in this direction. Here are just a few examples. Royal Roads University's Resilience By Design Lab (Victoria, BC), MIT's D-Lab, and the Stanford d-School plus the National Equity Project's Liberatory Design Process. Programs like the Creative Reaction Lab and Justice By Design look deeply and critically at the power structures built into community processes.[12]

In the climate change and community participation arena, the hi-tech means to acquire useful information about changing environmental conditions are frequently far too expensive or inaccessible, to be useful. Often the sites to be tested are far from the school buildings and the human habitation centers in need of the information. Pamela Silva Díaz's work as a National

Geographic Explorer engages her in collaboratively designing low-cost measurement devices usable by citizen scientists to identify the causes of mangrove death near their homes. The communities will gather the data and invite university experts to their design of solutions when needed. In Puerto Rico, the public University of Puerto Rico has multiple campuses, and several community outreach and involvement programs. Community knowledge and historical farming and environmental stewardship practices help to promote regenerative food security. Some campuses assist poorer communities with access to solar power (Javier and his professors), set up community schooling (Aula en la Montaña), and also help them by assisting with their taxes (to make sure they are getting benefits due to them).

The Role of Educator Expertise and Jargon

Similarly, pre-K-12 teachers bridge the academic and practical, community-held and scholarly knowledge. They do their best to translate what they can access into their teaching, but the education field is also full of jargon. We education experts are guilty of undermining trust this way, too. In many schools, the few teachers who have facility in Spanish, or the few Black teachers are constantly asked to translate. White, English-only teachers ask, "Can you talk to these parents for me? Help me write this text message? What are they asking me to do?" During a time of crisis, this layers on an additional job and its unique dimensions of cultural code-shifting stress. Parent Heejae Lim founded Talking Points in 2014, which is an easy translation app to ease and stimulate communication between schools and parents. Both parents and teachers are empowered by it. Another parent group, the Family Engagement Lab in San Francisco, created FasTalk, which not only translates into over 100 languages but also provides a platform for tips from teachers.[13]

But even with translation apps, the language educators use to talk about changes in learning is often obscure. The Fordham Institute "How to Sell SEL" study of 2,000 parents of both major parties and all demographic groups revealed that "social-emotional learning," and especially "SEL," doesn't sell. In fact, all parents preferred "life skills." While they had no objection to and are in favor of teaching (both directly and indirectly) "soft skills" such as empathy, kindness, sensitivity to other cultures, emotional awareness, risk-taking, self-discipline, goal-setting, and so on (especially if it doesn't "take time away" from "academics"), as soon as educators used phrases like social-emotional learning, and, even worse, soft skills, a sense of unease and mistrust drove parents to reject them and the educators who used the jargon.[14]

How can educators break free of these "I am the design expert in this field" mental models that, if they are not influencing us directly, have a hold on the institutions in which we work? If you are an education leader, make space for co-design and co-governance in your work. Remember, you are only as strong as the people around you. One co-benefit? You will be much happier if you don't feel you have to make all the decisions yourself, and collectively your organization will be more resilient. Another way for teachers to break free is to ally (converge) across disciplines with each other and with university educators and practitioners in various fields in teams that co-design. Conspire with students, parents, and grandparents to co-design how you yourself and your students see themselves using their own powers in the service of life's principles. Make your own design language. Is your way of change making diffuse? Distributed? Organic? Biocentric? Emancipated? Decolonized? What works for you? adrienne maree brown (2017) asks the essential questions, "how can we stay connected to our deeper purpose and intention toward life while engaged in adaptation and change? What is our vision and how can I hold to it in design?"[15] Let your own process unfold according to your principles and your creativity. Stop listening to the misleading narrative that there's time for creative work only in those schools "that don't have to worry about the testing," or are not "failed schools," or that power-full design only happens among the gifted or the wealthy or the polite. Design is one of the most important powers connecting intention and agency, helping us to unlearn helplessness, and create living solutions that are power-full expressions of trust in ourselves, in our relationships, and in life itself.

Design Is a Civic Process Leading to Regenerativity

In the age of climate disasters, we all need to think of ourselves and our communities as design hubs. Across all ages, all subjects, and all sectors, we are seeing fundamentally different (some new, some very old) and exciting ways of being citizens in communities. In her essay in *All We Can Save*, "Becoming a Climate Citizen," Kate Knuth posits that through the pain and grief, in anxiety and frustration, the most naturally true answer to the question, "what is the best thing I can do?" will create a renaissance of leaderfull democracy. With a renewed emphasis on citizenship, local and planetary, on inclusive processes, and emergence (not scale) as life-centric patterns of change, human civic engagement can counteract the entropic divisions driven by inequalities and partisan polarization fueled by algorithms and foreign adversaries. She believes that strengthening the institutional and cultural tools to enable everyone to contribute to life-centric collaborative change will reduce deaths from despair and outweigh policy preferences driven by greed.[16]

Puerto Rican-born climate justice educator and activist Elizabeth Yeampierre emphasizes the power of interrelated agency, "Leader-full means there is enough room for all of us. Seeing everyone roll in together is much more powerful than having one or two people speak for everyone. Being intergenerationally leader-full also generates the best ideas and solutions. We need to do this together, and we can do it lovingly."[17] As educators, we are creating the conditions for agency and design to flourish. Teachers lead with love. As always, five-point safety is critical, and the "lovingly" part matters. If you are involving people you do not know, are you all safer in your space or theirs? How is your invitation to participate–warm, welcoming, and energizing? Is every aspect of participation based on consent? What are the issues and interests that matter to the people, even children, present? What protocols can you establish or steps can you follow to welcome all voices and include everyone in a process that feels safe and that builds bridges for people who might otherwise hesitate or might disagree with one another? Is the space itself comforting and inspiring?

From the beginning and from the youngest ages children can engage in a virtuous cycle of civic activity, or designing with a group's well-being in mind. (See Chapter 9) In a moment we can dive into various approaches you can use, but let's stop and think about the power of design to teach life skills indirectly and directly, as well as other civic benefits. If we are engaged in bio-centric design and praxis as the mainstay of learning, there will be no difference between school and real life. When students feel the rush that comes with authentic civic responsibility, agency, and purpose, it infuses their lives with belonging, excitement, and good feelings that they want to repeat. My students often said, "design is hard work, but it doesn't feel that way." A glimmer of flow. Once they have successfully presented their idea for a solar-powered rainwater filtration and touchless hand-washing station to the town council and gotten the project into the town budget, changed a local ordinance to allow for solar panels on houses, or stopped the use of plastic bags (or plastic anything), or created a way to track COVID or for refugees to find free housing, or changed regulations to adapt lighting for the benefit of marine life ... they are more likely to present more ideas later. Their sense of belonging also will empower dissent, enabling them to hold systems accountable, and advocate leader-fully and powerfully for change. Their sense of place and pride in their civic responsibility grows every time they see their innovation in action.

Regenerative Citizenship Is Essential to Acting Beyond Futurephobia

Students involved in civic learning through design become good at noticing what is working (and not) at many levels even as they are deeply engaged, and this metacognitive ability to notice and reflect grows into a critical consciousness and self-awareness that is the basis of engaged citizenship. They learn how systems work and how they overlap. They see that systems of governance can change and adapt, too, and with a sense of confidence can challenge the injustices they see and influence civic learning and actions to remedy them. They begin to sense the dynamic tension between patience and urgency, and gain command over their use of time. Students begin to own their own stories and shape the world around them. Paolo Freire would have called this way of teaching the "praxis" of critical pedagogy—the practical knowledge that enables reflections and actions upon the world in order to transform it.[18] I call it regenerative citizenship. The agency to affect change beyond futurephobia.

Benefits of Design Agency for Youth (and Their Educators)

Even a little bit of agency, if it is achieved authentically and with real responsibility attached, sets off a positive and regenerative cycle of benefits. For one thing, students want to come to school. Because of their roles as creative companions with adults, they behave in more adult ways. They become excellent facilitators of collaboration and respectful conversation. They often describe a sense of responsibility for each others' growth and well-being, as if it comes with the territory. School officials notice attendance issues disappearing, unless there are extenuating circumstances, but officials in schools where co-design thinking is prominent can rest assured that there is usually a reason other than disengagement! Since students are engaged in meaningful and power-full work, disciplinary issues begin to disappear, and collaborative partnerships result in better peer-to-peer and adult relationship building. Adults begin to fundamentally trust the students as the students ably take on more responsibilities, and so those discipline issues that arise are more likely to be met with a "Why? What happened to you today?" rather than the meting out of punishments. Community organizations and agencies view the students as valued re-sources, members of the community with something unique and worthwhile to contribute.

Students engaging with authentic responsibility in the world can make their own decisions about what they need to do in the course of the day. In fact, when I found myself swimming in the "teacher as design hero" pool, this was one of the most important questions I added to the "power audit." Ask your students: what am I doing and deciding that you could do and decide? Their life orientation and self-directed mindset can be taught directly as well as indirectly by enga-ging them in authentic civic projects. As a learner guide, en-abler, coach or advisor, the teachers' role and responsibilities shift. The teacher will need to be sure that projects are au-thentic and challenging and drive learning deeper, as well as taking place in conditions safe for risk-taking. In their book *Empower*, Spencer and Juliani write, the teacher collaborates to seek or shape opportunities for the students to engage mean-ingfully, models adult co-creative civic behaviors, affirms them in the students, and co-creates an inspiring sense of community.[19] He also mentions that teachers help to provide the tools. Some teachers are afraid to step out into the world of design because they do not have the tools, either. Remember, there is nothing wrong with learning to use the Arduino the day before or SketchUp together with the students. But heads up, school leaders—there has to be flexibility and time for teachers and students to learn this way.

TIME, TIME, TIME

Time to build the relationships. Time to explore. Time to reflect. Time to change course, redefine, iterate. Time to slow down, listen, and feel. Is there time to be silent? A place to rest? There needs to be a place to go to calm and forgive oneself, to laugh with peers or adults, to counteract the urgencies of social media, disaster, trauma, and the pull of entropy. Time and place to think. Best if it can be outside, or in a room with a view. No static from phones or social media. Schools where design thinking guides the days generally do not have industrial assembly-line bell schedules. At Embark Education, OneStone and the Pacific School for Inquiry and Innovation, as just three examples among many, students create their own schedules, sometimes with the guidance of their advisor, sometimes on their own. They set up their own functional boundaries, and they own and assess them. Is this use of my time helping me to move toward my goals? Is it helping me go deeper or be more precise and clear? Is this "wandering and wondering time" expanding my thinking on this subject and enabling me to surface more questions? What past knowledge do I have that can shed light on this moment? Who do I need to talk to? Is there time to observe and learn to observe using all my senses? Time to imagine and create, to feel awe and savor it, to remember to say thank you? Thinking and feeling and reflecting is NOT inaction.

Why It Helps to Have a (Living) Process for Change in the Age of Climate Disasters

A process can provide the means to unleash ingenuity and achieve change when there is overwhelming complexity. When I first landed in Puerto Rico, ten days after María, I was staying with three school superintendents who had experience in disaster management. Our Puerto Rican friends were already steeped in pain, urgency and overwhelm. "This is so devastating and huge and complex and we are not sure where to begin … and the stakes are so high … ." There was no communication. No one knew how many school officials, faculty, or children would even be able to go to school, even IF any could be opened soon. No one knew the extent of the damage to the buildings or when the generators would fail. We met in eight different places over five days, sometimes chasing power and wifi in the middle of the day, all off site. It might take us hours to go a half mile in the city. I developed a mantra for us: "all we can do is all we can do." We arrived with different processes for managing change in a crisis, the four of us, but we clung to them. We tried to listen deeply and openly and shared what we could without trampling anyone else's processes. I feel strongly that the world is in a similar place of overwhelm now with regard to the injustices of climate change. We know the situation is bad and getting worse, and it is easy to become overwhelmed. It helps to own some tools when there's a storm upon us.

Every complex problem is multi-disciplinary and by the interconnected nature of things, brings different people and living beings together. A trusted design/change process allows people to collaborate across these divides. How can coastal resilience engineers communicate with psychologists and historians and urban planners and educators and neighborhood groups and elders and children and fishermen? A reliable and mutually trusted process provides a safe, clear, and understood "container," as Adam Kahane (2010) would put it, for the convergence to happen. It enables a sustained focus of creative energy (even while acknowledging pain and the presence of historical injuries) on the challenge. It gently demands seeing, hearing, and building on each others' strengths, challenging our own biases and assumptions, all as part of the process, not because one person's voice is better or cleaner or more academic than another. An accepted process is an expression of the concept of empowered love because it keeps people turning toward each other when they might otherwise remain fragmented in echo chambers and silos.

It is easy for children, youth, and their teachers and professors to become overwhelmed by the complexity and intensity of the world's challenges, too. But creative, collaborative, rooted, and empathic design/change processes can be very simple: Notice, Imagine, Plan, Do, or Feel, Imagine, Do, Share (dfcworld.org) and are accessible by very young children. When young children can engage authentically in the civic life of their communities, their sense of belonging and purpose creates joy, a sense of opportunity, and what Freire would call "civic courage." Having a process to aid in contributing to society and influencing positive change engenders both responsibility for others and self-actualization. Agency and efficacy, the ability and the confidence to make a difference, rests on having the design tools—knowing how to learn what needs to be learned and how to get things done.

A reliable design process facilitates a sense of security and builds confidence in regenerative relationships. Knowing HOW to drive change, how to challenge assumptions and biases, how to be guided and motivated by human feeling, how to create vision and consensus, how to surface the right problems at the right scale, how to tap into our own historical knowledge and inner drive, how to create the alliances needed to enact our ideas, enables us to disrupt oppressive power-impact flows and builds power-full resilience. The power of process unlocks the doors to an abundant life of belonging, collaborative problem seeking and difference making, shared restoration, renewal, and joy. And in the end, we may find ourselves significantly less fatalistic about the complexity of challenges like climate change.

As educators, we need to respect and love ourselves enough to open up the space to step back (dive in?) and see where we are on our own journey of life. It may take some time to figure out how to reconnect with your inner co-designer or, as some say, to let "the child's mind" in us unfold its wings. It may take some time to unlearn performative compliance-driven habits, and it will require companionship and practice and reflection to develop your own inner coherence and civic agency. Find other educator-learners you can join on this part of your journey. They are out there, hosting podcasts like Ben Freud's *Coconut Thinking* and Kyle Wagner's *Transformative Learning Experiences*, writing articles, hosting sessions on platforms like k20 or Getting Smart or What School Could Be, working with organizations like UNESCO, SDG Educators, ASEE (American Society of Engineering Educators), Big Picture Learning, k12lab's School Retool, or Project Zero's Justice by Design and Agency By Design. It may take some time and support to keep building and sustaining the ecosystems of relationships around you to support transformative design. Remember, the process you choose to use is just a toolbox. The tools do not have the agency to transform anything on their own, so the intention and worldview and relationality with which you use them makes all the difference. They will become part of you and how you see the world. Jeff Hopkins, founder and school leader of Pacific School for Inquiry and Innovation, put it best. "Design thinking isn't something we do at our school. It is who we are."

 Mending News!

Regenerative Springhouse Community School Offers Revitalizing Sessions for Adults

As it says on their home page, "Springhouse is an intergenerational learning community with life at its center. We are actively reimagining education and believe learning is a lifelong journey that should be centered around vitality, meaning, and cultivating wholeness to better serve the world's emerging needs." You might want to explore their classes and find some healing and inspiration. https://springhouse.org/

And let's not forget that our students will come to you with varying degrees of agency and self-efficacy. Be careful of your assumptions here. You might think that wealthy and privileged children have an elevated (perhaps inflated) sense of agency because they "have it made" or are headed for CEO-ship and leadership. But ... overly protected and micro-managed, many feel insufficient and ineffective. Decision-making and authentic responsibility *with consequences* scare them silly. Life outside the bubble scares them, too. Similarly, young people from underserved communities often know far more about persisting, self-control, caring for others, responsibility, and creative problem solving than they are given credit for. Many of them are so accustomed to being thought deficient in school, and that their contributions won't matter, that they don't bring their strengths forward. In both of these cases (and all in between), parents and educators working together to cultivate their own and youth agency and efficacy can make a tremendous difference. I have yet to meet students who did not feel stronger with design processes and mindsets and relationships—the tools for change—in their possession. Remember the kids who made the film that begins this book? The story about change they wanted to tell was how design thinking was helping them to believe they have a future.

Why You Haven't Seen a Design Process Graphic Yet

I have not focused on any particular process yet, and that is by design. If you focus on the process before identifying what values and principles the process represents, you can end up with less agency to change things in an equitable and power-full way, and the process itself becomes fixed and no longer "living." "Design Thinking" is already out there, widely used around the world in various contexts. Co-design thinking is a toolkit of incalculable value in empowered community resilience and disaster recovery, and it looks a bit different everywhere.

Once you see how effectively it can work, it is tempting to become very attached to *the* process." You might become so attached to teaching The Process, that you lose sight of the values and heart-thinking relational design culture you are co-creating, and the power flows could become counter-cultural or skewed. An example of this is what happens sometimes in the teaching of writing. In an effort to break it down into easy-to-understand parts, the Five Paragraph Essay becomes too formulaic, and a limiting end in itself, losing sight of the more liberating intellectual pursuit of ideas and evolution of the mind. Instead, think of our living (because it changes everywhere we do it) model of co-design pictured in Figure 8.4 as a *starting* place, simple tools that can be used as an extension of the funds of knowledge your students and their communities bring. Viewed, used, and reflected upon with critical consciousness of nested systems, position, and power, regenerative "design thinking" (not just a process but also the heart-thinking that goes along with it) can be a trusted collection of mindsets and methods to co-empower our shared resources.

FIGURE 8.4 A regenerative design thinking process

The community where you work may already have "tried and true" processes for bringing the community together to confront challenges, reflected in the way your students relate. Or, the process you and your community choose to use might look quite different. You might use one format for inquiry and another variation for problem seeking and solving. Another version for vision-making and consensus-building. You might emphasize or employ different elements of it at different times. Don't feel like you have to use all of the tools at once! The point is to own and iterate one or two processes that fit right culturally and that function well to connect and integrate our wisdom and creativity to influence the nested systems we inhabit.

A Critical Look at the History of Design Thinking

Like the communities in which you live and work, the design thinking model I started with has a history of its own. For one thing, professionals such as educators, architects, engineers, community planners, and public health officials have used some form of stakeholder-responsive design for centuries. In other words, these kinds of experts might get input from stakeholders before, during, and/or after the moment of designing solutions for them. If they did that, their efforts would generally land in the Design FOR domain of the Who Holds the Power of Design chart (Figure 8.3). The Creative Education Foundation's efforts to codify Creative Problem Solving processes date back to the 1940s. The UN's efforts to include children's voices in the decisions made affecting them go back to the 1950s. In the 1980s, IDEO's practice of "human-centered design" to generate creativity in business based on a form of empathy began gaining traction. Other scholars and practitioners used and wrote about it, many exploring new and different uses of related epistemologies and processes. When David Kelley codified a Design Thinking process, built it into the Hasso Plattner Institute of Design's "d-school" curriculum and open-sourced it to the world in 2005, it included "Empathize, Define, Ideate, Prototype, and Test" in that now famous wandering row of hexagons. The global need for a simple process to clarify complexity and take steps to embrace and influence change (and the imprimatur of Stanford, improved the likelihood that designed products and services would get purchased) was so great that it proliferated and became widely adapted, adopted, critiqued, and iterated, and is still evolving today.

The United Nations uses design thinking to create community well-being and systems in the Za-atari Refugee Camp (the largest in the world) and throughout their public-facing agencies. Big tech companies use it for innovation and team building. But it's not just them. NGOs, retail giants, healthcare, transportation, municipalities, and small businesses are using it, too. It's a rare business or government school that doesn't teach it now. It is by no means the only approach, but one that is useful because of its simplicity, and so it became the starting place for our toolbox of equitable change making and power-full eco-social resilience. Design thinking has changed a lot since I first started using it in a public policy class on community resilience, and changed even more once we began iterating it in Puerto Rico. Using design thinking ethically and responsibly means adapting it or dropping it altogether depending on the context. I frequently don't use the original terminology at all.

Co-design thinking (Designing WITH) is a toolkit of incalculable value in community resilience and disaster recovery. Community leaders and global innovators use it to generate vision and find paths out of wicked, sticky, and complicated "where do we begin?" challenges like climate change. Educators around the world have picked up on the potential of design thinking processes and mindsets to teach creative problem solving and to foster positive growth around the transformation—of school, community, and life. In some countries and regions (British Columbia, for one, Finland for another) it is built into centralized curricula, and fosters civic, collaborative, and positive engagement from the beginning of school, involving children in issues they care about. With the support of the k12lab at Stanford (and its spin-off centers for belonging, liberatory design, school space design, School Retool, and life design), and Harvard's Project Zero (and its spin-offs Justice By Design, Maker-centered Learning, and Agency By Design) teachers and students can be part of a community of thought leaders continuing to research, apply, and critique design thinking, even as they are using it to transform.

"Power Audit" the Process As You Go: Design-Critical Thinking

The more we understand about how design thinking works (and where it doesn't), the better able we will be to intentionally use parts of it or the whole of it in equitable, inclusive, and co-empowering ways. As we walk through this version, let's use a critical lens and audit the power dynamics within it. There is a graphic representation of this power audit in Resource 4. As we go, pay attention to the "meta" lesson in criticality, positionality, and power we are enacting, too. You and your students can extend this critical awareness to all of the systems and ecosystems they inhabit. Pay attention to the skills and mindsets, or the "co-benefits" (to borrow a term from health practice) of the different phases of this process. Here's the bottom line for our audit: identifying who owns those benefits will help us to map and make visible how power is flowing out widely rather than vertically, and encourage the customarily powerless become power-full with the agency to influence change.

If design thinking is new for you, you may be reassured by some new (and really old) favorites built in, such as the "4C" so-called "21st-century" skills: Collaboration, Creativity, Communication, and Critical thinking. When we run these through our critical review of design thinking, we begin to see even more clearly the ways in which regenerative community co-design thinking can teach them. In Resource 5, there is a more "skills focused" self-assessment rubric for helping to merge 4C goals and co-design thinking ones.

It is important to note here that educators can teach design thinking in parts, building these phases (and the mindsets and skills that go with them) separately into lessons throughout your curricula. Doing so will be important steps toward expanding your capabilities with "the tools," as you aim for at least one full design challenge per year or semester. Framing or bookending your curriculum with challenges meaningful to students gives purpose to their drive to deeply learn more content. All of this will be planting the seeds of an emerging culture of design and coherence relevant to your context, so that you too will be able to say, "design thinking is not something we do, but it is who we are." On that note, let's be clear. Like everything else that's regenerative, learning to teach design thinking is a lifelong journey, which you are not going to get from a book or a single workshop. But here is a place to begin.

How to Approach Co-design Thinking—Tips for Teachers

Use the rest of this chapter in conjunction with Resource 4, which helps to sort out graphically what the skills, mindsets, and co-benefits of each phase could be, as well as revealing the results of many power audits. You may also wish to consult other toolkits and guides to get a range of approaches to help you identify and modify the ones that will work best for you. I highly recommend OneStone's Design Toolkit, https://onestone. org/design-toolbox, and the National Equity Project and d-School's Liberatory Design toolkit found here https://www. nationalequityproject.org/frameworks/liberatory-design.

The original first phase of design thinking was called Discovery, often shortened to Empathy, in order to emphasize that this phase is all about learning about others' perspectives. Today, design educators often begin with Noticing one's own positional biases and preconceived ideas, identifying one's own strengths, as well as tuning in to the issues in our place and seeing what we care deeply about. In this launching segment, students become aware of the difficulties facing others and also attune to their own strengths and capabilities.

Gathering

We call this phase Gathering, so as to emphasize that no one is being "discovered" or uncovered, and that we will not push to empathize if that is emotionally fraught. Gathering is relational, and so interrelatedness and coherence is emphasized through the idea of compassion and "I/we can relate" also shapes motivation and purpose. This is also a time to gather up as a team, playing Superpowers and How Do I Belong in order to establish what we feel we can contribute and where we would like to grow.

The Gathering phase usually takes longest and lends itself well to being taught with special focus in many contexts because it is so rich with regenerative power. In addition to the foundational steps previously mentioned, it is characterized by divergent thinking, wide open and curious for all learning, careful observation, and deep listening, by slowing down to notice contextual details and tone and body language, and by gathering stories from those who are not usually listened to.

This is an opportunity to teach respectful inquiry and story-listening skills, as well as consentful data (of all kinds) gathering and documentation. Contextualized research and "content learning" happens throughout the design process, but especially in this phase, as designers are highly motivated to know more about the situations and other beings they care about. This is a good opportunity to guide learners toward both research skills and establishing their learning goals, including what I call "depth perception," or how to go deeper and when they will know when they know enough for now. Notice that we are not generating solutions at this point, but gathering up all the knowledge and local expertise that we can.

Turn to Resource 4 to see what the power audit for this Gathering phase turned up. We need to keep asking ourselves the questions, Who is the designer, at this moment? What language am I using to describe the people I am observing? What is my social position in relation to them? What is the Nature of our relationship? How might my own privilege affect how I ask and what I notice? How am I showing up? Have I adequately audited my own power in this situation? How have I invited others into this process with me? How have we addressed power dynamics and belonging in our team? What assumptions am I making about how others will answer my questions? How could that interfere with clean asking and whole listening? *These questions need to be addressed honestly before going any further into a design process.* To those of you who are thinking about teaching for the power to drive change , this kind of work in power literacy never ends. It is evolutionary because it changes the architecture of the relationships around us, and it needs to be taught and enacted every day. It will take some time to practice the work enough with yourself so that you can teach others. I am still learning.

A Word About Empathy

Empathy is a word often misunderstood in the design thinking process. More frequently, a kind of **compassion** emerges, where, importantly, an observer can imagine or relate to what it might be like to experience the world the way someone else does and then be moved to act. Notice how compassionate the young people who have contributed to this book are when it comes to the whole of our living family! This compassion underscores our interrelatedness and the emotional resonance engenders internal motivation and purpose, a drive to make a positive difference in another being's life. True fellow-feeling, or empathy, where you *actually feel* the same way another person is, tapping directly into your own emotional context and history and theirs, is a deep emotional commitment and usually only happens *authentically* in the context of a long-term, safe and trusting relationship. It is definitely desirable in collaborative thinking, but the reality is that it could put participants (i.e., your students and their families) in positions of emotional vulnerability. Consider this. From a position of privilege, you can return to safety and emotional calm with ease because you never really leave it. The pursuit of "empathy" can be something akin to a kind of "emotional tourism," where the privileged can take a jaunt through someone else's struggle, feel it for a moment maybe, and snap back into safe mode. It's a lot to ask of our design partners, too. Digging honestly into genuine feelings needs to be in the context of a deep, trusting relationship. With consent, with trust built over time, and with recognition of position and potential trauma, compassion can happen, and that is certainly enough.

Now that you're onto the rhythm of this, let's move on from Gathering through the rest of the co-design thinking process. Remember that once you feel you have a have *co-design* in your repertoire, you will be able to facilitate (your students will also) design experiences where your design partners are actually holding all of the power of design. I tried this "Designed BY" frame first with my students. Having centered oneself and one's team, gathered the expertise of your partners in design and sought out all voices, especially the typically silent(ced) ones, we have to converge all of our information in order to see which needs, concerns, strengths, attitudes, and resources emerge as priorities. This is a good opportunity to make thinking visible, through drawing or other arts, though often words make their appearance too.

Clarify

We call this phase "Clarify," because it seems more democratic than "Define," which is how many design thinking schemas move on. There is a lot of power in who gets to "define." If you are trying to identify patterns of response and feeling, clarity seems more accurate than "definition" anyhow. Working with our design partners, we want to look at all we have gathered and notice what patterns emerge. This is a very good opportunity to ask follow-up (clarifying!) questions, to go a little deeper with consent to touch feelings and underlying doubts and strengths. It is also an excellent chance to teach about making trustworthy inferences from evidence. We use a chart format where we first collect what people said and did, and from there infer how they think and feel. We don't draw a line between thinking and feeling. The storytellers are there to confirm and to hold the ones making inferences accountable and/or share in the process themselves.

Further, this is a chance to practice making our convergent (bringing it together) thinking visible. Figures 8.5 and 8.6 show two examples of how Bayamón Design Lab students reflected and clarified what they had learned from their design partners in the village. Making thinking visible is such an important learning skill in all disciplines (and can help to bring them together) that we rely on Harvard Project Zero's Agency By Design (free) Thought Routine and Making Thinking Visible in many learning contexts. http://www.agencybydesign.org/

FIGURE 8.5 Making feelings visible

FIGURE 8.6 "Power abuela," strengths of identity

Once you have some clarity about the emerging patterns of strengths and concerns among your community of co-designers, the next step could be to find the opportunities for design. In the old design thinking models, this was referred to as a "**problem statement.**" We prefer *opportunities*, to stay focused on asset thinking rather than deficit thinking), and to get out of savior mindsets and the linear problem-solution-problem-solution trap. Your students may well already be on this urgency driven, "gotta get the answer fast" treadmill. In co-design thinking, a fast answer is bound to be wrong. Slow down so they can notice when they are jumping to solutions and skipping over the foundational trust gained through an ethical Gathering and Clarifying process. Clarifying where the opportunities for design are with a framing statement also known as a "how might we ... ." statement opens the door for the concept of shared efficacy to bring about change, and keeps it open for all possible options, and that those options will also be living and changing. If your class has remained open to their design partners' hearts and thoughts, there might be more than one opportunity to pursue. Your class may divide further into teams focused on specific design opportunities (notice: not solutions yet!!! Just opportunities for design ...) at this point (or possibly later, after imagining).

The opportunity statement is meant to be an invitation to brainstorming. In fact, avoid putting a solution in it, which will it so narrow that it shuts down possibilities. This is also an opportunity to consider scale. If the opportunity is a local version of a global problem, that's okay! Emphasize what your design partners' needs or values are. Here's an example. If you are trying to improve virtual learning, you could say, "HMW co-create engaging virtual learning environments that build on youth creativity, confidence and connectedness?" It acknowledges that there are constraints and values youth concerns, but also enables their creativity. You may settle on more than one opportunity statement, which could reshape co-design teams based on their own motivations and findings.

Convergent thinking always runs the risk of trespassing on others' ways of thinking and being, so don't forget to check out

Resource 4 for what the power audit turned up! At the same time, take note of the co-benefits for your co-designers and for yourselves of regenerative design.

Imagine
Imagine, to avoid the jargony, "Ideation," brainstorms "beyond the box" solutions to the challenge/opportunity statements by using magical thinking and seeming impossibilities to permit wild ideas to thrive. Multiple methods can be used to unlock creativity as what works best for one creative team might not work best for another. There may be culturally rooted approaches to brainstorming that you should rely on. My students have referred to our multiple ideations as "Favretti's fun ways to get all the peanut butter out of the jar." I preferred "reaching for as many stars as we can," but seriously, the key to all creativity is to shut down the inner editor and stop judging. And to build up silliness. Use magical thinking. And don't do it all in one sitting. This is part of building design agency and divergent thinking that you can do anytime with any opportunity that comes your way.

For most people, going fast and alone but sitting in teams the first time around works well. More experienced ideators might be able to jump right into a trusted-team ideation session, but most kids are too concerned about being judged to do that right off. Also, your brain benefits from some fun warmup exercises and from breaks involving physical activity, so build that into your planning. One "starting point" possible series could look like this. A team game of "Fortunately, Unfortunately," making the silly story standing, and then when the teacher says "Action!" act out the last statement. Then get down to imagining/brainstorming. Everyone writes one phrase or 2–3 keywords or quick sketch on a post-it or one small piece of paper per idea. Ideate for 5 minutes, aiming for 10–15 ideas. Or, if lunch is happening in 10 minutes, make it a challenge … 25 ideas for lunch! A winning team?? The idea, as you are gleaning, is that we are not looking for great ideas. We are looking for a LOT of them.

The next session might focus on optimizing each idea you already have. Add two more ideas stemming out from one. Or, sort them into categories and add five more ideas. Optimize each others' ideas (great for practicing a "Yes, And ..." mindset and get out of our "But-heads."). A great warmup for this is 20 Circles (or squares). In two minutes, make 20 different faces, or pizzas, or cookies, or anything like that. Squares can be 20 houses. Upon reflection, the students will notice that the most effective strategy is to just change one element and *voi lá*! A new idea. Another strategy is to have teams ideate on other teams' challenge statements. Don't forget to celebrate! It's easy to power-audit ideation/imagining. Who is doing the imagining?

Building Consensus. After the wide-open divergence of idea generation, it is time to converge again. What will be the ideas or constellations of ideas that get tested? Here's an opportunity to develop more civic and relational skills—consensus-building. Coming to consensus is another danger zone where it is very easy to reproduce systemic biases and social threats. But the power relationships pre-existing the consensus building can be positively disrupted if we view this as another opportunity to enact true collaboration. Critically reflect with your students on whether voting in a small group would be inclusive or exclusive? How can we make sure that everyone involved is seen, fully listened to, and included?

An Idea is a shared gift. With a celebratory ceremony, everyone gives their gifts to the team. They let them go. I like to envision this like a milkweed pod or a dandelion puffing out its seeds on a breeze. Maybe some will germinate. Maybe not. There are no bad ideas. The full listening is full-on now, as ideas are explained and sorted, and sometimes added to--the collaborative imagining continues now. Educators and facilitators might hear, "YES! And ... then we could ..." or "What if we ..." or "If only we could ..." or "Then we would need to ..." but NO JUDGING. The totally magic ones go in the magic pile. The sorting will surface how ideas are related to each other, and may be combined like constellations into separate solutions, pathways, or initiatives. Some teams benefit from sketching as well as explaining verbally. Both the imagining and the consensus building parts of this phase represent an opportunity to connect with design partners to include their ideas, too, and their suggestions about which groups of ideas resonate the most. Sometimes the ideation is a large group event, and then teams may emerge to take on different approaches. No decision is made until everyone is heard and idea-constellations are built that everyone on the team can live with.

Build to Try

A quick **prototype** is just that—a quick **sketch**, often a 3d "sketch." This is not the camera-ready story-board, or the industry-ready blueprint. This phase of co-design thinking is a low-tech, low-investment absolutely essential way of making thinking visible and uncovering the potential pain points or sticky spots in the ideas. Here's an opportunity to reflect on repurposing—using found materials, or "clean garbage" to build out our ideas. Making it, even in sketch form, opens up a new kind of efficacy: we can effect change. We can put some-thing together and make it work. We can see where it fails. This phase can be very scary, especially because we are visualizing our ideas in real life with real consequences. It's an opportunity for you to help your students and their design partners see failing as learning. We can see what else needs to be done within or to a system to support our new impact or our vision. We can identify who can help us and invite them in. Remember all of the kinds of expertise that can help: Nature/life, com-munity experts, trained and credentialled experts … .

Humbly seeking input about the quick prototypes from all kinds of experts also puts your students and their design partners in the driver's seat. Their design partners are experts in their own experience, and their knowledge of place, identity, and history adds immeasurably to the co-benefits of design for all. The team will need to call on outside experts as well. In the village in Puerto Rico, a team of community members and students was looking at improving evacuation in times of flooding. They needed input not only from their community partners, who told them what they had experienced evacuating during Hurricane María, but also from the US Coast Guard and the Department of Education (remember the locked school sits on the highest ground). In figuring out whom to invite, the teams learned about the whole system of emergency response and evacuation. During the conversation with outside experts, they learned that some aspects of their prototype would work and some would need to be iterated. They developed partnerships that would help implement their new strategies. See Figure 8.7.

FIGURE 8.7 Working with US Coast Guard Sector San Juan

In the original model of design thinking, after prototyping comes the "test." Does it work? Where does it fail? And that's where the process loops to an earlier part of the process, sometimes ideating solutions again, returning all the way to gathering if needed. Humbly seeking expert input is part of the prototyping process. What is the purpose of quick prototyping if not to make your thinking visible or 3D, so that your whole team can see where it will fail and so that you can get input? I use "humbly seeking input" because that is the stance our students should be in, if their living solutions are evolving. A power audit might show that if they are arrogant or defensive about their solutions, they could be holding onto the power of design in such a way as to shut down the relational and trust-building potential of a reliable, shared co-design process. Who gets all the co-benefits, then? Think of the implications of this moment when co-designing learning experiences with your students. What are you holding on to that you could humbly let go?

Try Again

It's true that quick prototyping and input seeking might surface the need to repeat some of the steps. To keep things simple and emphasize not to skip this part, I've put it into a separate phase called "**Try Again**," even if you think it's "good enough." This also emphasizes that the process of change embodies change: learning, reframing, redirection, and redesign. How can our solutions be more sustainable? How could they be cheaper? How will they be maintained and changed? How are they fitting into or changing systems to move toward more ecological and socially just resilience? How can they more clearly fulfill the opportunity to adapt or mitigate? How could they respond more closely to the challenge/opportunity statement? or better reflect what resonated with our partners and what we learned from all of our experts? This is a chance to reflect on the importance of making mistakes for learning (without self-criticism), and also on the continuous change that is part of life. Iterating together helps keep the flow of power and co-benefits in the right hands, as we try again (and again) to make our solutions more feasible, more do-able, more sustainable, and more adaptable. Trying again together builds trust and relationships, as our design partner-experts know that the process is responsive to them.

Enact

"**Enacting**" is when additional relational life skills, like working with your partner organizations to implement the changes youth have co-designed, appearing in public to persuade the city council, and other critically important leadership and entrepreneurship experiences will emerge. Participating with your partner organizations to draw up action plans and budgets, and taking on responsibilities to see them through is a vital part of any design process, and a good opportunity to learn about ethical entrepreneurship. Learning communities need to see what they can do to be sure that there are funds available or accessible to move proposals forward. I did not draw up a Power Audit chart for this, because design contexts and outcomes will be so different from each other, but this is of course a moment in design (life) when systemic barriers and prejudices could kill the students' enthusiasm and agency. (See Chapter 10) Before you begin the project, you will need to be sure that there are many possibilities for enactment, and that you are, together with your students, thinking of many different perspectives on success.

Not every project is destined for implementation—in fact, often design thinking processes can be used to motivate depth of inquiry, or vision-making, or prioritizing complex issues and opportunities, and those outcomes ARE the implementation. Some projects won't pass the accountability measures or address the challenges in ways that will be feasible and sustainable. These will need more work or will go into the learning process pile.

Reflection and Celebration

Every step of the processes you use, and every project is worth reflecting on. Learning happens in multiple ways, and one of the most human is reflection. Individual and shared metacognition and recollection, with gratitude as a main stance (my students send thank-yous with specific examples to their design partners and teammates), and honest consideration of lessons learned is essential to agency, resilience, and long-term transformation. In Resource 5, you will find some examples of reflection questions and opportunities for self-assessment and gratitude.

Don't forget to celebrate! Design is fun and energizing!

Making Design Thinking Transformative

Many teachers and school systems, under time pressures of their own, teach design thinking as a process or, "*the* process of design," which can easily become another add-on initiative with a series of performative steps that has little transformative value. To prevent that, there are (at least) five beneficial situations you will want to aim for:

1. *Voluntary* deepening of engagement with co-design thinking at a pace led by faculty and students and community needs and potential. Often the joy and empowerment need to be witnessed, and the teacher-to-teacher "how do you set this up and know that it's working" needs to be shared before others can see how it could work in their context. "I want that for my kids" is the most common response after witnessing.

2. *Ongoing* professional learning and multi-generational reflection creates a regenerative cycle of shared growth. Internalizing design mindsets and habits takes time and practice. It is not going to happen in a one-shot (or even two or three), talking-head expert kind of transfer. A multi-age, multi-perspective, multi-disciplinary community of learners is best.

3. Organizations in your ecosystem that *authentically need and want* your youth participation. These might include valued cultural resources such as zoos, aquariums, parks, libraries, makerspaces, gardens or museums, ethnic organizations, government agencies, or local businesses.

4. Be sure that the *potential to influence change is actualized* as frequently as possible. Some inquiries remain as inquiries—they grow from student interests and wonderment and don't get implemented because that's not how they unfold. Build relationships and systems and networks that will prevent great ideas from going into the garbage.

5. Be sure that educators have *time and space to reflect and internalize* and that they have the *agency to create worlds with their students*. This means they will also need some flexibility to adapt time and space constructively in and outside of your school center. Some programs use intersessions, but the most integrated, adaptable schedule is ideal.

Remember, critical consciousness and adherence to life's principles of coherence, interrelatedness, regeneration, iterative change, and biodiversity make a co-design process power-full, and its purposeful use to expand justice and abundance makes it absolutely necessary in the age of futurephobia and climate disasters. Turn to the next pages to see how José Obregón tells the story of how design thinking saved his life.

Seeds for Planting

Everybody designs, but Nature is the best designer of all.

To co-create regenerative cultures of care and change, we can aspire to be bio-centric, democratized, and emancipatory in our designing, guided by the essential principles of life.

Design is not neutral, and can be used in such a way as to increase fragmentation, and to strengthen harmful structures and systems. Critical consciousness of the design processes you are using, while you are using them, helps to ensure that the co-benefits of design mindsets and habits are shared and ripple "horizontally" and multi-dimensionally through the web of interrelationship.

Regenerative design processes cannot be learned from a book, or even an active workshop, though that could function as a spark. Design proficiency is not a destination but a journey which, like life, continually evolves.

Notes

1 *Experimental Biology* 2019.
2 Wahl 2016. I have adapted Wahl's dimensions slightly.
3 Escobar 2017.
4 Fleming 2013.
5 Sanford 2020.
6 Manzini 2015.
7 Wahl 2016.
8 brown 2017.
9 Spencer and Juliani 2017.
10 Sanford 2020.
11 Silva Díaz 2021.

12 Royal Roads University Resilience By Design Lab https://resiliencebydesign. com/ MIT D-Lab https://d-lab.mit.edu/ Liberatory Design https://www. liberatorydesign.com/ and https://www.nationalequityproject.org/ frameworks/liberatory-design Creative Reaction Lab https://www. creativereactionlab.com/our-approach Justice By Design http://www.pz. harvard.edu/projects/justicexdesign

13 Talking Points https://talkingpts.org/ Family Engagement Lab and FasTalk https://www.familyengagementlab.org/

14 Tyner 2021.

15 brown 2017.

16 Knuth 2020.

17 Yeampierre 2020.

18 Freire 2018.

19 Spencer and Juliani 2017.

Interview: Jeltsin José Obregón

Jeltsin José Obregón, yes, he was named after Boris, is the dynamic young man who led El Pueblo Unido program during a gap year as it established opportunities for school transformation using design thinking in Puerto Rico. He attended community college in California and is now a full-time student at Berkeley. It was my honor to interview him in October of 2020.

Maggie Favretti:	Why do you say that "design thinking saved my life?"
José Obregón:	My freshman year, I went to a traditional high school, and my experience was not that great. For some classes, I did not have teachers who could teach, in my opinion. It was more them reading from the book or making us watch movies. They didn't seem to do much planning. To be fair, this public school was not supported. They didn't have a lot of resources … we didn't have books, or they were really trampled, or pages were ripped out … so they lacked resources, and a lot of the teachers were either teaching for the first time or they were substitute teachers, so they didn't have that much experience. And so they taught in the traditional way that they had learned … by the book, testing by the book, and stuff like that. I didn't like it, and I was kind of lost, to be honest.

The first thing I saw in my new school was when we went through the door of this huge garage. It was a garage. It used to be a car shop, so … . I went through there and I was like, "is this a real school?" (laughs) For me it was like, "what am I doing here?" I came from a school where we had hallways and many

DOI: 10.4324/9781003215806-11

classrooms, and now I have this huge garage, divided by whiteboards on z-racks. Some spaces didn't even have a divider, we said, "we're going to meet in this space, and this is where we're going to talk" and you could hear everyone when you were teaching. I think that created resilience in the students who were there because we got used to the noise, and we got used to working in any space. Literally anywhere, like on the floor. We could change it too. And that was really good for us to be designers because we were solving problems every single day.

MF: What was it like to be designing your school as you went along?

JO: That was messy at first. We had design thinking class every single day, and I remember that our first design challenge was to redesign the restaurant experience, and I was really taken up by creativity of it, thinking of new ideas, and the fact that we were building stuff and taking it apart, and building, and taking it away, and using "clean" garbage for prototyping ... if it was there, you could use it. I remember that every week it was a new iteration of the curriculum. We were designing it as we went. Every single year was a new iteration too. My first year, intersession was like that, and we were trying to apply design thinking to the regular classes, trying to be more project based instead of just tests, which really caught my attention, and I think that's why I focused more in school.

My second year we had Lab Days where you would make your own schedule as a student. So you would decide what you needed to do. Students would go to their homeroom, and our advisors would look at our schedule, and sometimes a teacher would request us to go to a class because we were behind. Or, if you were ahead you could go do something else. Another thing that we had was that during regular days, we always had a focused independent time (FIT) period, where we could read, or do homework—just focus on our own projects.

MF: What was design thinking like for you?

JO: I was really into art. And I was in this class called social design, really human-centric, where we were looking at social problems, and we would try to solve them using the arts. I remember we went to San Francisco, and one of the biggest problems here in the Bay Area is homelessness. We went to the Mission District, which is a heavily populated Latino and minority district, with a lot of arts there. There are the mission murals. You go through these little alleys and there's graffiti art, social justice art, which is really beautiful. This was another thing about design thinking. You got to learn outside of the classroom, to see the world how it is, and try to empathize. I remember I was into photography, and so was another classmate, and we thought OH! We can use photography to raise awareness, and this was the first time I thought I could do something that mattered. We decided to make a museum, where you went inside and around, surrounded by homelessness.

We had a problem, though. We really needed more pictures and we both had to work after school. So I said, "tomorrow, I'm going to take BART and go up to San Francisco and take pictures when I am supposed to be in school. Don't tell anyone." I was so into it that I went to San Francisco by myself. It was kind of scary, because I went to the place where homeless people live, and a lot of people are scared to walk there, because there are some people with mental illness, and you don't know who you're going to face. I was 15 and didn't know if I could handle that. But I went up to two people and interviewed them and really tried to empathize with them. That was my first experience with getting deep into "empathy." I asked these two people if I could interview them. They were immigrants from Honduras, and they had lost their family members, and they could not find work, and got depressed and addicted. And they made choices they regretted, but now their only choice was to live in a tent. Then I asked a veteran who was holding a sign, very respectfully, what led him to be in that position. Everyone gave very emotional responses and felt such strong regret. They let me record video, and so when we were designing the museum, we decided to put the video right in the center of the space, with black walls and the large prints of the photos. When we had Open House, I remember some people were crying. They got into the stories. This whole experience taught me so much about empathy and stories. And seeing the impact that it had led me to do other things, too.

Like when the school didn't have a baseball team, and I wanted to play baseball. I had to work with a lot of people. I pitched it to the administration four times, and each time they said, nope, iterate your budget again, and iterate your proposal. I had to talk to students again, ok, so how would your life change, how can we do this? I had to research where we could play. There were so many details I had never considered—that really taught me to do project management. I remember designing the team logo, and I'll never forget when we were playing our first game, seeing this on everyone's hats and uniforms, and on everyone there, and I thought, "Wow. It's so cool how you can build something from this little idea or prototype 'til you actually are seeing it in action." That was how I could imagine working in Puerto Rico.

I think these little projects help you build and expand your thinking so you could be able to solve these big problems in your community. I remember not understanding the importance at first, and I thought the first design challenges were stupid. What I did not realize was that I was learning a process that would make it possible to solve serious problems in the community, and that I've been able to do afterwards. Yeah. I still think all the time about the homeless situation now, and what more I could do. I think about how California is the 5th biggest economy in the world, if it were a separate country, so it has a lot of wealth and innovation. There are so many things that CA has done first. Both socially, and technologically. My girlfriend and I just started ideating as we were talking about it—she is also a design thinker—we were thinking about the different problems homeless people face, like addiction, and mental health, and what brought them to that situation.

Yes, you built them a house, but you've isolated them by design. So how do you help people in there? You have trauma, like homeless people who have come from war or violence, you have addiction, which sometimes comes from that, and depression too, and then just people who can't afford the rent, so how do you help them?? And how can you make solutions sustainable, so we're not just solving for the now, but also for the future?

MF: How did El Pueblo Unido Program get started in Puerto Rico?

JO: We were always learning how to use design thinking with community groups, either going there or inviting them in, so that they could use it to solve problems. That was amazing for me, as a student, to be teaching adults how to solve problems. So I really liked that, and that was when I thought I could educate people about it and empower them, too. So when Rob [Bolt] told me that he wanted to do something in Puerto Rico, I said "yes, I've read about the hurricanes in the news, I want to do something to help." I was the only senior in a group of juniors, and we designed this exchange with this public school in Puerto Rico. It was mainly all students doing it on this side, coached by Rob and this other parent, and then teachers and the principal on the other side in PR. We had to design everything about the trip ... how we would get there, where we would stay, how we would pay for it, what we would do with design thinking. We went to Puerto Rico in January 2018, but it was only the week before we went that we found out who we would be working with. Communication was terrible after the hurricanes. After we got back, we used lab days to figure out how to get them here to CA. That was a really good example of teachers and students co-designing education.

The first time we all met, we were with this one group of students who were totally quiet. Rob said, "go talk to them." I was the only Spanish-speaking student, so I was elected to translate and talk to everyone. Rob was looking at me like, "Go go go, you speak Spanish, you have to talk to them." But we found out that they had planned a welcome for us, including a surprise dance in Maritza's classroom, and it was really cool. On their side, they'd been planning all this, and we did not know about it. They definitely wanted to show us their culture, and that experience really made us excited about working together. They were amazing.

We did a course in design thinking with them, with the students who were selected by their teachers. It went well, but one of the most important things was that the teachers were seeing what it could do, and they got really involved. As we talked with them, they thought design thinking was an amazing way of learning and really wanted to know more about it.

When we got back, I was chosen to lead, and that was when Rob and I started talking about a gap year, but at that point, it was just to run the exchange. We divided our students into different responsibilities for designing their experience when they were with us, logistics, activities, housing, travel, and fund-raising. My role was to be the overall critic and support person—how are we going to do that? What else can we do? What have we missed? When they got there, I checked to be sure everything worked. It was very hard for me, both the design and implementation, because I was also doing so many other things—working, baseball, model UN, school, being a senior—I was so passionate about this exchange that I didn't make enough time for everything else. I had to drop out of some other things, but that was an important turning point for me. I committed to something I cared about even more. Other people were relying on me.

Once they were here, Maritza and the others, they wanted to know how to implement design thinking in their school. We were surprised by that. We never thought it would be a program about how to put design thinking into their school. Out of the exchange grew that question. How could we do design thinking in a very traditional public school that had been there for decades, in a system that is also very traditional? That was the big challenge. But they had a principal and a teacher who were deeply engaged. They were learning. Then you [the author] invited us to go to

Puerto Rico in April, to run that workshop with educators, and that was when I learned more about the PR system. The first time I went there, it was mostly about the exchange, but the second time, with you, it was much more about how could we do this here? I went into more of the classrooms and met more teachers, and began seeing more about how they teach and empathizing with them more. I was learning about Project Based Learning (PBL) and empathizing with the culture, and the education system, so I could see how I could help when I got there for my gap year.

MF: What a huge undertaking for your gap year! How was it for you?

JO: My experience was overall amazing. I have not yet met someone my age who went to a completely different place, to start something new in a completely different culture. That was a huge challenge. It was also a challenge for me because I was leading, in the real world, or trying to lead. I was the decision maker. And a lot of the decisions I was going to make were going to have an immediate impact on people. That was huge. And adults were trusting me to make those decisions. And some adults were looking at me, to see what I was going to do. In a critical way, like trying to test to see "if you can do it." There were many times when I went to important meetings and people would introduce me as a student, and not as the Executive Director of the program. And those were also people who were close to me. And I think that made me realize that I needed to tell them *and show them* that I'm capable of doing this and you can trust me.

The first intersession was the hardest because we had to find people in the community who would participate even though they've never seen this before and had no idea of the positive things that could happen. We had no idea what would happen. We had no idea how it would look in a public school. All the teachers' eyes were on the program, the PR Dept of Education's eyes were on the program, so we had a lot of pressure. And I remember on the first day of that intersession, one of the [career] Explorations, we thought we had all agreed but then they said, "oh we're not ready for the students." And we had arranged to bring the students to them. I texted them to let them know we were on our way, and they said, "oh. That's today?" And we had to deal with all of that, and right then I asked "what else can we offer for these students?" That problem came up in every single intersession—there was at least one Exploration or one teacher absence, so you had to solve it, right then and there, with no time for complaining.

MF: How was the experience of teaching teachers?

JO: Teaching teachers was one of the greatest experiences I have had so far. Teaching adults how to teach. It was ironic, if you think back to the beginning of how I got started with this. They taught me, but now I am teaching them how to teach in a different way. I gained a lot of confidence through teaching teachers and college professors, and I gained a lot of confidence in talking to adults. I felt more comfortable talking to adults than I did with students, for some reason, when I was in Puerto Rico. Teaching design thinking was my favorite part of my gap year.

MF: Anything you wish you had done differently?

JO: Of course there were things I wish I had done differently. We met with teachers one hour a week for six weeks, and a lot of them would come late, because they were cleaning up, talking with students, walking down from the 3rd floor, so then there was only 40 minutes left, and some would need to leave early. And I had to try to teach design thinking but also prepare them with what they were going to teach during the intersession. That I wish we had done differently. Of course if you had more time you could teach teachers many things, but seeing the results of the intersession made me really happy. I had spent day and night working on it, but then seeing the students, starting the first day, seeing the students working, designing, creating, solving problems, made me really proud. I never thought I could do this. There are so many feelings, it's hard for me to decide where to focus. Overall, I was really grateful to be able to teach adults, because that changed my way of thinking about how people can relate to each other. And now, even though I'll be nervous, I can go in front of a class or in front of a group and talk. Before, I was totally scared to do that, and now when I'm doing that, I feel like I'm in my zone.

MF: What happened next?

JO: After the Gap Year, I got to go to Maryland, to Frederick Community College, to teach design thinking to educators, to talk about the program. That was an incredible experience, to teach about design thinking in English, not in Spanish. And then I went to Harvard, with Ben Wild [Walkabout Education] and taught design thinking to graduate students in the school of education. As I saw more and did design thinking challenges more, I was iterating every single time and I became better at it. I also thought about how I was iterating all during my gap year—both the way I was working and in my personal life. The hardest thing was being away from my family and being away from my girlfriend. I wish I could go back in time and restructure how I worked, so I could have done other things. I just worked all of the time. But I didn't know how to work efficiently. I wish I could go back and learn Plena, or learn Bomba [two signature Afro-Caribbean dances]. I really wanted to learn that. But I know I'm going to go back.

MF: Overall reflections on design thinking?

JO: I think design thinking helps you to be resilient because you get accustomed to a lot of iteration, so you always keep trying. You get confidence in your problem solving, so when you face problems in your future, you collaborate to solve them instead of panicking or getting overwhelmed. And I think you can see that in Puerto Rico, I mean they went through a lot, with the hurricanes and the earthquakes, and poverty and government corruption, and now pandemic, but they collaborate and are resilient, especially the students at FMC. They had powerful messages about how they gained confidence through design thinking. Now they feel they can solve the problems of the world. I saw pictures of them going and cleaning the beaches during the pandemic. They put on their masks and went to the beach to start cleaning up the plastic and other stuff. That was a project that came out of one of the regular classes at FMC. So now when they learn about climate change, they go and do something. Now they know that together they can take on things that are big and scary.

Now that I am thinking about my own experience, going from learning in person to learning online during the pandemic, now that I'm a college student … what I learned in high school, in that garage with all the noise, learning that way, going to Puerto Rico to a traditional system, trying to change the system to learning in a different way, has helped me to be resilient right now when I am learning online. I try to think differently about how I can learn best, for myself. Try to change up my schedule every day. Build a pile of books to put my computer on so I can stand up because sitting down was making my knee hurt. That's the mentality of design thinking, where we don't spend a lot of time worrying about it but are constantly solving those little problems that we face. I think we are better problem seekers, too. We see them and fix them to keep making things better. It's a very positive way to be.

9 Power-full Positivity: Empowered Hope and the Positive Civic Action Cycle

How does the Positive Civic Action Cycle empower hope?
How does the Positive Civic Action Cycle bring people together?
How does the Positive Civic Action Cycle support mental health and overall well-being in the face of futurephobia?

As I sit down to write this chapter, Santiago Chile is preparing to host the first-ever Conference of Parties to the Escazú Agreement.[1] The first regional declaration of its kind, more than two-thirds of the 33 eligible Latin American and Caribbean countries have signed on, and over half have ratified it and filed with the United Nations. The Escazú Agreement, drafted in Costa Rica in 2018, and in effect since April of 2021, aims to guarantee implementation of the following: open access to environmental information (within 30-days of request), public participation in the environmental decision-making (open invitation by law), access to justice in policy making (including appeal and redress of harm), and access to protection for defenders of the land. This last provision is essential as Latin America is where Earth's homeland

DOI: 10.4324/9781003215806-12

defenders are most vulnerable to assassination and attacks. The Santiago Conference (Escazú COPS1) aims to strengthen the legislative, financial, and enforcement capacity of the signatories, including Indigenous people, who are co-hosts and full participants. How might our students engage with this new development?

 Mending News!

Co-hosting the Santiago Conference Will Be 20-Year-Old Indigenous Youth Leader Sumak Helena Sirén Gualinga

Gualinga grew up splitting her time between her father's land and people (Finland) and her mother's Kichwa Sarayaku family in the remote mountains of Ecuador, where Helena was born. The critical awareness she developed there of climate impacts as social impacts, too, led her to be a biocentric policy activist as a teen. She comes from a long tradition of Indigenous women fighting for the rights of women, of Indigenous people, and of our Mother Earth. Her mother and aunt, her grandmother and older sister are all activists, too. Gualinga has made a number of important films, with the production assistance of her father's family and of other environmental and Indigenous and natural rights organizations. Perhaps you and your students would like to connect with her.

By now over a billion people live in communities or countries with Climate Emergency Declarations. While the meaning of those declarations varies, in most cases they enable streamlined decision making around regulations on environmental polluters and financing for municipal climate-justice-forward projects. Hawai'i is the only US state to do it, though many municipalities have, including New York City (the nation's most populous) and small communities fighting for their lives, from Alaska to the Barrier Islands. Twenty-something Bhartendu

Pandey intends to use the new declarations to leverage his findings about climate and social injustice built into global urban planning. Instead of mapping unequal incomes and wealth distribution in cities, Pandey wrote his college thesis on mapping "infrastructure inequality" as the first step in any urban infrastructure design initiative. Communities with better lighting and drainage, better water quality and more green spaces, and better transportation alternatives and better school buildings attract people who can afford to pay more to live there. But infrastructure changes slowly and is very durable. Typically, infrastructure is designed to last 100 years. If climate and social justice is not taken into account in the redesign or new design of infrastructure, it will inhibit social progress and lock in climate and social injustice for generations. Pandey views this moment of increasing urbanization as our best chance to make a systemic difference using justice in infrastructure design.[2] How can our students be involved in furthering local climate emergency declarations so as to free up dollars and grant monies for local climate adaptations?

Puerto Rico has a chance to make moves in this direction, too, with the funding for school recovery and redesign just starting to trickle in. Their schools were, like most US public schools, designed for a sturdy industrial model of education, but many of them are unstable against earthquakes or they are broken since the earthquakes of early 2020. It is exciting to see how regenerative, "living" schools stateside are providing for the three E's communities are seeking: educational benefits, economic benefits, and environmental benefits. Here is an opportunity to bring together education and climate justice, in safe, healthy buildings that will pay for themselves (and then some!) over time and can serve as community health and climate (resilience) studios. Puerto Rico is a colony of the United States and so it can't sign on to the Escazú Agreement, even though island nations on either side of it have. But that doesn't need to stop its municipalities and its Department of Education from acting as if it has. It will not be able to afford to make every building a living building up to the biophilic standards of the Living Building Challenge.[3] But that doesn't mean it can't use

348 ◆ Power-full Positivity

those regenerative standards as a guide for those buildings it CAN renovate, and involve local communities and youth in the decision-making process.

Climate Courage Is Empowered Hope

Efficacy is the knowledge that you can effect change. Agency is exercising one's capabilities to act on the world around you. Power-full positivity is not just reframing, wishing, dreaming, or talking. It is not simply being optimistic because that feels better than giving in to despair. It is not hope for hope's sake, or a self-care meditation, although all of these are available to us anytime and pretty good tools to use as well. It is not even just the awareness that better worlds are possible, or that someone else is "working on it," though that certainly helps, too. Power-full positivity comes from both efficacy and agency, and empowers us to seek opportunities to make hoped for outcomes into realities. Having done something that matters, or being involved in something meaningful, being entrusted with the well-being of others in a community—this is hope built on the strength of those roots of regenerative power and nourished by the principles of life itself. Civic action, or doing something for the good of the whole, energizes a regenerative cycle of courage and empowered hope. During the design labs in Bayamón in 2019, students and teachers saw and felt something more of what's possible in school. Attendance of students and teachers during the intersessions climbed to nearly 100%. Disciplinary infractions were practically nonexistent. Teachers were asking, "how can I build this into everything I do?" In the video some of the students made in 2019, "Design Thinking Launches in Puerto Rico," (https://www.designed4resilience.org/puerto-rico), one student talks about how important it is to be co-designers of their education. All of the students interviewed in the making of the film said how they felt like they were making history. Education justice history. Many of them have stepped into leadership roles in their schools and communities, and into the host organization, the Center for Design-Thinking and Innovation in Education (CD-TIE) itself.

 **Mending News!**

CD-TIE Offers Design Thinking Certification Course

In collaboration with the UPR-Bayamón, San Juan-based CD-TIE has created an in-person series of thirty hours of free design thinking workshops for educators, complete with takeaway materials. Beginning with their first in-carnation as El Pueblo Unido Program, which co-created the intersessions that fostered design thinking across all departments and grades 7–12 in Escuela Francisco Manrique Cabrera in Bayamón, they have fostered an acquaintance with design thinking for over a hundred teachers in at least six schools around the island. Many of those have continued to design on their own, using the tools in new ways. Several of the students involved have become gap-year leaders and peer mentors, and teacher alumni can be fellows, using design thinking to keep the evolution of CD-TIE alive and regenerating. https:// www.elpueblounidoprogram.org/

Students like these embody the rhetorical question teacher, writer, and activist Mary Annaïse Heglar asks, "What if hope isn't what leads to action? What if courage leads to action and hope is what comes next?" Hope, joy, awe, humility, and the bold love and collective efficacy to energize and fuel our power to act again. Remember the banners the 6th graders in Whistler made, from Chapter 6? Those are the defiantly loving and hopeful outcomes from the strong feelings expressed in their poem below.[4]

Climate Change
By Zoe Kargl, Laura Hallisey, Moka Higashi,
Dinara Ilyasova, 6th grade
As the cold arctic ice melts,
the climate changes and erodes
Many creatures that used to roam
Now hide away
From the rising dangers of our changing planet
the scenery around us crumbles and changes
Ocean levels rise
Mountains fall
We as society can stop it all
For we are the change,
the kids who want to protect it all.

"We are the change." These young people, and the ones you are relating to in the other pages of this book, are building communities and creating worlds. Their leadership is full of empowered hope, and their future is leader-full. They are strong enough to act, even beyond the weight of future-phobia, because they have tapped into their shared re-generative powers and energized their co-agency. They are taking up their civic responsibility to safeguard the rights of others as well as their own. They are beyond resilient—they are defiant. To them, doing something that matters is re-generative because it encourages them to do it some more. Life creates the conditions for more life. Regenerative posi-tivity is the same way. Civic action creates hope creates courage creates action creates courage creates hope creates action, in a friendly and virtuous "power-full positivity cycle" of love and care that benefits communities and youth alike. The teachers who are on the journey with them are some of their most important allies. As educators, what can we do to support, guide, and be by their side, arm in arm, doing what good ancestors do?

FIGURE 9.1 The positive civic action cycle

Teachers and the Positive Civic Action Cycle

Teachers can initiate what I call a Positive Civic Action Cycle (Figure 9.1), which not only is regenerative in the sense that positive action leads to more positive action, but which also encourages greater engagement, deeper listening and learning, and adds to overall well-being. "Civic" in this sense means doing something for the common good. Students and teachers caught up in a positive civic action cycle start looking for more opportunities to contribute. Why? Because helping others has a positive physiological effect, and because this helps us to live with our legitimate concerns about the future. We are not "eliminating the negative by accentuating the positive," instead we are noticing our feelings and what they are telling us, processing them together in our web of safe relationships, using them to build up our sense of purpose, and *acting beyond* futurephobia in ways that are meaningful and healing. Varshini Prakash, Executive Director of the youth climate action revolution Sunrise Movement puts it this way. "The only failure would be to do nothing."[5]

Do Something

Doing something that matters is essential to create the positive and empowering feelings of belonging associated with purpose-full action. Think of a time when you worked on something with others to make a difference. What did that feel like?

One of the most frustrating things about being in school is the sensation that you are not doing anything. The emphasis is all on *potential* energy, which can lead to feelings of power-lessness and futurephobia. Self-doubt (maybe I have nothing to contribute) grows over time and also kinetic energy builds up into frustration (remember Chris? Why do I have to wait?). We need to get more kinetic energy, more relevant and purpose-full DOING into our learning, if we want it to be meaningful. As our friend the young solar engineer Javier Moscoso says, "you can always talk about ideas, but until you have actually connected two wires, you haven't actually done anything."

What can we do to keep learners in a regenerative action cycle of positivity? From the earliest ages, civic activity might be helping to clean up, looking out for each other, gardening and seed saving (remember Fabián?), making something for elders in exchange for stories, measuring rain, counting tree species or finding monarch butterfly eggs, graduating to older students' full-on climate innovation, community advocacy, decision-making, and leadership. All of it connects to and deepens some aspects of needed and relevant "content" learning, as well as adding valuable life skills. Together we can seek ways to become involved in co-creating and carrying out commitments to our brothers and sisters and other relations in the living world, and holding ourselves and others accountable to them.

When we are facilitating contributions to our living community, we are also facilitating belonging. In her beautiful book *Design for Belonging: How To Build Inclusion and Collaboration In Your Communities*, designer, educator, and researcher Susie Wise writes that in her numerous interviews with people about what belonging feels like, many of them said "they knew they were part of a community when they felt they were making a contribution."[6] Peter Block, author of *Community: The Structure of Belonging*, calls the different ways of supporting belonging "conversations." The first is the "invitation," and the last is "gifts," both given (contribution) and received. He writes, "belonging occurs when we tell others what gifts we receive from them."[7]

To support a feeling of abundance and belonging and to facilitate the Positive Civic Action Cycle, consider helping youth teams to create belonging using the concept of gifts and reciprocity. At the beginning of a project, invite teammates to write down along the edges of their big paper or whiteboard what gifts they bring, and what they would like to learn. I might write, "I can contribute compassionate listening, and I would like to learn how to be more comfortable about reaching out to people I do not know." In my design labs, I have found that this simple exercise (called "How Do I Belong") especially when it is done with humility and compassion, leads to greater cohesion and care for each other. Young people look out for each others' learning and growth this way, too. Success becomes a collective thing.

In the middle of a design process, there may come a time to share ideas. This is another opportunity for giving gifts to the team so that the students don't over identify with their own ideas, and friendships are not made or broken based on whose idea got the most support. And then of course, there is Block's best conversation of belonging—celebration and gratitude—*when we tell others what gifts we have received*. This can happen, of course, face to face; however, it is also a good practice for saying thank you and giving specific praise in writing. Each teammate writes to the others in gratitude and names the gifts received. A team is a very small community—a good place to learn and practice belonging and positive relational growth.

As a teenager, Sophia Kianni had already given significant gifts to the world. You know her as the founder of Climate Cardinals (Mending News p. 279). Before her 21st birthday, she had already served several years as Youth Advisor on Climate Change to the Secretary General of the UN, founded Climate Cardinals to translate research and information about the environment into as many languages other than English as possible, gave a ground-breaking TEDTalk on climate, power, and language, and was named among teens changing the world by a number of media outlets, including Forbes. VICE media named her person of the year in 2020. She attends Stanford, but has been a guest speaker at Yale and Harvard (twice). In 2022, Sophia was selected to co-chair the World Economic Forum's Generation Restoration Youth Hub, where she will be working with youth and practitioners from around the world to co-design a Nature and Climate Program focused on ecosystem restoration and assisting other youth to make a real impact. Of course she credits her parents with giving her young activism all the support and encouragement they could, but when I interviewed her back when she was just 19 and breaking onto the climate activism leadership scene, she said that her 6th-grade teacher (there it is again—6th grade) introduced her to civics and led to her to get involved in local issues she cared about. She liked it so much that she "just kept on doing that."[8]

Sophia's teacher en-couraged her to exercise her agency and gave her the option to choose something she cared about to practice making a difference. From there, her regenerative power has generated more energy and agency than Sophia ever predicted. High-schooler Ajahni Nedrick from Brooklyn tells a similar story of change, only at the neighborhood level, from the perspective of a character named George.

George was a high-school student who lived in San Antonio. He had great teachers who taught him the importance of environmental conservation and sustainability. He also lived in a very clean neighborhood. They would often see different people in their neighborhood looking at houses and taking pictures. A couple months later, George moved to New York City, and he was excited about the change to a new environment. What he did not expect was how dirty it actually was. The sidewalks were littered with trash, the subway rats feasted on thrown-out pizza crusts, and there were plastic bottles found in the drains on every corner. This was unacceptable for George. George noticed that there were never any trash cans around the neighborhood to keep it clean, and the animal waste made the neighborhood smell unpleasant.

George wanted to do something about this problem. The next month he convinced the people in the neighborhood to start keeping the neighborhood clean, including his co-workers and a community group that helped him get more trash cans in the neighborhood. They started recycling properly and cleaning up after themselves. A year went by and George realized that the neighborhood was cleaner than the year before. The air was fresher, there was less waste on the ground. In the end, George was glad that he was able to make a difference in his community and overall make a good environmental change.

George was glad. I wonder, if George had not had environmentally conscious teachers in San Antonio, would he have sought ways to "Befriend, Tend and Mend" as opposed to Fleeing or Freezing or just getting bummed out? As a youngster, would Sophia have had the courage, the self-efficacy to build a coalition of other young volunteers doing translations if she had not been given the en-courage-ment to engage in civic life and the practice of doing it? Would Sumak Helena Sirén Gualinga be leading a climate summit in Chile today if it weren't for the cycle of positive civic engagement she saw enacted in her family every day?

Cultivate a Culture of Befriend, Tend, and Mend to Stay Positive

When sudden shock disasters occur, the threat reaction defined by researchers and clinicians such as Leslie Davenport[9] as "Befriend and Tend" is in full view. Neighbors help neighbors, even if they do not otherwise know each other. People's sense that they are interconnected and in need of each other is strong. Community cooperation is at an all-time high. Climate change is a slow-growing existential threat with uneven consequences. It would be easy to maintain a kind of false positivity by pretending it won't be that bad next year. When our design lab students from Bayamón interviewed residents of one of the most hard-hit areas in Puerto Rico, they were surprised to find that many people there were not preparing for the next one. Recent studies have shown that it is emotionally harder to accept realities like climate impacts if you feel powerless to protect yourself and others. In our case, we found that some who were traumatized by the double hurricane needed to assure themselves that such a tragedy would simply never happen to them again. "We can't survive by going around expecting another disaster," they said. They were caught in an emotionally protective "Freeze" or "Flight" response, or maybe in a "bargaining" phase of their grief. Cultivating a habitual response of "Befriend, Tend and Mend" helps people in the teeth of climate change to accept and express their own feelings, and helps young people to act beyond futurephobia.

Befriend, Tend and Mend is a nurturing response to threats that emphasizes relationships and is nourished by love. It embodies a giving and collective attitude rather than an individualistic, "what's in it for me" attitude. It is easiest to adopt if you feel that you have some agency (at least collectively), and easiest to sustain if you do. Students in a public school in British Columbia shared that they wished more of their teachers would help them to teach their peers about recycling, for example, and appreciated tremendously the support (not just lip-service but action-based) of those teachers and school officials who *were* helping. I'm sure this feeling is widespread in schools around the world.

As Sena Wazer wrote in her personal contribution, the "Fight" response is needed, too, and is felt strongly in the activist community, but is very difficult to sustain over time. Exhaustion and "burnout" is a real possibility. The positivity engendered by Befriend, Tend and Mend communities in Puerto Rico who worked together well after the hurricanes was regenerative because it was rooted in collective power and love. The unifying positive force felt by those communities empowered them (en-couraged them) to eject a corrupt governor not even two years later. The feeling that people were acting on behalf of others, on behalf of the whole, gave them the strength to find the time, be creative, and make the sacrifices necessary to protest throughout the summer until they succeeded. The Sunrise Movement also emphasizes collaborative alignment and collective civic responsibility in their actions. With music from the heart, the shared purpose of climate action is framed as giving something to people and the environment, not taking things away (e.g., trucks and meat) by advocating for new jobs in the fastest-growing environmental sector, and economic invigoration through circularity.

One way that educators can help young people get ready for the new green economies is to participate in them at the school level. Youth involvement in participatory budgeting is a way to think about co-governance. School makerspaces and tech programs can host Culture of Repair organizations and multigenerational classes in repair, pre-loved clothing shops and innovative upcycling and integrated well-being programs such as Mabel Lassalle's Connecting Paths in Puerto Rico.

 Mending News!

Connecting Paths PR Heals, Upcycles, and Upskills

Mabel Lassalle blends together integrated mental health and well-being with circular economics and community well-being. She does it by teaching adults to sew! That's not all there is to it … they are sewing beautiful artisanal handbags and other items from used clothing, especially jeans, that would otherwise be thrown away. She gets donations of machines that the participants can "earn" to keep based on their follow-through and interest in continuing the program. Participants sell anything they make, learning financial literacy and entrepreneurship, skills they can transfer. Best of all, Mabel is creating a community of sustainability-minded people who are learning to take care of themselves through mindfulness and meditation, and to take care of each other and Earth—it's all part of the Connecting Paths. Could your students come up with a locally appropriate org like this? https://www.facebook.com/connectingpaths/

Additionally, actions like working with community members to facilitate reuse and recycling, like Ajahni's character George did, studying materials and making innovations in upcycling, and advocating for and engaging in local circular economies are just the start. Repair culture can also mean making amends for historical acts of violence and oppression, investigating and testing out giving economies and reciprocal ones (such as "Indigenomics"), researching the impacts of guaranteed housing or basic income or child care—all create a positivity cycle based on regenerative principles. Ecosystem restoration, species security, food and water conservation and care are consistent with the idea of Tend, Befriend and Mend, and easy to base localized curricula upon. The transfer of the positive action cycle idea of Befriend, Tend, and Mend to living eco-systems just makes sense.

Befriend and Tend in Anna, Texas

You may be thinking, this is a hard sell. We can't even get past "learning loss," banning books and history, and COVID-19 mental health impacts. Former librarian and lifelong maker Emily Burk runs the makerspace at the public high school in Anna, Texas. She wants to share with her students the do-it-yourself, repair it, "we got this" attitude she learned from her parents and grandparents. Her multi-faceted background helps her to answer the question, how do we include making and (re) generative maker mindsets to improve mental and emotional well-being throughout the curriculum by connecting it to the content and across age groups?

In his podcast on *Transformative Learning Experiences*, Kyle Wagner asked Emily how the "back to school" transition went.[10] "We were all curious about what we would be left with after all that zoom learning" and all those hours spent online." The teachers immediately noticed some upsetting trends in mental health and also acculturation. The administration hired a Social Emotional Learning (SEL) specialist, Barbara Coleman, who realized right away the limitations of teaching SEL as an add-on. She went to Burk and said, "It's just not working." Burk and Colman said simultaneously, "What if we try design thinking?" They knew that engaging kids *with each other* in the act of helping/playing with the younger kids would be good for them—but even they were surprised by how well it worked.

In a follow-up interview, they shared that, to protect children's confidentiality, they brought in the District counselor to talk about what he does and what he's learned in the school's play (therapy) lab.[11] High school students were provided with large sheets of paper and encouraged to list issues while he spoke. He addressed everything from social skills and attachment issues stemming from parental cellphone addiction, to abusive family situations and COVID isolation. Students, motivated by the resonance with their own experiences, and their desire to help "the little kids," formed teams and dove in.

Burk and Coleman found that the students' engagement was full on, and all the teachers' needed to do was keep asking, what problem is this solving? What do you actually want kids to do with it? How might this be used in play therapy? The students designed using "clean garbage" and for the most part low tech tools. Ideas that have been put into action so far include a "sensory buffet" for the youngest children to find what sounds, smells, textures, lights, colors, etc. are calming, fidget toys, a talking "monster," and games for youngsters to play that teach and engage them with each other. All of their ideas went on display for the play therapy counselors, who not only reviewed the ideas based on attractiveness/usefulness/effectiveness but also sustainability and durability.

Best of all, the aptly-named "Art of Giving" play design activity brought joy and the chance to "play" across age groups while both age groups learned important life skills and gained psychological insights themselves. The kids were so enthusiastic that they asked their other teachers if they could do something like this in their classes. The "Giving" culture and the contagious positivity cycle of Befriend, Tend, and Mend has now created its own beautiful problem—the makerspace calendar is overwhelmed by all the other curious and energized teachers who want to bring the magic of design thinking, the civic action positivity cycle and its SEL benefits to their own classes. Barbara Coleman said, "now I'm seeing opportunities for change *everywhere!*" The kids are, too, and that is an abundance of opportunities for collaborative success.

Co-creating a Civic Action Positivity Cycle for All

When you focus on the love and the regenerative civic actions that create community and generate change, courage, and hope in an outwardly spiraling positivity cycle, you are also opening up the possibilities for students to wonder, "how can I enact my values in school?" While there are no universal values, even across cultures most parents agree that they would like to know that their children are in a safe and caring space, where kindness is important, and from where their children will grow to be responsible citizens. Developing a Befriend, Tend, and Mend habit suits just fine for most parents as a starting place, and with of course plenty of opportunities for participation in local concerns (the appetite for this varies form culture to culture, too), it helps students to learn to give their gifts responsibly and to grow into being listened to and trusted as reliable members of something larger than themselves.

Some have asked me, "how do you teach about climate change without it becoming *political* and therefore contentious?" I like to quote Ronald Reagan, when he said, "Preservation of our environment is not a liberal or a conservative challenge—it's common sense."[12] Earth is our home and the mother of all of our mothers, conservative or liberal. Earth connects all of us and all living systems, worldwide. It was Richard Nixon who signed the Clean Air Act, the Clean Water Act, and the Environmental Protection Agency into being. Indeed, conservative values of independence (as in Do It Yourself (DIY) making and repair culture, and energy independence), national security (as in protecting our vulnerable military installations from climate impacts), prosperity (as in thriving into the future), family, and stewardship (as in protecting our assets as well as preserving God's creation) are also consistent with climate change teaching, so that if you begin by listening to what people care about, you can usually find places to connect. It was young Republicans who came up with the idea of taxing pollution (instead of profits), and many pro-family Republicans have joined the Young Conservatives for

Energy Reform (YC4ER) in horror about the effects that coal-fired power plants are having on their own and nearby communities.[13] In fact, according to Yale's recent surveys, attitudes toward actively addressing climate change have changed most significantly among Republicans (especially younger ones) in recent years. Now more than half of the total believe we should be doing something about it. This is not to say that everyone agrees, by far. But there might be some common ground.

Similarly, some teachers have worried about how to build a positive action cycle around climate change in communities where evangelical churches hold sway. There are role models to follow there, too. Katherine Hayhoe is one of the best-known evangelical leaders for climate action. Along with her husband, the pastor of Lubbock Bible Church, she co-authored *A Climate for Change: Global Warming Facts for Faith-Based Decisions.* Her widely viewed TED Talk includes her belief that "after thousands of conversations over the past decade … that just about every person in the world already has the values they need to care about a changing climate. They just haven't connected the dots."[14] The Rev. Canon Sally Bingham, of Interfaith Power & Light, makes connecting the dots easier. She says that saving creation is the calling of all humans, as it is to save each other. Her motto is "Love God; Heal Earth," also the title of her book presenting the views of twenty-one faith leaders on "our sacred duty to protect the environment."[15]

African-American civic and church leaders can help to build a positivity cycle around climate action with Black youth, too. The Rev. Dr. Ambrose Carroll leads the African-American Baptists from West Oakland, and his Green the Church movement has "combined theology with ecology" and teamed up with the NAACP and the Urban League to surface and discuss health issues relating to environmental racism, such as asthma, cancer, and COVID-19 and how Black and Brown church communities have been disproportionately affected. He calls the Black churches the "sleeping giant" in the climate action movement.[16] Reverend Carroll's leadership is an example of how local actions focusing on issues people care about can bring people of different parties and beliefs together. The shared "tending and mending" is stimulating the "befriending," the interrelationship that makes communities strong and resilient and able to hold together to respond to harm and bring about positive changes.

Role Models and Preparation for the Green Justice Future

Teachers can find allies from within the community and from outside of it to provide motivation and examples of how kids can see that "people like me" care about Earth, too. African-American activist and policy influencer Van Jones braided together racial and climate justice into an economic business model he named the Green Collar Economy (his book on the subject was a bestseller). He's looking at how rapidly jobs in the solar and wind sectors are growing, and the need for skilled tradespeople and youth leaders and entrepreneurs who can establish pathways to economic stability for people of color in the United States.

One of the first things to do in your school or university's community is to learn who is there, and how they might contribute to a cycle of positive engagement. (See also Chapter 6) Where are your potential allies? Who shares basic values about what we hope for our children? Are there already organizations in place that mentor or apprentice young people? Are there community colleges or universities nearby? Are there tech-based organizations that could assist young people like Gunav, who by third grade is already envisioning ways to use AI to improve the health of the planet ... or maybe he can assist them!? Do you live in a disaster-prone area? Are there government agencies at any level that are monitoring the environment or social justice issues? Opportunities for citizen science? Any solar installation and maintenance companies? That's a sector that is predicted to double in size over the next few years. What are the problems they are facing? Who are the distant role models (perhaps celebrities, authors, business leaders, etc.) and the local role models, perhaps spiritual or community leaders or teachers? What do your students care about? Is there a way to create a "home-grown" leadership, economic, and education cohort based on that? Young people who might stay in their community to add their agency to its regenerative capacity?

In Hawaii, the only state to declare a climate emergency so far, Ma Ka Hana Ka 'Ike (In Working One Learns), is part of a mostly Indigenous community on Maui whose learning continuum encourages youths to become empowered by focusing their agency on caring for their community. They learn purpose-full life skills, relevant knowledge, and traditional cultural practices, as well as job skills, leadership, and entrepreneurship. Emphasizing the regenerative Nature of their work, they are encouraged to stay and become staff for the program and to remain as community leaders and Earth's defenders.[17]

Local Action Brings People Together in Cycles of Positivity

Imagine if the school district itself were a "role model," leading by example? Imagine if the home-grown talent pool gave students the opportunity to see that "people like us" are successfully leading with love? Imagine if students felt that their school was committed to their environmental safety, for life? Imagine if that "school" became a community-wide learning and change hub/studio and talent magnet? Think big and celebrate small gains.

A focus on students and trusted community networks linked by shared values and connection points made Virginia Beach City Public schools into a fully sustainable district. The full story is told in the excellent Green Schools Network anthology *Trailblazers for Whole School Sustainability* (2022), but let me just say this much. If I told you that a large public school district with 86 schools and about 67,000 students in a conservative district in Virginia would become a leader in how districtwide sustainability can be achieved, you might not believe me. Sustainability Officer Tim Cole was originally hired on as a new construction project manager. Then he was called back into active military service in Iraq. As an original member of

SEAL Team 6, Cole knows something about risk and threats. He was preparing for an action when it occurred to him that the biggest threat facing his children and grand-children was "our collective inability to maintain a symbiotic relationship with one another and the environment. In that moment, I realized that we, as a school division in Virginia, could have a larger, more significant impact if we adopted a holistic approach that encompassed more than just buildings and operations."[18] Cole gives a lot of credit to his superintendent's team, who shared his vision and helped him build the community and school alliances needed for focusing on buildings, transportation, and food supply as well as involving students and teachers in the effort. They try to stay focused on the "triple bottom line" of benefits: money-savings, environmental safety, and a more holistic and coherent learning framework. There are strong links to the Willow School's Three E's: Environment, Education, and Economics, leading to a regenerative cycle of positivity.

How the Positive Civic Action Cycle Promotes Well-Being Through Agency

In the Positive Civic Action Cycle, courage feeds hope, and hope feeds courage, and agency feeds both and is fed in return. In living systems, the sun gets it all energized. But what gets the regenerative cycle going? What gives young people (or any people, for that matter) the courage to act in the first place? To use their regenerative power to act *beyond* futurephobia, and un-do its grip of powerlessness? And what are the beneficial effects on them as a result of their action? We had a "both-and" moment several years ago, during a class reflection on how we might co-design for well-being in contrast to how my students felt that school was stressing them out. In the process of clarifying what we meant by well-being, we came up with the seven elements of well-being that stem from love, trust, and safety, shown in its shorthand, "aid to memory" version in Figure 9.2. After you look at it, we can expand on it.

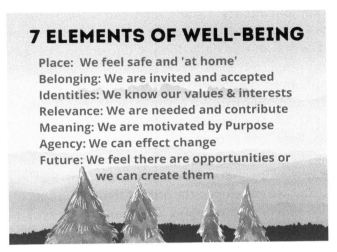

7 ELEMENTS OF WELL-BEING

Place: We feel safe and 'at home'
Belonging: We are invited and accepted
Identities: We know our values & interests
Relevance: We are needed and contribute
Meaning: We are motivated by Purpose
Agency: We can effect change
Future: We feel there are opportunities or
we can create them

FIGURE 9.2 Seven elements of well-being, rooted in love, trust, and 5-point safety, of course

Safety and trust. I am seen, reflected, accepted, and loved. I feel physically, emotionally, socially, culturally, and environmentally safe, and feel connected to others who are equally kept safe. Trust is at the center because it influences all the other elements and in turn, they influence it. Without trust, school cannot effectively support growth.

Sense of place and belonging. This is my/our space, where I feel connected and "at home." I am welcomed and invited to participate with my whole self. I/we can dissent safely, can make demands on systems. I/we interrelate and know how social, cultural, and ecological systems are nested here and how I/we can contribute to and influence them.

Identities and values. My identities and values are known and appreciated. We develop shared intentions that prioritize our relationships with people and our home planet ecosystems.

Relevance and responsibility. I am/we are needed and contribute to something larger than myself/ourselves. Civic action directly fuels this aspect of our well-being and the next three.

Meaning and purpose. I/we feel internally motivated and revitalized by caring, relationships, interests, or other emotional connections and commitments that give me/us a sense of purpose and a reason to engage.

Efficacy and agency. I know I/we can make a difference and influence or drive change and we practice justice through design and action in our daily lives. Civic action energizes what Paolo Freire referred to as "civic courage." This helps us to feel power-full about the future.

Future and opportunity. I/we know there are opportunities for me or I/we can create them. We know how to co-create and sustain systems and communities of care.

These elements, co-created with youth, have become the basis of my intention to guide learning experiences that encourage agency. After we developed the idea of the "6-P" roots of our (re) generative power, we overlaid the elements of well-being on them and were moved by the inseperable coherence. (See Figure 9.3) In a circular and interrelated fashion, our well-being becomes a source for our agency to drive change, and in turn, our regenerative powers are a source for our well-being. We had named at least a significant portion of what energizes both courage and hope in the "action cycle" of regenerative positivity.

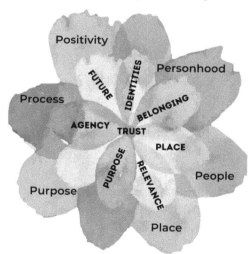

FIGURE 9.3 The co-flourishing of regenerative agency and well-being

Teaching With Well-Being and Power Frameworks in Mind

Agency and Well-Being, courage, and hope, each facilitating the growth of the other, and embodied in civic action. Since everything is related and everything we do is relational, we felt better once we had seen how these interconnected elements can energize a regenerative cycle of well-being and agency at the same time. We could see how purpose-full and empowered civic action could actually help us to heal inside, and to deepen our relationships, too. We began to feel we were close to the heart of what "regenerative learning" is all about, and to feel that we now owned our intention and our commitments to co-design, to "take up our civic space." These elements are the framework, the purpose, and the direct benefits of regenerative learning design. When we got to that point, some students (and adult allies!) shared these reflections:

1. From a high school senior: It's harder to be creative when you're fuzzy about what the beneficial outcomes should be. I feel more inspired and creative now that I feel more certainty about what we are up to, and that also makes me feel more certain that it will work.
2. From a 9th grader: I worry that I might not be good enough. Just seeing this sign and being part of civic actions like the "how do we belong" project makes me feel like maybe I have something to contribute.
3. From a teacher: I feel like I can use this as a rubric for my own "positive civic action" projects. If we have set them up well, all of the six powers will be exercised and the well-being benefits will flow, and then kids will want to keep doing civic actions because it feels good.
4. From a community design partner: It really helped me to understand what your priorities and underlying goals are. Now I feel like I can work from my side of the bridge.
5. From a parent: What parent wouldn't want this for their kids?

"Civic actions," or "doing something for the good of the whole," can begin with something small and informal, like noticing and encouraging classmates to welcome the friendly overtures of the new student with cerebral palsy and helping to ensure that every project and every class event is fully welcoming. Or something small and formal, like Superpowers or the "how do we belong" team-building exercise or classroom practices such as "disagree agreeably" discussion protocols and power audits, or a spring cleanup of the local stream. Once you can feel the positivity growing, often as an outgrowth of a shared reflection on how this agency to act feels, educators can gradually expand the number of "players," the depth of learning, and the responsibilities involved. Is there a need within the school system, such as there was at Anna, TX? Is there an area nearby that is undergoing ecological change? Does the schoolyard have enough shade? Are temperatures rising to unhealthy levels in the neighborhood? Is there access to fresh food and clean water? How about housing? Sanitation? From simple inquiry and citizen science projects to participation in design and implementation of community infrastructures (gardens, parks, energy innovations) and systems to adapt and mitigate climate impacts and other unjust situations, the positive civic action cycle generates even more benefits. The more we engage in civic actions, the more we begin to see that *additional* specific positive co-benefits are attached to learning through civic action. They grew from and informed our relationships with ourselves and others and Earth, as well as supporting our ability to generate positive action even in potentially overwhelming situations like climate change.

Other Positive Co-Benefits of the Civic Action Cycle

Pride

One of the co-benefits we can assign to the positivity cycle is pride. As climate educator and author Elin Kelsey puts it, "when we act on behalf of the common good we feel proud, and that pride is important to environmental engagement." It turns out that, according to a Princeton University study, pride is a much stronger motivator for environmental action than guilt.[19] This is not surprising, since we tend to avoid uncomfortable emotions and move toward ones that make us feel good. The young men from Brooklyn who contributed to this book, Dubar, Raymond, and Ajahni, all expressed pride, either directly or through their story characters, in acting on behalf of their communities. The pride people feel while engaged in civic action is also attached to their sense of purpose and meaning, and contributes to their feelings of belonging, as well.

Feeling Good

Acting out of care and compassion for someone, human or not, releases into the body the same well-feeling hormones (mainly oxytocin) that create joy and happiness. Our body knows when we are engaged in civic positivity, and it makes us want to do more of it and deepens our social interactions. This hormone also reduces stress and anxiety. The reaction is slightly more pronounced in women than men, but the benefits are the same.[20] This is how Befriend, Tend, and Mend seeds the most long-term benefits.

Social/Ecological Capital: Reduced Fragmentation and Increased Cooperation

We've already noted the importance of thinking ecologically about our social systems, too. Fragmentation, of school from community and humans from Nature, men from women, and children from adults and elders, wastes human capacity to do our part. In Place-Based Education, climate activist and educator David Sobel writes about the symbiosis of school and community. Just try to improve a school significantly without community support, he says. Instead, schools should be seen as "engines for the public good," and young people as social resources.[21] Co-operation is human nature, asserts *Nature: Human Behavior* (2018),[22] contrary to what we sometimes hear in the hyper-individualistic capitalist narratives. It's easier to achieve and better for our health and for the health of our communities. Sobel continues, "when schools focus only on how education benefits the individual, they become the enemy of the community. They educate young people to leave, and so fulfill the prophecy that these places are doomed."[23] Communities receive just as much benefit from engaging with and listening to youth voices and ideas as the young people do, and local communities are the right scale for youth to achieve impact.

Communities could wait a long time for policymakers to agree on what needs to be done, but environmental education and civic action can become a community-wide learning experience that changes attitudes and drives change—communities can become cultures of change with a feeling of shared responsibility and agency and a change-maker or learning community identity of their own. We know that the biggest driver of community change is peer acceptance or positive peer pressure. When others near you are putting up their own micro-solar grids, when they are standing up for their rights to clean air and gathering the data to back it up, neighbors join in. And when young people are doing the inviting, adults usually say yes. Young people and their adult allies have created co-ops and revolving funding for better access to food, community water-filtration, advocacy groups against pollution and in favor of environmental and holistic education, better street lighting, urban tree planting and solar maintenance projects. They serve as data collectors, drone operators to reveal violators of environmental regulations, and organize as defenders of Earth. Our oldest relative, our mother of all our mothers needs all of us to respond.

Compassion and Self-Compassion in the Positive Civic Action Cycle

We've seen how compassion is good for our health. And we've established that acting for the common good is also good for us and feels good, too. Poet and essayist Emily Johnston writes in *All We Can Save*, "in truth, serving the world's needs is the only thing that I have seen consistently lighten that fear and grief and anger in others. ... there is, perhaps oddly, joy in this work. It's made me more deeply alive and connected, with a clearer perspective on what matters, and has surrounded me with friends who share my care for the world. At any moment, we can choose to show up."[24] The need to protect others is not only human. Animals (and plants! remember the rhizosphere?) do this too.

The compassion instinct is very strong, and since it makes us feel good to do it, since it draws energy from action and power from life itself, how can we avoid the cycle speeding up and spinning beyond our ability to sustain? Young social and climate activists are asked to appear everywhere, advocate, protect, speak, write, demonstrate, and convene. They are lightning rods for hate-bots and bullies. They are often excluded from the seats of decision-making and so feel they are fighting against huge, harmful, and intractable systems of degenerative power without commensurate weight. Their threat response has been the opposite of disengage (flight or freeze). These are the fighters. As educators, how can we be better co-conspirators, not by becoming overwhelmed ourselves, but by befriending and tending to each other and our activist peers and students? How do we know when the civic actions we are taking are enough?

Positive Civic Action Cycle and Learner Esteem

Regenerative learning re-sets the goalposts. It is not about winning, or earning the best grades or the most money, or even saving life on Earth as our measure of success, but thriving. And in order to thrive, we must be participating in the world in such a way as to contribute to others thriving, too. As artist and climate justice activist Favianna Rodriguez wrote, "… it's time to write a new story. I cannot heal my community or myself without healing the planet; and we cannot save the planet without healing injustice."[25] Life creates the conditions for more life. In *Thrive: The Purpose of Schools In a Changing World*, authors Valerie Hannon and Amelia Peterson suggest that thriving is the result of flourishing relationally in the natural environment at four interdependent levels: Global, Societal, Interpersonal, and Intrapersonal.[26] Thriving should clearly be the purpose of schooling, but there are systemic educational injustices that are trapping learners in a futureless zone with little agency to do anything about it.

Grading, Sorting, and the Failure Trap

"There is no hope in there for me," said one of the students in Dr. Camille Farrington's study featured in her book *Failing At School.*[27] Her research, combined with decades of similar studies, showed that typical school grading policies (a numerical grade made up of some combination of homework, in-class work, tests, papers, and effort, with less credit for late work) is primarily used for sorting students into levels, or tracks, and promoting them to college (or not). In every case, among those students who already command opportunity access and those very far from it, typical grading policies undermined depth and engagement, emphasized external measures as the main motivator, and resulted in a labeling process that undermined self-esteem even if the student was receiving A's. If you watched Rachel Wolfe's *Losing Ourselves*, you saw how grading policies and external measures left the "highest performing" students undereducated and bereft of internal motivation. As you might also have noticed, typical grading policies are "status-affirming," in the sense that students who have different abilities, or who have challenges with work or family or illness or systemic oppression and environmental injustice do less well on their standardized tests and on their grades. Research also shows definitively that "stereotype threat" is real, and Black and Latinx, LGBTQ+ youths and others furthest from opportunity expend significant emotional and cognitive energy being concerned about whether or not they will "measure up" or let down their demographic group.

Farrington's research went on to reveal that most learners caught in the failure trap (even if they were simply *afraid* of failing, of not being "good enough") were not clear about and not at all involved in how the grade was arrived at or which were the more important areas to focus on for growth. In fact, most felt that academic growth for them was not possible. If they had missed some school, or if they had failed a quarter or missed several assignments, they knew that the grading policy was stacked against them. Indeed, they extrapolated that to their lives, and assumed that they were just "not one of the good people."[28]

In Farrington's research, which did not include regenerative learning environments, learners were significantly more likely to succeed if they were in schools that were offering choices (a bit of agency) within the curriculum to make it more relevant to learners' lives, used growth mindset grading (highly proficient, proficient, not proficient yet) on very clear and consistent (from teacher to teacher) learning goals, were allowed to alter their grades with after-the-fact improvement, when teachers valued their historical and cultural contexts and brought learners' own contributions to the fore, and viewed learners as assets to the school and their families and communities as funds of knowledge (Luis Moll's terminology).[29] Students were much more likely to attend those schools (or those classes) and felt that they could grow and improve and succeed. I keep asking myself, then why do we keep hold of the old mechanistic grading policy? Whose interests is it serving? And even in the 'growth mindset' typical schools, what parts of the grading policy are holistic and bio-centric in design? How do students show their relational caring, their living systems thinking, their design and power literacies, their collaborative gift-giving and taking to effect positive civic change and collective success? Which approach will situate them best to take up their space, so to speak, in the positive civic action cycle that builds courage and hope?

Environmental Education's Positive Impact on Academic Behavior

In 1998, the State Education and the Environment Roundtable (SEER) commissioned a study across 12 states and 40 schools that were integrating the environment into their curricula, kindergarten through grade 12. The results were clear. Those students who participated in ecologically oriented curricula and the civic actions that went along with it noticed significant improvements in depth of learning across all disciplines, in critical thinking, problem-solving, and decision-making. The students' enthusiasm for school and engagement in learning, as well as

374 ◆ Power-full Positivity

their student self-esteem (seeing themselves as a "good student") and their persistence through difficulties all improved. All participating schools observed better behavior overall, and one in particular, Hotchkiss Elementary in Dallas noted a drop from 560 disciplinary referrals per year down to 50 by the time the environmental education program was fully implemented.[30] Seeing themselves as fully engaged in school and seeing themselves "as students," represented a significant improvement over the usual deficit mindsets that have students believing that the reason behind every setback is that they are not capable, or "good." It turns out that environmental education that also builds agency through action is a good way of opening the door to growth mindsets and self-esteem, both foundational for academic engagement.

The Impact of Agency and Accountability in the Positive Civic Action Cycle

One of the most significant aspects of agency in regenerative learning is working together in order *to establish and be accountable to what matters*. In Shane Safir's spectacular book *Street Data*, she tells the story of the BALMA project, which was not only transformative for her students, but for herself and her colleagues. I've mentioned that you should read this book before, but if you haven't yet, it's ok to put this one down and read Chapter 5, "Redefine Success." It's about Agency and how to measure what matters. I will not be able to do justice to her work here, work which she calls developing "a pedagogy of voice." To oversimplify, Safir had developed a summer Law Academy with her diverse urban public school, and in the process met her dynamic thought partner of Afro-Cuban descent who taught at a nearby, mostly White, affluent private school. Together they hatched the BALMA project, which brought students from both worlds together to investigate equity in education. Over months, they visited with each other, shared readings and discussions, and prepared a presentation to a large audience from both communities.

But how did they know it "worked?" Safir goes on to say, "If we accept that success can be defined by a metric ... we will find ourselves forever suspended in a hamster wheel, chasing external solutions, curricula, and validation. But if we believe that every student is more than a number (or a "trauma story")—is in fact a complex, layered human being with endless potential, brilliance, and access to cultural wealth ... we can choose a pedagogy that transforms everything from our classrooms to our adult cultures to our policies." What happens when we adopt such a stance and engage learners directly in positive civic action, perhaps in the transformation of their school and community? How can we tell what they are gaining, when so much of the instruction is indirect, and so much of frameworks are abstract? Safir argues that the *real equity work begins "when we redefine success as the cultivation of student agency* and realign our measures of success to this goal." Taina Gomez, a graduate of the program, took the lessons of BALMA into her work, now serving as a public defender in Solano County, CA. She reflected, "it was empowering to take ownership of my own education. Even though you had to look at structural inequalities and systemic injustice, you felt empowered knowing that you didn't have to sit silently with it." BALMA project teacher Rex de Guia observed, "not only were our students 'on par,' but they *outperformed,* and not only outperformed, but they made changes to the system, to the institution, and played a significant role while they were there." Instead of being passive consumers, the BALMA project students were co-creating their learning and regeneratively creating their worlds.

The Positive Cycle of Reflection

A lot of human learning is indirect. Students learn a lot from school and their teachers that teachers don't teach them directly. Sometimes called a "hidden curriculum," it is layered and complex, and always filtered through the learners' own contextual and experiential lenses. What regenerative learning does is to make visible the positive aspects of civic agency so that they can be reflected upon, celebrated, and renewed. Learners can't learn agency, eco-citizenship, and life from a book, or by passively receiving direct instruction in it from a teacher. As a result, the most important tools an educator has to see developing are observation and reflection. You need to see/hear what students are doing and how they are doing it, notice their affect and body language, and ask them. Asking is important because it signals that you care about what they think. It says, "I want to hear your voice." How you ask can have many layers of approach.

Individual Reflection

How do you measure Agency? Well-being? How is a student doing with drawing on their own resources of regenerative power? It is very good to know how they are feeling about these elements before you begin working on a civic action together, but after you establish a level of trust (so, not Day 1). This will be a baseline. It can be a survey on a Likert scale, from strongly agree to strongly disagree, and it needs to be done in private, sharing results only with you. You can always encourage written comments or questions they would like to pursue. Read these carefully, and follow up sensitively if you see there are red flags. (see Resource E) On the surveys I did in Puerto Rico, they tended to feel very low efficacy to make a difference, had not learned much about climate change, and did not feel that their ways of learning were valued, but felt pretty good about peer and teacher love. They also did not like thinking about the future. Be sure to keep your questions positive! Instead of asking them to respond to the statement, "my teachers do not value my ways of learning," state, "my ways of learning are valued here." After just two weeks of the Design Labs in Puerto Rico, learners' low results had climbed significantly, as had their attitudes about their well-being and potential for future opportunities.

I always interview learners, too, for a private session about agency and well-being. Sometimes these conversations are formally scheduled and sometimes they are not. Have your questions of the week ready, so that you are prepared to do both. One of my favorites is, "when was the last time you felt you could make a difference? How did that happen and what was it like?" Almost always, it involves other people, and so mutuality, relationality, teamwork, diversity, and belonging questions and conversations follow. Similarly, "how often do you feel encouraged to build your own knowledge (instead of passively receiving information from your teachers)," results in elevating an awareness of power structures in their lives and how together we might be able to "move the needle." And then there's this question, "What would you want to keep in mind when *you* are facilitating this activity?" Prepared by the conversations we had in Puerto Rico, young people there became key participants in facilitating faculty learning and institutional change, energizing a regenerative cycle of agency that creates more agency and empowered hope.

Some of my richest, most fun conversations with students are around setting their own learning goals and aspirations. I usually have some of my own, either based on the curriculum I am responsible for, what I can predict they will need to know to address the challenge they have chosen, or what skills I have observed they've been working on, but I never dictate. These usually emerge from the discussion, and a little brainstorm on what they already know and feel confident that they can do, as well as where they would like to do more. What would they like to change? How would they like *to be changed?* I am often surprised (why should I be?) by with a little practice, how good students become at goal-setting and at determining what might indicate progress in that area. As an essential life skill, checking in with oneself and one's learning and being able to articulate that, at least to oneself, cannot be underestimated. "What did you learn that you did not expect to learn?" gives young people a chance to discuss how indirect lessons and gifts came their way and enriched their experience and impact. Learners of all ages quickly embrace this as an empowering part of a positive life design cycle, a creation of their own lesson/action/life plan, that enables us to have agency to act "outside of the box," with people and the rest of the living community outside of the typical school, and beyond futurephobia.

Students are encouraged to make and keep a journal in whatever medium suits them, in which they construct their own rubrics for reflection. I also am careful to ask them what else they want to tell me, what questions I should be asking, what questions they would like to ask me or other students. They exercise their agency in this completely, though only parts of it are private. Going back to "how do I belong" gifts-given and received, some of the best personal growth happens through the stories told collectively. Other people on the team are encouraged to weigh in on each other's learning. When you start this from a young age, personal growth is a relational part of collective success (we learn in relation, after all!). And did I tell you that in regenerative learning success is almost always a collective thing? I didn't need to.

Collective Success

We are at our most power-full when we are functioning together. For that reason, frequently shared reflections—for me it is part of our closing ritual every day—keep us focused on the indirect learning, sharing the accomplishments and setbacks of the day, maybe reframing and renaming them as victories, staying joyful and celebrating the small shared steps we take toward our big goals keep the positive civic action cycle pumping away like a heart at the center of our collective agency. Shared purpose, belonging, a sense of place and coherence grow when we act with love—in unity (not uniformity) of diverse perspectives. This is the "meaning" most humans crave. This is how we disrupt whole systems, when we see how leader-full and power-full we are together. We have such unstoppable agency when we know we are part of something bigger than ourselves. That's when we reach for transformation. Being accountable to that whole, to oneself-in-relation, to community, and to the mother of all of our ancestors and of ourselves, Earth—this is how we 'measure' thriving. Are we thriving together? How are we contributing? What gifts are we being given in return? Are we ready to jump at the level of the Escazú Agreement and hold regions accountable? Or municipalities and state governments accountable for inequities in infrastructure that could last for generations? An awareness of our collective power enables us to decide how we want to participate.

Regenerative learning focuses on collective strengths (regenerative powers) and how they can be used to elevate kindness, interrelatedness, love, coherence, and well-being, or as one student put it, "a feeling of being lifted up." Regenerative "schools" are already reinventing themselves (or starting from scratch) and joining learning ecosystems that are in fact webs of civil society committed to thriving, or flourishing at all levels, and this offers spectacular opportunities for agency—civic action beyond futurephobia—and power-full positivity.

Seeds for Planting

The Positive Civic Action Cycle is based on the idea that doing something positive for others, or the "Befriend and Tend" threat response, generates many benefits, including the desire to do it again. Benefits include: empowered hope and courage, individual and collective agency to act beyond futurephobia, pride, feelings of well-being, improved learner self-esteem, and levels of academic engagement, to name some.

The Positive Civic Action Cycle can bring people together across many kinds of boundaries including political and spiritual ones by finding common civic values upon which to act together.

The Positive Civic Action Cycle generates authentic accountability and civic responsibility, and an ability to reflect on indirect lessons and successes.

Educator guidance and authoritative (not authoritarian) expertise in observation and inquiry as well as co-creating goals help to maintain mutually energizing momentum to learn deeply and engage fully in reflective practice lifelong.

Together, we can act beyond futurephobia.

Notes

1 For more information on the Escazú Agreement, see here: https://environment-rights.org/the-escazu-agreement/ for more about the Escazú COPS1, see this https://dialogochino.net/en/climate-energy/52871-chile-hosts-first-summit-on-the-escazu-agreement/

2 Barthendu Pandey, '21 Infrastructure Inequality https://environment.
yale.edu/news/article/built-infrastructure-inequality-challenge-urban-
sustainability-environmental-justice?utm_source=YaleToday&utm_
medium=Email&utm_campaign=YT_Yale%20Today%20Alum%20no
%20Parents_4-18-2022
3 Living Building Challenge https://living-future.org/lbc/ Founder Jason
McLennan's TEDTalk on Living Buildings https://www.youtube.com/
watch?v=gSMecC6pcGo
4 These 6th graders, attend the Myrtle Philip Community School, serving
mostly Lil'wat and Skwxwú7mesh youth according to a learning framework based on Indigenous principles of collective attunement, collaboration, learning from diverse perspectives, empathy, and co-agency. https://
www.sd48myrtlephilip.org/
5 Sunrise Movement: We Are The Climate Revolution is one of the largest
US-based youth-led climate advocacy and policy-watch groups. With over
400 hubs for change around the US, Sunrise carries some weight! https://
www.sunrisemovement.org/
6 Wise 2022.
7 Block 2008.
8 Kianni 2020.
9 Davenport 2017.
10 Burk 2022.
11 Burk et al 2022.
12 Reagan 1984.
13 Karelas 2020.
14 Hayhoe 2018.
15 Bingham, 2009.
16 Karelas 2020.
17 Ma Ka Hana Ka 'Ike, at https://www.hanabuild.org/
18 Cole 2022.
19 Kelsey 2020.
20 Davenport 2017.
21 Sobel 2013.
22 Davenport 2017.
23 Sobel 2013.
24 Johnston 2020.
25 For a glimpse of Favianna Rodriguez's power-full work, visit https://
favianna.com/
26 Hannon and Peterson 2021.
27 Farrington 2014.
28 Farrington 2014.
29 The Funds of Knowledge Toolkit based on Luis Moll's work is essential for
thinking about community- or place-based learning projects. https://
www.k12.wa.us/sites/default/files/public/migrantbilingual/pubdocs/
Funds_of_Knowledge_Toolkit.pdf
30 Sobel 2013.

10 An Invitation to Possibilities: Creating Power-full Regenerative Learning Communities and Networks

What can we create together?
What comes next?

Adam Robb taught for 15 years in typical schools in Alberta, Canada. Trained as a social studies teacher, he was handed textbooks on the first day of school and told that the table of contents would make a good outline for his course. His students should "know" everything in it by the end of the year. Right away, Adam began to notice how alienated HE felt by this approach. His students were not faring any better. They were frustrated by the gap between the curriculum and their lives, the hierarchical pedagogy that went with it, and the feeling that it was a pointless waste of time. Even Canada's efforts at reconciliation with Indigenous peoples, its efforts to acknowledge its past to reshape its present, were becoming mechanical and unfelt. The community was undergoing a big "visioning"

DOI: 10.4324/9781003215806-13

project, however, wondering what their town could be like in 30 years. Robb and his students "let the place name the curriculum" and went to work. They mapped their community. They gathered stories and photos and hopes and concerns. They sought out voices rarely consulted and met up with people in positions of power. They documented, made their thinking visible, and collaborated with their community design partners every step of the way.

Everyone was excited to participate and to receive the students' recommendations, which included feasible steps in view of climate justice to make the community more inclusive and sustainable. But even though the town officials could see the ecological and social benefits to the students' plan, and could see the potential long-term savings and resilience, even though they knew about the importance of committing to the students as relevant and engaged citizens, they had already contracted with a consultant, at a cost of … . and so … . One of the students vented, "That's it. I'm never getting involved in the town again."

Robb made sure the project didn't die this way, though, by encouraging the students to find the biggest friendly platform they could find to share their story and their recommendations. When they first approached the Living Futures Conference, organizers said, "but this is a REAL conference." I can't print what Robb probably felt at that time, but he was soon able to convince them that the students were real, too. In the end, they got onto the main stage and the place was packed, eager to hear what young people had to say. The students put their home community under the microscope, in a way, to which the municipal leaders responded by including a number of students in the next school design committee.

Hope is a mutual commitment. People have to know that they will be listened to and taken seriously before they risk their hope, to say nothing of their time and effort. Hope comes with action that builds agency and belonging. Commitments are fundamentally relational, but our typical schools and governments function in ways that break up relationships. Hierarchies, silos, time confetti, external demands driving curricular decisions—all of this undermines agency, and without agency, we are powerless to deal with the many critical existential challenges of our day. There is a big gap between what we know works, what helps students learn well and feel well, what causes them to engage and be motivated, what drives learning deep, and what happens on a daily basis in most typical schools.

For the most part, teachers feel little agency to do anything about that. Robb noticed that his students were graduating with extremely low esteem and little confidence and that their adult lives would carry any meaning or purpose. They confessed that they did not know how to engage, how to make a difference, or even how to have a meaningful conversation. They viewed themselves (and each other) as a long list of static deficits instead of being full of abilities, possibilities, and dynamic growth potentials. They did not think they had much interest in being responsible citizens, let alone ones who could take on Settler Colonial-Indigenous reconciliation. They felt little attachment to any community. In general, they felt hopeless. Robb says, "I tried everything to change the system from within. I studied and applied systems change theory. I even tried to change the way we thought about the use of space. Nothing worked. Bottom line? I just felt that if I put in more hours, I would be able to get the kids what they needed in spite of it all. I left heartbroken that I was walking away from them, but in the end, I needed to survive. That was the real bottom line."[1] Robb didn't go far. Just far enough that he could co-create Howl https://www.experiencehowl.com/, a program based on regenerative life principles viewed through Indigenous understandings and civic actions that build agency. Open to those just finishing school, it's a gap-year experience that tries to fill in the gaps. Young people who have been through the experience are a testament to its regenerativity—many of them return to teach in it, counsel students thinking about applying, and offer professional learning to teachers.

What if the purpose of school was actually to engage people of all ages in the co-creation and tending of interrelated, living communities of coherence, belonging, and agency?

Would that necessitate a name change from "school" to reflect that learning doesn't stop at grade 12 or 16? And that learning might take place in many different contexts with a curriculum named by the place?

Would it open up, emancipate, democratize, and distribute the way we think about learning ecosystem infrastructure and processes? Empower hope and resilience?

Would it open possibilities to re-root deeply into our relationships with our Mother Earth and with other humans as the source of our human agency to be, well, fully human and living in right relation with all our relations?

And could a revolutionary but not at all new emphasis on interrelationship benefit from technologies used as tools to heal fragmentation and expand empathy and compassion?

Could it help to heal the wounds we are living in and to secure a future for us all?

Imagine a learning ecosystem (or it might be called something else) where the goals were clear. Health. Interrelationship. Biodiversity. Change. Regenerativity. In this ecosystem, everyone knows what their learning experiences stand for because everyone participates in the conversation and the positive cycle of civic action all of the time. No waiting. No waste. No disposable people, relatives, or sacrifice zones.

Let's imagine the possibilities together.

What if the purpose of school was actually to engage people of all ages in the co-creation and tending of interrelated, living communities of coherence, belonging, and agency? How would our recruitment, preparation, and sustenance of educators evolve to match?

There are very many frustrated teachers (and school admin!) out there. Some are in schools. Some are biding their time. Some are just starting out. Some are burning out. Nonetheless, it is understandable, writes education-change-agency theorist Elliott Eisner, if a bird raised in a bird cage doesn't hop right out when the door is opened. And I have found a similar phenomenon in my work in liberatory and agency-building education. There is a kind of security in the cage. A kind of serenity in knowing you are going to just stop fighting. You know where the boundaries are. You feel, like Adam Robb and I did (and most of the teachers in this situation we call typical school do), that if you just work harder at managing the effects of the cage, your students will be ok. Parents share this burden. You don't know whether what's outside of it is worth the risk.

How do we invite ourselves and others out of the cage? Would this necessitate a new way of thinking about how students are invited into them and at what cost? Can higher education adapt so as to admit students based on the new purposes and definitions of collective success and thriving?

And are we ready to co-create new approaches to teacher preparation, healing, and sustenance?

Would community colleges and other institutions of specialized learning engage even more deeply and convergently with the multi-disciplinary challenges of their local and global contexts? Could they become host studios of regenerative change?

Let's imagine the possibilities together.

I wonder if the new purpose of school would change the way we think about work and success? Could that also be guided by a shared, regenerative purpose in which a better world for future generations (seven of them, at least) is always in the front of our minds?

Could it be that belonging and well-being, living with purpose and citizenship, caring for and listening to Earth and each other is the highest purpose and the meaning of being human?

Are these possibilities worth the risk? Are these possibilities achievable?

Alexis and Tinti Deya Massol thought so when they began the fight back in the 1980s against the mining companies that were getting ready to strip Adjuntas (Puerto Rico) of her natural beauty and pollute the whole region. They were headed for becoming a sacrifice zone. Starting with two or three friends who were willing to commit, the Massols began a relatively new model of community action. Tinti was a teacher, and so educating her neighbors about nature, pulling in all the available environmental and scientific research (and explaining it in accessible language), and building on the community's sense of culture and place came naturally to her. The second time they met, many more people came, and brought music and dance, and a way of gathering that was rooted in *el batey* traditions and fun. The energy they produced resulted in the founding of Casa Pueblo, dedicated to using all kinds of knowledge to drive change for climate and social justice. In the end, the protests became a movement, and the mining companies have not returned to Puerto Rico.

Today, Alexis and Tinti's son Arturo Massol teaches at the UPR-Mayagüez and runs Casa Pueblo. It is both a science and society learning center and a model to use science and local knowledge to generate change. Casa Pueblo is a gathering place. Its focus, after the defeat of the mining companies, shifted to the significance of solar energy. It has been a slow but steady process, starting with a micro-grid around the plaza, involving local businesses there. Change is uncomfortable. Some wanted to stay connected to the fossil fuel-powered grid and use their gas-powered generators when the power goes out (as it does frequently) because they knew how that works and where the pitfalls are. The double hurricanes and the troubles with the grid since then have convinced many.

After the hurricanes, thanks to Casa Pueblo's efforts and the eco-citizenship of the plaza business leaders, power in Adjuntas went back on very early. As people sought them out for charging batteries and phones, the businesses benefited. A sense of community pride increased. While the rest of the island continues to struggle piecemeal to install solar micro-grids, Adjuntas is becoming energy secure. There are enough businesses saving money on their electricity now that they are able to subsidize residential expansion in a cycle of positive eco-citizenship. Energy is power. Power is power.

Education is power, too, as Javier Moscoso (and Culebra!) and professors like Marcel Sitiriche who continue to expand the support for solar sovereignty and energy security can attest. And Alexis and Tinti based their whole movement on the wealth of community knowledge in combination with the local universities and their contributions, too. There is a forest near Adjuntas, which Casa Pueblo manages (on behalf of the government) and has turned into the teaching forest known both as El Bosque del Pueblo (the forest of the people) and Bosque Escuela (Forest School). Learning from nature and restoring relationships within it calls for regenerative heart-thinking and reciprocity. Learners of all ages bring curiosity, open hearts and their own knowledge, and they receive love and wisdom from Earth herself in the forest hillside. They leave more human and whole.[2]

What if the purpose of school was actually to engage people of all ages in the co-creation and tending of interrelated, living communities of coherence, belonging and agency?

What can you commit? Can you commit to regenerative, community-building action? Listening to those who are rarely heard? Can you put down roots in this movement and be nourished by it?

You can decide what level of commitment is best for you. Do you prefer to stand aside and stay out of the way? That's okay, too. Resources for change come in many forms. What resources do you have? What you already know is that a gift given is a gift received. What are your gifts? Which of the 6P's of regenerative power are your strongest roots? Which are emerging? Are you a parent, a policy-maker (both?)? Are you involved in higher education or job training or education for adults? Are you a community organizer? A school board member? Admin or teacher? Do you run a non-profit organization or a small business? Do you work in government? Are you a student? An elder?

Maybe you can commit to a real conversation, one that involves more listening than speaking, and seeks common ground. One that allows people to tell their truths and uses metaphors to help them. Maybe the metaphor will *be* the "common ground" in which to root relationships of civic belonging and creative agency.

Maybe you can commit to learning more about learning from life and wondering how regenerative learning communities of care and coherence can evolve. Can you help prepare the soil?

388 ◆ An Invitation to Possibilities

Are you a person with lots of money and a desire to leverage education in the effort to secure a future on Earth, the only planet where we can thrive? Can you afford NOT to spend your privilege investing in a future for us all? Perhaps you'll fund and co-create a Regenerative Learning Center for those who want to teach and lead this way. OneStone (Chapter 8) is a private school in Boise, Idaho, which is free for all who attend. Students there use design thinking to design for good and to design the school itself. Everything it does is consistent with what it stands for: we believe in the power of students. Students are at every decision-making table. They never had to compromise their values to seek funding, the majority of which is provided by a single foundation that also believes in the power of students—but you have to work hard to find their names. Can you break out of the traditional impact and scale, credit-competitive, "what's in it for me" funding models? Funders, consider investing in the possibilities of life.

Education policymakers, can you commit to the new purpose of school? Can you do what it takes to foster the growth of bio-centric school infrastructures and place-based, purpose-filled curricula? Consider getting us off the treadmill of industrial schooling and monocultural standardization.

Interrelated Networks of Regenerative Agency

Everything is interrelated. It's much harder to knock down a forest than a single tree because it is connected both below and above ground with living networks. We are always more powerful when we "roll in" together. How can we connect to thrive?

Educators, parents, and student leaders still "in the cage" may need to feel their agency, feel the positive civic action cycle, and then either step out or shove the door open and call the others out, too. What if we created something like HOWL for them? Where, instead of the usual "professional development," teachers/admin/students engaged directly with the communities where they work and live in partnership to address climate justice and other challenges? How would that experience influence the opportunities they co-create with "their" kids? Could they then become networked regenerative change makers?

Could your university become an interconnected hub for change? Many are joining together already. Youth Designing Climate Resilience is a bi-country, bi-university, ten-community action-research project. The action part of it is a positive civic action cycle that is rooted in both school and community. Six schools of various types in British Columbia, and four in Puerto Rico are finding out what their students care about with regard to their living environment and climate justice impacts. Taken together, they are building a community of care. In their own communities, they are bringing together relevant organizations and agencies to bring about change, and in the process driving engagement, learning, and interrelatedness deeper. If all goes well, educators AND youth will enact their learning and regenerate more. Will it bring about greater well-being and help people of all ages to act beyond futurephobia? Might it release us from the cage? There are hundreds of programs like this already underway. SeaGrant is just one example, helping to make regenerative learning happen, connecting university and community schooling with wisdom from the sea all around the coasts of the United States and her territories. Can we help these schools to link up and learn from each other?

A quick google search of regenerative educator networks turns up more than a few options. The map at https://learn. ecovillage.org/course/regenerative-schools/indicates that regenerative learning is a global movement. Can we make sure that we are not trying to co-create new networks of eco-communities using old market models and social stratifications?

Imagine the possibilities, if the purpose of school was *actually* to engage people of all ages in the co-creation and tending of interrelated, living communities of coherence, belonging, and agency?

Are you willing to let that be your purpose too? How will you weave your thread into the collective fabric of meaning?

Our Mother Earth is asking for us to care for her with the same generosity of spirit that she has cared for us.

UNESCO has asked the education sector, all of it, to stop "business as usual" and focus on the four great existential challenges: equality, fragmentation, democracy, and climate.

It is the time for us to come home to ourselves and our earthly family. To renew our connection to life and to each other. Our ancestors and our offspring are asking us what kind of ancestors *we* are going to be.

Futurephobia can paralyze us, but education is one of the most powerful levers we have to get us unstuck. Educators, reach for the heart-knowing connected to our Mother Earth, that living part of us that understands more beautiful worlds are possible, and know this: when faced with extinction, teach closer to the roots of life. When faced with powerlessness, teach agency. Learn from those who know, and cultivate the soil rich with the interrelatedness and coherence of life into which our roots of agency can grow. Plant the seeds and help them flourish, but don't try to make your garden look like everyone else's. Don't even try to make it look the same as it did yesterday. Remember that living beyond futurephobia is not a destination, it is a learning journey, lifelong. The good news is that it is already happening and that we are not alone. Our Mother Earth has given us everything we need. Let's turn toward each other and all of our relations and see what we can create together.

Notes

1 Robb, Adam and Maggie Favretti. *Personal Interview*, 24 April 2022. Here is how to access his regenerative gap-year program, Howl. https://www.experiencehowl.com/
2 This story was shared with me by one of Casa Pueblo's many fans, Dr. Eduardo Lugo, in a personal interview on 26 April 2022.

Acknowledgments

I am, because all of you are. No one can produce a book without whole villages and families and inspirational thought partners and readers and for me, anyway, just the right light and fresh air coming in the window, a beautiful place to walk, a timer to make me get up and move around, and soul-friends and families and just the right husband to keep me nourished and whole. I couldn't have gotten started without the big inspiration from youth in Puerto Rico, and could not have kept going without the joyous rechargings of old friendships and the excitement and contributions of new folks met (and new books read!) along the way. And on that note, I don't have a very good memory, and so I am already afraid that this acknowledgment will let someone down ... and could never match up to my gratitude for the collective effort that made this book possible. A super-special thank you to the forgiving souls whose names somehow got left out. You are the best!

From the beginning, Lauren Davis, editorial director of Routledge's Thames & Hudson Eye On Education series, believed in this project and gave me wise guidance and enthusiastic encouragement and assigned a crack team of copyeditors. I'm grateful to my former colleague, David Sherrin, for introducing us. For everyone who laid eyes on any part of this book, or had conversations about it over zoom or over a cup of tea—you have made the book much much better and a collective success. Thank you.

The hurricane crisis in Puerto Rico also blew in Rob Bolt and José Obregón, who set up an exchange around design thinking between their school in California and Esc. Francisco Manrique Cabrera in Bayamón. El Pueblo Unido Program (now the Center for Design Thinking and Innovation in Education) created two-week intersessions called Design Labs, and I was able to launch several community-oriented design thinking labs there. I am additionally grateful to Maritza Sierra, Evelyn Sanchez, Glendali Delgado, and the other "FMC" teachers and parents and collaborators such as Felix Alemar and Cybel Betancourt for their friendship and hospitality and guidance. And most especially I am grateful to the youth of EPU and FMC for their honesty and trust. The students in the design labs, who ultimately became the driving inspiration for this book, were helped by community leaders Milly Chévere Ortiz and Waldemiro Velez and their neighbors in Ingenio, Toa Baja, and Christine Nieves Rodriguez in Mariana. LCDR Jesse Harms, LT Courtney Wolf, MST3 Angel Davila and ENS Stacy Urreola from the US Coast Guard, Sector San Juan, with the support of CAPT Eric King, gave us expert insight into disaster risk management Search and Rescue, and recovery. A host of willing officials from the PR Department of Education participated and saw to it that they followed up on youth solutions when they could. All of them met with the design lab numerous times, sometimes under challenging circumstances, and made the whole thing possible. The film the students made about how design thinking was helping them to envision a future would not have been possible without the support of Puerto Rico community and youth story-powered filmmaker Margaret Mair, and environmental activist filmmaker Patrick Lynch, who came to Puerto Rico with production support from Cecily Tyler and Docutribe. My friends Stephan Schweighofer, Christine Boyer, Ben Wild, and Peg Cioffi came from Austria and New York, respectively, to join in.

I am grateful to the AASA (the School Superintendents' Association) and Lynne Shain, my former Ass't Supe, who sent me into the catastrophic situation ten days after María, to "see if you can do some good." And I might not have been able to return to Puerto Rico after the first visit without the endeavors of Gloria Viscasillas to bring design thinking to the entrepreneurship education programs Fundación Banco Popular supports, which brought me back twice in 2018. After that and until now, I could not go to Puerto Rico at all without the generous support of family and friends, and the collaborative partnership of ResilientSEE-PR. Its Boricua bad-ass founder Yanel DeAngel is a force of nature. She is an inspirational and award-winning architect and now Principal & Managing Director at Perkins and Will (Boston), a wonderful mom, and in her "spare" time manages to lift up women, youth, and minoritized leaders in climate-and-justice-forward design. She created ResilientSEE, whose mission is to provide pro bono design and planning assistance to Puerto Rican communities as they make moves toward social, environmental, and economic resilience, one community at a time. I am also deeply grateful to their AREA Research team, whose financial and legal support makes the Design Ed 4 Resilience and ResilientSEE-PR 501(c)(3) sisterhood go. Without them (and the Canadian SSHRC funds), the unique participatory action research collaboration "Youth Designing Climate Resilience" with Canada's Royal Roads University and UPR-Mayagüez, creating a "data-trail" to demonstrate that what I'm talking about in the book actually works, would also not be possible.

I don't have the pages to name all of the students and teachers and community-action-oriented friends who have taught me about living and learning and working in a disaster-affected colony in crisis (Puerto Rico), but here are the ones who have given me the most time, patience, friendship, Boricua magic, thought partnership, creative companionship, and in many cases, a place to work and a roof over my head. They are teachers, parents, engineers, artists, community leaders, business innovators, program founders, and directors, and they have read and written pages in this book, created regenerative schools and community centers, hosted classes and workshops, and set up design labs and other programs that have and are saving people's lives: Miguel Camacho, María Elena Velásquez, Eduardo Lugo-Hernández, Sandra Soto Santiago, Nyvea Silva, Pamela Silva Díaz, Chris Papadopoulos, Marcel Castro-Sitiriche, Jesse and Frankie Harms, Linda Holcman, Sheykirisabel Cucuta Gonzalez, Maria Christian, Roberto Micheri, Glorimar Ripoll, Rosaura Orengo, Mabel Lassalle, Cecilio Ortiz-Garcia y Marla Pérez-Lugo, Milly Chevére Ortiz, Waldemiro Velez Soto, Ada Monzón, Monica Perez Nevarez, Soraya Sesto, Dana Montenegro y Angiemille Latorre, Cybel Betancourt, Rob Bolt, Maritza Sierra, Evelyn Sanchez, Felix Alemar, Glendali Delgado, Xion Lucca Torres, María Gabriela Huertas Diaz, María Rolón, Helga Maldonado, Minerva De Jesús, y Nancy De Jesús. Mis hermanos y hermanas, les estoy sumamente agradecida. Estoy con ustedes en solidaridad mientras creamos los mundos sanadores de justicia, plenitud y abundancia que sabemos que están en camino. Por el amor y la vida y nuestra madre Tierra. Abrazos.

A big thank-you to the teachers, parents, and school leaders who helped to gather the beautiful contributions from their students who love and learn from our oldest relative of all. My neighbor and friend Tara King Clark, Roberta Kubik of the Myrtle Philip Community School, Joseph C. Rice of Nawayee Center School, Sean McFadden of Brooklyn's Eagle Academy for Young Men II and their Green Team, María Elena Velásquez of Edison School in Caguas, PR, Kavitha Jakher of Army Public School in Hisar, India, and Yerko Sepúlveda of Hawken Upper School in Cleveland, Ohio. Huge hugs for the young people who put themselves out there with their poetry, stories, artwork, or who, like the young folks at Aula en la Montaña, are creating a better world with their love for Earth, their gardens, and their communities—your truths guide this book.

I continue to be inspired by my young adult co-conspirators and contributors, and am very grateful for their time, their ideas, their enthusiasm for Earth, and for the potential in all of us. They are creating the worlds we want to live in. Engineers Javier Moscoso Cabrera, Natalia Ospina, and Christine Groves. Ogiek Community leader, journalist, and nurseryman, David Warren. Génesis Ramos, Gabriela Otero Andino, Isabel Colón, Alana Gallart, José Obregón, and the entire Impacto Juventud crew, grabbing hold of the arc of justice with their whole weight. Farmer-educator-researcher-community builders, Amanda Martinez, Gavrielle, and Remi Welbel. Sophie Bardetti, navigating gracefully across borders and languages. Nick Cain, Jr. Blackfoot leader, pluralist, and climate and justice activist, Sunrise activist Sena Wazer and Climate Cardinal founder Sophia Kianni, are all devoting themselves to our shared future at the state and global levels. All of these young change makers deserve special attention, but one who has been teaching me for a long time and who has influenced me deeply in her role as a learner-teacher and friend-mentor (frientor?), whose high school truth shines in the 30-minute documentary *Losing Ourselves*, is Rachel B. Wolfe. She pulled the covers off what it means when you say, "high-performing school." She remains a keen observer of society and a journalist keeper of conscience. Shine On.

I am so fortunate that my life has been a journey of learning shared with amazing colleagues and students. I am moved to thank the thousands of students collectively who did more to teach me about learning and life than any classes about education could have. They say you never forget your first classes. Two of those classmates have stayed with me on this journey, Jonathan Fendelman, whose love of the outdoors launched my thinking about youth agency and reconnecting children with their biocollective family back when I was mostly still a child myself, and Beatrice Sevcik Gibney, a stalwart supporter of youth creativity and agency and education justice—a clearer of static and spender of privilege to make space in the world for what matters. You're a superb mom and great friend. You make me possible.

I am proud to say that my k12 teaching career was spent beside incredibly beautiful souls with whom I have shared purpose and created meaning, whose insights, inspirations and questions are indelible, and whose companionship in thinking deeply about who we are and how that's expressed in what we do keeps me going. Richard "Doc" Seubert, the late Michele Forman (she is no less a part of this conversation), Stephen Mounkhall, Pamela Kroll, Kami Wright, Liz Johnson Simmons, Lisa Yokana, Christine Boyer, Amanda Filley, Ken Bonamo, and all of the colleagues too many to name whose mutual support and shared purpose energizes me ... we make worlds together.

I am deeply thankful for my thought partners along the journey of the book, who have talked through ideas, read sections, helped me learn, and shared in the love I feel for this and the next seven generations. In British Columbia, Resilience By Design Lab's Austin Lang and RBDLab founder and climate studies professor Robin Cox, education leader Irene Corman and design thinker Susan Crichton, are working together on colonialism in Canada and how justice in design can facilitate the repair. In Minneapolis, Indigenous school and Philips Indigenous Education network director Joseph C. Rice generously supported me and the book with his ideas clarifying best practices and the meaning of coherence, interrelatedness, and decoloniality from his perspective, as well as patiently pointing out my Western-educated, White-lady blind spots. I am deeply grateful to you all for your help in keeping the prophecy of the Rainbow Warriors in the front of my consciousness.

Idea-sharing groups pitched in, too—the d-school k12 Designing Your Life constellation called into being by Gabrielle Santa-Donato, one of the brightest stars, a group whose most enthusiastic and idea-generating regulars included folks from OneStone and also Alex Campell from Elizabethton City Schools and Laura Cole from GSE Dallas. I am grateful to my colleagues from the ethics-based Indian International School in Sharjah (UAE), led by Sheela George and including Neeta Dua, Swapnaja Deshpande, who helped me put together my original global Futurephobia thinking and feeling group and continue as bright stars lighting the way. Friends like climate activists Innocent Deckoks from Nairobi and from New York and CT, Madelaine Eppenstein, Stephen Seward, Peg Cioffi, and CDR Brian Maggi (USCG) were also regulars in the original Futurephobia group and continue as guides and creative companions.

And then I am renewed and re-made by the people, mostly educators of both the formal and informal (parent) varieties, who are the hosts of conversations about the future of learning and just societies from around the world. They have given me ideas, shared information and stories publicly, and spent fun hours imagining how things could be different. Many many thanks to Trevor Soponis, Loni Berqvist, Matt Barnes, Gholdy Muhammad, Nuestra Escuela, Tim Logan, Ivan Cestero, Jammie Menlo, Emily Burk and Barbara Coleman, Miguel Gonzalez, Ayana Verdi, Mark Biedron, Adam Robb, Pam Moran, Elizabeth O. Crawford, and Carla Marschall, the Crew at Hopewell City Schools, Jenny Finn, Jim McCue, Jason Swanson, Luis Martínez-Fernández, Alexis Massol at Casa Pueblo, Kyle Wagner, Benjamin Freud, Charlotte Hankin and at *Getting Smart*, Tom Vander Ark, Nate McClennan, Mason Pashia, and Rashawn Carruthers. Kyle, Nate, and Benjamin, thanks for the beautiful questions you posed to me on your podcasts, and Benjamin, thank you for your insightful and uplifting comments on the book and also in our podcast conversation with Nate! Mason and Shawnee, I love that you love poetry and music. Thank you for your reading and support, too!

And then there are the closest ones, who are with me every step of the way, cheering from near and far. There's my Heidelberg family, most especially the Herrmannspahns, Andreas, Uli Rahn, Felix und Nele, and the Groches, Isabel, Dieter und Max, and Isabel's parents Günther und Armgard Klein, and my Thadden (Humanitarian) Schule colleagues Traute Werner, Irene Schubert and Martin Döpp. There's my Normandy family, Jean-Paul et Christiane LeGravey, and then of course my Italian family of Favrettis, Piols, e Agostinos. There's my empowering #SheLeadsEdu family—thank you Pam Moran and Jody Britten and Lisa Yokana and our posse of supersmart women! There's my sister Emily Macdonald and her family in Michigan, my late brother Giovanni and his beloved friends from all over the place–all of you must have been cheering VERY loudly, because I could hear you all the way from here!

My Mystic, CT family also cheered me on and endured long talks about this futurephobia business on the river and at outdoor picnics and walking through COVID together—thank you Janis and Andy Mink, Pete Tebeau and Nancy Graham, Pieter and Linda Visscher, Kris Kuhn, Millie White (and thank you, Amy, for your help with the Notes), Danielle Egan, Tara King Clark, Tysen Naughton, Tom and Candy Sanford, Carl Kaufmann, and all of the crew who share my love of the Mystic River Estuary so much that you put up with all my thinking out loud and gave me love and friendship in return.

I needed to be alone a lot to write this book, and so my Middlebury, VT family swung into helping mode, deeply discounting rentals, making space in their homes, helping me with everything from broken smoke alarms to going for walks and family dinners. Middlebury is my tap-root place, and you all are the reason. Many thanks to Dan and Diane Dapolito, Bettina Matthias, Stefano Mula, Neil and Judy Bicknell, Ilaria Busdraghi and Pieter Brucke, Eric and Helen Covey, Tim and Imelda Forman, John Hunisak, Perrine Terry, Jack Brown, Dick Forman, and Adam Mahady—your friendship and the knowledge that you are there, even if I am being a hermit and we are not spending a lot of time together, has sustained me through a challenging process. Frankie Dunleavy and Dana Yeaton, and Vanessa and Greg, thank you for making me a part of your family. All those shared ideas and laughs and walks and that good food and love and the joy of welcoming Josiah to the world, these moments with you are some of my greatest delights.

I am thankful for my parents, Rudy and Joy, who have been through this book-writing business before, and whose generous love and loud cheering helped me stay focused as the deadline neared. Their respect for the Earth and her inhabitants, their love for community, and interest in maintaining their role as connectors of past and present and future shaped my worldview. I am, because of you. I am thankful for my daughter Sarah, whose insights and opinions have helped me to understand the world through her eyes and have guided my growth since I was HER present age. Her scientific mind and her kinship with trees, her work as a steward of the land and forests, and her love and affection bring me great joy and gives me the best reason of all to write this book. Thank you for your love, and for your confidence in me! I am, because of you. I am grateful for Paul's daughter Meredith, whose devotion to her Dad has shined on me, too, so I know she's cheering, and that if I am away being a hermit to write this book he will get frequent phone calls and a visit or two. So Paul. How do you thank the person of your heart, the bedrock of your sanity, the one who has unilaterally spent the most of himself to husband this book into being? My gratitude runs so deep and full it's hard to catch. I love you. You have heart-thought with me about the young folks who inspire us both, given me the space to go off and dive in deeply, and listened to all the parts of this book as they were coming together. It won't be news to you. You have welcomed me into your being and nested in mine. I am, because of you.

References

Abrams, Zara. 2019. "Puerto Rico, Two Years After Maria: The Aftermath of the Aftermath." 1 September 2019. Vol 50 No. 8 *American Psychological Assoc.* https://www.apa.org/monitor/2019/09/puerto-rico

Adefarakan, Temitope nd. "Integrating Mind, Body and Spirit Through the Yoruba Concept of Ori: Critical Contributions to a Decolonizing Pedagogy." *Sharing Breath, Embodied Learning and Decolonization.* Athabasca University Press. https://read.aupress.ca/read/sharing-breath/section/c53bd62e-abaf-4bd3-859d-20cf02db467a

Andrews, Peter. 2015. *Natural Sequence Farming.* Australia. Website. https://www.nsfarming.com/

Bailey, Elizabeth Tova. 2016. *The Sound of a Wild Snail Eating.* Chapel Hill, NC: Algonquin Books.

Behrendt, Jammie and Maggie Favretti. *Personal Interview.* February 2022.

Bell, Brenda, John Gaventa, and John Peters, Eds. 1990. Myles Horton and Paolo Freire, *We Make the Road By Walking: Conversations On Education and Social Change.* Philadelphia: Temple University Press.

Benyus, Janine, in Johnson and Wilkinson, Eds. 2020. "Reciprocity," In *All We Can Save: Truth, Courage, and Solutions for the Climate Crisis.* New York: One World.

Benyus, Janine. 2002. *Biomimicry: Innovation Inspired By Nature.* New York: HarperCollins.

Berger, Ron. 2021. "Our Kids Are Not Broken." *The Atlantic*, 20 March 2021. https://www.theatlantic.com/ideas/archive/2021/03/how-to-get-our-kids-back-on-track/618269/

Bigelow, Bill. 1996, quoted in Sobel, David. *Place-Based Education: Connecting Classrooms and Communities.* Orion, 2013. 2nd Edition.

Bingham, Sally G. 2009. *Love God, Heal Earth: 21 Leading Religious Voices Speak Out On Our Sacred Duty to Protect the Environment.* Pittsburgh: St. Lynn's Press.

Bir Sethi, Kiran 2009. "Kids, Take Charge." *Ted/India Video.* November 2009. https://www.youtube.com/watch?v=n3DJwCyrZas

Block, Peter 2008. *Community: The Structure of Belonging.* San Francisco: Barrett-Koehler Publishing.

Blow, Charles M. 2012. "I Know Why the Caged Bird Shrieks." *New York Times Opinion.* 19 September 2012.

Bly, Robert. 2004. *Kabir: The Ecstatic Poems*, Versions by Robert Bly. Boston: Beacon Press.

Bridges, Earl, and Craig Martin. 2022. "San Juan Puerto Rico: After The Storm." *The Good Road, Season 2, Episode 203*. January 3, 2022.

brown, adrienne maree. 2017. *Emergent Strategy: Shaping Change, Changing Worlds.* Chico, California: AK Press.

Brown, Brené. 2021. *Atlas of the Heart: Mapping Meaningful Connection and the Language of Human Experience.* New York: Random House.

Bruni, Frank. 2015. *Where You Go Is Not Who You'll Be: An Antidote to the College Admissions Mania.* New York: Grand Central Publishing.

Burgess, Eleanor 2019. *The Niceties*. United Kingdom: Concord Theatricals.

Burk, Emily and Kyle Wagner. 2022. *Transformative Learning Experiences*. Podcast. 5 January 2022. Access on Apple or Spotify.

Burk, Emily, Barbara Coleman, and Maggie Favretti. *Personal Interview*. 12 January 2022.

Burke, Susie E. L., Ann V. Sanson, and Judith Can Hoorn, "The Psychological Effects of Climate Change on Children," *Current Psychiatry Reports*, 20, 35 April 11, 2018. 10.1007/s11920-018-0896-9

Cantor, Pamela and Linda Darling-Hammond, and others. 2020. "How the Science of Learning and Development Can Transform Education: Initial Findings," *Science of Learning and Development Alliance*. May 2020. https://5bde8401-9b54-4c2c-8a0c-569fc1789664.filesusr.com/ugd/eb0b6a_24f761d8a4ec4d7db13084eb2290c588.pdf

Caraballo-Cueto, José. 2021. *Aprovechamiento académico y el cierre de escuelas en Puerto Rico. A Technical Report*. https://www.researchgate.net/publication/343636485_APROVECHAMIENTO_ACADEMICO_Y_EL_CIERRE_DE_ESCUELAS_EN_PUERTO_RICO

Carter, President Jimmy. 1994. *An Outdoor Journal: Adventures and Reflections, The Carter Collection*. Fayetteville: University of Arkansas Press.

Caruthers, Rashawn and Tom Van Der Ark, "Operation Breakthrough: Changing Life Trajectories From Birth to Citizenship" *Getting Smart*. 12 January 2022.

CDC, "Helping Patients Cope With Traumatic Events." https://www.cdc.gov/masstrauma/factsheets/professionals/coping_professional.pdf

Cioffi, Peg and Maggie Favretti 2022. *Personal Interview*. Explore Walkabout's anti-racist model here: https://walkabout.org/

Climent Belda, Xabier and Aaron Kudja, Dir. 2019. "Mariana Pa'lante. 31 min." https://www.amazon.com/Mariana-PaLante-Xabier-Climent-Belda/dp/B082MRM5ZN

Coates, Ta-Nehisi. 2015. *Between The World and Me*. New York: Spiegel and Grau.

Cole, Tim. 2022. "From LEED to Leader: Virginia Beach City Public Schools Sets the Bar for Divisionwide Sustainability," In *Trailblazers for Whole School Sustainability: Case Studies of Educators In Action*, Jennifer Seydel, Cynthia L. Merse, Lisa A. W. Kensler and David Sobel eds. (New York: Routledge), 254–270.

Coleman, Rep, Bonnie Watson, and Task Force Chair. 2019. "Ring The Alarm: The Crisis of Black Youth Suicide in America." *Congressional Black Caucus, Emergency Task Force on Black Youth Suicide and Mental Health*. December 2019. https://watsoncoleman.house.gov/uploadedfiles/full_taskforce_report.pdf

Command Z Productions. 2019. *Puerto Rico Schools Launch Design Thinking*. Cecily Tyler, docutribe. 4 minutes. https://vimeo.com/338790507 (English subtitles) https://vimeo.com/338874017 (Spanish) Also see: https://www.designed4resilience.org/puerto-rico

Costanza-Chock, Sasha. 2020. *Design Justice: Community-Led Practices to Build the Worlds We Need*. Boston: MIT Press.

Curtin, Sally C. "State Suicide Rates Among Adolescents and Young Adults Aged 10–24, United States 2000–2018". National Vital Statistics Report Volume 69, No. 11. https://www.cdc.gov/nchs/data/nvsr/nvsr69/nvsr-69-11-508.pdf

Czikszentmihalyi, Mihaly. 1991. *Flow: The Psychology of Optimal Experience*. New York: HarperCollins, 1991.

Dalrymple, Louis, Cartoonist. 25 January, 1899. *US Library of Congress*. https://commons.wikimedia.org/wiki/File:School_Begins_1-25-1899.JPG

Damon, William. 2008. *The Path to Purpose: Helping Our Children Find Their Calling in Life*. New York: Free Press.

Davenport, Leslie 2017. *Emotional Resiliency in the Era of Climate Change: A Clinician's Guide*. London: Jessica Kingsley Publishers.

de la Torre, Saturnino and María Candida Moraes. 1997. *Sentipensar: Fundamentos y estrategias para reencantar la educación*. UNESCO/Edicion Aljibe.

Ebby, Will 2022. "Climate Matters: Vermont's Disingenuous Energy Portfolio." *Addison County Independent*, April 14 2022.

Ellison, Ralph. 1995. "What These Children Are Like." (1963), In *The Collected Essays*, John F. Callahan ed. (New York: Modern Library), 555.

Escobar, Arturo. 2017. *Designs for the Pluriverse: Radical Interdependence, Autonomy, and the Making of Worlds*. Durham, NC: Duke University Press.

Eskreis-Winkler, L., et al., 2019. "A Large-Scale Field Experiment Shows Giving Advice Improves Academic Outcomes for the Advisor." *Proceedings of the National Academy of Science*, 116(30), 14808–14810. 10.1073/pnas.1908779116

Experimental Biology. "Study shows dogs can accurately sniff out cancer in blood: Canine cancer detection could lead to new noninvasive, inexpensive ways to detect cancer." *ScienceDaily*. ScienceDaily.com, 8 April 2019. www.sciencedaily.com/releases/2019/04/190408114304.htm

Farrington, Camille. 2014. *Failing At School: Lessons for Redesigning Urban High Schools*. New York: Teachers College Press.

Favretti, Maggie, et al., 2021. "Community Designers: A Pilot Virtual Community Co-Design Symposium." *American Society of Engineering Education* (ASEE). Conference Paper, July, 2021.

Fielding, Randy. 2021. "Learning Communities Change the Paradigm." *Getting Smart*. 11 November 2021. https://www.gettingsmart.com/2021/11/11/learning-communities-change-the-paradigm/?utm_source=Smart+Update&utm_campaign=f0d19e083b-SMART_UPDATE_2021_11_11&utm_medium=email&utm_term=0_17bb008ec3-f0d19e083b-32139545

Fleming, Rob. 2013. *Design Education for a Sustainable Future*. New York: Routledge.

Fothergill, Alice and Lori Peek. 2015. *Children of Katrina*. Austin: Texas University Press.

Freire, Paolo. 2018. *Pedagogy of the Oppressed*, 50th Anniversary Edition. London: Bloomsbury.

Fried, Robert 2005. *The Game of School: Why We All Play It, How it Hurts Kids, and What it Will Take to Change It*. San Francisco: John Wiley & Sons.

García, Emma and Elaine Weiss, 2019. "US Schools Struggle to Hire and Retain Teachers," and other articles in "The Perfect Storm In the Teacher Labor Market." Series. *Economic Policy Institute*, April 16, 2019. https://www.epi.org/publication/u-s-schools-struggle-to-hire-and-retain-teachers-the-second-report-in-the-perfect-storm-in-the-teacher-labor-market-series/

Gast, John, Painter. *American Progress*. 1872. *Autry Museum of American Art*. Los Angeles, CA.

Getting Smart Staff. "Teaching Design Thinking to Hack School and Design for Complexity." *Getting Smart*, October 11, 2018. Accessed: https://www.gettingsmart.com/2018/10/teaching-design-thinking-to-hack-school-and-prep-for-complexity

Glass, Thomas E. 2019. "Where Are All the Female Superintendents?" AASA The School Superintendents Association. https://aasa.org/schooladministratorarticle.aspx?id=14492

Gottfried, Jeffrey. 2020. "Americans' News Fatigue Isn't Going Away--About Two-Thirds Still Feel Worn Out." *Pew Research*. February 26, 2020. https://www.pewresearch.org/fact-tank/2020/02/26/almost-seven-in-ten-americans-have-news-fatigue-more-among-republicans/

Grant-Thomas, Andrew. "Editor's Introduction, Issue One." *Othering & Belonging: Expanding the Circle of Human Concern*. http://otheringandbelonging.org/editors-introduction/

Gregoire, Carolyn. 2013. "The 75-Year Study That Found the Secrets to a Fulfilling Life." *Huffington Post*. 23 August 2013. https://www.huffpost.com/entry/how-this-harvard-psycholo_n_3727229

Haidt, Jonathan. 2006. *The Happiness Hypothesis: Finding Modern Truth in Ancient Wisdom*. New York: Basic Books.

Hammond, Zaretta. 2015. *Culturally Responsive Teaching & The Brain: Promoting Authentic Engagement and Rigor Among Culturally and Linguistically Diverse Students*. Thousand Oaks, CA: Corwin.

Hannon, Valerie and Amelia Peterson. 2021. *Thrive: The Purpose of Schools In A Changing World*. Cambridge: Cambridge University Press.

Hattie, John. 2008. *Visible Learning*. London: Routledge. Also in "Hattie Ranking: 252 Influences And Effect Sizes Related To Student Achievement." https://visible-learning.org/hattie-ranking-influences-effect-sizes-learning-achievement/

Havel, Vaclav. 1991. *Disturbing the Peace: A Conversation with Karel Huizdala*. New York: Penguin.

Hawken, Paul. 2007. "To Remake the World." *Orion Magazine*, May-June 2007. https://orionmagazine.org/article/hawken-article-may-june-text-in-place/

Hawken, Paul. 2021. *Regeneration: Ending the Climate Crisis in One Generation*. New York: Penguin.

Hayhoe, Katharine. 2018. "The Most Important Thing You Can Do To Fight Climate Change: Talk About It." *TEDWomen* November 2018. TED Video. 17:03. https://www.ted.com/talks/katharine_hayhoe_the_most_important_thing_you_can_do_to_fight_climate_change_talk_about_it?language=en

Hirsch, Eric and Emerick Scott. 2006. "Teacher Working Conditions Are Student Learning Conditions: A Report on the 2006 North Carolina Teacher Working Conditions Survey." *Center for Teaching Quality*. https://www.teachingquality.org/wp-content/uploads/2018/04/Teacher_working_conditions_are_student_learning_conditions.pdf

Hobson, Brittany. 2021. "Manitoba elder Dave Courchene Jr., founder of Indigenous education centre, dies at 71" *Toronto Star* December 8, 2021.

Hodges, Tim. 2018. "School Engagement is More Than Just Talk." *Gallup Education*, October 25, 2018. https://www.gallup.com/education/244022/school-engagement-talk.aspx

Hofstede, Geert, et al., 2010. *Cultures and Organizations: Software of the Mind*. McGraw-Hill. Quoted in Hammond 2015.

hooks, bell. 1994. *Teaching To Transgress: Education As the Practice of Freedom*. New York: Routledge.

hooks, bell. 2009. *Belonging: A Culture of Place*. New York: Routledge.

Hutchins, Giles and Laura Storm, 2019. *Regenerative Leadership: The DNA of Life-Affirming 21st century Organizations*. Wordzworth.

ISAAC School 6th grade exhibit "Community Faces: Humanizing the Immigrant Label." Video https://eleducation.org/resources/community-faces-humanizing-the-immigrant-label-a-better-world-project

Jackson, C. Kirabo, et al., 2020. "Who Benefits From Attending Effective Schools? Examining Heterogeneity in High School Impacts." *National Bureau of Economic Research(NBER)*. WORKING PAPER 28194 DOI 10.3386/w28194 December 2020. https://www.nber.org/papers/w28194

Johnson, Ayana Elizabeth and Katharine Wilkinson, Editors. 2020. *All We Can Save*. New York: One World.

Johnston, Emily N. 2020. "Loving A Vanishing World." In *All We Can Save*, Johnson and Wilkinson Eds. (New York: One World), 256–265.

Jones, Zachary 2017. *Worldchangers Handbook: A Young Person's Guide to an Impactful Life*. Zachary Jones.

Kahane, Adam. 2010. *Power and Love: A Theory and Practice of Social Change*. San Francisco: BK (Berrett-Koehler) Publishers.

Kaminsky, June. "Four Directions." *First Nations Pedagogy Online*. Website. https://firstnationspedagogy.ca/fourdirections.html

Karelas, Andreas. 2021. *Climate Courage: How Tackling Climate Change Can Build Community, Transform the Economy, and Bridge the Political Divide in America*. Boston: Beacon Press.

Kelly, Diann Cameron. 2009. "Civic Readiness: Preparing Toddlers and Young Children for Civic Education and Sustained Engagement." *National Civic Review*. Wiley Online Library, 22 January 2009. https://doi.org/10.1002/ncr.234 https://onlinelibrary.wiley.com/doi/abs/10.1002/ncr.234

Kelsey, Elin. 2020. *Hope Matters: Why Changing the Way We Think Is Critical To Solving the Environmental Crisis*. Vancouver: Greystone.

Kianni, Sophia and Maggie Favretti. *Personal Interview*. 7 October 2020.

Kimmerer, Robin Wall. 2003. *Gathering Moss: A Natural and Cultural History of Mosses*. Corvallis, OR: Oregon State University Press.

Kimmerer, Robin Wall. 2020 (text 2013). *Braiding Sweetgrass: Indigenous Wisdom, Scientific Knowledge, and the Teachings of Plants*. Minneapolis, MN: Milkweed.

King, Jr., Dr. Martin Luther. 2010. *Where Do We Go From Here: Chaos Or Community?* 1967. Beacon Press Legacy Edition. Boston: Beacon Press.

Klein, Naomi. 2021. *How To Change Everything: The Young Humans Guide to Protecting the Planet and Each Other*. Atheneum, 2021.

Knuth, Kate. 2020. "Becoming a Climate Citizen." In *All We Can Save: Truth, Courage, and Solutions for the Climate Crisis*, Johnson and Wilkinson eds. (New York: OneWorld).

Kristof, Nicholas, and Sheryl WuDunn. 2009. *Half the Sky: Turning Oppression into Opportunity for Women Worldwide*. New York: Random House.

Kristofferson, Matthew. 2022. "Ozone Exposure Linked to Cognitive Decline in Older Adults, YSPH Study Finds." *Yale School of Public Health*, January 13, 2022. https://ysph.yale.edu/news-article/ozone-exposure-linked-to-cognitive-decline-in-older-adults-ysph-study-finds/

Landry, Christopher, director. 2022. *Joanna Macy and the Great Turning*. Video Project. 26 minutes.

Leiserowitz, Anthony, et al., 2021. "Climate Change in the American Mind, September 2021." *Yale University and George Mason University. New Haven, CT: Yale Program on Climate Change Communication* https://climatecommunication.yale.edu/publications/climate-change-in-the-american-mind-september-2021/

Lent, Jeremy. 2021. *The Web of Meaning: Integrating Science and Traditional Wisdom to Find Our Place in the Universe.* Canada: New Society Publishers.

Liebel, Manfred. 2020. *Decolonizing Childhoods: From Exclusion to Dignity.* Bristol, UK: Policy Press.

Limón, Ada. "A Name" from *The Carrying: Poems.* Milkweed Editions, 2018. Copyright 2018 by Ada Limón. Reprinted with the permission of The Permissions Company LLC on behalf of Milkweed Editions, milkweed.org

Lorde, Audre. 1977. "The Transformation of Silence into Language & Action." *Paper delivered at the Modern Language Association's "Lesbian and Literature Panel,"* Chicago, Illinois, December 28, 1977.

Love, Bettina. 2019. *We Want To Do More Than Survive: Abolitionist Teaching and the Pursuit of Educational Freedom.* Boston: Beacon Press.

Maldonado, Helga. 2022. *Facebook post,* 25 March 2022.

Manzini, Ezio. 2015. *Design, When Everybody Designs: An Introduction to Design for Social Innovation.* Cambridge, Massachusetts: The MIT Press.

Marks, Elizabeth, et al., "Young People's Voices on Climate Anxiety, Government Betrayal and Moral Injury: A Global Phenomenon." Available for pre-print download at SSRN: https://ssrn.com/abstract=3918955 or http://dx.doi.org/10.2139/ssrn.3918955

Marschall, Carla and Elizabeth O. Crawford. 2022. *Worldwise Learning: A Teacher's Guide to Shaping a Just, Sustainable Future.* Thousand Oaks, CA: Corwin.

Martínez-Fernández, Luis and Maggie Favretti. *Personal Interview.* February 20, 2022.

McCabe, G. 2008. "Mind, body, emotions and spirit: reaching to the ancestors for healing." *Counseling Psychology Quarterly,* 21(2), 143–152.

McGilchrist, Iain. 2021. "Healing the Divided Brain." In *Kumar and Cenkl, Transformative Learning.* Canada: New Society Publishers.

Menakem, Resmaa. 2017. *My Grandmother's Hands: Racialized Trauma and the Pathway to Mending Our Hearts and Bodies.* Las Vegas: Central Recovery Press.

Michaels, F. S. 2011. *Monoculture: How Our Story is Changing Everything.* Canada: Red Clover Press.

Minero, Emelina. 2017. "When Students Are Traumatized, Teachers Are, Too." *Edutopia.* October 4, 2017. https://www.edutopia.org/article/when-students-are-traumatized-teachers-are-too

Modan, Naaz. 2021. "Survey: 48% of Teachers Considering Job Change." *k12Dive,* 24 November, 2021. https://www.k12dive.com/news/survey-48-of-teachers-considering-job-change/610477/

Mooney, Chris, et al., November 7, 2021 "Countries' Climate Pledges Built on Flawed Data, Washington Post Investigation Finds." *Washington Post.*

Moran, Pam and Ira Socol 2019. "Timeless Learning: Remaking Space and Time In Any School." *Big Questions Institute Webinar.* 19 July 2021. https://bigquestions.institute/timeless-learning-webinar

Morris, Monique. 2018. *Pushout: The Criminalization of Black Girls in School.* New York: New Press.

Muhammad, Gholdy. 2020. *Cultivating Genius: An Equity Framework for Culturally and Historically Responsive Literacy*. New York: Scholastic.

Myers, Sarah P. *Personal email*, Jan 22, 2022. US Forest Service, Black Hills National Forest.

National Academies of Science, Engineering, and Medicine, 2017. *Listening Tour Summer 2017*. Several Reports have emerged, and can be accessed here: https://www.nationalacademies.org/our-work/measuring-community-resilience

National Academies of Science, Engineering, and Medicine. *Building and Measuring Community Resilience: Actions for Communities and the Gulf Research Program*. 2019 https://www.nationalacademies.org/our-work/measuring-community-resilience

Nichols, Wallace. 2014. *Blue Mind: How Water Makes You Happier, More Connected, and Better At What You Do*. Abacus.

Nieves Rodriguez, Christine. 2020. "Community Is Our Best Chance." In *All We Can Save*. Ayana Elizabeth Johnson and Katharine K. Wilkinson, Eds. (New York: One World), 363–368.

Nixon, Dr. Charisse. "Can We Induce Learned Helplessness?" *Penn State Erie and the Director of the Ophelia Project*. N.d., Access: https://www.youtube.com/watch?v=gFmFOmprTt0

Nugent, Ciara. 2021. "75% of the Young People Around the World are Frightened of the Future Because of Climate Change." *TIME*. 14 September, 2021. https://time.com/6097677/young-people-climate-change-anxiety/

O'Brien, Naomi and Lanesha Tabb. 2020. *Unpack Your Impact: How Two Primary Teachers Ditched Problematic Lessons And Built a Culture-Centered Curriculum*. San Diego: David Burgess Consulting.

Park, Maximilian. "Emotional Intelligence From a Teenager's Perspective." https://www.youtube.com/watch?v=MbmLNr89L-A

Parks, Rosa and Gregory J. Read. 1994. *Quiet Strength: The Faith, The Hope, and the Heart of a Woman Who Changed a Nation*. Zondervan.

Pashia, Mason. 15 November 2021. "How Sustainable is Your District? Using the GreenPrint from the Green Schools National Network." *Getting Smart*.

Penniman, Leah in Johnson and Wilkinson 2020. "Black Gold." In *All We Can Save: Truth, Courage, and Solutions for the Climate Crisis*. New York: One World.

Pierce, Natalie. 2019. "It's Not Just the Protests. Here's How Young People Are Helping The Planet." *World Economic Forum*, April 18, 2019. https://www.weforum.org/agenda/2019/04/its-not-just-the-protests-heres-how-young-people-are-fighting-for-the-planet/

Pope Francis. 2015. *Laudato Si': Encyclical Letter On Care for Our Common Home*. Vatican City: Libreria Editrice Vaticana.

Quinn, Daniel. 1995. *Ishmael: A Novel*. New York: Bantam Books.

Ray, Sarah Jaquette. 2020. *A Field Guide to Climate Anxiety: How to Keep Your Cool on a Warming Planet*. Oakland: University of California Press.

Reagan, Ronald. 1984. "State of the Union Address." 25 January 1984. *Ronald Reagan Presidential Foundation* https://www.reaganfoundation.org/ronald-reagan/reagan-quotes-speeches/state-of-the-union-2/

Rice, Joe. 2020. "Nawayee Center School: A Conversation with Joe Rice." *Education Reimagined*. 4 February 2020. https://education-reimagined.org/conversation-joe-rice/

Rice, Joe, and Maggie Favretti. *Personal Interview*, March 2022.

Richard, Leider. 2015. *The Power of Purpose*. San Francisco: Berrett-Koehler.

Rico, Sofia. 2021. "Aula en la Montaña: A New Educational Initiative in the Center of the Island." *Noticel*, 24 January 2021. https://www.noticel.com/la-calle/top-stories/20210124/aula-en-la-montana-una-nueva-iniciativa-educativa-en-el-centro-de-la-isla/

Riley, Shantal. 2022. "Lake Superior's Forever Chemicals: Indigenous Tribes Around the Lake Depend on Fishing to Survive–But the Fish are Contaminated." *Washington Post Magazine*, 12 January, 2022. https://www.washingtonpost.com/magazine/2022/01/12/lake-superior-forever-chemicals/

Rizo, Mike. 2022. "El Valor." *USFS sponsored panel, Nature of Cities Festival*, 30 March 2022.

Robbins, Jim. 2015. *The Man Who Planted Trees: The Story of Lost Groves, the Science of Trees, and A Plan to Save the Planet*. New York: Spiegel and Grau.

Robinson, Ishmael. 2021. "Creating a Culturally Responsive Math Curriculum for the Elementary Grades." *Edutopia*, 7 May, 2021. https://www.edutopia.org/article/creating-culturally-responsive-math-curriculum-elementary-grades

Robinson, Sir Ken. 2010. "Sir Ken Robinson at Full Sail University: Teachers Are Like Gardeners." Video. Youtube. https://www.youtube.com/watch?v=aT_121H3kLY&t=11s

Roy, Arundathi. 2003. *War Talk*. Cambridge, MA: South End Press.

Safir, Shane and Jamila Dugan. 2021. *Street Data: A Next Generation Model for Equity, Pedagogy, and School Transformation*. Thousand Oaks, CA: Corwin.

Sahlberg, Pasi. 2021. *Finnish Lessons 3.0*. New York: Teacher's College Press.

Salama, Jordan. 2020. "Are We 'Generation Screwed?' Not Necessarily." *National Geographic*, October 13, 2020. https://www.nationalgeographic.com/magazine/article/are-we-generation-screwed-not-necessarily-coming-of-age-amid-covid-19

Sanford, Carol. 2020. *The Regenerative Life: Transform Any Organization, Our Society, and Your Destiny*. Boston: Nicholas Brealey Publishing.

Satterlee, Cynthia. 2022. Posted on edutopia instagram by @gwenblumberg 11 January 2022. https://www.instagram.com/p/CYmWls1vHaQ/?utm_medium=copy_link

Scharmer, Otto. 2016. *Theory U: Leading From the Future As It Emerges, Revised Edition*. Oakland, CA: Berrett-Koehler.

Schwartz, Judith D. 2020. "Water Is a Verb," In Johnson & Wilkinson, eds. *All We Can Save: Truth, Courage, and Solutions for the Climate Crisis*. (New York: One World), 312–318.

Segarra-Alméstica, E., et al., 2021. "The Effect of School Services Disruptions on Educational Outcomes After Consecutive Disasters in Puerto Rico." *Natural Hazards Center Public Health Report Series*, 2. Boulder, CO: Natural Hazards Center, University of Colorado Boulder. https://hazards.colorado.edu/public-health-disaster-research/the-effect-of-school-services-disruptions-on-educational-outcomes-after-consecutive-disasters-in-puerto-rico

Seydel, Jennifer, et al., *Trailblazers for Whole School Sustainability: Case Studies of Educators In Action*. New York: Routledge.

Shah, Komal. 2021. *Raise Your Hand: A Call for Consciousness in Education*. New Degree Press.

Shivaram, Deepa. 2021. "Pediatricians say the mental health crisis among kids has become a national emergency." *NPR* 20 October 2021. https://www.npr.org/2021/10/20/1047624943/pediatricians-call-mental-health-crisis-among-kids-a-national-emergency

Silva Díaz, Pamela 2021. "Design for Climate Resilience." *Engineering for Change*. September 13, 2021. https://www.engineeringforchange.org/news/design-climate-resilience/

Singer, Tania. 2015. "How to Build a Caring Economy." *World Economic Forum*. 24 January 2015. https://www.weforum.org/agenda/2015/01/how-to-build-a-caring-economy/

Skene, K., et al., 2022. "Can Guidance During Play Enhance Children's Learning and Development in Educational Contexts?" A Systematic Review and Meta-Analysis. *Child Development*.

Sobel, David. 2013. *Place-Base Education: Connecting Classrooms and Communities*, 2nd edition. np: Orion.

Socol, Moran and Ratliff 2018. *Timeless Learning: How Imagination, Observation, and Zero-Based Thinking Change Schools*. San Francisco: Jossey-Bass.

Solnit, Rebecca. 2009. *A Paradise Built In Hell: The Extraordinary Communities That Arise In Disaster*. New York: Penguin.

Spencer, John and A. J. Juliani. 2016. *Launch: Using Design Thinking to Boost Creativity and Bring Out the Maker in Every Student*. San Diego, CA: Dave Burgess Consulting.

Spencer, John and A. J. Juliani 2017. *Empower: What Happens When Students Own Their Own Learning*. No location. IMpress Books, Dave Burgess Consulting, Inc.

Sullivan, Jessica, Leigh Wilton, and Evan Apfelbaum 2020. "Adults Delay Conversations About Race Because They Underestimate Children's Processing of Race," *Boston University*, Journal of Experimental Psychology: General, published online Aug. 6, 2020.

Taylor, Denny. 2020. "Parents and Teachers As First Responders During the COVID-19 Pandemic." https://static1.squarespace.com/static/5abc153cb1059858310b37e1/t/5ecd5c6995a4d74aea8628e8/1590516842716/Parents_and_Teachers_as_First_Responders_During_the_COVID-19_Pandemic.pdf

Taylor, Shelley E. 2006. "Tend and Befriend: Biobehavioral Basis of Affiliation Under Stress." *Current Directions in Psychological Science*, December 1 2006. 10.1111/j.1467-8721.2006.00451.x

Ted Dintersmith. *What School Could Be*. Princeton University Press, 2018.

Thomashow, Mitchell. 2020. *To Know the World: A New Vision for Environmental Learning*. Boston: Massachusetts Institute of Technology (MIT).

Thompson, R. 2018. *Gardening for health: a regular dose of gardening*. Clinical medicine (London, England), 18(3), 201–205. 10.7861/clinmedicine.18-3-201

Thunberg, Greta. 4 November 2021. https://twitter.com/GretaThunberg/status/145629 5342253740037 Full tweet:"#COP26 has been named the most excluding COP ever. This is no longer a climate conference. This is a Global North greenwash festival. A two week celebration of business as usual and blah blah blah".

Tutu, Archbishop Desmond and Rev. Mpho Tutu, Douglas C. Abrams, Ed. 2014. *The Book of Forgiving: A Fourfold Path for Healing Ourselves and Our World*. New York: HarperCollins.

Tyner, Adam, et al., August 2021. *How to Sell SEL: Parents and the Politics of Social-Emotional Learning*. New York: Fordham Institute and YouGov. https://fordhaminstitute.org/

sites/default/files/publication/pdfs/20210811-how-sell-sel-parents-and-politics-social-emotional-learning.pdf

Ungar, Michael. 2018. *Change Your World: The Science of Resilience and the True Path to Success.* Toronto: Sutherland House.

Upton, John. 2015. "Media Contributing to 'Hope Gap.'" *Climate Central.* 28 March 2015 https://www.climatecentral.org/news/media-hope-gap-on-climate-change-18822

US EPA 2015. *Indoor Air Quality.* EPA https://www.epa.gov/report-environment/indoor-air-quality

Vander Ark, Tom, et al., 2020. *The Power of Place: Authentic Learning Through Place-Based Education.* Thousand Oaks, CA: Corwin, 2020.

Vander Ark, Tom and Emily Liebtag. 2021. *Difference Making at the Heart of Learning: Students, Schools and Communities Alive With Possibility.* Thousand Oaks, CA: Corwin.

Van Der Kolk, Bessel, MD. 2014. *The Body Keeps The Score: Brain, Mind, and Body in the Healing of Trauma.* New York: Penguin Books.

Van Horn, Gavin, Robin Wall Kimmerer, and John Hausdoerffer. 2021. *Kinship: Belonging In a World of Relations.* 5 Volumes. Libertyville, IL: Center for Humans and Nature.

Van Osch, Thera 2013. "Towards a Caring Economic Approach." Netherlands, *OQ Consulting.* https://oqconsulting.eu/wp-content/uploads/2020/04/The-Economy-of-Care.pdf

Wagner, Kyle. LinkedIn, December 15, 2021. *Transformative Learning Experiences with Kyle Wagner, promoting Episode 25 with Yvette Larson: How to Let Go and Build Future Mindsets.* Podcast available here: Listen on Spotify: https://spoti.fi/3EWB98I Listen on Apple: https://apple.co/33xAZ9W

Wahl, Daniel Christian. 2016. *Designing Regenerative Cultures.* Axminster, England: Triarchy Press.

Wahl, Daniel Christian. 2017. "From Control & Prediction to Conscious Participation, Foresight, and Anticipation." *Medium,* April 17, 2017. https://designforsustainability.medium.com/from-control-prediction-to-conscious-participation-foresight-anticipation-3fae231cbdc7

Watson, Dyan, Hagopian, Jesse, and Wayne Au, Editors. 2018. *Teaching for Black Lives.* Milwaukee, WI: Rethinking Schools.

Weissbourd, Richard. 2016. "Parents Say Good Grades Trump Kindness … at Least that's what Kids Think." *Harvard Graduate School of Education.* 6 December 2016. https://www.gse.harvard.edu/news/16/12/parents-say-good-grades-trump-kindness-least-thats-what-kids-think

Wheatley, Margaret. *Turning to One Another: Simple Conversations to Restore Hope to the Future.* Second Edition. San Francisco: Berrett-Koehler, 2009.

Williams, Florence. 2017. *The Nature Fix: Why Nature Makes Us Happier, Healthier, and More Creative.* Norton.

Williams, Jeremy. 2021. *Climate Change Is Racist: Race, Privilege, and the Struggle for Climate Justice.* London: Icon Books.

Wise, Susie. 2022. *Design For Belonging: How To Build Inclusion and Collaboration In Your Communities.* California: 10 Speed Press.

Wolfe, Rachel. *Losing Ourselves.* Youtube video. June 26, 2014. 31:46. https://www.youtube.com/watch?v=9Wr7OPT5R2M

Worth, Katie. 2021. *Miseducation: How Climate Change Is Taught In America.* New York: Columbia Global Reports.

Yeampierre, Elizabeth. In *All We Can Save: Truth, Courage, and Solutions for the Climate Crisis*, Ayana Elizabeth Johnson and Katharine K. Wilkinson, eds. (New York: One World), 128.

Yoder, Kate. 2021. "It's Not Just You. Everyone is Googling Climate Anxiety." Grist. October 4, 2021. https://grist.org/language/climate-anxiety-google-search-trends/

Zelikova, Jane. 2020. "Solutions Underfoot." In Johnson & Wilkinson, Eds. *All We Can Save: Truth, Courage, and Solutions for the Climate Crisis*. (New York: One World), 287–292.

For Product Safety Concerns and Information please contact our EU
representative GPSR@taylorandfrancis.com
Taylor & Francis Verlag GmbH, Kaufingerstraße 24, 80331 München, Germany

For Product Safety Concerns and Information please contact our EU
representative GPSR@taylorandfrancis.com
Taylor & Francis Verlag GmbH, Kaufingerstraße 24, 80331 München, Germany

www.ingramcontent.com/pod-product-compliance
Ingram Content Group UK Ltd.
Pitfield, Milton Keynes, MK11 3LW, UK
UKHW021427080625
459435UK00011B/182

* 9 7 8 0 4 1 5 8 5 1 0 2 2 *